Earthworm Ecology

Edited by

Clive A. Edwards

SOIL
AND WATER
CONSERVATION
SOCIETY

Soil and Water Conservation Society
Ankeny, Iowa

S^t_L

St. Lucie Press

Boca Raton Boston London New York Washington, D.C.

Library of Congress Cataloging-in-Publication Data

Catalog information may be obtained from the Library of Congress

Table of Contents

Preface

Charles Darwin was the first scientist to bring earthworms to the attention of scientists and the general public, more than a century ago. Darwin noted the importance of earthworms in breaking down dead plant materials, recycling the nutrients they contain, and turning over soil. His book *The Formation of Vegetable Mould through the Action of Worms* (1881) summarized his conclusions on earthworms, reached after 40 years of observation and experimental work. In his book, he expressed the opinion that "earthworms have played a most important part in the history of the world." The importance of his personal contributions to our knowledge of earthworms cannot be stressed enough and led to a great upsurge of work on the morphology, histology, and taxonomy of earthworms in the late 19th and early 20th centuries.

However, it was only in the last 25 years that interest in and research into the ecology and biology of earthworms has peaked. Much of this work was summarized by Edwards and his coauthor in their book, *The Biology and Ecology of Earthworms* (first edition 1972, second edition 1977, third edition 1995), and by Lee (1985) in his book, *Earthworms: Their Ecology and Relationships with Soil and Land Use.* In recent years, interest in earthworm ecology and the importance of earthworms to soil fertility has been increasing at an extremely rapid rate and so has research into the subject. This is evidenced by the increases in the numbers of references quoted by the authors of *The Biology and Ecology of Earthworms* in the three editions that have appeared. In 1972, they quoted 565 references; in the second edition (1977), 674; but in the third one, there were more than 1500. This probably represents only a third of those published up till this time.

The present book, *Earthworm Ecology*, owes its origin to the Fifth International Symposium on Earthworm Ecology, held in Columbus, Ohio, United States, in July 1994. At this symposium, attended by more than 220 scientists from 38 countries, 165 research presentations were made and most of these are being published in a special volume of the journal *Soil Biology and Biochemistry.* However, in the eight sessions held at the symposium, each session was opened with an invited review paper by a distinguished scientist and concluded with a final overview of the subject and conclusions by a second such scientist. These 16 invited papers have been edited to form the material presented in this volume. There are eight sections in this book covering all of the major aspects of earthworm ecology, including earthworm diversity, behavior physiology and general ecology and their roles in nutrient cycling, soil maintenance, plant growth, and environmental and waste management, with two chapters on each topic.

These contributions by distinguished earthworm scientists represent a state-of-the-art summary of the ecology and importance of earthworms, in both natural ecosystems and agroecosystems, and should be invaluable to soil scientists in all relevant disciplines as well as to farmers, students, and members of the general public interested in the long-term maintenance of soil structure and fertility.

Clive A. Edwards
The Ohio State University
Columbus, Ohio

Earthworm Taxonomy, Diversity, and Biogeography

Earthworms and Earth History

S. James
Department of Biology, Maharishi International University, Fairfield, Iowa

E arth history is traditionally the domain of geologists and various paleo-disciplines (paleontology, paleoecology, paleoclimatology, paleobotany, etc.). However, the history of biology is sprinkled with research on the connections between present-day biogeography and ecology on one hand and earth history on the other. Such research may divided into three broad categories. First, there is application of data derived from life forms of the present to questions of earth history. For example, the use of phylogenetic trees in combination with distributional data can provide insights into the history of land-area relationships, as done in the field of vicariance biogeography (Wiley 1988). We may be able to claim that earthworms were of some importance in the early development of plate tectonic theory, and therefore of vicariance biogeography, since the former has been very important to the ascendance of the latter. The Oligochaete systematist Michaelsen named an earthworm genus after Wegener in honor of Wegener's work toward an understanding of the distributions of earthworms (Michaelsen 1933). It is possible that the two men (office neighbors at the University of Hamburg) discussed earthworm distributions, providing Wegener more evidence for his then-radical theory. Many other groups of organisms have been used in arguments supporting or refuting various hypotheses about events of the past (Wiley 1988; Humphries and Parenti 1986; Rosen 1985; Liebherr 1988).

One can also find a significant thread of research on the contributions of living things to global processes. In its boldest version, this latter area is the Gaia Hypothesis (Lovelock 1988), but numerous more mundane examples can be found in the literature on biogeochemical cycles, trace gas fluxes, and other topics relevant to global climate models.

1-884015-74-3/98/$0.00/$.50

For example, earthworms may influence land forms. Charles Darwin (1881) described a process by which earthworms may increase rates of soil erosion and thus the rates of change of land topography. This has not been thoroughly researched, and there is some evidence that earthworms may reduce rates of soil erosion (Hopp 1946; Sharpley and Syers 1977) in agricultural land. Nooren et al. (1995) suggest that earthworms can increase rates of clay loss from an African soil, creating nutrient-poor sandy topsoils. Lavelle and Martin (1992) hypothesized that by protecting soil organic matter against oxidation, earthworms could have an important influence on atmospheric carbon dioxide levels. Because carbon loss from soils is an important contribution to the elevation of atmospheric carbon dioxide levels, any organisms capable of reversing or moderating that trend should be investigated closely.

A third way in which earth history plays a significant role in field biology is in the understanding of ecological interactions and of taxon distributions. For example, the presence of a particular taxon and its unique ecological contributions to the community of one site, but its absence from another, could be interpreted as due to differences in history. Perhaps the taxon could exist in the latter site, but did not get there. Thus it may not be some ecological or evolutionary necessity that determines certain characteristics of the system, but rather a historical accident. Both of the research projects I will outline below contain examples of this.

Of these three connections of earth history to modern biology, I would like to focus on two, the first and the last. These may be stated briefly as using modern organisms to learn about the history of the earth, and viewing modern distributions and ecology as the outcomes of an interaction between evolutionary and large-scale abiotic processes. My purpose in this chapter is to outline some of the ways that research on earthworm systematics and biogeography can contribute to the broader subject of earth history, and vice versa. To accomplish this I will be reviewing two recent research projects and the methods I have used. On the way through these discussions I will suggest that those of us working on earthworm systematics and biogeography can profit from close attention to some of the recent developments in organizing one's ideas and analyzing data.

The first project has to do with the usefulness of earthworms in studying the geological history of the earth, with particular reference to movements of land masses. It began from two pieces of biogeographical data: First, that earthworms (except peregrines) are absent from mid-oceanic volcanic islands, indicating that they may experience great difficulty crossing salt water (Stephenson 1930), and second, that there are endemic earthworms on some Caribbean islands. The possibility of over-water dispersal has been debated in the past, particularly in relation to the endemic species of the subantarctic islands (Michaelsen 1911;

Stephenson 1930; Lee 1959). I saw an opportunity to test the hypothesis of no over-water dispersal in a general way, and to use it, if supported, to argue that earthworms are biogeographical model organisms. By model organism in this context I mean one whose dispersal is so poor that its distribution can be viewed as entirely determined (in this case) by past land connections and vicariance events introducing salt-water barriers between land areas.

If transoceanic dispersal has been negligible in earthworm history, then earthworm phylogenies can be used to unlock many earth historical riddles, such as the geological evolution of complex areas like the Caribbean Basin and the archipelagoes of the western Pacific Ocean. This application of phylogeny follows from the simplest form of allopatric speciation. The biotas of the separated areas will have evolutionary histories mirroring the fragmentation history of the land. Post-fragmentation dispersal muddles the land area cladogram derived from the hypothesized phylogenetic tree of the organisms. Therefore a low- or no-dispersal taxon is preferable to one able to cross the barrier (Noonan 1988; Sober 1988). In spite of this rather obvious conclusion, most of the work to date in the field of historical biogeography has focused on relatively vagile organisms, such as reptiles, birds, and insects.

Biogeography comes in many forms, and it will be convenient to define what kinds of biogeography we are dealing with. Ball (1975) described three phases of the science of biogeography. The first is the empirical or descriptive phase, in which the basic data are collected. At this point, one knows where the taxa are, and there may be some synthesis, such as the definition of the classical biogeographic provinces (e.g., Nearctic, Ethiopian). Then comes an attempt to explain the distribution. The narrative phase is the result. A plausible story is given, one which seems to fit the evidence fairly well. Work to date on the subject of oceanic island earthworm distributions has achieved this much, leaving room for an analytical approach.

Analytical biogeography requires that hypotheses be formulated and their predictions tested. This is now the standard against which manuscripts and research proposals are judged, almost regardless of the need for descriptive work as a foundation. If the collection of basic biogeographical data is not driven by some higher aim, the project is not really a scientific enterprise. In this context I would like to describe the fundamentals of one of my research programs, the biogeography of earthworms in the Caribbean Basin.

As mentioned above, it appears that earthworms have rarely or never crossed salt water (other than the salt-water-tolerant species inhabiting seashores). This could lead to a narrative (the reason they do not occur on such islands is that they cannot cross salt water) or to a statement of a hypothesis. One could state as a hypothesis that earthworms cannot survive or do not have natural means of transport across bodies of salt water. This is testable, though it would be difficult to release test worms or cocoons by all possible means of conveyance (rafting vegetation, logs, on debris in violent cyclonic storms, and so on), and even harder to track their fates. It may be easier to test the predictions of the hypothesis.

The hypothesis that earthworms cannot survive natural means of transport across bodies of salt water predicts that land areas arising from mid-oceanic uplift of submerged rock or from volcanic eruption should not have earthworms. Obviously, this hypothesis arose from the observation that such islands either lack earthworms or only harbor earthworms widely distributed by human agricultural activity. It is tested by examining islands conforming to the modes of origin just mentioned, and about whose earthworm fauna little or nothing is known. The Lesser Antilles fit this description. These islands constitute a fairly strong test, since they are close to one another and to potential sources of colonization, unlike the Hawaiian archipelago and the islands of the Mid-Atlantic Ridge. There is ample evidence that other taxa have colonized the Lesser Antilles from South America and from the Greater Antilles and other islands to the north (Humphries and Parenti 1986), so it would not be particularly surprising to find yet another group of organisms doing the same.

The general pattern of occurrences of earthworms on the Lesser Antilles has been presented elsewhere (Fragoso et al. 1995). No earthworms other than peregrine species were found on the southern Lesser Antilles or the small volcanic islands north of Guadeloupe. Many new species endemic to their islands were found on Guadeloupe, Dominica, Martinique, and St. Lucia (James 1996, unpub. data; Moreno unpub. data). Based on a preliminary estimate of the phylogenetic relationships of the species involved, at least nine successful dispersal events would be required to establish the earthworm faunas of those four islands. If so, this is a very dense cluster of dispersal events in the middle of the archipelago, furthest from sources of colonization. However, earthworms have failed to colonize the Lesser Antilles by over-water dispersal from nearby land masses populated with indigenous earthworms. There is no evidence that the South American earthworm fauna has spread northward into the Lesser Antilles, or that the elements of the earthworm fauna of the Greater Antilles, particularly Puerto Rico and the Virgin Islands, have dispersed to the east and south.

The Guadeloupe–St. Lucia axis poses a challenge to the conclusions that otherwise would be reached easily from the data from other islands. Without recourse to an analytical approach, the challenge cannot be met, because hypotheses of dispersal are logically unfalsifiable. Any distribution could arise by post-fragmentation dispersal, if one allows sufficient complexity of dispersal history. In this case, progress will only come from testing the hypothesis that the distributions are the result of vicariance, since it is logically conceivable that such a hypothesis could be rejected. That is the next stage in my work, approaches to which are vicariance biogeography and the acquisition of molecular data.

If for the time being one can accept that over-water dispersal can be ignored as a factor in earthworm distribution to islands or between any two land areas separated by salt water, then earthworms are nearly ideal indicators of past land area connections. Their evolutionary history will mirror these past connections, since the severing of the land connection isolates populations of species. From the perspective of vicariance biogeography, these isolating or vicariating events are the primary factors of interest in the history of the flora and fauna of land areas. Dispersal is seen as a source of noise in the data, analogous to homoplasious character evolution (Sober 1988). Vicariance biogeography represents a system of formulating hypotheses that predict distribution patterns based on underlying historical models (Wiley 1988). The underlying historical models have to do with creation of barriers to genetic exchange. Any species, earthworms included, could be affected by the fragmentation of a range due to climatic, geologic, or other processes.

Thus, it should be possible to make a very good mapping between the branch points on an earthworm cladogram and the separations of the land masses on which earthworm taxa occur. In the jargon of vicariance biogeography, one replaces the terminal taxa on the phylogenetic tree with the names of the collection locations to make an area cladogram. A geological model provides a predicted area cladogram, which can then be compared to the biologically-derived one. The success of this approach depends heavily on very good phylogenetic analysis and on having the data set as free as possible from dispersal-induced noise.

It should be clear that any analytical biogeography of this sort absolutely requires a prior phylogenetic analysis (Wiley 1988). Ball (1975) pointedly remarked that earthworms had nothing to offer to biogeographical analysis because the treatment of the data available at his time of writing was too superficial. Unfortunately, very little has changed since then, and taxonomic revisions continue to be made without any such explicit phylogenetic analysis.

Earthworm taxonomists have been so few in number, and apparently so isolated from their counterparts working on other taxa, or perhaps so overworked doing basic taxonomy, that many of the concepts and methods long in use by other breeds of systematist are unfamiliar to earthworm specialists. With one exception (Jamieson 1988), all the higher-level systematics research on earthworms is based on classical methodology. This is not to say that the classical method was bad, but that "new" methods, particularly cladistic analysis (Hennig 1966; Sudhaus and Rehfeld 1992), have emerged since the older generation of earthworm specialists were trained. Unfortunately, very few of those specialists have taken advantage of the revolution in systematics that has taken place in their lifetimes.

Because the current estimates of earthworm phylogeny at all levels are potentially suspect, either from lack of data or obsolete analytical methods applied to good data, the tremendous potential for biogeographical inference using earthworms cannot be tapped. We have the opportunity to make a breakthrough, one in which modern technologies and techniques will generate research of interest to a broad range of systematists and biogeographers.

Among the most important and promising modern techniques is the ability to obtain DNA sequence and other forms of molecular data quickly and cheaply (Sambrook et al. 1989; Sanger et al. 1977; Hillis et al. 1993). DNA sequence information offers the prospect of large numbers of characters (each base position is one character with four possible states), a choice of genes with various rates of evolution for various times since divergence, and the welcome avoidance of many old arguments about homology and stability of various morphological characters (but of course introduces some new problems). More than avoiding the thoroughly debated homology/stability questions, an independent data set for one's taxa of interest allows one to attack the character evolution questions in an objective way.

On the other hand, the use of DNA sequence data requires learning new techniques, both in the laboratory and at the computer. Sequence data also have homology problems and weighting considerations, but these are common to all forms of life and are the subject of a very active field of investigation.

The role of molecular data in systematics and analytical biogeography will be increasing. This is not to say that morphological characteristics will be discredited, but that they will be supplemented by the molecular evidence in a combined analysis (e.g., Wheeler et al. 1993; Omland 1994). The two types of data do not always agree, but this problem is also general to all forms of life. Quite a bit of work is being done to develop methods for quantifying the degree of incongruence between molecular and morphological data (Swofford 1991; Thomas and Hunt 1993; Bull et al. 1993; Omland 1994) and guidelines for performing combined analyses. Therefore one benefits from the work of many more people than just those who work on one's own taxon of interest.

The field of earthworm systematics is long overdue for reinvigoration and an influx of ideas and techniques new to many of us. Good classical systematics will never lose its fundamental value, and it is the foundation for the standards of publication often ignored by modern authors. However, a century of work by a small but dedicated group has failed to resolve such fundamentals as the definitions of families (e.g., Sims 1980). To date, only Jamieson (1988) has offered a rigorous analysis of this problem, and his work largely seems to have been ignored. The higher-level systematics of earthworms seems to be a very good area in which to apply molecular data.

Biogeographical contributions from earthworm phylogeny need not be confined to questions involving taxa separated by oceanic barriers. In general, earthworms are slow to disperse, mating is highly localized, and populations may be easily isolated. If we take as an example the earthworm fauna of New Zealand, we see that in mountainous regions there can be tremendous overall species diversity, even though the number of species in any one site may be small (Lee 1959). Thus, the possibility exists to investigate the phylogeny of the earthworms of a single land area in relation to many potential fragmentations and re-annealings of ranges due to geological, hydrological, or climatological processes. While the noise in the data may be greater than in the case of transoceanic questions, it should still be as good as or better than the data derived from other taxa widely cited in the biogeographical literature.

The question of how to learn about the history of the earth from earthworm phylogeny and biogeography is worth asking only because we have reason to believe that the history of life is linked in many ways to the history of the earth. On the other hand, have earthworms been affected by historical processes, and on what scales of time and space? Certainly much of the distributions of higher earthworm taxa can be illuminated by study of the history of the earth's crust. What appears in the present as anomalous disjunct distributions can be understood as the results of the fragmentation of a continuous distribution. At other time scales, one can examine the impacts of other events of earth history on earthworm distributions. Glaciation is one example.

The second project I would like to use as an illustration of biogeographical research looks at the distributions of North American earthworms in relation to the maximal extent of the Wisconsin (Würm) glaciation and asks how the process of post-glacial recovery affects the composition of earthworm faunas at different points from south to north. It also addresses some alternatives to the conventional wisdom on this subject.

This project concerns where the worms are (basic descriptive biogeography) and why they are there (moving in the direction of analytical biogeography). It also hopes to provide some basis for figuring out the larger modern ecological consequences of the processes affecting earthworm distributions.

Work to date on the subject of glaciation and earthworm distributions has resulted in extensive fundamental distributional data (Gates 1977; Reynolds 1994, 1995) and a plausible explanation for the patterns (Gates 1977; Reynolds 1994), leaving room for an analytical approach. Analytical biogeography requires that hypotheses be formulated and their predictions tested. For example, one could state as a hypothesis that earthworms cannot survive beneath glaciers.

This is testable, though it would be difficult to release test worms at the under-side of a glacier, and even harder to go back and look for them. One may prefer to examine the predictions of the hypothesis: there should be no native earth-worms in areas recently uncovered by receding glaciers, regardless of preglacial history of earthworm presence on that site.

However, even if the observed distributions are in accord with the above historical model (the glaciers made it impossible for earthworms to be there), this does not prove a causal link. In the present case, there are other alternative explanations which must be considered. First, it is conceivable that modern-day earthworms in North America are not capable of surviving the climate any farther north than they presently occur. Second, it is conceivable that North American earthworms were present farther north prior to colonization of North America by peoples from Europe, but that European earthworms (or some com-bination of European worm invasion and habitat destruction) eliminated native species by competition. We need only make the additional hypothesis that cli-mate affects the outcome of the process of competition, rendering it possible for native species to persist in the southerly areas.

To meet these complaints against what seems a simple and obvious narrative explanation, I conducted experiments and made several altitudinal transects to test the hypothesis of climate limitation. Transects are comparative, not experi-mental in nature, and so do not constitute as strong a class of evidence. To address the competition question, I designed and implemented competition ex-periments based on the deWit replacement series used in plant competition (deWit 1960).

A detailed account of the results from these experiments would not be ap-propriate for this volume, and at this writing, the analysis of the data is not complete. Tentatively, the bulk of the evidence favors abiotic historical factors as explanations for the modern earthworm distributions: Glaciation removed earthworms from those areas once covered by ice or underlain by permafrost in periglacial areas, and the worms have been very slow to diffuse northwards. I hesitate to use the word "disperse" since there appear to be few events in the normal course of the earthworm life cycle that promote dispersal, other than coming out for a crawl after heavy rains. Using estimates of rates of spread obtained from The Netherlands (Marinissen and van den Bosch 1992), 10,000 years is enough for some peregrine earthworms to advance 60 to 100 km. Thus one would predict range expansions of 100 to 200 km since maximal extent of the ice in the Northern Hemisphere.

Range expansion rates may differ among species, for various reasons, in-cluding modes of reproduction and niche. For example, epigeic species may have a higher natural rate of diffusion than oligohumic endogeics. If true, this would result in something analogous to a chromatographic fractionation of earthworm faunas. Should such a pattern emerge, earthworm ecological functions will be differently represented in the natural vegetation of locations along north-south transects crossing the limits of native earthworms. This should have some impact on ecosystem processes. The extreme case would be in the northern regions where no earthworms are present and forest litter layers are quite deep. The contribution I tried to make to the question of how glaciation (or any other historical factor important to a species distribution) affects earthworm distributions was to remove the question from the narrative domain, and to try to formulate and test hypotheses. Those hypotheses tested were either the predictions of the central hypothesis (in the present case, that glaciation made impossible the occupation of ice-covered lands) or alternatives to the central hypothesis. While negative data are never as satisfying as positive, and can be overturned by a single positive datum, broad-scale events are often amenable only to investigation by a process of elimination of alternatives.

Much earthworm biogeography has been directed to the distributions of peregrine species (e.g., Reynolds 1995). Completely different historical agents, such as patterns of human migration and horticultural and agricultural trade routes, would seem to be involved. Totally different ecological concerns emerge: Are species absences due to historical factors alone or due to incompatibilities between sites and species? Are the present distributions of the peregrine species determined by their transport history or by ecological factors? To what extent is habitat disturbance involved in successful establishment of peregrines? Does it make sense to talk of species associations when the species found together may have nothing more in common than a collection of travelers in a train station? Are there forms of data, such as molecular data, that will allow one to trace the origins of populations of peregrine species to areas of origin? The task of bringing rigorous scientific methodology to this area will require much thought and may yield insights into the connections between ecology and human history.

Earthworm systematics has been making its primary contributions to the work of people whose interests lie in ecology, agriculture, and other fields in need of a coherent classification of earthworm species. This is due in part to the service functions of the field and to the lack of specialists. However, with use of the new types of data and analytical methods discussed above, it should soon be possible to move towards providing the robust phylogenies required for good biogeography. The potential for contributions to the understanding of the earth's history and its interactions with the history of biotas is great. There may be few other terrestrial taxa so widely distributed, so ancient, and so amenable to collection and study as earthworms. When one also considers the high degree of endemicity of earthworm species, it is a wonder that scientists working on biogeographical questions have not already taken advantage of the marvelous research opportunities in earthworm systematics and biogeography.

REFERENCES CITED

Ball, I. 1975. Nature and formulation of biogeographic hypotheses. Syst. Zool. 24:407–430.

Bull, J.J., J.P. Huelsenbeck, C.W. Cunningham, D.L. Swofford, and P.J. Waddell. 1993. Partitioning and combining data in phylogenetic analysis. Syst. Bio. 42:384–397.

Darwin, C. 1881. The formation of vegetable mould, through the action of worms, with observations on their habits. Murray, London.

de Wit, C.T. 1960. On competition. Versl. Landbouwk. Onderz. 66:1–82.

Fragoso, C., S.W. James, and S. Borges. 1995. Native earthworms of the north neotropical region: Current status and controversies. In P. Hendrix (ed.), Earthworm ecology and biogeography in North America. CRC Press, Boca Raton, Florida.

Gates, G.E. 1969. On the earthworms of Ascension and Juan Fernandez Islands. Breviora 323:1–4.

Gates, G.E. 1971. On reversions to former ancestral conditions in megadrile oligochaetes. Evolution 25:245–248.

Gates, G.E. 1972. Burmese earthworms. Trans. Amer. Phil. Soc. NS 62(7):1–326.

Gates, G.E. 1977. More on the earthworm genus _Diplocardia_. Megadriogica 3:1–48.

Hennig, W. 1966. Phylogenetic systematics. University of Illinois Press, Urbana.

Hillis, D.M., M.W. Allard, and M.M. Miyamoto. 1993. Analysis of DNA sequence data: Phylogenetic inference. Meth. Enzymol. 224:456–487.

Hopp, H. 1946. Earthworms fight erosion, too. Soil Cons. 11:252–255.

Humphries, C.J., and L.R. Parenti. 1986. Cladistic biogeography. Clarendon Press, Oxford.

James, S.W. 1996. Nine new species of _Dichogaster_ (Oligochaeta: Megascolecidae) from Guadeloupe (French West Indies). Zoologica Scripta 25(1):21–34.

Jamieson, B.G.M. 1988. On the phylogeny and higher classification of the Oligochaeta. Cladistics 4:367–401.

Lavelle, P., and A. Martin. 1992. Small-scale and large-scale effects of endogeic earthworms on soil organic matter dynamics in the humid tropics. Soil Biol. Biochem. 24: 1491–1498.

Lee, K.E. 1959. The earthworm fauna of New Zealand. New Zealand Dept. of Scientific and Industrial Research Bulletin 130. Wellington, New Zealand.

Liebherr, J.K. 1988. General patterns in West Indian insects, and graphical biogeographic analysis of some circum-Caribbean _Platynus_ beetles (Carabidae). Syst. Zool. 37: 385–409.

Loope, L.L., O. Hamann, and C.P. Stone. 1988. Comparative conservation biology of oceanic archipelagoes. BioScience 38:272–282.

Lovelock, J. 1988. The ages of Gaia: A biography of our living earth. Norton and Company, New York.

Marinissen, J.C.Y., and F. van den Bosch. 1992. Colonization of new habitats by earthworms. Oecologia 91:371–376.

Maury, R.C., G.K. Westbrook, P.E. Baker, Ph. Bouysse, and D. Westercamp. 1990. Geology of the Lesser Antilles. pp. 141–165. In G. Dengo and J.E. Case (eds.), The Caribbean region. Geological Society of America, Boulder, Colorado. The Geology of North America, Volume H.

Michaelsen, W. 1911. Zur Kenntnis der Eodrilaceen und ihrer Verbreitungsverhältnisse. Zool. Jahrb. Abt. f. Syst. 30:527–572.

Michaelsen, W. 1933. Die Oligochaetenfauna Surinames mit Erörterung der verwandtschaftlichen Beziehungen der Octochatinen. Tijdschr. Ned. Dierk. Vereen. 3:112–131

Nakamura, M. 1990. How to identify Hawaiian earthworms. Chuo University Research Notes. No. 11, pp. 101–110.

Noonan, G.R. 1988. Biogeography of North American and Mexican insects, and a critique of vicariance biogeography. Syst. Zool. 37:366–384.

Nooren, C.A.M., N. van Breemen, J.J. Stoorvogel, and A.G. Jongmans. 1995. The role of earthworms in the formation of sandy surface soils in a tropical forest in Ivory Coast. Geoderma 65:135–148.

Omland, K.E. 1994. Character congruence between a molecular and a morphological phylogeny for dabbling ducks (*Anas*). Syst. Biol. 43(3):369–387.

Patterson, C. 1981. Methods of paleobiogeography. pp. 446–489. In G. Nelson and D.E. Rosen (eds.), Vicariance biogeography: A critique. Columbia University Press, New York. 593 pp.

Pindell, J.L., and S.F. Barrett. 1990. Geological evolution of the Caribbean region; a platetectonic perspective. pp. 405–432. In G. Dengo and J.E. Case (eds.), The Caribbean region. Geological Society of America, Boulder, Colorado. The Geology of North America, Volume H.

Reynolds, J.W. 1994. The distribution of the earthworms (Oligochaeta) of Indiana: A case for the post-Quaternary introduction theory for megadrile migration in North America. Megadrilogica 5:13–32.

Reynolds, J.W. 1995. Status of exotic earthworm systematics and biogeography in North America. In P. Hendrix (ed.), Earthworm ecology and biogeography in North America. CRC Press, Boca Raton, Florida.

Rosen, D.E. 1975. A vicariance model of Caribbean biogeography. Syst. Zool. 24:431–464.

Rosen, D.E. 1985. Geological hierarchies and biogeographical congruence in the Caribbean. Ann. Mo. Bot. Gard. 72:636–659.

Roughgarden, J. 1990. Origin of the eastern Caribbean: Data from reptiles and amphibians. In D. LaRue and G. Draper (eds.), Trans. 12th Caribbean Conf., St. Croix, USVI Miami Geol. Survey.

Sambrook, J., E.F. Fritsch, and T. Maniatis. 1989. Molecular cloning, a laboratory manual, 2nd edition. Cold Spring Harbor Laboratory Press, New York.

Sanger, F., S. Nicklen, and A.R. Coulson. 1977. DNA sequencing with chain-terminating inhibitors. Proc. Natl. Acad. Sci. USA 74:5463–5467.

Savage, J.M. 1982. The enigma of the Central American herpetofauna: Dispersals or vicariance? Ann. Missouri Bot. Gard. 69:464–547.

Sharpley, A.N., and J.K. Syers. 1977. Seasonal variation in casting activity and in the amounts and release to solution of phosphorus forms in earthworm casts. Soil Biol. Biochem. 9:227–231.

Sims, R.W. 1980. A classification and the distribution of earthworms, suborder Lumbricina (Haplotaxida: Oligochaeta). Bull. Br. Mus. (Nat. Hist.) Zool. Ser. 39(2):103–124.

Sober, E. 1988. The conceptual relationship of cladistic phylogenetics and vicariance biogeography. Syst. Zool. 37:245–270.

Stephenson, J. 1930. The Oligochaeta. Clarendon Press, Oxford.

Sudhaus, W., and K. Rehfeld. 1992. Einfuehrung in die Phylogenetik und Systematik. Gustav Fischer, New York.

Swofford, D.L. 1991. When are phylogeny estimates from molecular and morphological data incongruent? pp. 295–333. In M.M. Miyamoto and J. Cracraft (eds.), Phylogenetic analysis of DNA sequences. Oxford University Press, New York. 358 pp.

Swofford, D.L., and G. Olsen. 1990. Phylogeny reconstruction. pp. 411–502. in D.M. Hillis and C. Moritz (eds.), Molecular systematics. Sinauer, Sunderland, Massachusetts. 588.

Tajima, F. 1993. Unbiased estimation of evolutionary distance between nucleotide sequences. Mol. Biol. Evol. 10:677–688.

Talavera, J.A. 1990. Claves de identificacion de las lombrices de tierra (Annelida: Oligochaeta) de Canarias. Vieraea 18:113–119.

Thomas, R.H., and J.A. Hunt. 1993. Phylogenetic relationships in *Drosophila*. A conflict between molecular and morphological data. Mol. Biol. Evol. 10:362–374.

Wheeler, W.C., P. Cartwright, and C.Y. Hayashi. 1993. Arthropod phylogeny: A combined approach. Cladistics 9:1–39.

Wiley, E.O. 1981. Phylogenetics. Wiley Interscience, New York.

Wiley, E.O. 1988. Parsimony analysis and vicariance biogeography. Syst. Zool. 37:271–290.

The Status of Earthworm Biogeography, Diversity, and Taxonomy in North America Revisited with Glimpses into the Future

2

John W. Reynolds
Oligochaetology Laboratory, Lindsay, Ontario, Canada

n a recent discussion of the distribution of earthworms in North America, Reynolds (1994a) discussed the three steps of biogeographical theory. The first step is *descriptive* or *faunistics*, the gathering of facts and enumeration of animals in an area, including research and literature surveys. This step, although seldom achieved, seeks to present a clear distributional picture of all the animals in all areas. The second step is the *classification of data*, or grouping of the distributional data according to as many different points of view as a particular investigation may find necessary, including a comparison of distributional ranges of phylogenetically related groups. This step also analyzes the fauna of a geographically, ecologically, or historically uniform area. The third and final step, *causal analysis*, tries to explain the reason for the present distribution as it has been presented. It is from this step that the principles of biogeography emerge. At present, in North America, we are probably somewhat between the first two stages with megadriles (Reynolds 1975a, 1976a, 1994a).

The study of the status quo of animal distributions and of the grouping of these distributions according to different principles is a study of momentary phenomena. Faunistic and regional zoogeography is basically static zoogeog-

1-884015-74-3/98/$0.00/$.50
©1998 by CRC Press LLC

raphy; present distributions are the result of processes that move the animals in space and as a consequence of which the distributional picture changes with the passage of time. Thus, causal zoogeography is identical to dynamic zoogeography. Causations of distributions are dynamic processes. As long as our inquiry probes into the reasons for the arrival and settling of a species in a certain area, we are within the field of dynamic zoogeography. As soon as we ask ourselves why and how an animal is able to live in a particular area, we leave dynamic zoogeography; as a matter of fact, we leave zoogeography entirely, and our question receives an answer along ecological lines. For example, the lack of an animal species in a certain area may be caused by ecological (it cannot exist there) or zoogeographical (it has not arrived there) reasons. The answers pertaining to dynamic zoogeography are often ecological, but here ecological cause is followed by movement, individual or population, of the subject. When the ecological cause is followed by a positive or negative response of the organism or population and when a spatial shift is *not* involved, the whole phenomenon is within the sphere of ecology. When distributional phenomena change over a longer time span, and when the functional relationships of the organism and the environment result in adaptive changes, we come to the meeting ground of dynamic zoogeography and evolutionary studies. The latter, however, are usually assigned to the taxonomist, for evolutionary changes are most easily discerned by noting morphological changes. Lindroth (1962) expressed the relationship of these two disciplines as follows: Zoogeography always depends on taxonomy to know *what* to study; but taxonomy also depends on zoogeography, since geographic speciation is the accepted norm of the formation of its basic working unit.

Every animal species originated from a few ancestors in a limited area; if a particular species is now found to be widespread, it must of necessity have reached parts of its present range at an earlier period. The first aspect of dynamic zoogeography pertains to *dispersal*. If we know the details of dispersal processes, we can explain much about the presence or absence of animals. Dispersal may result as a by-product of other important phenomena belonging to the biological habits of the animal, or it can result from distinct, adaptive characteristics of the species that directly assist dissemination into wider areas. In dispersal study, both the intrinsic abilities of an animal to spread and the opportunities the environment offers for spreading are equally important. Although every animal species has the capability to migrate, dispersing individuals must find a suitable area in which to settle and reproduce through many generations. When one studies the process of settling, or colonization, one must scrutinize the ecological factors that make existence possible in a given area, as well as the adaptations and limitations of a species—structural, physiological, behavioral, population dynamical, etc.—which enable it to start a new population and survive (successfully) in the newly colonized area. Factors of dispersal as well as factors of existence in an area influence the size, extent, and dynamism of the distributional range of the animal.

James (1995, this volume) took a coincidently similar approach when he elaborated on the concepts of Ball (1975). Ball had three phases of biogeographic methodology: (1) empirical or descriptive, (2) narrative, and (3) analytical approach. James concentrated his discussion on two points: (1) DNA sequence information and (2) biogeographical research related to glaciation. I have very limited personal experience with DNA research but for more than two decades (Reynolds 1973d, etc.) I have advocated this approach, but have never had the opportunity to follow it up. It now appears that James, his colleagues, and their students have the means to do so and oligochaetology should benefit from the results of their work.

The second topic is one on which I have devoted considerable time and activity over the years. My earthworm research has concentrated on presenting wide-ranging political (state/provincial) surveys (Table 1). James and others are using this information and by going back to some of these areas, and knowing what species should be present, are conducting more specific studies, i.e., using transects.

EARTHWORM BIOGEOGRAPHY, DIVERSITY, AND TAXONOMY

In the second part of this chapter I wish to discuss the advances and innovations in oligochaetology during the past two years, particularly wherein I had some involvement. For a number of years I have had the opportunity to know, as a journal referee and editor, sometimes more than a year or two in advance, what would appear in the literature regarding earthworm biogeography, diversity, and taxonomy and I should like to summarize some of my relevant impressions.

Biogeography

North America

Canada—In the past two years considerable advances have been made in the distributional reports of earthworms for many regions of North America. In 1992, Reynolds and Reynolds presented the first complete picture of the megadrile distributional patterns in Quebec. Several earlier reports (Reynolds 1975a,b,c, 1976) presented segments of the Quebec earthworm pattern, but it was not until recently (Reynolds and Reynolds 1992) that the whole province was considered.

In this report 19 species were recorded for the province and *Sparganophilus eiseni* was reported for the first time from two widely separated collections more than 700 km east of any previously known records.

Scheu and McLean (1993) presented the first report of earthworm distribution for wide-ranging areas of southern Alberta. In their paper, they reported eight species with *Lumbricus rubellus* for the first time from the province. They also included considerable discussion on the ecological aspects of the species present.

One of the more interesting and surprising reports was by two Russian scientists working in Siberia and the Yukon (Berman and Marusik 1994). Until their paper appeared there were no published reports on earthworms from the Canadian territories. They found *Bimastos parvus, Dendrobaena octaedra,* and *Dendrodrilus rubidus* in the far north. They also went into great depth to present their views on earthworm migration, isolated populations, and earthworm introduction in the far north to try and explain why the Siberian megadrile fauna is lacking in the Yukon.

United States—The last two years have seen considerable expansion of our knowledge of earthworm distribution in the United States. Reynolds (1994b) recorded 37 species in the state of Indiana, ten of which were reported for the first time. In North Carolina (Reynolds 1994d), he reported 42 species where ten were also reported for the first time from the state. In another Atlantic coastal state, Virginia (Reynolds 1994f), 37 species were reported with six species being recorded for the first time. Later in the year, the earthworm distributions in two more southern states were published, Florida (Reynolds 1994g) and Mississippi (Reynolds 1994h). In the case of the state of Florida, there were 51 species and three subspecies reported in eight families. Seven of these were reported for the first time from Florida. In the case of Mississippi, 27 species were recorded and ten of these were reported for the first time. The earthworm distributional patterns of several other states and provinces are currently in preparation.

A significant publication (Coates et al. 1995) presents the scientific and common names plus distributional ranges for all the groups in the Clitellata and Aphanoneura.

The first attempt to present a regional view of the earthworms present in continental North America was by Reynolds (1975a, 1976a). During the past 20 years, there have been many advances and additional available data for many regions (states and provinces) in North America. The results of much of this additional data are presented in recent papers (Reynolds 1994a, 1995), which include the latest earthworm taxonomic and distribution maps.

The first table of regional earthworm surveys in North America was made by Reynolds et al. (1974). Since that time, he and others have made wide-ranging collections in North America, resulting in numerous publications of the distribution of various species of earthworms in North America. An updated version of that table appeared in Reynolds (1994i). Additional reports made this year require a revised table (Table 1) which will include all species and not just the exotic Lumbricidae as presented in Reynolds (1995).

Other Countries

The recent past has seen a considerable expansion of our knowledge of megadrile distribution on other continents as well. For instance, de Mischis (1992, 1993) has continually expanded the distributional records for Argentina. Late in 1993, the first survey of the earthworms of Swaziland appeared (Reynolds 1993). This survey, undertaken many years ago, reported seven species from that small African country. More recent surveys, undertaken on three trips during 1992 and 1993, contributed to the first survey of the earthworms of Bangladesh (Reynolds 1994c) where 14 species were reported and speculation on the possible presence of an additional 28 species was discussed.

Two trips I made to Belize during 1993 produced the first survey and report of earthworms from that country (Reynolds and Righi 1994). This first brief survey reported three species from Belize: *Dichogaster bolaui* and *Pontoscolex corethrurus* and a new species, *Eodrilus jenniferae*. Additional samples have been obtained subsequently (Reynolds and Guerra 1994) and future collecting trips (January 1995) will soon present a clearer picture of the presence and distribution of megadriles in this country.

Diversity

There has been considerable data published recently on earthworm diversity. During the summer of 1993, many North American students and scientists gathered in northern Georgia for a workshop (*Earthworm Ecology in Forest, Rangeland, and Crop Ecosystems in North America*) on the current status of various aspects of earthworm research on this continent (Fender 1995; James 1995; Reynolds 1995). The work of our colleagues in Central America and the Caribbean was also presented (Fragoso et al. 1994). A summary of their papers, which also includes the latest information on earthworm biogeography and taxonomy in North America, is described in the next section of this paper.

In the autumn of 1993, Bøgh published an interesting and innovative paper on *Identification of Earthworms: Choice of Method and Distinction Criteria*. In this paper, he discussed the use of electrophoretic techniques in the identification of earthworm species. One of the immediate benefits of this approach is the potential accurate determination of juveniles and fragments. One of the more pleasing aspects in this paper was the confirmation of the separation of the *caliginosa* complex which the late Gordon Gates and I have long advocated. The morphological criteria developed by Gates (1972) borne out in many of my surveys throughout North America were supported in this paper by Bøgh.

Two years ago, I prepared a paper for the 25th Anniversary of the School of Environmental Science at Sambalpur University in Orissa, India. The book published from that occasion, *Advances in Ecology and Environmental Science*, honored M.C. Dash, who has made many valuable contributions to the understanding of the Enchytraeidae in North America and India. In recent years, he has undertaken research with megadriles to examine the role of Indian species in vermicomposting. My contribution to this book was a paper on the diversity and distribution of all megadrile families in North America based on my surveys on this continent since 1967 and this was accompanied by an updated series of maps illustrating these distributional patterns (Reynolds 1994a).

During June 1994(e), Reynolds prepared an article on the *Earthworms of the World*. The topics of this paper included global distribution, barriers to migration, habitat requirements, and functions of earthworms in the soil. Sometimes those who write in an esoteric or narrow field fail to stand back and present their work in a more general and readable fashion of this type.

Taxonomy

For a field of science as limited as oligochaetology, we are fortunate to have a series of books which bring together all the description citations and type depositions of earthworms in one place, i.e., *Nomenclatura Oligochaetologica* and the three supplements prepared to date (Reynolds and Cook 1976, 1981, 1989, 1993). The third supplement (*N.O. Supplementum Tertium*) which records new taxa up to December 31, 1992 indicates that 739 genera, 40 subgenera, and 7254 species have been described. The fourth supplement, *N.O. Supplementum Quartum*, currently in preparation (Reynolds and Cook 1998) has a further 250 new species described. From my editorial, reviewing, and refereeing work, I am sure that this number will more than double in the next year. Some of the most exciting discoveries are the presence of nearctic species in the far reaches of North America where they have not been previously recorded, for example, Fender's and McKey-Fender's work on *Bimastos* and *Arctiostrotus* in the northwestern United States and southwestern British Columbia (Canada) as well as James's discoveries of *Argilophilus* and *Diplocardia* in the southwestern United States.

I have alluded briefly to the workshop held in northern Georgia in July 1993 at which most of the North American earthworm researchers and their students were present (Hendrix 1995). Four of the presentations were focused on biogeography and taxonomy. The topics were divided along taxonomic and biogeographical lines. All of the taxonomic papers were accompanied by continental range maps for genera and in some cases species or groups of species.

The first paper in the book was *Status of Exotic Earthworm Systematics and Biogeography in North America* (Reynolds 1995). This paper deals primarily with the Lumbricidae and generally excludes the nearctic genera *Bimastos* and *Eisenoides*. The section on historical perspectives traces the associations and classifications of authors from Linnaeus (1758) through Mršić (1991). The reasons for the frequent shifting and lumping of certain species inter- and intragenerically are discussed. This frequent realignment by taxonomists has created many nomenclatural and taxonomic problems for researchers for many years. This discussion also includes the contributions and activity in North America (Gates, Fender, Reynolds, and Cook) which is frequently lacking in some European reports. Some portions of the biogeographical section are reported here along with an updated Table 1.

The second paper was entitled *Systematics, Biogeography, and Ecology of Nearctic Earthworms from Eastern, Central, Southern, and Southwestern USA* (James 1995). This paper deals with five families, two of which are monospecific, e.g., Lutodrilidae (*Lutodrilus multivesiculatus*) and Komarekionidae (*Komarekiona eatoni*). The family Sparganophilidae is monogeneric with 12 species. The Lumbricidae centers on the two nearctic genera, *Bimastos* and *Eisenoides*, having nine and two species, respectively. James's Megascolecidae (Acanthodrilidae *sensu* Gates and Reynolds) is restricted to the genus *Diplocardia* and its 42 species. James's ecological section included discussions of population studies, emphasizing the lack of community studies and economic applications. As in all papers in this book, there is a concluding section on the author's view as to future earthworm research imperatives.

The third paper addressed *Native Earthworms of the Pacific Northwest: An Ecological Overview* (Fender 1995). It deals with a group of earthworm (Megascolecidae, Argilophilini) which are unfamiliar to most people. Fender hits the nail on the head when he states that the Pacific northwest possesses the most "rich, varied, and interesting, but highly underreported" earthworm fauna. There is a vast amount of collected data, waiting to be analyzed, and taxa to be described. Fender discusses the historical biogeography, ecology, and variation of this group of little known oligochaetes. His research imperatives center on the need for ecological studies and descriptions of species.

The final taxonomic paper is entitled *Native Earthworms of the North Neotropical Region: Current Status and Controversies* (Fragoso et al. 1995). For those of us working exclusively in North America, the lists of earthworm species and many of the authors cited in the paper may not be familiar, although the early works cited in their historical perspective include researchers such as

Table 1. Regional earthworm surveys in North America

Region	Number of species	Number of units (%) surveyed[1]	Reference(s)
Alabama	28	75	Reynolds (1994i)
Alberta	6	30	Scheu & McLean (1993)
Arkansas	21	29	Causey (1952, 1953)
Connecticut	21	100	Reynolds (1973c)
Delaware	14	100	Reynolds (1973a)
Florida	54	85	Reynolds (1994g)
Georgia	42	75	Reynolds (prep.)
Illinois	32	45	Harman (1960)
Indiana	37	100	Reynolds (1994b)
Louisiana	17	100	Harman (1952), Gates (1965, 1967)
Maryland	26	100	Reynolds (1974b)
Massachusetts	21	100	Reynolds (1977a)
Michigan	20	64	Snider (1991)
Mississippi	27	77	Reynolds (1994h)
Missouri	21	27	Olson (1936)
Montana	8	14	Reynolds (1972)
New Brunswick	13	100	Reynolds (1976d), Reynolds & Christie (1977)
New York	20	47	Olson (1940), Eaton (1942)
North Carolina	42	79	Reynolds (1994d)
North Dakota	5	15	Reynolds (1978b)
Nova Scotia	15	100	Reynolds (1976d)
Ohio	22	63	Olson (1928, 1932)
Ontario	19	96	Reynolds (1977)
Oregon	25	70	MacNab & McKey-Fender (1947), Fender (1985)
Prince Edward Island	12	100	Reynolds (1975b)
Quebec (south shore)	15	100	Reynolds (1975b,c,d, 1976b)
Quebec (north shore)	19	86	Reynolds & Reynolds (1992)
Rhode Island	11	100	Reynolds (1973b)
South Dakota	3	3	Gates (1979)
Tennessee	41	100	Reynolds et al. (1974), Reynolds (1977c,d, 1978a)
Virginia	37	77	Reynolds (1994f)
Washington	22	40	Altman (1936), Fender (1985), MacNab & McKey-Fender (1947)
Yukon	3	100	Berman & Marusik (1994)

[1] Units are counties, districts, parishes, etc.

Beddard, Benham, Cognetti, Eisen, Gates, and Michaelsen, who are familiar earthworm taxonomists to all. In the oral presentation, we were introduced to many new taxa (genera and species) which are about to be described. Unfortunately, many of these have not yet been published and will not be included in order to protect the nomenclatural status of the names, i.e., to avoid presenting *nomena nuda* (see Fragoso and Fernández 1994). The authors explained in great detail the biogeography, ecology, and taxonomy of the earthworms from this region. Their research imperative includes intensive sampling in the region, analysis of phylogenetic affinities, and earthworm taxonomic keys, which are easier to use.

In their list of the earthworm fauna of the north Neotropical region, Fragoso et al. (1995) indicated the absence of any written report on earthworms from Belize (formerly British Honduras). Twice during 1993, before and after the Georgia Workshop, I had the opportunity to work in this small Central American country and collect earthworms. The results of these collections were published in a paper by Dr. Gilberto Righi and myself wherein two well-known species (*Dichogaster bolaui* and *Pontoscolex corethrurus*) are reported along with a new species, *Eodrilus jenniferae*. Aside from the description of a new species and the first record of earthworms from Belize, this paper includes a discussion on the retention of *Eodrilus* and *Diplotrema* as separate and distinct genera based on four criteria. We also continue with a suggestion for distinguishing four closely related genera: *Eodrilus*, *Notiodrilus*, *Acanthodrilus*, and *Microscolex*. Our solution for distinguishing these genera will undoubtedly spark some discussion in the future by Fragoso and others, and as a result of these debates we should come closer to achieving the research imperatives we all espoused in the discussions and presentations at the workshop.

PRESENTATIONS ON EARTHWORM TAXONOMY, DIVERSITY, AND BIOGEOGRAPHY AT THE FIFTH INTERNATIONAL SYMPOSIUM

The first earthworm ecology paper in this session at ISEE 5 was presented by Dr. A.G. Viktorov of the Russian Academy of Science in Moscow, titled *Diversity of Polyploid Races in the Family Lumbricidae*. My personal experience has been limited to one contribution akin to this topic (Reynolds 1974a), but Viktorov has included in his literature the fundamental works by Omodeo (1951, 1952, 1955, and 1956) and Muldal (1952). One reference by Jaenike is included, as well as many Russian references. This literature review along with his own research indicates three significant findings: (1) genome mutation in Lumbricidae for polyploids and diploids is essentially equal, (2) polyploid races appear to occupy the outer margins of the species range, and (3) when diploid and polyploid races are sympatric they utilize different ecological niches. The data presented by Dr. Viktorov are based on limited studies, 58 species belonging to 12 genera *vis-à-vis* 400+ species and 25+ genera globally (Reynolds 1995). Nevertheless, Dr. Viktorov does summarize his published findings (Viktorov 1988, 1989), which have probably had limited previous distribution.

The second paper in this session was presented by Dr. Victor V. Pop of the Institute of Biological Research (Cluj-Napoca, Romania), titled *Earthworm-Vegetation-Relationships in the Romanian Carpathians*. In reviewing Dr. Pop's paper, I was reminded of some of my own early work (1970, 1971, 1972b,c) before I began extensive earthworm surveys throughout North America (see Table 1). The results produced in this eastern European study are similar to those we found in eastern North America. The data for Dr. Pop's interpretation of the earthworm-vegetation-soil relationships are based on more than 300 collection sites gathered and analyzed over more than 20 years. His correlation analysis, in the Romanian Carpathians, appears to illustrate two contradictory points: (1) at the single species level, generally, lumbricids tend to show little preference for certain vegetation or soil types and (2) certain earthworm community patterns are characteristic for certain biotypes. Generally, he found that slightly acid to neutral soils are inhabited by more complex earthworm communities. Also, the earthworm communities with the greatest biodiversity were those with the greatest percentage of endemic species. Dr. Pop's research suggests that grassland earthworm communities are more heterogeneous and difficult to characterize. The overall findings of Dr. Pop confirm the existence of true earthworm communities based on vegetation and soil relationships at the ecosystem level.

A poster presentation was titled *The Earthworms of Baño Ore, Luquillo Experimental Forest, Puerto Rico*, by Dr. Sonia Borges and Monica Alfaro of the Universidad de Puerto Rico-RUM (Mayagüez, PR). This presentation increases our understanding of earthworm communities in the Neotropics and, in particular, the eastern corner of Puerto Rico. One of the surprising results is the low species density and limited species diversity. Statistical analyses indicate no significant differences between earthworm density and biomass and forest association and soil depth. Our recent limited surveys in Belize (Reynolds and Righi 1994; Reynolds and Guerra 1994) showed similar results, but we expect future collections will alter our initial findings.

Another poster presentation was by Dr. Catalina de Mischis of the Universidad Nacional de Córdoba, titled *A Preliminary Survey of the Earthworms of the Reserva Hídrica Dique La Quebrada, Córdoba, Argentina (Annelida, Oligochaeta)*. This represents the fifth of a series of contributions to the knowledge of the earthworm fauna in the Republic of Argentina made by Dr. de Mischis. The results of her study remind me very much of my work in Tennessee (Reynolds 1970, 1971, 1972c) wherein I examined woodland and grassland habitats at the Oak Ridge Reserve and in the Great Smoky Mountains National Park. There is one striking contrast between this study in Argentina and those of east Tennessee. Dr. de Mischis collected only exotic species (Lumbricidae and Megascolecidae) in her study *vis-à-vis* similar exotic species in these two families plus nearctic Lumbricidae (*Bimastos* and *Eisenoides*) and Acanthodrilidae (*Diplocardia*). De Mischis also points out the similarity of her findings to those of Reynolds and Reinecke (1976) in the Kruger National Park.

A poster titled *Size Shift in the Mexican Earthworms Species Balanteodrilus pearsei: A Possible Case of Character Displacement* was presented by Carlos Fragoso and Patricia Rojas of the Instituto de Ecología (Xalapa, Mexico). Character displacement has been recorded for many different animal groups in the past, generally as a result of available food reserves or behavioral differences. These authors present the first report of this phenomenon in earthworms. They examined three species of the genus *Balanteodrilus*, two of which are new and as yet undescribed. Dr. Fragoso and his colleague have determined that *B. pearsei* is indeed a very common species in the eastern Mexican tropics and its size difference is not a random condition but probably as a result of (1) response to poor food sources, (2) character displacement resulting from past long-term competition, and (3) reproductive character displacement or reinforcement. In the mid-1970s I noticed a similar occurrence in *Lumbricus festivus* populations, present in Quebec and British Columbia, but was unaware of character displacement or its causes or effects at that time (Reynolds 1977c). We have recently noticed a possible second report of a size shift in earthworms (*L. rubellus*), which results from a possible case of character displacement (Reynolds and Mayville 1994).

Another poster was presented by Hulton B. Wood (USDA Forest Service, Riverside, CA) in association with K.L. Oliver and Dr. Sam W. James, titled *Relict Megascolecidae and Exclusion of Lumbricidae from Basalt-Derived Soils in Southern California*. In an earlier study, Wood and James (1993) suspected earthworm species diversity differed between basalt and non-basalt-derived soils. This research set out to examine these suspicions and they determined that relict species (Acanthodrilidae) and the peregrine species of Lumbricidae were absent from basalt-derived soils. They believe several factors may have influenced the exclusion of these groups of earthworms from these soils, e.g., predation, topography, soil chemistry, and soil physics. My research experience was an early study in the Haliburton Highlands of central Ontario (Reynolds 1972d; Reynolds and Jordan 1975).

The final poster was titled *"Grassroots" Earthworm Collecting in Jamaica,* presented by Caton Gauthier and Mary Appelhof of Flowerfield Enterprises (Kalamazoo, MI). Not since the early years of this century, when the Rev. Hilderic Friend was contributing his short notes to the earthworm literature (1890–1930), have "amateurs" been seen in publishing in the scientific literature. The background of these authors is in the practical and educational vermicomposting fields. In their presentation, they described their five-stage project to educate the people of Jamaica in basic concepts of biology with the aid of increasing their practice in habitat conservation and the environmental benefits of earthworms. I am pleased to see the advances made by this team because I was consulted on several occasions during the formulation of this project. This project appears to be well on its way to a successful conclusion and has some similarities to our *Earthworm Biology and Vermicomposting Workshops* held annually at Sir Sandford Fleming College. This is not surprising, since Mary Appelhof attended our workshop in 1993 and Caton Gauthier in 1994. I have long been an advocate for periodically presenting our science in a more popular vein, i.e., Reynolds (1994e), so this information could be more accessible.

FUTURE TRENDS AND RESEARCH IMPERATIVES IN EARTHWORM TAXONOMY

One of the major problems for earthworm taxonomy in North America has been the paucity of scientists, all living in isolation. Many individuals have dabbled in earthworm research, but their contributions can frequently be counted on one hand. For two promising scientists, tragic death came early, before their potential impact could be realized (William Murchie and Richard Tandy).

Gordon Gates, the "dean" of earthworm taxonomy and systematics, died in 1987. Although he began publishing in 1926, it was not until the latter part of his career that he devoted much time to the earthworms of North America and the Lumbricidae.

Prior to 1950, there were Frank Smith (publication period, 1885–1937) and Henry Olson (publication period, 1928–1940), who made contributions to taxonomy and distribution, respectively. In the last few decades, Dorothy McKey-Fender and William Fender have been concentrating on the taxonomy and distribution of the native and exotic earthworm fauna of the west coast of North America, and Sam James on the endemic species of the southeastern and plains areas.

Since 1972, I have collected earthworms widely throughout North America, alone and with the aid of my colleagues at the Tall Timbers Research Station. The results of these collections have been published as distributional data primarily, with minimal contribution to systematics *sensu stricto*. Reynolds and Cook (1977, 1981, 1989, 1993, 1998) in the *Nomenclatura Oligochaetologica* series have brought together in one source the necessary reference data for anyone involved in the taxonomy and nomenclature of earthworms.

With this limited background, I suggest the following priorities for research and funding support.

Training of Taxonomists

For more than two decades (Reynolds 1973d; Reynolds et al. 1974), I have stated continually that the scarcity of competent earthworm systematists/taxonomists was detrimental to ecologists and others. The normal institutions which employ these types of specialists and encourage their development, e.g., museums and departments of agriculture, have not done so in North America since Smith worked for the Illinois Natural History Survey in the early 1900s. There must be a concerted effort to support this type of research, before we are left without any competent specialists in our field. I see only four colleagues at ISEE 5 who attended the colloquium in Prague in 1973: Clive Edwards, Andrei Pokarzhevskii, Adriaan Reinecke, and myself. The large number of colleagues here who are actively working on various aspects of earthworm biogeography and taxonomy is most gratifying and bodes well for our future.

Parthenogenesis in Taxonomy

The other major exotic group of earthworms in North America (Megascolecidae, pheretimoid groups) has long been plagued with taxonomic problems, which resulted from widespread parthenogenesis in its species (Gates 1972b). There is parthenogenesis within the Lumbricidae. One study recently has shown that localized populations of *Octolasion tyrtaeum* (Jaenike et al. 1980, 1982; Jaenike and Selander 1985) exhibited parthenogenesis. Previously, taxonomic problems with some morphs of what is now *Dendrodrilus rubidus* may be attributable to parthenogenesis. This area of research needs more attention.

Earthworm Surveys

From Table 1 we can see that, in spite of what has already been accomplished, there are major areas of North America in which earthworm surveys are totally lacking. In certain areas where native species still exist, there is the considerable potential for discovery of new species. Any new species in the Lumbricidae will probably come from the native genera *Bimastos* and *Eisenoides*, or a new genus. Additional new species might be expected to occur in other nearctic genera such as *Arctiostrotus*, *Diplocardia,* and *Komarekiona.*

Life Histories

It is amazing that for the nearly 8,000 oligochaetes (Reynolds and Cook 1993), modern, updated, life history studies have been made on only a few species, i.e., fewer than 20. Lee (1992) has suggested that only about six lumbricids and six tropical species have been studied in sufficient detail to provide adequate information. Some of the information gathered on common Lumbricidae was done at a time when species lumping occurred, i.e., factors attributed to *Allolobophora caliginosa* which included several species and thus accounted for the range of data, *vis-à-vis* specific values for other species.

Modern Techniques

One area which was considered for years, but only recently had any evidence to support its potential, is electrophoresis. Bøgh (1993) illustrated that certain species were different, i.e., *Aporrectodea tuberculata* and *Ap. turgida* are distinct species, and demonstrated how to identify species from fragments. This area of research should be followed, and will probably help with areas of confusion.

Earthworms for Waste Management

The concept of recycling and composting has gained increasing acceptance over the past two decades. The contributions of earthworms to vermicomposting have been imported to industrialized and non-industrialized countries. We have restricted our efforts to only a few species (*Eisenia foetida*, *Eudrilus eugeniae*, *Perionyx excavatus*, etc.), but with almost 4,000 megadrile species available to us, we must search for additional species that may be harnessed to assist in the decomposition and transformation of our waste products into useful materials.

Earthworms for Environmental Monitoring

The ability of many earthworm species to accumulate heavy metals and various pesticides offers us opportunities to trace the movement of these materials in the soil. One of our microdrile species, *Tubifex tubifex*, has been used as a biological indicator in polluted waters for decades.

We need to conduct research on uptake mechanisms, distribution, and concentration of these chemicals in various types of earthworm tissues. In addition we need to know how to interpret our findings as they relate to our daily lives.

All of these types of activities require accurate determination of species, and hence the continual need for well-trained taxonomists.

Plain Language and Less Esotery

I have long advocated the necessity for our scientific information to be more accessible to the general non-scientific community. We are a small group of scientists working with limited finances and materials. We have suffered from not following the example of entomologists and ornithologists. These disciplines have advanced more rapidly because of the contributions of "amateurs" and general collectors. In the early part of this century, we had one such person, the Rev. Hilderic Friend, who was turned aside and dismissed by the specialists of the day. He was a good naturalist, but his contributions were ridiculed and discounted. I believe that if he had been helped and encouraged, his work might have had a greater impact on oligochaetology as we know it today. Many of our conventions were established for sound reasons, but we must take time to explain these to our newer colleagues. I was pleased to see that non-specialists with limited technical experience are taking the opportunity to attend this conference and make presentations. Hopefully, with the proper guidance and encouragement, others will present papers at future symposia.

During the past three years, I have been writing a column for *The Wormletter* under the banner "Ask the worm doctor," in which I have tried to answer questions from worm growers, vermicomposters, and those with a general interest in recycling and the environment. I embarked on this venture because I was tired of seeing the same old misinformation being repackaged and redistributed as recent new information, e.g., the old Henry Hopp material of the late 1940s reprinted by Garden Way in the 1970s with absolutely no revisions or updating. This is only one of many such examples. In recent discussions with Stephen White, who is editor of the *Worm Digest*, I am pleased to learn that they are prepared to present their journal as a vehicle to get our various scientific findings to a much wider audience.

CONCLUSIONS

In this paper, I have tried to relate my past experience to the topic of this session. Circumstances beyond the control of some of our colleagues necessitated their cancellation at the last minute. Those who have been able to attend and present their papers and posters have given us hope for the resurgence of earthworm taxonomy and a glimpse into what lies ahead. I thank the Organizing Committee for giving me the opportunity to present the closing lecture for the first session of this 5th International Symposium on Earthworm Ecology.

REFERENCES CITED

Altman, L.C. 1936. Oligochaeta of Washington. *Univ. Wash. Publ. Biol.* 4(1), 1–137.

Ball, I.R. 1975. Nature and formulation of biogeographical hypotheses. *Syst. Zool.* 24(4), 407–430.

Berman, D.I., and Y.M. Marusik. 1994. On *Bimastos parvus* (Oligochaeta: Lumbricidae) from Yukon Territory (Canada) with notes on distribution of the earthworms in north-west North America and northeast Siberia. *Megadrilogica* 5(10), 113–116.

Bøgh, P.S. 1992. Identification of earthworms (Lumbricidae): Choice of method and distinction criteria. *Megadrilogica* 4(10), 163–174.

Causey, D. 1952. The earthworms of Arkansas. *Proc. Arkansas Acad. Sci.* 5, 31–42.

Causey, D. 1953. Additional records of Arkansas earthworms. *Proc. Arkansas Acad. Sci.* 6, 47–48.

Coates, K.A., S.R. Gelder, J. Madill, J.W. Reynolds, and M.J. Wetzel. 1995. Common and scientific names of aquatic invertebrates from the United States and Canada: *Clitellata* and *Aphanoneura* (Phylum Annelida). *Amer. Fish. Soc. Spec. Publ.* (in press).

Eaton, T.H. 1942. Earthworms of the northeastern United States: A key, with distribution records. *J. Wash. Acad. Sci.* 32(8), 242–249.

Fender, W.B. 1985. Earthworms of the western United States. Part. I. Lumbricidae. *Megadrilogica* 4(5), 93–129.

Fender, W.B. 1995. Native earthworms of the Pacific Northwest: An ecological overview. In *Ecology and biogeography of earthworms in North America* (P.F. Hendrix, ed.), pp. 53–66. Lewis Publishing, Boca Raton, FL.

Fragoso, C., and P.R. Fernández. 1994. Earthworms from southwestern Mexico, New Acanthodriline genera and species (Megascolecidae, Oligochaeta). *Megadrilogica* 6(1), 1–12.

Fragoso, C., S.W. James, and S. Borges. 1995. Native earthworms of the north neotropical region: Current status and controversies. In *Ecology and biogeography of earthworms in North America* (P.F. Hendrix, ed.), pp. 67–114. Lewis Publishers, Boca Raton, FL.

Gates, G.E. 1965. Louisiana earthworms. I. A preliminary survey. *La. Acad. Sci.* 28(1), 12–20.

Gates, G.E. 1967. On the earthworm fauna of the Great American desert and adjacent areas. *Gt. Basin Nat.* 27(3), 142–176.

Gates, G.E. 1972a. Toward a revision of the earthworm family Lumbricidae. IV. The trapezoides species group. *Bull. Tall Timbers Res. Stn.* No. 12, 146 pp.

Gates, G.E. 1972b. Burmese earthworms. An introduction to the systematics and biology of megadrile oligochaetes with special reference to southeast Asia. *Trans. Amer. Philos. Soc.* 62(7), 1–326.

Gates, G.E. 1979. South Dakota does have earthworms! *Megadrilogica* 3(9), 165–166.

Harman, W.J. 1952 A taxonomic survey of the earthworms of Lincoln Parish, Louisiana. *Proc. La. Acad. Sci.* 15, 19–23.

Harman, W.J. 1960. Studies on the taxonomy and musculature of the earthworms of central Illinois. Ph.D. dissertation, University of Illinois, Champaign, 107 pp.

Hendrix, P.F. 1995. *Ecology and biogeography of earthworms in North America.* Lewis Publishers, Boca Raton, FL, 244 pp.

Jaenike, J., and R.K. Selander. 1985. On the co-existence of ecologically similar clones of parthenogenetic earthworms. *Okios* 44(3), 512–514.

Jaenike, J., S. Ausubel, and D.A. Grimaldi. 1982. On the evolution of clonal diversity in parthenogenetic earthworms. *Pedobiologia* 23(3–4), 304–310.

Jaenike, J., E.D. Parker, and R.K. Selander. 1980. Clonal niche structure in the parthenogenetic earthworm *Octolasion tyrtaeum. Amer. Nat.* 116, 196–205.

James, S.W. 1995. Systematics, biogeography and ecology of earthworms from eastern, central, southern and southwestern USA. In *Ecology and biogeography of earthworms in North America* (P.F. Hendrix, ed.), pp. 29–51. Lewis Publishers, Boca Raton, FL.

Lee, K.E. 1992. Some trends and opportunities in earthworm research or: Darwin's children—the future of our discipline. *Soil Biol. Biochem.* 24(12), 1765–1771.

Lindroth, C.H. 1962. Foreword. In *Taxonomy and geography* (D. Nichols, ed.), pp. 3–5. Syst. Assoc. Publ., London.

Linnaeus, C. 1758. *Systema Naturae. Regnum Animale* (10th ed.). 824 pp.

MacNab, J.A., and D. McKey-Fender. 1947. An introduction to Oregon earthworms with additions to the Washington list. *Northwest Sci.* 21(2), 69–75.

de Mischis, C.C. 1992. The first record of the species *Amynthas diffringens* (Baird 1869) (Oligochaeta: Megascolecidae) in the province of Cordoba (Argentina). *Megadrilogica* 4(8), 143–144.

de Mischis, C.C. 1993. A contribution to the knowledge of megascolecid fauna (Annelida, Oligochaeta) from the province of Cordoba, Argentina. *Megadrilogica* 5(2), 9–12.

Mršič, N. 1991. *Monograph on earthworms (Lumbricidae) of the Balkans.* Slovenska Akademija Znanosti Umetnosti, Ljubljana, 757 pp.

Muldal, S. 1952. The chromosomes of the earthworms. I. The evolution of polyploidy. *Heredity* 6, 55–76.

Olson, H.W. 1928. The earthworms of Ohio, with a study of their distribution in relation to hydrogen-ion concentration, moisture and organic content of the soil. *Bull. Ohio Biol. Surv.* 4(2), Bull. 17, 47–90.

Olson, H.W. 1932. Two new species of earthworms for Ohio. *Ohio J. Sci.* 32, 192–193.

Olson, H.W. 1936. Earthworms of Missouri. *Ohio J. Sci.* 36(2), 102–193.

Olson, H.W. 1940. Earthworms of New York state. *Amer. Mus. Nov.* No. 1090, 9 pp.

Omodeo, P. 1951. Problemi zoogeografici ed ecologici relatici a limbrichi peregrini, con particolare riguardo al tipo di reprouzione ed alla struttura earriologica. *Boll. Zool.* 18, 117–122.

Omodeo, P. 1952. Cariologia dei Lumbricidae. *Caryologia* 4, 173–178.

Omodeo, P. 1955. Cariologia dei Lumbricidae. II. Contributo. *Caryologia* 8, 137–178.

Omodeo P. 1956. Contributo alla revisione dei Lumbricidae. *Arch. Zool. It.* 41, 129–212.

Reynolds, J.W. 1970. The relationship of earthworm distribution and biomass to soil type in forest and grassland habitats. *Agron. Abs.* 1970, 161.

Reynolds, J.W. 1971. The effect of altitude, soil moisture and soil acidity in earthworm (Oligochaeta: Acanthodrilidae and Lumbricidae) density, biomass and species diversification in *Liriodendron tulipifera* L. stands in two areas of east Tennessee. *Assoc. Southeast. Biol Bull.* 18(2), 52.

Reynolds, J.W. 1972a. A contribution to the earthworm fauna of Montana. *Proc. Mont. Acad. Sci.* 32, 6–13.

Reynolds, J.W. 1972b. The relationship of earthworm (Oligochaeta: Acanthodrilidae and Lumbricidae) distribution and biomass in six heterogeneous woodlot sites in Tippecanoe County, Indiana. *J. Tenn. Acad. Sci.* 47(2), 63–67.

Reynolds, J.W. 1972c. The activity and distribution of earthworms in tulip poplar stands in the Great Smoky Mountains National Park, Sevier County, Tennessee (Acanthodrilidae, Lumbricidae and Megascolecidae). *Bull. Tall Timbers Res. Stn.* No. 11, 41–54.

Reynolds, J.W. 1972d. Earthworms (Lumbricidae) of the Haliburton Highlands, Ontario, Canada. *Megadrilogica* 1(3), 1–11.

Reynolds, J.W. 1973a. The earthworms of Delaware (Oligochaeta: Acanthodrilidae and Lumbricidae). *Megadrilogica* 1(5), 1–4.

Reynolds, J.W. 1973b. The earthworms of Rhode Island (Oligochaeta: Lumbricidae). *Megadrilogica* 1(6), 1–4.

Reynolds, J.W. 1973c. The earthworms of Connecticut (Oligochaeta: Lumbricidae, Megascolecidae and Sparganophilidae). *Megadrilogica* 1(7), 1–6.

Reynolds, J.W. 1973d. Earthworm (Annelida, Oligochaeta) ecology and systematics. In *Proc. 1st Soil Microcommunities Conf.* (D.L. Dindal, ed.), pp. 95–120. U.S. Atomic Energy Comm., Natl. Tech. Inform. Serv., Springfield.

Reynolds, J.W. 1974a. Are oligochaetes really hermaphroditic amphimictic organisms? *Biologist* 56(2), 90–99.

Reynolds, J.W. 1974b. The earthworms of Maryland (Oligochaeta: Acanthodrilidae, Lumbricidae, Megascolecidae and Sparganophilidae). *Megadrilogica* 1(11), 1–12.

Reynolds, J.W. 1975a. Die biogeographie van Noorde-Amerikaanse (Oligochaeta) noorde van Meksike-I. *Indikator* 7(4), 11–20.

Reynolds, J.W. 1975b. Les Lombricidés (Oligochaeta) des Îles-de-la-Madeleine. *Megadrilogica* 2(3), 1–8.

Reynolds, J.W. 1975c. Les Lombricidés (Oligochaeta) de la Gaspésie, Québec. *Megadrilogica* 2(4), 4–9.

Reynolds, J.W. 1975d. Les Lombricidés (Oligochaeta) de Î'Ile d'Orléans, Québec. *Megadrilogica* 2(5), 8–11.

Reynolds, J.W. 1975e. The earthworms of Prince Edward Island (Oligochaeta: Lumbricidae). *Megadrilogica* 2(7), 4–10.

Reynolds, J.W. 1976a. Die biogeographie van Noorde-Amerikaanse (Oligochaeta) noorde van Meksike-II. *Indikator* 8(1), 6–20.

Reynolds, J.W. 1976b. Catalogue et clé d'identification des lombricidés du Québec. *Nat. Can.* 103(1), 21–27.

Reynolds, J.W. 1976c. The distribution and ecology of the earthworms of Nova Scotia. *Megadrilogica* 2(8), 1–7.

Reynolds, J.W. 1976d. A preliminary checklist and distribution of the earthworms of New Brunswick. *N.B. Nat.* 7(2), 16–17.

Reynolds, J.W. 1977a. The earthworms of Massachusetts (Oligochaeta: Lumbricidae, Megascolecidae and Sparganophilidae). *Megadrilogica* 3(2), 49–54.

Reynolds, J.W. 1977b. The earthworms (Lumbricidae and Sparganophilidae) of Ontario. *Life Sci. Misc. Publ., Roy. Ont. Mus.*, 141 pp.

Reynolds, J.W. 1977c. The earthworms of Tennessee (Oligochaeta). II. Sparganophilidae, with the description of a new species. *Megadrilogica* 3(3), 61–64.

Reynolds, J.W. 1977d. The earthworms of Tennessee (Oligochaeta). III. Komarekionidae, with notes on distribution and biology. *Megadrilogica* 3(4), 65–69.

Reynolds, J.W. 1977e. Le ver québécois (*Lumbricus festivus*) envahit la Colombie-Britannique. *Can. Field-Nat.* 91(4), 395–396.

Reynolds, J.W. 1978a. The earthworms of Tennessee (Oligochaeta). IV. Megascolecidae, with notes on distribution, biology and a key to the species in the state. *Megadrilogica* 3(7), 117–129.

Reynolds, J.W. 1978b. A contribution to our knowledge of the earthworm fauna of North Dakota. *Megadrilogica* 3(8), 148–149.

Reynolds, J.W. 1993. On some earthworms from Swaziland (Oligochaeta: Glossoscolecidae, Megascolecidae, Microchaetidae and Octochaetidae). *Megadrilogica* 5(1), 1–8.

—Reynolds, J.W. 1994a. The distribution of earthworms (Annelida, Oligochaeta) in North America. In *Advances in ecology and environmental science* (P.C. Mishra et al., eds.), pp. 133–153. Ashish Publication, New Delhi.

Reynolds, J.W. 1994b. The distribution of the earthworms (Oligochaeta) of Indiana: A case for the Post Quaternary Introduction Theory for megadrile migration in North America. *Megadrilogica* 5(3), 13–32.

Reynolds, J.W. 1994c. The earthworms of Bangladesh (Oligochaeta: Megascolecidae, Moniligastridae and Octochaetidae). *Megadrilogica* 5(4), 33–44.

Reynolds, J.W. 1994d. Earthworms of North Carolina (Oligochaeta: Acanthodrilidae, Komarekionidae, Lumbricidae, Megascolecidae, Ocnerodrilidae and Sparganophilidae). *Megadrilogica* 5(6), 53–72.

Reynolds, J.W. 1994e. Earthworms of the world. *Global Biodiversity* 4(1), 11–16.

Reynolds, J.W. 1994f. Earthworms of Virginia (Oligochaeta: Acanthodrilidae, Komarekionidae, Lumbricidae, Megascolecidae and Sparganophilidae). *Megadrilogica* 5(8), 77–94.

Reynolds, J.W. 1994g. Earthworms of Florida (Oligochaeta: Acanthodrilidae, Eudrilidae, Glossoscolecidae, Lumbricidae, Megascolecidae, Ocnerodrilidae, Octochaetidae and Sparganophilidae). *Megadrilogica* 5(12), 125–141.

Reynolds, J.W. 1994h. Earthworms of Mississippi (Oligochaeta: Acanthodrilidae, Lumbricidae, Megascolecidae, Ocnerodrilidae and Sparganophilidae). *Megadrilogica* 6(3), 17–29.

Reynolds, J.W. 1994i. Earthworms of Alabama (Oligochaeta: Acanthodrilidae, Eudrilidae, Lumbricidae, Megascolecidae, Ocnerodrilidae and Sparganophilidae). *Megadrilogica* 6(4), 35–46.

—Reynolds, J.W. 1995. The status of exotic earthworm systematics and biogeography in North America. In *Ecology and biogeography of earthworms in North America* (P.F. Hendrix, ed.), pp. 1–28. Lewis Publishers, Boca Raton, FL.

Reynolds, J.W., and D.S. Christie. 1977. Additional records of New Brunswick earthworms. *N.B. Nat.* 8(3), 25.

Reynolds, J.W., and D.G. Cook. 1976. *Nomenclatura Oligochaetologica*, a catalogue of names, descriptions and type specimens of the Oligochaeta. University of New Brunswick, Fredericton, 217 pp.

Reynolds, J.W., and D.G. Cook. 1981. *Nomenclatura Oligochaetologica Supplementum*

Primum, a catalogue of names, descriptions and type specimens of the Oligochaeta. University of New Brunswick, Fredericton, 39 pp.

Reynolds, J.W., and D.G. Cook. 1989. *Nomenclatura Oligochaetologica Supplementum Secundum*, a catalogue of names, descriptions and type specimens of the Oligochaeta. *New Brunswick Mus. Monogr. Ser. (Nat. Hist.)*, No. 8, 37 pp.

Reynolds, J.W., and D.G. Cook. 1993. *Nomenclatura Oligochaetologica Supplementum Tertium*, a catalogue of names, descriptions and type specimens of the Oligochaeta. *New Brunswick Mus. Monogr. Ser. (Nat. Hist.)*, No. 9, 39 pp.

Reynolds, J.W., and D.G. Cook. 1998. *Nomenclatura Oligochaetologica Supplementum Quartum*, a catalogue of names, descriptions and type specimens of the Oligochaeta. *New Brunswick Mus. Monogr. Ser. (Nat. Hist.)*, (in prep.).

Reynolds, J.W., and C.A. Guerra. 1994. Two species of earthworms newly reported from Belize, C.A. (Oligochaeta: Glossoscolecidae and Megascolecidae). *Megadrilogica* 5(10), 122–124.

Reynolds, J.W., and G.A. Jordan. 1975. A preliminary conceptual model of megadrile activity and abundance in the Haliburton Highlands. *Megadrilogica* 2(2), 1–9.

Reynolds, J.W., and P.N. Mayville. 1994. New earthworm records from Rainy River District in northwestern Ontario (Oligochaeta: Lumbricidae). *Megadrilogica* 6(2), 13–16.

Reynolds, J.W., and A.J. Reinecke. 1976. A preliminary survey of the earthworms of the Kruger National Park, South Africa (Oligochaeta: Glossoscolecidae, Megascolecidae and Octochaetidae). *Wet. Bydraes, P.U. vir C.H.O. (B)* No. 89, 19 pp.

Reynolds, J.W., and K.W. Reynolds. 1992. Les vers de terre (Oligochaeta: Lumbricidae et Sparganophilidae) sur la rive nord du Saint-Laurent (Québec). *Megadrilogica* 4(9), 145–161.

Reynolds, J.W., and G. Righi. 1994. On some earthworms from the Belize, C.A. with the description of a new species (Oligochaeta: Acanthodrilidae, Glossoscolecidae and Octochaetidae). *Megadrilogica* 5(9), 97–106.

Reynolds, J.W., E.E.C. Clebsch, and W.M. Reynolds. 1974. The earthworms of Tennessee (Oligochaeta). I. Lumbricidae. *Bull. Tall Timbers Res. Stn.* No. 17, 1–133.

Scheu, S., and M.A. McLean. 1993. The earthworm (Lumbricidae) distribution in Alberta (Canada). *Megadrilogica* 4(11), 175–180.

Snider, R.M. 1991. Checklist and distribution of Michigan earthworms. *Mich. Academician* 24, 105–114.

Tandy, R.E. 1969. The earthworm genus *Pheretima* Kinberg, 1866 in Louisiana. Ph.D. dissertation, Louisiana State University, Baton Rouge, 155 pp.

Viktorov, A.G. 1988. Polyploidy of earthworm populations at area edges. In *Soil biology of northern Europe* (D. Krivolutskil, ed.), pp. 103–105. Nauka, Moscow (in Russian).

Viktorov, A.G. 1989. Ecology, caryology, and radiosensitivity of di- and polyploidy earthworms. Ph.D. dissertation. Moscow, Inst. Evol. Anim. Morph. Ecol., USSR Acad. Sci.

Earthworm Biology, Ecology, Behavior, and Physiology

Factors Affecting Earthworm Abundance in Soils

3

J.P. Curry

Department of Environmental Resource Management, University College, Dublin, Ireland

E arthworm populations show a considerable amount of variability in time and space, with mean densities and biomass ranging from less than 10 individuals and 1 g m^{-2} to more than 1,000 individuals and 200 g m^{-2} under favorable conditions. However, within particular climatic zones, earthworm assemblages, with fairly characteristic species richness, composition, abundance, and biomass, can often be recognized in broadly different habitat types such as coniferous forest, deciduous woodland, grassland, and arable land. There is a considerable volume of literature describing the earthworm communities of such habitats and much of this has been summarized by Lee (1985). There is also a considerable volume of information describing the influence of various environmental and management factors on earthworm populations, but in comparison with insects, where the population ecology of many species has been subjected to quantitative analysis, earthworm population ecology is still largely at a descriptive stage. There are many reasons for this disparity, including the relative ease with which key life history parameters of many insects can be studied compared with those of earthworms. The objective of this paper is to review, in a mainly descriptive way, the main factors influencing earthworm abundance. These, presented in a highly schematic way in Figure 1, fall into two broad categories; namely, external factors which determine the habitat (climate, soil, vegetation and litter supply, and management) and the biotic interactions within the communities to which earthworms belong (competition, predation, parasitism and disease, and food relations).

1-884015-74-3/98/$0.00/$.50
©1998 by CRC Press LLC

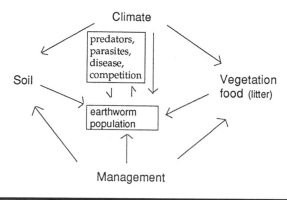

Figure 1. Factors influencing earthworm abundance.

CLIMATE

Climate affects earthworms directly by influencing their biology and life processes, and indirectly through its effects on their habitat and food supply. Temperature is a factor of primary importance in that it determines individual metabolic rates and, on a global scale, it can have a major role in determining patterns of earthworm distribution and activity. The range of temperatures within which earthworms can function is narrow, with upper lethal temperatures being rather low (25–35°C) and optimum temperatures typically being in the range 10–20°C for cool temperate species and 20–30°C for tropical and subtropical species (Lee 1985). Few species can tolerate temperatures below 0°C, although many species have behavioral and/or physiological adaptations that enable them to survive unfavorable periods in areas with strongly seasonal climates.

Temperature may be a factor of primary importance in determining the composition and structure of earthworm communities (Lavelle 1983; Lavelle et al. 1989). Faster organic matter decomposition rates at higher temperatures result in decreased litter availability, and litter-feeding epigeic and anécique earthworm populations tend to be depleted in tropical soils compared with those in temperate soils. With increasing temperatures, endogeic species which can utilize resources of increasingly lower quality through more efficient digestive processes involving mutualistic interactions with ingested soil microflora are favored. Thus, in Mediterranean and humid tropical areas, oligohumic species which are able to feed on soil poor in organic matter are found deep in the soil profile. These are typically K-strategists—large in body size and slow-growing with low fecundity and mortality rates. However, very large endogeic species such as *Octochaetus multiporus* in New Zealand and *Megascolides australis* in Australia appear to be more common in temperate than in tropical soils (Lee, pers. comm.). Thus, while large body size is an adaptation which facilitates feeding on nutrient-poor soil, in warmer soils body size may be constrained by increased energy demand for respiration, resulting in a severely limited energy supply for tissue production from a low-energy diet.

High temperatures are often associated with moisture shortages. Seasonal earthworm mortality in temperate soils has generally been attributed to moisture stress rather than to temperature extremes (e.g., Gerard 1967; Phillipson et al. 1976). Indeed, the overwhelming importance of soil moisture in determining earthworm distribution and activity has been demonstrated frequently. In a recent survey of earthworms in a range of agricultural soils, with annual rainfall varying from 230 to 1,150 mm, in southern Australia, rainfall explained more of the variance in earthworm numbers than any other variable (Baker 1998). Optimum soil moisture content varies for different species and ecological groups, and within species there appears to be a considerable capacity to adapt to local conditions (Lee 1985). In general, earthworms are most active at moisture tensions approaching field capacity (~10 kPa), while activity declines rapidly as the moisture tension exceeds 100 kPa and ceases for most species below permanent wilting point (1,500 kPa) (Lavelle 1974; Nordström 1975; Nordström and Rundgren 1974; Baker et al. 1993).

While adapted populations in areas with strongly seasonal climates have the capacity to survive periods of drought, they nevertheless suffer heavy mortality, particularly among juveniles that are unable to escape desiccation by moving deeper into the soil and becoming inactive (e.g., Gerard 1967). The severity and duration of summer drought impose severe constraints on the duration of earthworm activity and undoubtedly influence both the overall population density and biomass which can be attained in situations where growth and development are restricted to relatively short periods in autumn and spring.

SOIL PROPERTIES

Many studies have attempted to relate earthworm distributions to a range of soil physical and chemical parameters, often with inconclusive results. Apart from soil moisture, the soil properties which appear to be of most importance include texture, depth, pH, and organic matter.

Medium-textured soils appear to be more favorable than sandy soils or soils of high clay content (Guild 1948). Nordström and Rundgren (1974) reported a positive relationship between clay content and the abundance of *Aporrectodea caliginosa*, *A. longa*, *A. rosea,* and *Lumbricus terrestris* in 15 forest, pasture, and heath soils in Sweden, with clay contents ranging from 5 to 20%, while stepwise multiple regression indicated a positive relationship between clay content and the numbers and biomass of introduced (*Aporrectodea*) species in 113 pasture soils in southern Australia (Baker et al. 1992). Decreasing population densities of *A. caliginosa* were linked with increasing proportions of sand and gravel in Egyptian soils (Khalaf El-Duweini and Ghabbour 1965), while low earthworm densities (max 73 m^{-2}) occurred in sandy and silty coastal grassland sites in Co. Wexford, Ireland, compared with similarly managed loam soils (max 516 m^{-2}) (Cotton and Curry 1980b). While texture could have a direct effect on earthworm activity in the case of abrasive gravelly soils, more often the influence of texture may be indirect, through its effect on moisture relationships. Heavy, poorly drained clay soils may become anaerobic in areas of high rainfall while light sandy soils are prone to drought.

The depth of soil has been shown to be a significant factor governing earthworm distributions in temperate (Philipson et al. 1976) and tropical (Fragoso and Lavelle 1992) forest soils, and lack of a sufficient depth of aerobic soil could be a factor limiting the establishment of deep-burrowing species in soils reclaimed after mining (e.g., Curry and Cotton 1983).

Earthworms are generally absent from very acid soils (pH <3.5) and are scarce in soils with pH <4.5. While there are considerable differences between species in their preferred pH, the majority of temperate climate species are found in the range 5.0–7.4 (Satchell 1967; Bouché 1972). Other edaphic factors which have been linked with earthworm distributions include Ca, Mg, and N content (Fragoso and Lavelle 1992), while populations can be adversely affected by high salt concentrations which can occur for example in irrigated soils (Khalaf El-Duweini and Ghabbour 1965).

The nature and quality of the soil organic matter are determined largely by the litter input from the vegetation. Litter from grass, herbaceous plants, and deciduous trees growing on base-rich fertile soils is generally of high quality with C:N ratios approaching or less than 20:1, while the vegetation on impoverished acidic soils produces tough, unpalatable litter, low in nutrients (C:N ratio >60:1) and unfavorable for earthworms. The organic matter which provides the food base for the earthworm community is vitally important in determining their distribution and abundance, and soil organic matter content can sometimes be a good predictor of earthworm abundance. For example Hendrix et al. (1992) reported a highly significant correlation between earthworm density and soil organic C content over a range of sites in Georgia, U.S.A., including a wide variety of soil and vegetation types and management histories.

PREDATION

Earthworms are in the diets of hundreds of species of animals, vertebrates, and invertebrates, but the quantitative impact of predation on populations has not been studied intensively. Most attention has been given to birds which can be highly visible and sometimes severe predators on earthworms. Bengtson et al. (1976) excluded golden plovers (*Pluvialis apricaria*) from small plots in an Icelandic hayfield in May/June and reported that numbers and biomass of earthworms (*A. caliginosa* and *Lumbricus rubellus*) were more than twice as high after 22 days in the protected plots than in adjacent areas exposed to predation. Observations of feeding plovers showed that about 100 lumbricids m^{-2} could be expected to be taken over the experimental period, a figure which agreed closely with the results of the exclusion experiment.

Golden plover predation was also the subject of a study by Barnard and Thompson (1985), who compared earthworm populations in areas enclosed by nets with those in unprotected control areas in English pasture at the beginning and end of a three-month period (December to March). Earthworm densities declined by 46% and 71% in unprotected young and old pastures respectively, while density increased by 11% and 14% in corresponding enclosures. At the feeding rates observed, the authors estimated that golden plover predation could account for about 50% of the differences recorded while the other 50% was attributed to predation by other birds, foxes, and badgers which were also affected by the nets.

Earthworms were classified as a main food source for blackbirds and a regular food for songthrushes in France (Granval and Aliaga 1988), while heavy predation by gulls, starlings, and magpies has been reported in New Zealand grassland (Moeed 1976). Earthworms comprised more than 90% of the food mass ingested by black-headed gulls when they were readily available on the soil surface following autumn cultivation in Switzerland (Cuendet 1983). About 10% of the total earthworm biomass was made available by cultivation, and 25–33% of this was taken by gulls. In a similar study conducted in southwestern Ontario, the impact of ring-billed gull predation on earthworms in freshly plowed land was also found to be negligible (Tomlin and Mille 1988).

Many Insectivora (Mammalia) prey extensively on earthworms. Moles (*Talpa europaea*) consume 18–36 kg of prey annually per individual in Britain; at least half and sometimes as much as 100% of this prey consists of earthworms, depending on their availability (Mellanby 1966; Raw 1966; Funmilayo 1979). Large quantities of mutilated worms are stored in caches within their fortresses for future use.

Earthworm feeding is also prevalent among shrews (Soricidae), with earthworms comprising 0–60% of the diet of the common shrew (*Sorex araneus*) in British grassland, depending on the season (Pernetta 1976b). At a daily consumption rate of 1.5–5 g fresh mass per individual (Pernetta 1976a), a field population of 10–20 shrews per ha in mixed grassland and woodland habitat could consume 15–100 g fresh mass ha^{-1} day^{-1} or 0.5–3.7 g m^{-2} yr, equivalent to somewhere in the order of 1–5% of the mean earthworm biomass in such habitats.

Among the Carnivora, the European badger (*Meles meles*) and the red fox (*Vulpes vulpes*) are major earthworm feeders. The badger is highly specialized behaviorally as a predator of *L. terrestris*, and its population density seems to depend heavily on earthworm availability (Kruuk and Parish 1982). Adult badgers were estimated to consume 130–200 *L. terrestris* each per night in mixed deciduous woodland, pasture, and arable land in England (Kruuk 1978), but annual consumption by the badger population was estimated to be less than 5% of the total earthworm biomass available, and the effect on the earthworm population was deemed to be negligible. The red fox shows similar foraging behavior in relation to *L. terrestris* and can have a catch rate of up to 10 worms per minute (Macdonald 1983).

Invertebrate predators of earthworms include centipedes (Chilopoda) and ground beetles (Carabidae). On the basis of an exclusion experiment, Judas (1989) concluded that birds, shrews, and rodents did not affect earthworm abundance in a German beechwood, but chilopods and carabids, at the population densities recorded for the study area, could potentially have a significant impact on the earthworm population.

Available evidence does not suggest that predation has a major long-term influence on earthworm population dynamics in most habitats, although short-term population reductions may sometimes occur following periods of intensive feeding by birds such as golden plover. A notable exception is the case of the New Zealand flatworm (*Artioposthia triangulata*) which has recently become established in Ireland and Scotland and other areas in northwestern Europe where it is capable of causing severe reduction in earthworm numbers and of bringing about major changes in community structure (Blackshaw 1995; Blackshaw and Stewart 1992).

DISEASE AND PARASITISM

A wide variety of parasitic and pathogenic organisms have been recorded from earthworms (Lee 1985); these include bacteria, fungi, protozoans, rotifers, platyhelminths, nematodes, mites, and dipterous larvae. Many are parasites of earthworm predators, and in some cases earthworms are secondary hosts in which the parasites complete part of their life cycle. The effects of many of these organisms on their earthworm hosts are not well understood and are generally not considered to be significant, but some are known to be harmful. Larvae of the cluster fly (*Pollenia rudis*) parasitize and kill lumbricids in Europe and North America (Walton 1928; cited by Lee 1985), while Kingston (1989) attributed high summer mortality in *A. caliginosa* and *L. rubellus* at least partially to larvae of *Calliphora dispar* in irrigated pasture in Tasmania. Earthworms in non-irrigated land were not similarly affected because the population was isolated from the parasite by being quiescent 12–20 cm below the soil surface.

An anoetid mite, *Histiosoma murchiei*, was reported to parasitize cocoons of *Allolobophora chlorotica* and to a lesser extent *Eiseniella tetraedra* in Michigan, U.S.A. (Oliver 1962); the mites feed on and destroy the developing worms. Anoetid mites are common in wet habitats, and infection rates in *A. chlorotica* cocoons were consistently around 40% in a heavily forested area subject to spring floods. This parasite has also been reported from a peaty, poorly drained pasture in the Strødam nature reserve, Denmark (Gjelstrup and Hendriksen 1991) where about 20% of the cocoons of *A. caliginosa* and about 7% of those of *L. terrestris* were found to be parasitized.

COMPETITION

Earthworm populations can be influenced by any animals whose activities affect their habitat conditions and food supply. These could include grazing animals in grassland and termites in tropical and subtropical habitats, which can drastically influence the nature and quality of organic matter available to earthworms. In a broad sense, earthworms could be regarded as being in competition with such animals for food; however, the term "competition" in the strict ecological sense is usually reserved for interactions between and within closely related species.

Interspecific competition is thought to play a major part in determining the structure of earthworm communities (Bouché 1983; Lavelle 1983), and there are plausible arguments in support of this view. Despite the relative paucity of species (1–16) in most earthworm assemblages, a considerable amount of niche separation is apparent, suggesting ecological adaptation to permit the coexistence of potentially competing species. Phillipson et al. (1976), for example, found evidence for ecological separation in time and space and differences in food preferences among the ten species present in an English beechwood, and concluded that these differences were important in reducing interspecific competition. Lavelle (1983) considered that differences in patterns of vertical distribution and in body size are most important in achieving niche separation in tropical soils, while horizontal and temporal separation and feeding specialization are the main factors in temperate soils. He concluded that competition is greater in temperate soils where populations tend to be concentrated close to the surface, because there is heavy dependence on litter as a food source and the depth of soil that can be exploited is reduced by smaller body size. In tropical regions, by contrast, where higher temperature conditions favor microbial activity and enhanced levels of interaction between fauna, microflora, and organic matter, a greater diversity of food resources can be utilized, permitting the occurrence of a wider range of earthworm sizes, greater depth distribution in the profile, and reduced competitive pressure.

In the absence of supporting evidence, differences between species are not in themselves indications of niche differentiation resulting from competition (Begon et al. 1990), and there is little direct evidence for interspecific competition among earthworms in the field. The few experimental studies which have been conducted (e.g., Dalby et al. 1996) have given largely inconclusive results. A decline in native species has been linked with the establishment of introduced lumbricid species in cultivated areas of Australia, New Zealand, and South Africa (Barley 1959; Martin and Charles 1979; Reinecke and Visser 1980), but there is no direct evidence that this decline has been caused by interspecific competition. Likewise, James (1991) reported a reduction in native *Diplocardia* spp. following invasion of tallgrass prairie in Kansas, U.S.A., by *A. caliginosa* and *Octolasion cyaneum*. In cases where the vegetation and soil have been altered radically, such trends may largely reflect inability of native species to adapt to the new conditions, but in cases where no such disturbance has occurred competitive replacement is at least a possibility.

Interspecific competition in the field is notoriously difficult to detect, but the apparent absence of current competition does not mean that it is unimportant as a factor influencing community structure and population density. Competition may occur only occasionally, or not at all, at present, because natural selection in response to competition in the past may have favored avoidance of competition through niche differentiation (the "ghost of competition past"; Connell 1980). Thus, unsuccessful competitors may have been eliminated already, and mature, present-day communities may comprise species which are able to coexist with little or no competition. Furthermore, competition need not be continuous or intense to be important, as competition for scarce resources at critical stages in the life cycle could have important consequences for species populations.

Interspecific interactions may not necessarily always have negative effects on one or more of the interacting species. For example, Temple-Smith et al. (1993) found that *A. longa* gained more weight in the presence of *A. caliginosa* than in single species culture, while decomposing leaf bundles at the entrance of *L. terrestris* burrows provided favorable microsites for *Dendrodribus rubidus* in English woodland (Phillipson et al. 1976). However, in the longer term the litter-burying activities of anécique species such as *L. terrestris* are bound to adversely affect populations of epigeic species by reducing their food supply.

There is more general agreement on the importance of intraspecific competition in determining earthworm populations. There may be some situations in which competition is for resources other than food, as was reported when *L. terrestris* was cultured at increasing densities with adequate food in fixed volumes of soil (Butt et al. 1994), but in most natural habitats intraspecific competition is likely to be for food (Satchell 1967; Daniel 1992).

FOOD

There is little doubt that earthworm populations are often food-limited: This is evident from the fact that populations often increase following organic amendment. The response to organic amendments can be particularly marked in disturbed habitats of low organic matter content (Edwards 1983; Lofs-Holmin 1983), but significant population increases can also occur in favorable habitats such as permanent pasture, following the application of high-quality organic materials such as animal manures (Curry 1976; Cotton and Curry 1980a,b; Edwards and Lofty 1982a). In the absence of other constraints it is likely that the earthworm carrying capacity of most habitats could be increased considerably by increasing the food supply. Hartenstein and Bisesi (1989) estimated from laboratory studies conducted by Hartenstein and Amico (1983) that a *L. terrestris* biomass of up to 0.5 kg m^{-2} could be sustained under conditions of unlimited food supply in soil irrigated with livestock wastes.

The main source of the organic matter on which earthworms feed is litter from above-ground plant parts in most ecosystems, although dead roots and rhizodeposition can also be important sources. Some species, including *A. chlorotica*, are found in close association with roots, and some species are known to ingest living roots (Baylis et al. 1986). Earthworm populations in woodlands can be limited by the amount and continuity of the litter supply; this was apparent, for example, in afforested coal-mine dumps in Germany where epigeic species (*Dendrobaena* spp., *L. rubellus*) flourished when a well-developed litter layer was present, but declined in importance when the litter layer was depleted by the action of anécique species such as *L. terrestris* (Dunger 1989). Zicsi (1983) concluded that continuity of food supply was of cardinal importance in determining the suitability of deciduous woodlands in central Europe for the survival of large-bodied, anécique earthworms. However, it appears to be the quality rather than the actual quantity of litter which most often limits earthworm populations (Satchell 1967; Boström and Lofs-Holmin 1986; Swift et al. 1979).

Much of the litter input into soil is poor in nutrients with N, in particular, often being in scarce supply. Satchell (1963) calculated that the N requirement of the *L. terrestris* population in an English deciduous woodland (c. 100 kg ha^{-1} yr^{-1}) was at least equivalent to, and was possibly in excess of, the supply from litter. Nitrogen is often considered to be the critical factor limiting earthworms in many ecosystems, both temperate (Satchell 1967) and tropical (Lee 1983).

Nitrogen content can be a useful indicator of food quality when comparing widely different litters but may be less useful as a predictor of earthworm performance on more palatable residues from agricultural crops and deciduous trees (Table 1). Boström and Lofs-Holmin (1986) and Boström (1987, 1988), for

Table 1. Tissue production in relation to food (mg fresh mass g^{-1} dry mass). Values in parentheses are corrected to allow for growth in unamended soil

	Lumbricus terrestris	Aporrectodea caliginosa	Mixed spp.
Grass, *Lolium perenne* 1.5% N (Boyle, 1990)	82–251	17–69	118–320
Grass, *Festuca pratensis*			
roots 0.8% N (Boström and Lofs-Holmin 1986)		53 (17)	
shoots 1.7–2.2% N (Boström 1987, Boström and Lofs-Holmin 1986)		182 (152)–247	
decayed 2.2–2.4% N (Boström 1987)		187–225	
Willow, *Salix burjatica* 1.8% N (Curry and Bolger 1984)	180–250		
Barley, *Hordeum distichum* 0.7–2.9% N (Boström 1987, Boström and Lofs-Holmin 1986)		74 (39)–224 (206)	
Barley, decayed 1.1–1.2% N (Boström 1987)		242–255	
Barley residues in field (Andersen 1983)			120–180
Lucerne, *Medicago sativa* 2.4–4.0% N (Boström 1987, Boström and Lofs-Holmin 1986)		106 (76)–132	
Lucerne decayed 2.2–2.9% N (Boström 1987)		175–249	

Table 2. Growth rates in peat/mineral soil cultures under different feeding regimes (From Boyle 1990) (mg ind^{-1} d^{-1} ± S.E.)

	Lumbricus terrestris	n	Aporrectodea caliginosa	n
Milled grass				
on the surface	18.9 ± 1.2 a	7	5.2 ± 1.6 a	6
mixed in	6.2 ± 1.4 b	6	2.7 ± 0.7 a	7
Chopped grass				
on the surface	17.7 ± 2.3 a	7	2.1 ± 0.6 b	8
mixed in	8.0 ± 2.2 b	6	1.2 ± 0.2 b	5

Means in the same column followed by the same letter do not differ significantly (P < 0.05, ANOVA and t tests).

example, found no consistent relationships between N content and the growth rate of *A. caliginosa*, cultured in soil amended with plant materials ranging from 0.37% N to 4% N, although adult growth rates and cocoon production rates were significantly lower on unfertilized barley straw (0.35% N) than on meadow fescue (2.57% N) and lucerne (2.3% N) residues.

Particle size has an important influence on the quality of plant materials as food for endogeic species such as *A. caliginosa* (Boström and Lofs-Holmin 1986), but not for large anécique species such as *L. terrestris* (Table 2). Boyle (1990) reared juvenile *L. terrestris* and *A. caliginosa* in mixed culture (1 *L. terrestris* + 1 *A. caliginosa* per 1-liter container) in a peat/mineral soil medium with chopped (8-mm pieces) or milled (<1 mm) ryegrass (*Lolium perenne*) provided as a food source. The worms were kept for 18–19 weeks at 15°C and grass (1 g DM) was either added to the soil surface or mixed into the soil every two weeks. Predictably, in view of its endogeic feeding habits, *A. caliginosa* grew faster on milled grass than on chopped, while for *L. terrestris,* which gathered up the food and dragged it into the mouth of its burrow, particle size was unimportant. Also predictably, *L. terrestris* fared better when the food was placed on the surface where it could be easily located and concentrated, but rather more surprisingly this was also the case to a lesser extent (P <0.10) for *A. caliginosa*. It may be that *A. caliginosa* benefited by gaining access to concentrations of decaying grass residues in *L. terrestris* burrows. However, its growth rate was low, compared with those recorded when *A. caliginosa* was reared individually under comparable conditions (Boström and Lofs-Holmin 1986), suggesting that *A. caliginosa* was at a net disadvantage as a result of its association with *L. terrestris*.

In addition to its nutrient content, litter quality is influenced by factors such as carbohydrate content and the concentrations of phenolic compounds (especially tannins) which reduce palatability (Satchell and Lowe 1967). The presence of toxins can also have adverse effects; for example, high mortality of juvenile *A. caliginosa* feeding in soil mixed with fresh lucerne residues was attributed to the glucoside saponin (Boström and Lofs-Holmin 1986; Boström 1988). Fresh litter is usually not acceptable to earthworms but must undergo a period of weathering before being eaten. Factors involved include leaching of feeding inhibitors, softening of hard tissues, and microbial degradation (Satchell and Lowe 1967; Wright 1972). The role of the soil microflora is important not only in increasing palatability but also in enhancing nutrient content (Waters 1951; Wright 1972; Cooke and Luxton 1980). This is particularly important in the case of lignified, nutrient-poor litter, such as straw, which undergoes a marked increase in N content when incubated in the soil (Boström 1987; Curry and Byrne 1996). The importance of microbial action in enabling endogeic earthworms to persist in tropical soils low in organic matter, through mutualistic association with ingested soil microflora, has also been established (Lavelle et al. 1989).

Litter ingestion rates are sometimes used as a basis for assessing limitations likely to be imposed on populations by the food supply; however ingestion rates tend to be very variable, reflecting differences in food quality and palatability, and for this reason rates of tissue production per unit litter input may be more useful. Data from a number of studies, mostly conducted in the laboratory under favorable conditions, but also including some field studies (Andersen 1983; Curry and Bolger 1984), are summarized in Table 1. Tissue production rates ranged from 17 to 255 mg fresh mass per g dry mass of ingested food in the case of *A. caliginosa*, representing production to consumption ratios (P/C) of 0.3–4.3% on a dry mass basis. The corresponding values for *L. terrestris* were 82–251 mg g^{-1} and P/C 1.4–4.2%. Boström and Lofs-Holmin (1986) included data for earthworm growth rates corrected for growth in unamended soil; this was not necessary in the case of the Curry and Bolger (1984) and Boyle (1990) studies because earthworms lost weight in the unamended peat or peat-mineral soil media used in those cases. Earthworms grew faster on barley and lucerne residues that had been buried in the soil for 1–3 months prior to the commencement of the feeding trials (Boström 1987), but this pretreatment had no effect on performance on milled *Festuca* residues, which presumably were acceptable with little or no weathering.

Table 3 summarizes data from a three-year study of the earthworm population in a winter cereal field at Lyons, Co. Kildare, Ireland (Curry et al. 1995), while the estimated food requirement of the population is compared with the food supply in Table 4. Twelve species were recorded, the most abundant being *A. chlorotica* (60–65% of adult numbers) and *A. caliginosa* (19–25% of adults).

Table 3. Tissue production and N requirement of the earthworm, in a winter cereal field (Curry et al. 1995)

	1988	1989	1990
Mean population density (nos m^{-2})	346	471	353
Mean biomass (g^{-2})	61	57	59
Tissue production (g^{-2})	68–156	87–210	89–137
N requirement for production (g^{-2})	1.2–2.8	1.5–3.8	1.6–2.5
N loss via excretion etc. (g^{-2})	3.6	3.3	3.0

Although population densities and biomass fluctuated considerably over the period of study, the mean annual values were fairly stable (Table 3). Annual tissue production values were 1.1–3.7 times the mean biomass, depending on the method of calculation. The estimates for N turnover, via excretion and mucus production, are derived from ^{15}N laboratory studies conducted with juvenile *L. terrestris*. The main sources of organic matter input to the soil were post-harvest crop residues, autumn-applied cattle slurry, and roots. Crop residue and slurry inputs were estimated, on the basis of six 50 × 50 cm samples collected in September 1990, as 484.2 ± 199.5 (S.E.) g DM m^{-2}; the mean N content of this material was 1.25%. Root inputs can be substantial but are difficult to quantify. No direct measurements are available in the present case, but tentative estimates can be made based on the results of studies which have traced the fate of ^{14}CO$_2$-labeled photosynthate in growing cereal plants. Keith and Oades (1986) and Jensen (1994) calculated that the total amount of C translocated belowground during the growing season in wheat and barley was equivalent to approximately one third of the C contained in harvested grain and straw. Harvested dry matter at Lyons amounted to about 1,500 g m^{-2}, suggesting that the total input of organic matter to the soil via the roots could be in the order of 500 g DM m^{-2}. Assuming that 40% of this is lost through root respiration (Jensen 1994), the

Table 4. Food requirement and supply for the earthworm population in a winter cereal field

	g DM m^{-2}	g N m^{-2}
Litter (stubble, cattle slurry)	484	6.1
Roots and rhizodeposition*	300	5
Requirement for maintenance and production	340–1050	4.6–7.1

* Estimated; cf. pp. 49–50.

amount available for root development and rhizodeposition (turnover of fine roots and carbohydrate exudates) could be about 300 g DM m^{-2}. Rhizodeposition could account for about half of this, the remainder being located in macroroots. Studies on N turnover in spring barley in Sweden indicated that the quantity of N allocated to roots was equivalent to about 25% of that removed at harvest (Andrén et al. 1990); on this basis the total N input to the soil from roots at Lyons could be about 5 g m^{-2}. Thus, the total input from aboveground litter and roots could be in the order of 800 g DM and 11 g N m^{-2} annually, with most of this becoming available to decomposer organisms in the autumn. Other potential food sources for the earthworm population are reingested casts, microbial biomass, and soil organic matter, which could include significant quantities of nutrients recycled from dead earthworm tissues. Assuming an average tissue production rate of 200 mg fresh mass per g dry mass organic input (Table 1), the input needed to sustain tissue production by the earthworm population at Lyons could be in the range 340–1,050 g m^{-2} yr^{-1}, while the estimated N requirement was 4.6–7.1 g m^{-2} (Table 3). If the actual tissue production and food requirement values fall in the lower part of this range, as seems likely in a cool temperate soil, then the figures suggest a reasonable match between food supply and demand. However, only a proportion of the organic matter input is likely to be available to earthworms. Litter bag studies indicate that, at most, 34% of crop residues are utilized by earthworms (Curry and Byrne 1996), while there is likely to be severe competition from other organisms for organic inputs in the form of rhizodeposition. Thus, it is unlikely that the level of population biomass recorded could be sustained for long under continuous arable cropping.

LAND MANAGEMENT

Human activities can drastically alter the soil environment and influence earthworm populations directly by physical disturbances and indirectly by altering the physicochemical environment and the food supply. Some of the main ways in which activities such as mining, deforestation and afforestation, arable cropping, pesticide use, and water management may influence earthworms are briefly reviewed below.

Mining and Industrial Wastes

Mining and industrial waste sites present conditions which are extremely hostile to biological activity (Ma and Eijsackers 1989; Hossner and Hons 1992; Logan 1992). Features of unameliorated sites, likely to inhibit earthworm establishment, include lack of organic matter, poor physical structure, compaction, poor drainage and unfavorable moisture conditions, excessive fluctuations in surface temperatures, and extreme acidity resulting from the reduction of sulphides and other materials in tailings ponds. Most soil-dwelling earthworms avoid low pH soils, although epigeic species such as *Lumbricus eiseni* and *Dendrodrilus/ Dendrobaena* spp. may be found in surface litter even in very acid soils. Very alkaline wastes such as pulverized fly ash (PFA) and wastes following Al extraction with NaOH from bauxite can also be toxic to soil fauna (Satchell and Stone 1977; Southwell and Majer 1982; Eijsackers et al. 1983). High salinity is probably the main reason for PFA toxicity; this declines to harmless levels after weathering for 2–3 years (Townsend and Hodgson 1973). Mine tailings from low-grade copper and uranium mining can also be highly saline (Nielson and Peterson 1973).

Metal toxicity can seriously impede the rehabilitation of mine spoil, adversely affecting revegetation and litter decomposition processes. Earthworms can tolerate fairly high levels of most heavy metals (Ireland 1983) although depression in numbers close to a copper refinery has been reported (Hunter and Johnson 1982). Metals in ionic form pose greater risks than organically bound forms (Malecki et al. 1982), and adverse effects are more likely in acidic soils (Ma 1988).

Prerequisites for earthworm re-establishment in severely degraded soils include the amelioration of adverse conditions such as low pH, the stabilization of the physicochemical environment, and the provision of a suitable food supply. Liming and organic matter amendment can counteract the effects of acidity and metal toxicity and facilitate the initial stages of earthworm establishment, but long-term community development depends greatly on the nature and extent of revegetation and the litter supply.

The rate and extent of population establishment vary depending on factors such as the extent of initial disturbance and depopulation, the size and shape of the area affected, the degree and kind of restoration work carried out, and the availability of colonizers. In the case of rehabilitated coal mining dumps in the former German Democratic Republic, earthworm establishment reflected the main features of vegetation succession (Dunger 1989). Early colonizing species such as *A. caliginosa* and *Dendrodrilus/Dendrobaena* spp. made their appearance when an herb layer had developed and litter had begun to accumulate. The development of a shrub layer and well-developed litter layer was accompanied by the appearance of large population densities of *Dendrodrilus/Dendrobaena* spp., and later *L. rubellus,* whose activities rapidly reduced the litter layer. By the time a closed tree canopy had developed, anécique species such as *L. terrestris* were well established, and during the transition to a fully woodland stage, further immigration of species occurred. Under optimum conditions the woodland stage with a species-rich and abundant earthworm fauna commenced 20–25 years after rehabilitation, but little earthworm community development occurred on acidic, infertile dumps.

Earthworm population establishment can occur quite rapidly in grasslands on mined sites restored to a high level of fertility. Purvis (1984) reported population densities in sites restored for 5 years or longer comparable with those in unmined sites in the English Midlands. However, earthworm biomass was low because large, deep-burrowing species were scarce: *L. terrestris* in particular was still largely confined to the edges of reclaimed fields after 10 years. Significant earthworm populations (9–10 spp., c. 270 ind. m^{-2}) were also found in 5–6-year-old productive grass leys on cutover peat in Ireland, although under less favorable conditions, earthworm establishment occurred much more slowly (Curry and Cotton 1983).

Since natural rates of earthworm dispersal into new habitats are low, at most 10–15 m yr^{-1} and no more than 2–3 m yr^{-1} for many species (Dunger 1969; Hoogerkamp et al. 1983; Marinissen and van den Bosch 1992), passive dispersal in water, in soil, with plants, by machinery, and by animals plays an important part in the colonization of rehabilitated land (Dunger 1989; Marinissen and van den Bosch 1992; Curry and Boyle 1995). In large tracts of land, and in situations where passive dispersal is inadequate, the process of earthworm establishment can sometimes be greatly accelerated by deliberate introductions (Vimmerstedt and Finney 1973; Stockdill 1982; Hoogerkamp et al. 1983).

Once a sustainable plant community has been established, most reclaimed soils can in time support a relatively stable earthworm population, but one which is likely to be constrained to a greater or lesser degree by site limitations. Thus, population densities and biomass in grasslands on reclaimed cutover peat are lower than those found in comparable grasslands on mineral soils, with *L. terrestris* being particularly scarce (Curry and Cotton 1983; Curry and Boyle 1995). In this and perhaps in many other examples of rehabilitated sites, an important factor limiting community development may be the restricted depth of biologically active soil.

Deforestation

Many temperate forest species adapt well to grassland on cleared deciduous forest sites. With the disappearance of the litter layer, there is a decline in epigeic species, but anécique and endogeic species benefit from improved soil fertility and food quality, and temperate grasslands tend to support greater earthworm biomass than do temperate forest soils (Lee 1985). Tropical forest earthworms are affected more drastically by deforestation. Most tropical forests are on nutrient-poor soils and have predominately epigeic earthworm populations, which largely disappear following forest clearance; in more nutrient-rich soils where endogeic and anécique species are more abundant, some may survive (Fragoso and Lavelle 1992). However, when adapted species are available for recolonization, high earthworm population densities may become established under suitable conditions. Lavelle and Pashanasi (1989) reported earthworm biomass of up to 153 g m^{-2} comprised almost entirely of the endogeic peregrine species *Pontoscolex corethrurus*, in pastures of cleared forests in Peruvian Amazonia.

Afforestation

The response of grassland earthworms to afforestation depends on the tree species planted and the quality and quantity of litter produced. Muys et al. (1992) compared five broad-leaved forest stands planted 20 years previously on meadow with a nearby meadow and two old forest stands. Significant differences between sites could be observed in litter decomposition rates, in the thickness and quality of the surface organic (Ao) layer, and in earthworm biomass and community structure. These effects were attributed to the quality and quantity of the annual litter produced in the various stands. Under *Quercus palustris*, which produces relatively unpalatable, poor-quality litter, earthworm biomass had diminished and the process of litter accumulation and moder humus formation had commenced.

Coniferous afforestation on fertile soil is accompanied by a marked impoverishment of the earthworm fauna, reflecting poor litter quality, declining pH, and deterioration in soil structure. Preliminary sampling in Woodville wood, a mixed oak woodland in Co. Offaly, indicated the presence of a moderate earthworm population of 40–60 g m^{-2} biomass comprising a mixture of epigeic, endogeic, and anécique species, while in areas which had been cleared and planted with conifers (mainly Norway spruce, *Picea abies*) 40–50 years ago, earthworms were scarce or absent (<10 g m^{-2}). The earthworms which were recorded comprised mainly *Dendrobaena* and *Dendrodrilus* spp., with occasional specimens of *Aporrectodea* and *Allolobophora* spp.

Cultivation

Earthworm populations in arable land are generally lower than those in undisturbed habitats, but not always so. The level of direct mortality associated with cultivation depends on the severity and frequency of soil disturbance. Plowing per se does not appear to cause serious mortality: Cuendet (1983) estimated that 5–10% of the earthworm biomass was brought to the surface by plowing, about 25% of this being mortally wounded. Rotary cultivation has much more drastic effects, decreasing earthworm numbers in a Swedish grass ley soil by 60–70% (Boström 1988). However populations recover fairly rapidly (within one year in the Swedish case) if the disturbance is not repeated. Larger, anécique species such as *L. terrestris* and *A. longa* that require a supply of surface litter and have relatively permanent burrows are the species most adversely affected by re-peated soil disturbance, while smaller endogeic species such as *A. chlorotica* and *A. caliginosa* are less affected and can benefit from plowed-in crop residues (Edwards 1983; Lofs-Holmin 1983). Tropical earthworms have little tolerance for cultivation (Lal 1987). Earthworms, especially the larger deep-burrowing species, are favored by minimum tillage and direct drilling compared with con-ventional methods of cultivation (Gerard and Hay 1979; Edwards and Lofty 1982b; Hendrix et al. 1986, 1992).

Indirect effects of cultivation that are likely to adversely affect earthworms include greater variability in surface soil temperature and moisture regimes in the absence of a permanent vegetation cover, reduced litter input, and more rapid oxidation of crop residues (Balesdent et al. 1988). Under these conditions earth-worms may experience severe food limitations, and population density and bio-mass are likely to reflect the quality and quantity of crop residue input (Hendrix et al. 1992). Populations benefit from tillage practices which return a high pro-portion of crop residues to the soil, particularly when the residues remain on the soil surface, and from crops such as cereals where significant amounts of resi-dues are left behind compared with root crops where most of the plant produc-tion is removed (Edwards 1983; Lofs-Holmin 1983; Hendrix et al. 1986).

Manures and Fertilizers

Earthworm population responses to mineral fertilizers can be variable. Gener-ally, the effects of moderate levels of application are positive, reflecting in-creased litter quality and quantity (Gerard and Hay 1979; Edwards and Lofty 1982a; Lofs-Holmin 1983; Boström 1988), but populations may be depressed by heavy applications of N (Nowak 1976). Adverse effects of some nitrogenous fertilizers such as sulphate of ammonia appear to be due to soil acidification. Ma et al. (1990) reported severe depression in earthworm numbers in some grass-land field plots which had been treated with various types of nitrogenous fertil-izers over a period of 20 years. The degree of depression reflected pH reduction, with ammonium sulphate and to a lesser extent sulphur-coated urea having most marked effects.

Organic manures benefit earthworms by providing additional food, by their mulching effects, and by stimulating plant growth and litter return. Farmyard manure is a particularly beneficial form of organic amendment (Edwards and Lofty 1982a; Lofs-Holmin 1983), but heavy applications of animal wastes as semi-liquid slurry containing high levels of ammonia and organic salts can be toxic (Curry 1976; Andersen 1980). Any adverse effects of moderate slurry applications are transitory, and the net population response is positive (Curry 1976; Cotton and Curry 1980a,b; Unwin and Lewis 1986).

Pesticides and Pollutants

Earthworms can be exposed to pesticides and other hazardous chemicals while moving through and ingesting contaminated soil, or by ingesting contaminated litter. Varied responses to pesticides have been reported, ranging from little or none to very severe depression in numbers depending on the species concerned, the chemicals used, the rates, methods, and frequency of application and other factors which are often not well understood (Edwards and Thompson 1973; Brown 1977; Lee 1985). Among the older pesticides, lead arsenate and mercuric chloride were highly toxic, as are soil fumigants such as DD, chloropicrin, methyl bromide, and carbon tetrachloride. Chlordane, heptachlor, and toxaphene are also very toxic and have been used as vermicides, but few of the other organochlorines affect earthworm populations to any significant degree at normal rates of application. Of the organophosphates, phorate and ethoprop are most toxic at normal rates of application, while others, including fonofos, parathion, and thionazin, can be moderately toxic. Carbamate insecticides, notably aldicarb, carbaryl, carbofuran, and methiocarb, are very toxic to earthworms (Stenersen et al. 1973; Stenersen 1979; Martin 1976; Edwards 1980, 1983; Clements et al. 1986), as are benomyl and some related fungicides (Stringer and Wright 1976; Lofs-Holmin 1981). Herbicides do not appear to be directly toxic to earthworms, but can have indirect effects by altering plant cover and food supply and the microclimate at the soil surface.

It is unlikely that occasional applications of even the most toxic compounds have very serious consequences, but their repeated use over a long period can. Long-term use of copper fungicides for disease control drastically reduced earthworm numbers in an English orchard (Raw 1962), and frequent treatments with large doses of insecticides (mainly phorate) over a period of 20 years eliminated earthworms from grassland plots (Clements et al. 1991).

Other potentially hazardous chemicals include heavy metals in metal smelter emissions, in landspread sewage sludge, and in landspread pig slurry containing Cu and Zn. Metals in organic wastes are not considered to be toxic to earthworms (Hartenstein et al. 1980; Malecki et al. 1982), but Cu toxicity has been suggested as the likely reason for low earthworm numbers in land heavily con-taminated with pig slurry (van Rhee 1977; Ma 1988; Curry and Cotton 1980).

Soil Water Management

As already mentioned, earthworm populations and activity are often restricted by unfavorable soil moisture conditions. Irrigation of dry soils has resulted in significant extension of the range of lumbricid species (Barley and Kleinig 1964; Reinecke and Visser 1980) and can allow at least some species to remain active during the hot dry summer weather in South Australia (Baker 1995). However populations are not always higher in irrigated land than in non-irrigated dry land. Earthworms in irrigated pastures may suffer high summer mortality due to sur-face compaction and poaching by grazing animals and to parasitism (Kingston 1989), while high salinity resulting from excessive irrigation can also limit populations in some situations (Khalaf El-Duweini and Ghabbour 1965). Con-versely, drainage and reclamation of wetlands such as polders and peat soils create conditions suitable for earthworm establishment (van Rhee 1969; Curry and Cotton 1983), while drainage of water-logged soils in high-rainfall areas of southeastern Australia resulted in a significant increase in abundance of *A. caliginosa* (Baker 1995).

CONCLUSIONS

In undisturbed sites which support relatively "stable" earthworm assemblages, the abundance and diversity of the earthworm fauna are determined primarily by the interactions of climate and soil. These factors determine the physicochemical parameters of the soil environment, the nature of the vegetation that can be supported, and the quantity and quality of the litter it produces. On a global scale, temperature is the climatic variable of greatest significance, since it deter-mines metabolic rates and the diversity of food resources that can be exploited, but on a more local scale moisture restrictions often determine patterns of dis-tribution and activity.

Earthworms are often exposed to high rates of predation and are subject to pathogen and parasite attack, and there may be times when predation especially can significantly depress population density. However, in situations where popu-lations are not constrained by physicochemical environmental factors, food sup-ply, notably the quality and quantity of the litter input, is the factor which most frequently limits earthworm abundance.

Competition for food is generally believed to be important in determining earthworm abundance, but there is little information on the nature of this competition and the frequency with which it occurs. Available evidence suggests that interspecific competition has been minimized through niche differentiation; when it occurs it is probably diffused in nature and may not have a major influence on population trends. By contrast, intraspecific competition may be common following periods of rapid population growth and may operate in a density-dependent manner so as to adjust population density to the available food supply.

Most, if not all, earthworm species appear to undertake surface migrations to a greater or lesser degree (Mather and Christensen 1992), but the significance of this behavior for population processes is not known. If, as Mather and Christensen suggest, migration is primarily a resource-seeking activity, it could be important in enabling the population to locate more suitable habitats when conditions become unfavorable. Migration is undoubtedly significant in the colonization of new habitats, although active migration may often be less important in this regard than passive dispersal (cf. p 52).

There has been little debate about the relative importance of density-dependent and density-independent factors in determining earthworm abundance. While there is a lack of critical information on earthworm population dynamics, some of the conclusions which have emerged from studies of soil insects such as the garden chafer, *Phyllopertha horticola*, may be relevant (Milne 1984). Most of the time when populations are low, natural control is due to the combined effects of weather, which is always density-independent in its action, and interspecific competition, predators, parasites, and disease, which may be density-independent or weakly density-dependent, but rarely if ever strongly density-dependent in action. Under favorable conditions, when the earthworm population is able to "escape" from these natural control mechanisms, the population will ultimately be "regulated" by intraspecific competition acting in a strongly density-dependent manner.

Virtually any form of human intervention will influence earthworm populations, often adversely when the intervention is disruptive, as in the cases of mining and mechanical cultivation. One aspect of human intervention with potentially important consequences is accidental or deliberate introduction of exotic species that could dramatically change abundance and species composition, possibly to the detriment of native species, and influence soils and plant production. However, there is considerable scope for promoting earthworm activity through management practices that remove constraints, such as low pH and unfavorable moisture conditions, which minimize the adverse effects of cultivation and pesticide use, and which increase the food supply through organic amendment and increased crop residue return to the soil.

REFERENCES CITED

Andersen, C. 1980. The influence of farmyard manure and slurry on the earthworm population (Lumbricidae) in arable soil. In D.L. Dindal (ed.). *Soil Biology as Related to Land Use Practices*, pp. 325–335. EPA, Washington.

Andersen, N.C. 1983. Nitrogen turnover by earthworms in arable plots treated with farmyard manure and slurry. In J.E. Satchell (ed.). *Earthworm Ecology—from Darwin to Vermiculture*, pp. 139–150. Chapman & Hall, London.

Andrén, O., T. Lindberg, U. Boström, M. Clarholm, A.-C. Hansson, G. Johansson., J. Lagerlöf, K. Paustian, J. Persson, R. Pettersson, J. Schnürer, B. Sohlenius, and M. Wivstad. 1990. Organic carbon and nitrogen flows. In O. Andrén, T. Lindberg, K. Paustian, and T. Rosswall (eds.). *Ecology of Arable Land—Organisms, Carbon and Nitrogen Cycling. Ecological Bulletin* (Copenhagen) 40, 85–126.

Baker, G.H. 1998. The ecology, management and benefits of earthworms in agricultural soils, with particular reference to southern Australia (this vol.).

Baker, G.H., V.J. Barrett, P.J. Carter, P.M.L. Williams, and J.C. Buckerfield. 1993. Seasonal changes in the abundance of earthworms (Annelida : Lumbricidae and Acanthodrilidae) in soils used for cereal and lucerne production in South Australia. *Australian Journal of Agricultural Research* 44, 1291–1301.

Baker, G., J. Buckerfield, R. Grey-Gardiner, R. Merry, and B. Doube. 1992. The abundance and diversity of earthworms in pasture soils in the Fleurieu peninsula, South Australia. *Soil Biology and Biochemistry* 24, 1389–1395.

Balesdent, J., G.H. Wagner, and A. Mariotti. 1988. Soil organic matter turnover in long-term field experiments as revealed by carbon-13 natural abundance. *Soil Science Society of America Journal* 52, 118–124.

Barley, K.P. 1959. The influence of earthworms on soil fertility. I. Earthworm populations found in agricultural land near Adelaide. *Australian Journal of Agricultural Research* 10, 171–178.

Barley, K.P., and C.R. Kleinig. 1964. The occupation of newly irrigated lands by earthworms. *Australian Journal of Science* 26, 290–291.

Barnard, C.I., and B.A. Thompson. 1985. *Gulls and Plovers. The Ecology of Mixed-Species Feeding Groups*. Croom Helm, London.

Baylis, J.P., J.M. Cherrett, and J.B. Ford. 1986. A survey of the invertebrates feeding on living clover roots (*Trifolium repens* L.) using ^{32}P as a radiotracer. *Pedobiologia* 29, 201–208.

Begon, M., J.L. Harper, and C.R. Townsend. 1990. *Ecology: Individuals, Populations and Communities*, 2nd ed. Blackwell, Oxford.

Bengtson, S.-A., A. Nilsson, S. Nordstrom, and S. Rundgren. 1976. Effects of bird predation on lumbricid populations. *Oikos* 27, 9–12.

Blackshaw, R.P. 1995. Changes in populations of the predatory flatworm *Artioposthia triangulata* and its earthworm prey in grassland. *Acta Zoologica Fennica* 196, 107–110.

Blackshaw, R.P., and V.I. Stewart. 1992. *Artioposthia triangulata* (Denby, 1894), a predatory terrestrial planarian and its potential impact on lumbricid earthworms. *Agricultural Zoology Reviews* 5, 201–219.

Boström, U. 1987. Growth of earthworms (*Allolobophora caliginosa*) in soil mixed with either barley, lucerne, or meadow fescue at various stages of decomposition. *Pedobiologia* 30, 311–321.

Boström, U. 1988. *Ecology of Earthworms in Arable Land: Population Dynamics and Activity in Four Cropping Systems*. Report No. 34, Department of Ecology and Environmental Research, Swedish University of Agricultural Sciences, Uppsala.

Boström, U., and A. Lofs-Holmin. 1986. Growth of earthworms (*Allolobophora caliginosa*) fed shoots and roots of barley, meadow fescue and lucerne. Studies in relation to particle size, protein, crude fibre content and toxicity. *Pedobiologia* 29, 1–12.

Bouché, M.B. 1972. *Lombriciens de France: Écologie et Systématique*. Insitut National de la Recherché Agronomique, Paris.

Bouché, M.B. 1983. The establishment of earthworm communities. In J.E. Satchell (ed.). *Earthworm Ecology—from Darwin to Vermiculture*, pp. 431–448. Chapman & Hall, London.

Boyle, K.E. 1990. The ecology of earthworms (Lumbricidae) in grassland on reclaimed cutover peatland and their impact on soil physical properties and grass yield. Ph.D. thesis, National University of Ireland.

Brown, A.W.A. 1977. *Ecology of Pesticides*. Wiley, New York.

Butt, K.R., J. Frederickson, and R.M. Morris. 1994. Effect of earthworm density on the growth and reproduction of *Lumbricus terrestris* L. in culture. *Pedobiologia* 38, 254–261.

Clements, R.O., B.R. Bentley, and C.A. Jackson. 1986. The impact of granular formulations of phorate, terbufos, carbofuran, carbosulfan and thiofanox on newly sown Italian ryegrass (*Lolium multiflorum*). *Crop Protection* 6, 389–394.

Clements, R.O., P.J. Murray, and R.G. Sturdy. 1991. The impact of 20 years' absence of earthworms and three levels of N fertilizer on a grassland soil environment. *Agriculture, Ecosystems and Environment* 36, 75–85.

Connell, J.H. 1980. Diversity and the co-evolution of competitors, or the ghost of competition past. *Oikos* 35, 131–138.

Cooke, A., and M. Luxton. 1980. Effects of microbes on food selection by *Lumbricus terrestris*. *Revue d'Écologie et de Biologie du Sol* 17, 365–370.

Cotton, D.C.F., and J.P. Curry. 1980a. The effects of cattle and pig slurry fertilizers on earthworms (Oligochaeta, Lumbricidae) in grassland managed for silage production. *Pedobiologia* 20, 181–188.

Cotton, D.C.F., and J.P. Curry. 1980b. The response of earthworm populations (Oligochaeta, Lumbricidae) to high applications of pig slurry. *Pedobiologia* 20, 189–196.

Cuendet, G. 1983. Predation on earthworms by the black-headed gull (*Larus ridibundus* L.). In J.E. Satchell (ed.). *Earthworm Ecology—from Darwin to Vermiculture*, pp. 415–424. Chapman & Hall, London.

Curry, J.P. 1976. Some effects of animal manures on earthworms in grassland. *Pedobiologia* 16, 425–438.

Curry, J.P., and T. Bolger. 1984. Growth, reproduction and litter and soil consumption by *Lumbricus terrestris* L. in reclaimed peat. *Soil Biology and Biochemistry* 16, 253–257.

Curry, J.P., and K.E. Boyle. 1995. The role of organisms in soil restoration, with particular reference to earthworms in reclaimed peat in Ireland. *Acta Zoologica Fennica* 196, 371–375.

Curry, J.P., and D. Byrne. 1996. The role of earthworms in straw decomposition in a winter cereal field. *Soil Biology and Biochemistry*.

Curry, J.P., and D.C.F. Cotton. 1980. Effects of heavy pig slurry contamination on earthworms in grassland. In D.L. Dindal (ed.). *Soil Biology as Related to Land Use Practices,* pp. 336–343. EPA, Washington.

Curry, J.P., and D.C.F. Cotton. 1983. Earthworms and land reclamation. In J.E. Satchell (ed.). *Earthworm Ecology—from Darwin to Vermiculture,* pp. 215–228. Chapman & Hall, London.

Curry, J.P., D. Byrne, and K.E. Boyle. 1995. The earthworm population of a winter cereal field and its effects on soil and nitrogen turnover. *Biology and Fertility of Soils* 19, 166–172.

Dalby, P.R. 1996. Competition between earthworms in high rainfall pastures in the Mount Lofty Ranges, South Australia. Ph.D. thesis, University of Adelaide.

Dalby, P.R., G.H. Baker, and S.E. Smith. 1995. Influence of species interactions and soil disturbance on growth and survival of three lumbricid earthworms in a pasture soil. *Soil Biology and Biochemistry* (in press).

Daniel, O. 1992. Population dynamics of *Lumbricus terrestris* L. (Oligochaeta : Lumbricidae) in a meadow. *Soil Biology and Biochemistry* 24, 1425–1431.

Dunger, W. 1969. Fragen der natürlichen und experimentellen Besiedlung Kulturfeindlicher Böden durch Lumbriciden. *Pedobiologia* 9, 146–151.

Dunger, W. 1989. The return of soil fauna to coal mined areas in the German Democratic Republic. In J.D. Majer (ed.). *Animals in Primary Succession: The Role of Fauna in Reclaimed Lands,* pp. 307–337. Cambridge University Press, Cambridge.

Edwards, C.A. 1980. Interactions between agricultural practice and earthworms. In D.L. Dindal (ed.). *Soil Biology as Related to Land Use Practices,* pp. 3–14. EPA, Washington.

Edwards, C.A. 1983. Earthworm ecology in cultivated soils. In J.E. Satchel (ed.). *Earthworm Ecology—from Darwin to Vermiculture,* pp. 123–137. Chapman & Hall, London.

Edwards, C.A., and J.R. Lofty. 1982a. Nitrogenous fertilizers and earthworm populations in agricultural soils. *Soil Biology and Biochemistry* 14, 515–521.

Edwards, C.A., and J.R. Lofty. 1982b. The effect of direct drilling and minimal cultivation on earthworm populations. *Journal of Applied Ecology* 19, 723–734.

Edwards, C.A., and A.R. Thompson. 1973. Pesticides and the soil fauna. *Residue Reviews* 45, 1–79.

Eijsackers, H., N. Lourijsen, and J. Mentink. 1983. Effects of fly ash on soil fauna. In Ph. Lebrun, H.M. André, C. Gregoire-Wibo, and G. Wauthy (eds.). *New Trends in Soil Biology,* pp. 680–681. Dieu-Brichart, Ottignies-Louvain la-Neuve.

Fragoso, C., and P. Lavelle. 1992. Earthworm communities of tropical rain forests. *Soil Biology and Biochemistry* 24, 1397–1408.

Funmilayo, O. 1979. Food consumption, preference, and storage in the mole. *Acta Theriologica* 24, 379–389.

Gerard, B.M. 1967. Factors affecting earthworms in pastures. *Journal of Animal Ecology* 36, 235–252.

Gerard, B.M., and R.K.M. Hay. 1979. The effect on earthworms of ploughing, tined cultivation, direct drilling, and nitrogen in a barley monoculture system. *Journal of Agricultural Science, Cambridge* 93, 147–155.

Gjelstrup, P., and N.B. Hendriksen. 1991. *Histiostoma murchiei* Hughes and Jackson (Anoetidae) as a parasite in the cocoons of some Danish earthworms. In R. Schuster and P.W. Murphy (eds.). *The Acari Reproduction, Development and Life History Strategies,* pp. 441–445. Chapman & Hall, London.

Granval, P., and R. Aliaga. 1988. Analyse critique des connaissances sur les prédateurs de lombriciens. *Gibier Faune Sauvage* 5, 71–94.

Guild, W.J.McL. 1948. Studies on the relationship between earthworms and soil fertility. III. The effect of soil type on the structure of earthworm populations. *Annals of Applied Biology* 35, 181–192.

Hartenstein, R., and L. Amico. 1983. Production and carrying capacity for the earthworm *Lumbricus terrestris* in culture. *Soil Biology and Biochemistry* 15, 51–54.

Hartenstein, R., and M.S. Bisesi. 1989. Use of earthworm biotechnology for the management of effluents from intensively housed livestock. *Outlook on Agriculture* 18, 72–76.

Hartenstein, R., E.F. Neuhauser, and J. Collier. 1980. Accumulation of heavy metals in the earthworm *Eisenia foetida*. *Journal of Environmental Quality* 9, 23–26.

Hendrix, P.F., B.R. Mueller, R.R. Bruce, G.W. Langdale, and R.W. Parmelee. 1992. Abundance and distribution of earthworms in relation to landscape factors on the Georgia Piedmont, U.S.A. *Soil Biology and Biochemistry* 24, 1357–1361.

Hendrix, P.F., R.W. Parmelee, D.A. Crossley, Jr., D.C. Coleman, E.P. Odum, and P.M. Groffman. 1986. Detritus food webs in conventional and no-tillage agroecosystems. *Bioscience* 36, 374–380.

Hoogerkamp, M., H. Rogaar, and H.J.P. Eijsackers. 1983. Effects of earthworms on grassland on recently reclaimed polder soils in the Netherlands. In J.E. Satchell (ed.). *Earthworm Ecology—from Darwin to Vermiculture*, pp. 85–105. Chapman & Hall, London.

Hossner, L.R., and F.M. Hons. 1992. Reclamation of mine tailings. *Advances in Soil Science* 17, 311–350.

Hunter, B.A., and M.S. Johnson. 1982. Food chain relationships of copper and cadmium in contaminated grassland ecosystems. *Oikos* 38, 108–117.

Ireland, M.P. 1983. Heavy metal uptake and tissue distribution in earthworms. In J.E. Satchell (ed.). *Earthworm Ecology—from Darwin to Vermiculture*, pp. 247–265, Chapman & Hall, London.

James, S.W. 1991. Soil, nitrogen, phosphorous and organic matter processing by earthworms in tallgrass prairie. *Ecology* 72, 2101–2109.

Jensen, B. 1994. Rhizodeposition by field-grown winter barley exposed to $^{14}CO_2$ pulse-labelling. *Applied Soil Ecology* 1, 65–74.

Judas, M. 1989. Predator-pressure on earthworms: Field experiments in a beechwood. *Pedobiologia* 33, 339–354.

Keith, H., and J.M. Oades. 1986. Input of carbon to soil from wheat plants. *Soil Biology and Biochemistry* 18, 445–449.

Khalaf El-Duweini, A., and S.I. Ghabbour. 1965. Population density and biomass of earthworms in different types of Egyptian soils. *Journal of Applied Ecology* 2, 271–287.

Kingston, T.J. 1989. *Aporrectodea caliginosa* and *Lumbricus rubellus* populations under irrigated and dryland pastures in northern Tasmania. In P.P. Stahle (ed.). *Proceedings of the 5th Australasian Conference on Grassland Invertebrates Ecology*, pp. 199–205.

Kruuk, H. 1978. Foraging and spatial organisation of the European badger, *Meles meles* L. *Behavioural Ecology and Sociobiology* 4, 75–89.

Kruuk, J., and T. Parish. 1982. Factors affecting population density, group size and territory size of the European badger, *Meles meles*. *Journal of Zoology* (London) 196, 31–39.

Lal, R. 1987. *Tropical Ecology and Edaphology*. Wiley, New York.

Lavelle, P. 1974. Les vers de terre de la savane de Lamto. In F. Athias, G. Josens, P. Lavelle, and R. Schaefer (eds.). *Analyse d'un Écosystème Tropicale Humide: la Savane de Lamto* (*Côte d'Ivoire*). *Les Organismes Endogés de la Savane de Lamto. Bulletin de Liaison des Chercheurs de Lamto* (*Paris*), no special, 5, 133–166.

Lavelle, P. 1983. The structure of earthworm communities. In J.E. Satchell (ed.). *Earthworm Ecology—from Darwin to Vermiculture,* pp. 449–466. Chapman & Hall, London.

Lavelle, P., and B. Pashanasi. 1989. Soil macrofauna and land management in Peruvian Amazonia (Yurimaguas, Loreto). *Pedobiologia* 33, 283–291.

Lavelle, P., I. Barois, A. Martin, Z. Zaidi, and R. Schaefer. 1989. Management of earthworm populations in agroecosystems: A possible way to maintain soil quality? In M. Clarholm and L. Bergström (eds.). *Ecology of Arable Land. Perspectives and Challenges,* pp. 109–122. Kluwer, Dordrecht.

Lee, K.E. 1983. The influence of earthworms and termites on nitrogen cycling. In Ph. Lebrun, H.M. André, C. Gregoire-Wibo, and G. Wauthy (eds.). *New Trends in Soil Biology,* pp. 35–48. Dieu-Brichart, Ottignies-Louvain la-Neuve.

Lee, K.E. 1985. *Earthworms. Their Ecology and Relationships with Soils and Land Use.* Academic Press, Sydney.

Lofs-Holmin, A. 1981. Influence in field experiments of benomyl and carbendazim on earthworms (Lumbricidae) in relation to soil texture. *Swedish Journal of Agricultural Research* 11, 141–147.

Lofs-Holmin, A. 1983. Earthworm population dynamics in different agricultural rotations. In J.E. Satchell (ed.). *Earthworm Ecology—from Darwin to Vermiculture,* pp. 151–160. Chapman & Hall, London.

Logan, T.J. 1992. Reclamation of chemically degraded soils. *Advances in Soil Science* 17, 13–35.

Ma, W.-C. 1988. Toxicity of copper to lumbricid earthworms in sandy agricultural soils amended with Cu-enriched organic waste materials. In A. Quispel and H. Eijsarkers (eds.). *Ecological Implications of Contemporary Agriculture. Ecological Bulletins* (Copenhagen) 39, 53–56.

Ma, W.-C., and H. Eijsackers. 1989. The influence of substrate toxicity on soil macrofauna return in reclaimed land. In J.D. Majer (ed.). *Animals in Primary Succession—the Role of Fauna in Reclaimed Lands,* pp. 223–244. Cambridge University Press, Cambridge.

Ma, W.-C., L. Brussard, and J.A. de Ridder. 1990. Long-term effects of nitrogenous fertilizers on grassland earthworms (Oligochaeta : Lumbricidae): Their relation to soil acidification. *Agriculture, Ecosystems and Environment* 30, 71–80.

Macdonald, D.W. 1983. Predation on earthworms by terrestrial vertebrates. In J.E. Satchell (ed.). *Earthworm Ecology—from Darwin to Vermiculture,* pp. 393–414. Chapman & Hall, London.

Malecki, M.R., E.F. Neuhauser, and R. Loehr. 1982. The effect of metals on the growth and reproduction of *Eisenia foetida* (Oligochaeta, Lumbricidae). *Pedobiologia* 24, 129–137.

Marinissen, J.C.Y., and F. van den Bosch. 1992. Colonization of new habitats by earthworms. *Oecologia* 91, 371–376.

Martin, N.A. 1976. Effect of four insecticides on the pasture ecosystem. V. Earthworms (Oligochaeta : Lumbricidae) and Arthropoda extracted by wet sieving and salt flotation. *New Zealand Journal of Agricultural Research* 19, 111–115.

Martin, N.A., and J.C. Charles. 1979. Lumbricid earthworms and cattle dung in New Zealand pastures. In T.K. Crosby and R.P. Pottinger (eds.). *Proceedings of the 2nd Australasian Conference on Grassland Invertebrate Ecology,* pp. 52–54. Government Printer, Wellington.

Mather, J.G., and O. Christensen. 1992. Surface migration of earthworms in grassland. *Pedobiologia* 36, 51–57.

Mellanby, K. 1966. Mole activity in woodlands, fens and other habitats. *Journal of Zoology* (*London*) 149, 35–41.

Milne, A. 1984. Fluctuations and natural control of animal populations, as exemplified in the garden chafer *Phylopertha horticola* (L.). *Proceedings of the Royal Society of Edinburgh* 82B, 145–199.

Moeed, A. 1976. Birds and their food resources at Christchurch International Airport, New Zealand. *New Zealand Journal of Zoology* 3, 378–390.

Muys, B., N. Lust, and P. Granval. 1992. Effects of grassland afforestation with different tree species on earthworm communities, litter decomposition and nutrient status. *Soil Biology and Biochemistry* 24, 1459–1466.

Nielson, R.F., and H.B. Peterson. 1973. Establishing vegetation on mine tailings waste. In R.J. Hutnik and G. Davis (eds.). *Ecology and Reclamation of Devastated Land,* Vol. 2, pp. 103–115. Gordon and Breach, New York.

Nordström, S. 1975. Seasonal activity of lumbricids in southern Sweden. *Oikos* 26, 307–315.

Nordström, S., and S. Rundgren. 1974. Environmental factors and lumbricid associations in southern Sweden. *Pedobiologia* 14, 1–27.

Nowak, E. 1976. The effect of fertilization on earthworms and other soil microfauna. *Polish Ecological Studies* 2, 195–207.

Oliver, J.H. 1962. A mite parasite in the cocoons of earthworms. *Journal of Parasitology* 48, 120–123.

Pernetta, J.C. 1976a. Bioenergetics of British shrews in grassland. *Acta Theriologica* 21, 481–497.

Pernetta, J.C. 1976b. Diets of the shrews *Sorex araneus* L. and *Sorex minutus* L. in Wytham grassland. *Journal of Animal Ecology* 45, 899–912.

Phillipson, J., R. Abel, J. Steel, and S.R.J. Woodell. 1976. Earthworms and the factors governing their distribution in an English beechwood. *Pedobiologia* 16, 258–285.

Purvis, G. 1984. Earthworm recolonization of open cast coal mine sites restored to agriculture and comparison with populations on unmined agricultural grassland. Technical Report MRPITR 184-2 to the National Coal Board, U.K.

Raw, F. 1962. Studies of earthworm populations in orchards. 1. Leaf burial in apple orchards. *Annals of Applied Biology* 50, 389–404.

Raw, F. 1966. The soil fauna as a food source for moles. *Journal of Zoology* (*London*) 149, 50–54.

Reinecke, A.J., and F.A. Visser. 1980. The influence of agricultural land use practices on the population densities of *Allolobophora trapezoides* and *Eisenia rosea* (Oligochaeta) in southern Africa. In D.L. Dindal (ed.). *Soil Biology as Related to Land Use Practices,* pp. 310–324. EPA, Washington.

van Rhee, J.A. 1969. Inoculation of earthworms in a newly drained polder. *Pedobiologia* 9, 128–132.

van Rhee, J.A. 1977. Effects of soil pollution on earthworms. *Pedobiologia* 17, 201–208.

Satchell, J.E. 1963. Nitrogen turnover by a woodland population of *Lumbricus terrestris*. In J. Doeksen and J. van der Drift (eds.). *Soil Organisms,* pp. 60–66. North Holland, Amsterdam.

Satchell, J.E. 1967. Lumbricidae. In A. Burges and F. Raw (eds.). *Soil Biology,* pp. 259–322. Academic Press, London.

Satchell, J.E., and D.G. Lowe. 1967. Selection of leaf litter by *Lumbricus terrestris*. In O. Graff and J.E. Satchell (eds.). *Progress in Soil Biology,* pp. 102–119. North Holland, Amsterdam.

Satchell, J.E., and D.A. Stone. 1977. Colonisation of pulverized fuel ash sites by earthworms. *Publicationes del Centro Pirenaico de Biologia Experimental* 9, 59–74.

Southwell, L.T., and J.D. Majer. 1982. The survival and growth of the earthworm *Eisenia foetida* (Lumbricidae: Oligochaeta) in alkaline residues associated with the bauxite refining process. *Pedobiologia* 23, 42–52.

Stenersen, H. 1979. Action of pesticides on earthworms. Part. 1. The toxicity of cholinesterase-inhibiting insecticides to earthworms as evaluated by laboratory tests. *Pesticide Science* 10, 66–74.

Stenersen, J., A. Gilman, and A. Vardanis. 1973. Carbofuran: Its toxicity to and metabolism by earthworms (*Lumbricus terrestris*). *Journal of Agricultural and Food Chemistry* 21, 166–171.

Stockdill, S.M.J. 1982. Effects of introduced earthworms on the productivity of New Zealand pastures. *Pedobiologia* 24, 29–35.

Stringer, A., and M.A. Wright. 1976. The toxicity of benomyl and some related 2-substituted benzimidazoles to the earthworm *Lumbricus terrestris*. *Pesticide Science* 7, 459–464.

Swift, M.J., O.W. Heal, and J.M. Anderson. 1979. *Decomposition in Terrestrial Ecosystems.* Blackwell, London.

Temple-Smith, M.G., T.J. Kingston, T.L. Furlonge, and R.B. Garnsey. 1993. The effect of the introduction of the earthworms *Aporrectodea caliginosa* and *Aporrectodea longa* on pasture production in Tasmania. Proceedings of the 7th Australian Agronomy Conference, Adelaide, p. 373.

Tomlin, A.D., and J.J. Miller. 1988. Impact of ring-billed gull (*Larus delawarensis* Ord.) foraging on earthworm populations of south-western Ontario agricultural soils. *Agriculture, Ecosystems and Environment* 20, 165–173.

Townsend, W.N., and D.R. Hodgson. 1973. Edaphological problems associated with deposits of pulverized fuel ash. In R.J. Hutnick and G. Davis (eds.). *Ecology and Reclamation of Devastated Land,* Vol. 1, pp. 45–56. Gordon and Breach, New York.

Unwin, R.J., and S. Lewis. 1986. The effect upon earthworm populations of very large applications of pig slurry to grassland. *Agricultural Wastes* 16, 67–73.

Vimmerstedt, J.P., and J.H. Finney. 1973. Impact of earthworm introduction on litter burial and nutrient distribution in Ohio strip-mine spoil banks. *Soil Science Society of America Proceedings* 37, 388–391.

Waters, R.A.S. 1951. Earthworms and the fertility of pasture. *Proceedings of the New Zealand Grassland Association* 13, 168–175.

Wright, M.A. 1972. Factors governing ingestion by the earthworm *Lumbricus terrestris* (L.) with special reference to apple leaves. *Annals of Applied Biology* 70, 175–188.

Zicsi, A. 1983. Earthworm ecology in deciduous forests in central and southeast Europe. In J.E. Satchell (ed.). *Earthworm Ecology—from Darwin to Vermiculture,* pp. 171–177. Chapman & Hall, London.

Earthworm Biology and Ecology— A Case Study: The Genus *Octodrilus* Omodeo, 1956 (Oligochaeta, Lumbricidae), from the Carpathians

4

Victor V. Pop
Institute of Biological Research, 48 Republicii Street,
3400, Cluj-Napoca, Romania

THE LUMBRICID GENUS *OCTODRILUS* FROM THE CARPATHIANS

The genus *Octodrilus* includes a well-defined group of lumbricid species and has a relatively simple history. Örley (1895) established the genus *Octolasion* for lumbricids with eight widely paired rows of setae, regardless of pigment. Pop (1941, 1944), on phylogenetic considerations, modified the diagnosis of the genus, keeping in it only species without red pigment. Omodeo (1956), based mostly on the number of spermathecae, divided the genus into the subgenera *Octolasium* and *Octodrilus*, which were raised to the rank of genera by Bouché (1971). Zicsi (1986), based on the position of male pores, divided the latter into the genera *Octodrilus* and *Octodriloides*. For the time being, I consider them subgenera.

1-884015-74-3/98/$0.00/$.50
©1998 by CRC Press LLC

65

In this conception, the genus *Octodrilus,* Omodeo (1956) includes medium-sized to very large earthworms, without pigment in hues of grey or brown, with widely paired setae, four pairs of seminal vesicles, and five to eight pairs of spermatheca. Clitellar organs are highly constant and characteristic for this species.

Most of the *Octodrilus* species have a relatively limited distribution area in Central and Eastern Europe or in North Africa. Endemic species occur in the Alps, Carpathians, and Dinaric Mountains. Very few species, however, such as *Octodrilus complanatus,* are widely distributed in Europe.

The genus *Octodrilus* is difficult to handle because of many closely related species, often improperly described, with overlapping diagnostic characters. At least 54 *Octodrilus* species have been described to date (Zicsi 1984; Pop 1989: Mršic 1991). In the Romanian Carpathians, 11 species and 7 subspecies are known (Pop 1941, 1948, 1978; V.V. Pop 1991; Zicsi and V.V. Pop 1984) (Table 1, Figure 1). Very little has been known about the general biology and ecology of *Octodrilus* species. They mostly occur in remote mountain regions, mainly on limestone, in which their sampling is very difficult. Therefore, the study of the *Octodrilus* species has been neglected.

During 20 years of research in the Carpathians, within different programs aiming at the study of the structure of montane ecosystems, I have collected very rich samples of earthworms belonging to the genus *Octodrilus.*

Some of the local populations, especially those in the Apuseni Mountains, raised difficult taxonomical problems, especially concerning the variability of characters. The taxonomical studies have led to more theoretical ones, such as the speciation, followed by ecological studies, both in the field and laboratory. The research direction which took shape has succeeded in covering a large range of topics concerning this interesting group of earthworms.

Results of this research have been presented at previous International Symposia on Earthworm Ecology. These include (i) the first attempt to separate *Octodrilus* species by means of numerical taxonomy (the Darwin Centenary Symposium on Earthworm Ecology, Grange-over-Sands, 1981); (ii) the theoretical background of *Octodrilus* species discrimination, based on a hypothesis of accelerated insular-like speciation (the Michaelsen Memorial Symposium on Terrestrial Earthworms, Hamburg, 1987); and (iii) the structure of earthworm communities and the role of large *Octodrilus* species in building up vermic characters in mountain soils (the Rosa Symposium, Bologna, 1985; ISEE 4, Avignon, 1990; the 11th International Colloquium on Soil Zoology, Jyväskylä, 1992; and ISEE 5, Columbus, Ohio, 1994).

Here the aim and a summary of main results of this research, published or not, are presented. Much data remain to be published.

Table 1. The *Octodrilus* species from the Carpathians

Octodrilus Omodeo, 1956		Male pores	Sperma-thecae	Tubercula pubertatis	Clitellum	Segments	Typhlosole ending	Length mm	Diameter mm
O. aporus	V.V. Pop, 1989	15	6	30–40	29, 30–40	207–273	155–163	275–460	14–18
O. bihariensis	V.V. Pop, 1989	15	6	29–38	29–37	98–256	72–158	94–240	4–8
bihariensis	V.V. Pop, 1989	15	6	29–38	29–37	98–195	72–120	94–143	4–7
b. rendzinicola	V.V. Pop, 1989	15	6	29–38	29–37, 38 (28). 29–	185–256	125–158	126–240	7–8
O. compromissus	Zicsi & V.V. Pop			29–37	36, (37)	125–206	90–136	63–195	3–7
c. minimus	V.V. Pop, 1989	15		29–37	29–36	125–161	90–111	66–105	3–4
c. compromissus	V.V. Pop, 1989			29–37	(28). 29– 36, (37)	161–206	116–136	63–193	4–7
O. exacystis	(Rosa, 1896)			30–38	29, 30–37, 38	100–252	88–162	60–310	4–10
e. meziadensis	V.V. Pop, 1989	15	6	30–38	30–37	100–187	88–118	60–135	4–5
e. exacystis	V.V. Pop, 1989			30–38	29, 30–37, 38	160–225	125–152	103–310	6–9
e. oresbius	V.V. Pop, 1989			30–38	29, 30–37, 38	180–259	140–162	140–290	6–10
O. frivaldszkyi	(Örley, 1880)	15	6	29–37	28, 29–36, 37	189–262	147–170	200–400	8–15
O. lissaensis	(Michaelsen, 1891)	15	6	29–36	29–36	98–150		80–150	4–5
O. ophiomorphus	V.V. Pop, 1989	15	6	30–38	29, 30–37, 38	202–263	155–174	225–420	10–16
O. permangus	V.V. Pop, 1989	15	6	30–39	29, 30–38, 39	232–262	155–179	320–720	11–17
O. robustus	(Pop, 1973)	15	5	30–38	29–38	224–253	164–170	200–300	13–15
O. transylvanicus	Zicsi & V.V. Pop, 1984	16–19	6	30–37	29–36	91–156	78–98	40–70	4–6

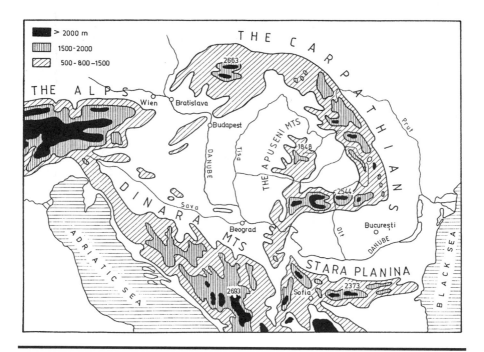

Figure 1. Species of the *Octodrilus* genus from the Carpathians. Anterior end, lateral view. a—*Octodrilus aporus*; b—*O. frivaldszkyi*; c—*O. compromissus*; d—*O. exacystis*.

The Carpathians

The Southern and South-Eastern Carpathians, belonging to the Alpino-Carpathic orogenic system, in Romania form a 900-km-long, 35–150-km-wide mountain chain with a median altitude of 840 m and the highest peak of 2,544 m (Figure 2). The main vegetation belts, consisting of oak (*Quercus petraea*), beech (*Fagus sylvatica*), and spruce fir (*Picea abies*) forests and subalpine-alpine grassland, are developed on cambisols, argiluvisols, and spodosols, with islands of mollisols.

Taxonomy of the Genus *Octodrilus*

Species discrimination or separation in the genus *Octodrilus* is a difficult task because of the close resemblance of many species. Many authors, when describing new species, have not clearly indicated the range and variation of diagnostic characters. Moreover, as these characters were interpreted differently, complex species difficult or impossible to delimit on objective criteria have resulted.

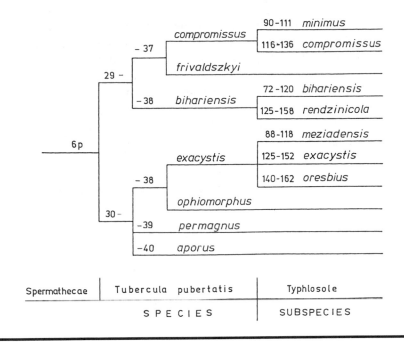

Figure 2. The Carpathians in the Alpine mountain system (after V. Mihailescu 1963).

The synthesis of the genus *Octodrilus* and its separation into the two sub-genera *Octodrilus* and *Octodriloides* presented by Zicsi (1986) clarify many aspects of species discrimination. Nevertheless, the genus *Octodrilus* remains difficult because of the many closely related species with overlapping diagnostic characters.

Variability of Characters

The systematic status assigned to different *Octodrilus* populations depends on the range we allow in variability of characters. Thus, assuming a wide variability of clitellar organs, some of the species described could be combined to form a single species, but by limiting the variability allowable, they could be regarded as distinct species or, in certain cases, as subspecies of polytypic species.

Due to the present lack of agreement on the taxonomic significance of some characters of lumbricid species, and even of genera, I have studied the variability of morphologic and anatomic characters in a proper material of *Octodrilus* (approximately 2,000 specimens) from almost the whole range of known species.

In addition to my own material kept with the Institute of Biological Research in Cluj-Napoca, I studied my father's, Professor V. Pop, collection at the University of Cluj-Napoca, Prof. A. Zicsi's collection at the Eötvös Lorand University in Budapest, and Michaelsen's collection in Hamburg.

Statistical processing of data on the variability of characters in local populations of the *Octodrilus* species from the Carpathians and the Alps, correlated with available data on other species of the genus, leads to the following ordination of their diagnostic value within the genus *Octodrilus* (V.V. Pop 1991):

at (sub)genus level:	position of male pores
at species level:	number and position of spermathecae
	position of tubercula pubertatis
	position of clitellum
	presence/absence of dorsal pores
	setal ratio
	shape of calciferous glands
at subspecies level:	extension or length of typhlosole
	number of segments
	body size and mass

Other characters are also important but of lower discriminatory value.

Two kinds of *Octodrilus* species were recorded in the Carpathians: (i) widely distributed species, like *Octodrilus exacystis* and *O. compromissus*, found in a range of different habitats and displaying a wide variability in non-specific characters (size, segment number, typhlosole ending); they are seemingly polytypic species, and (ii) endemic species, like *Octodrilus frivaldszkyi* or *O. aporus*, which are confined to small distinct habitats mainly on Mesozoic limestone; these appear to be monotypic species, with limited variability of characters.

Taxa Discrimination and Identification of Species

Taxa discrimination has to be based on a thorough examination of the variability of the diagnostic characters in local populations.

The position of the male pores, either on segment 15 or behind this segment, has allowed Zicsi (1986) to separate the newer genus *Octodriloides* from the former genus *Octodrilus*. Our studies support this separation, but for the time being, only at the subgenus level.

The constancy in sexual characteristics, like the number and position of the spermathecae, the position of the tubercula pubertatis, and, to a certain extent, the position of the clitellum, was confirmed statistically and was considered to be the main diagnostic characters at species level (Pop 1989, 1991).

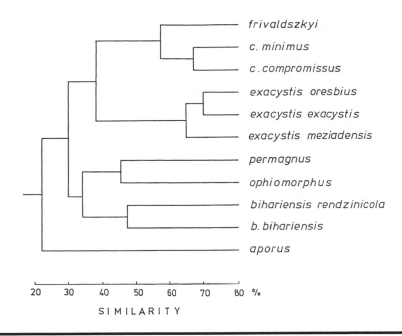

Figure 3. Pattern of *Octodrilus* taxa discrimination by the main diagnostic characters.

The position of the tubercula pubertatis seems to have particular good diagnostic value at the species level. I have never found any local species population with variable positions of the tubercula pubertatis, as occurs in other lumbricid genera. When differences of even one segment in the position of tubercula pubertatis occurred in the same sample, there were other differences as well, which allowed the separation of the individuals into distinct taxa.

On the basis of a study of the variability of characters in more than 1,500 individuals, it is a justifiable conclusion to recognize as many *Octodrilus* species as there are positions of tubercula pubertatis (Figure 3).

Subspecies discrimination presents another difficult taxonomic task. Subspecies in lumbricids have so far been recognized on classical criteria. According to Mayr (1971) "a subspecies is an aggregate of phenotypically similar populations of a species inhabiting a geographic subdivision of the range of the species and differing taxonomically from other populations of the species." That is, a subspecies has a character of spatial unity, a subdivision of a species in the dimensions of longitude and latitude.

However, habitat differences may be achieved over small distances in the case of insular distributions of biotopes in mountain regions. In many areas of the Carpathians, patchy distribution patterns of biotopes are evident. Islands of soils developed on limestone are surrounded by soils developed on acid parent material, and forest islands are surrounded by grassland areas. Soils, valleys, and vegetation act as barriers, so there is scope for allopatric, accelerated, insular-like speciation.

If we admit that insular speciation exists in these mountains, we must also accept a similar process of subspecies differentiation. Widespread species, inhabiting multiple kinds of biotopes, show clear morphological differences in the framework of species diagnostic characters. Taxonomic differences among subspecies concern mostly characters related to the size of worms, i.e., length, number of segments, and ending of the typhlosole. The location of the typhlosole ending, which is a very constant character in local populations and positively related with the size and number of segments, proved to be a convenient character for subspecies discrimination according to the "75 per cent rule" (Mayr et al. 1953).

The shape and length of the typhlosole may have an ecological significance as an adaptation to the quality and quantity of food. The size of the earthworm, which is positively related to the typhlosole ending, could also be regarded as an adaptation to soil conditions. In these mountains, the smaller species generally dwell in more compact soils under grassland, while the larger ones tend to inhabit looser forest soils. Thus, statistically delimited groupings of local populations might be regarded as also having different ecological requirements, and might therefore be considered as distinct subspecies.

Based on the above ordination of the diagnostic value of characters, I described, from a relatively small area in the Apuseni Mountains, five new *Octodrilus* species, seven new subspecies, and amended the diagnoses of three species (V.V. Pop 1989; Zicsi and V.V. Pop 1984) (Table 1). This number of newly described taxa suggested that the Apuseni Mountains should be considered as an active speciation center of the genus *Octodrilus*.

The validity of the species and subspecies delimitations was checked using a multiple character analysis without previous subordination of the diagnostic value of the characters. Following Sims (1969), I used the simple Sheal's method (1964). The dendrogram drawn according to Mountford (1962), used in classifying taxa (Figure 4), resembles very much the key drawn for delimiting taxa by the main diagnostic characters (Figure 3).

The dendrogram shows the existence of two groupings of species. The first group with *O. frivaldszkyi*, *O. compromissus*, and *O. exacystis* has conspicuous dorsal pores and a somewhat shorter (9 segment) tubercula pubertatis and clitellum. The second group of species has inconspicuous dorsal pores and longer

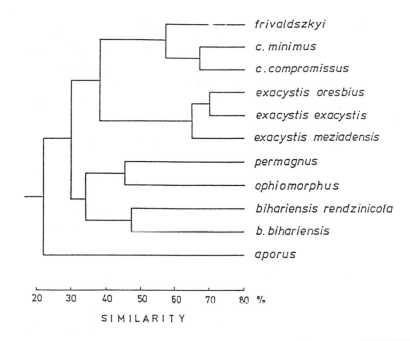

Figure 4. Classification of *Octodrilus* taxa from the Apuseni Mountains by means of multiple character analyses.

clitellar organs (10–11 segments). *Octodrilus aporus*, with no dorsal pores, has a separate position.

Even though it is only a phenotypical tree, not a phylogenetical one, the dendrogram suggests a truly divergent position of the four large *Octodrilus* species, namely *O. frivaldszkyi, O. aporus, O. ophiomorphus,* and *O. permagnus,* and the high probability that their discrimination is objective.

In describing the new species, or in delimiting the range of characters for the already described species, I adopted a rigorous statistical procedure. Thus, tables with statistically processed data are part of the description. The type series, in the majority of taxa dealt with here, had tens or even hundreds of individuals. The type populations and the holotypes, as well as the neotype for *O. frivaldszkyi,* have been selected to match as nearly as possible the arithmetic mean value of the numeric characters of the whole type series. Thus, the "nomenclatural type" or the "name bearer" of newly-described or emended taxa corresponds to the "morphological" or the "biological" types. It is important to note that such a selection avoids hazardous designation of holotypes from marginal, overlapping populations of taxa.

Insular-Like Accelerated Speciation in Octodrilus

The large number of endemic *Octodrilus* species that are patchily distributed in small areas of the Carpathians, as well as in the Alps and Dinara Mountains, could be explained by a process of insular-like speciation (Pop 1994).

The following conditions are considered to favor accelerated insular-like speciation:

- stenobiontism (species which tolerate only narrow variations of environmental factors) regarding montane habitats on Mesozoic limestone;
- insularity of these habitats, leading to geographical and reproductive isolation;
- the size of populations, which is an essential factor, as most of the isolated *Octodrilus* populations are rather small, thus enhancing the probability of quick genetic changes;
- low dispersal ability, earthworms being almost sedentary forms;
- the existence of parthenogenesis, indicated by indirect morphologic features. This kind of reproductive isolation might also be an accelerating factor for species segregation, since a mutation is more easily preserved and spread within a population, in the absence of genetic recombination through biparentalism.

The Apuseni Mountains are seemingly one of the most prolific speciation centers of the genus. Timing of the Alpino-Carpathian orogenesis (i.e., raising of the mountains) and phytohistorical data support the idea that endemic *Octodrilus* species were able to survive the Pleistocene glaciations in Carpathian refuges. Distinct *Octodrilus* lines are found in the limestone areas of the Carpathians, the Alps, and the Dinara Mountains.

Ecology of the Genus *Octodrilus*

Earthworm Communities Dominated by Octodrilus Species

As discussed above, two groups of *Octodrilus* species could be distinguished, namely a group of widely distributed, usually acid-tolerant, medium-sized species, and a group of endemic species, usually calcophilous or confined to limestone areas, which are medium-sized to very large species (Pop 1985; Pop, in press).

The great majority of the *Octodrilus* species was recorded in the vegetation belt of beech or beech-hornbeam forests, more rarely in mixed beech spruce-fir forests, as well as in corresponding grasslands (Pop 1982).

Beech (*Fagus sylvatica*) is the main forest tree in Romania, occurring on both aspects of the Carpathians and forming a distinct vegetational belt, both as mixed beech-spruce-fir or beech-hornbeam forests. The obvious individuality of Carpathian beech forests justifies their placement in an independent phytosociological alliance, namely *Symphyto cordato-Fagetum* Vida 59, *Fagion dacicum* Soó 62.

The earthworm fauna of the Carpathian beech forests differs correspondingly from that of similar biotopes in the Alps or Dinara Mountains. In this forest, biotopes are found to be the majority of Carpathian endemics, and as a particular feature, some of the largest lumbricids known.

The earthworm communities, previously referred to as synusia (Pop 1982, 1985, 1987), comprise two main structural patterns, related to the nature of the substrata (igneous-crystalline versus limestone-dolomite rocks), which are reflected in peculiarities of the soils and, within certain limits, some features of the phytocenoses.

The structural pattern of these earthworm communities, viewed in a broad, "ecological" sense, is maintained by a substitution process of ecologically similar species, which are, as a rule, vicariants, i.e., they exclude each other. This substitution process was found mainly at the level of the same ecologic categories, namely epigeic (surface living), endogeic (living in the depth of soil), and anecique (vertical migrator) species. Their ratio is related closely to soil properties and composition of vegetation cover.

The two main community types were tentatively named by characteristic species, following Casagneau's procedure (1961) when defining *Collembola synusia* in the Pirinei Mountains.

The earthworm community with *Octodrilus compromissus–Dendrobaena byblica* (Table 2) is characteristic of beech and mixed beech-spruce fir forests, with oligobasic cambic, spodic or argillic soils, with acid mull, developed on igneous or crystalline acid parent material.

The species *Dendrobaena alpina* is often present, but *D. byblica* could be partially substituted by *Dendrobaena clujensis* or *Dendrobaena veneta*. In places with deeper soils the endogeic *O. compromissus* or *Octodrilus exacystis* dominate the earthworm biomass. The large species, characteristic for the second community, occur sporadically and at low density.

The earthworm community with *Octodrilus frivaldszkyi* (Table 3) is very characteristic for beech or mixed beech-hornbeam forests, with rendzinas or cambic eu-, mesobasic soils (= brown earth), with calcic mull on limestone or dolomite (Pop 1985, 1987). This community type also occurs, very rarely, in the neighboring acid soils.

Table 2. Structure of earthworm communities with *Octodrilus compromissus–Dendrobaena byblica* in forest ecosystems with acid soils from the Carpathians

Species	Oak B.P. 1	2	Beech hornbeam B.E. 3	4	Beech A.B. 5	6	7	8	Fir-beech B.F. 9	Fir B.P. 10
Allolobophora caliginosa (Savigny, 1826)										
A. dacica (Pop, 1938)										
A. georgii (Michaelsen, 1890)										
A. mehadiensis (Rosa, 1895)										
A. rosea (Savigny, 1826)										
Dendrobaena alpina (Rosa, 1884)										
D. byblica (Rosa, 1893)										
D. clujensis (Pop, 1938)										
D. octaedra (Savigny, 1826)										
D. rubida (Savigny, 1826)										
Fitzingeria platyura (Fitzinger, 1833)										
Lumbricus polyphemus (Fitzinger, 1883)										
L. rubellus (Hoffmeister, 1843)										
Octolasion lacteum (Örley, 1885)										
Octodrilus c. compromissus (Zicsi & Pop, 1984)										
O. exacystis exacystis (Rosa, 1896)										
O. e. oresbius (V.V. Pop, 1989)										

B.P. = brown podzolic soil, B.E. = brown earth, A.B. = acid brown soil, B.F. = brown forest soil.

Similarity %: ☐ 0   ▨ 0–10   ▧ 10.1–20   ⊟ 20.1–40   ▦ 40.1–60   ■ 60.1–100

Table 3. Structure of earthworm communities with *Octodrilus frivaldszkyi* in forest ecosystems on limestone from the Carpathians

Species	Soil Site									
	R	T.R.	B.E.							P.B.
	1	2	3	4	5	6	7	8	9	10
Allolobophora dacica (Pop, 1938)				▤	▨		▨			■
A. georgii (Michaelsen, 1895)									▨	
A. rosea (Savigny, 1826)									▨	
Dendrobaena alpina (Rosa, 1884)	▨									
D. byblica (Rosa, 1893)	▨	▤	▨				▨	⊞	▤	▨
D. clujensis (Pop, 1938)	⊞								▤	
D. rubida (Savigny, 1826)										
Lumbricus polyphemus (Fitzinger, 1883)			▨	▨			▤			
L. rubellus (Hoffmeister, 1843)								▨		
Octolasion lacteum (Örley, 1885)			▨	▨			▤		▨	
Octodrilus aporus (V.V. Pop, 1989)				⊞						
O. bihariensis (V.V. Pop, 1989)	▨									
O. compromissus (Zicsi & Pop, 1984)		▤		▨					▤	
O. exacystis (Rosa, 1896)				▨						
O. frivaldszkyi (Örley, 1880)	⊞								⊞	▨
O. ophiomorphus (V.V. Pop, 1989)		■	■	■	■			▨		
O. permagnus (V.V. Pop, 1989)							▤			▤

R = rendzina, T.R. = terra rossa, B.E. = brown earth, P.B. = podzolic brown earth.

Similarity %: ☐ 0 ▨ 0–10 ▨ 10.1–20 ▤ 20.1–40 ⊞ 40.1–60 ■ 60.1–100

The community is dominated by the giant species of *Octodrilus,* namely *O. frivaldszkyi, O. aporus, O. ophiomorphus,* or *O. permagnus,* reaching 40–70 cm in length. These very large species, observed to be vertical burrowers or anecique worms, are vicariants, but one of them is always present.

Lumbricus polyphemus, considered to be an anecique or vertical migrator, seems to be one of the characteristic species of this type of earthworm community. However, in some places it is replaced by a large population of the giant *Octodrilus* species (Pop 1980).

Characteristic epigeic forms are the red-pigmented *Dendrobaena byblica* and/or *D. clujensis.* The presence of the small *D. alpina* is determined by the presence of spruce trees.

Endogeic, medium-sized worms are *Octodrilus compromissus, O. exacystis, Allolobophora dacica,* and/or *Octolasium lacteum.*

The substitution of the ecologically similar species seems to follow a certain zonality along the Carpathian range. In the south-western part (Mehedinti, Cerna, and Retezat Mountains), *Allolobophora* species substitute for the endemic *Octodrilus* species. Here the very large (40–80 cm long) *A. robusta* substitutes for the giant *Octodrilus* species, while *A. mehadiensis* occurs instead of medium-sized *Octodrilus* species. In the northern part of the Eastern Carpathians, the *Octodrilus* species are replaced by *Allolobophora carpathica.*

Biogeographic and geochronologic timing could explain the perfection of the functional relation between earthworm community types, vegetation, and soil type. Long coevolution and coadaptation of the beech-earthworm association might also explain the perfection of these relations (Pop 1982).

Earthworm Communities with Octodrilus Species in Grassland Ecosystems (Table 4)

The earthworm communities with *Octodrilus* species (Table 4) in soils developed under grassland display a less interesting structure. In areas with acid soils only, the relatively widespread *O. exacystis* and *O. compromissus* were found. In limestone areas, endemic species, such as *Octodrilus bihariensis* and *Octodrilus exacystis meziadensis,* typify the local peculiarities.

Seasonal Dynamics of Earthworm Communities with Octodrilus frivaldszkyi

The Padis karstic plateau, situated in the middle of the Apuseni Mountains (Figure 2), a quite large limestone area, covered by beech forests, with patches of fir tree forests (on acid rocks), represents the typical habitat for *Octodrilus frivaldszkyi* and *O. bihariensis,* two of the most interesting species of this ge-

Table 4. Structure of earthworm communities with *Octodrilus* species in grassland ecosystems from the Carpathians

Species	T.R. 1	T.R. 2	E.B.E. 3	E.B.E. 4	C.A. 5
Allolobophora caliginosa (Savigny, 1826)	▒		▒		
A. dacica (Pop, 1938)	▒		▒		
A. rosea (Savigny, 1826)	▓		☰		
Dendrobaena byblica (Rosa, 1893)			▒		
D. clujensis (Pop, 1938)	▒		▒		
D. rubida (Savigny, 1826)				▒	
Lumbricus polyphemus (Fitzinger, 1883)	▒		▒		
L. rubellus (Hoffmeister, 1843)			▒		
Octolasion lacteum (Örley, 1885)			☰		
Octodrilus b. bihariensis (V.V. Pop, 1989)					■
O. b. rendzinicola (V.V. Pop, 1989)		☰			
O. c. compromissus (Zicsi & Pop, 1984)				☰	
O. e. exacystis (Rosa, 1896)	⊞	⊞			
O. e. oresbius (V.V. Pop, 1989)		⊞	▓		

T.R. = terra rossa, E.B.E. = brown earth, C.A. = colluvial-alluvial.

Similarity %: ☐ 0   ▒ 0–10   ▓ 10.1–20   ☰ 20.1–40   ⊞ 40.1–60   ■ 60.1–100

nus. These species also indicate the presence of other endemic soil-dwelling invertebrates.

The scientific importance of several well-known caves, as well as the peculiar terrestrial flora and fauna of the central part of the Apuseni Mountains, have led to preliminary studies for making a nature reserve of the Padis karstic area. It is in this framework that I have studied the structure of the earthworm communities.

In 1979, the seasonal earthworm dynamics were studied at three representative sites, namely in a beech forest (Padis), a mixed beech-spruce fir forest (Pârâul Ponor), and a spruce fir tree forest (Calineasa).

In the beech forest from Padis, the peculiar, obvious, vermic characters developed in the soil by the giant *Octodrilus frivaldszkyi* and the large *Octodrilus bihariensis* were first recorded (Pop and Postolache 1987).

Here only the seasonal dynamics of the earthworm community that was dominated by *Octodrilus* species, from the beech forest, is presented. Mean data for the other two sites studied are given only for comparison of the earthworm biomass.

Site—The Padis karstic plateau, Bihorului Mountain, the Apuseni Mountains, 1,300 m altitude, S-SW aspect, 20% slope, beech forest (As. *Symphyto cordati– Fagetum* Vida 1959, facies with *Allium ursini*). The soil is a cambic rendzina with calcic mull and the following profile: O (2–0 cm), Am (0–25 cm), AmBv (25–36 cm), BvR (36–46 cm), and R (46 cm+).

Methods—A stratified random sampling program was drawn up, involving sampling earthworm populations at monthly intervals during May–October 1979 (months without snow cover).

Earthworms were expelled by formalin, from nine sample units each 50 cm × 50 cm surface area. Biomass was estimated by weighing the worms preserved in 4% formalin. Comparative weighing of worms, with and without emptying the gut content, showed that the loss of weight through preservation in formalin corresponds approximately with the weight of the gut content.

Earthworms were identified to species level, and each species divided into three age groups (adult, subadult, juvenile).

Microclimatic Dynamics—Seasonal dynamics of air and soil temperature (OLF litter stratum, A horizon at 0–5, 5–10, and 10–15 cm) are presented in Figure 5. Air temperature ranges between 11° and 15°C. Soil temperature shows two maxima, in June and in September. Soil moisture, more constant in deeper horizons, exhibits a somewhat similar seasonal dynamics.

Seasonal Dynamics of Earthworm Community—Five species are present at the study site (Table 5). The community structure is that described as a "community with *Octodrilus frivaldszkyi*" in the previous section. *Octodrilus frivaldszkyi* is one of the giant species, characteristic of the limestone areas in these mountains, and is often associated with the endogeic *O. bihariensis rendzinicola*.

D. alpina, a small epigeic worm, is mostly characteristic of coniferous forests in the Carpathians. The study area has sparse fir trees, which explain the presence and low density of this species.

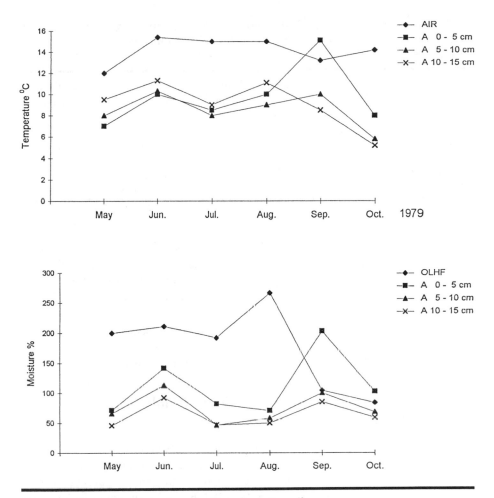

Figure 5. Seasonal dynamics of microclima in soil.

D. byblica and *D. clujensis*, which are red-pigmented, epi-endogeic worms, are common in the beech and fir tree forests of the Carpathians. The biomass of the community is dominated throughout the year by the two *Octodrilus* species (Figure 6). The seasonal dynamics of mean density and biomass of individual species are summarized in Figures 7 and 8.

It should be noted that the biomass of 256 g/m² is the highest earthworm biomass recorded to date in the Carpathians. For comparison, Table 6 shows the biomass recorded in two neighboring forest sites, investigated at the same time

Table 5. Characters with ecologic significance of lumbricid species in the beech forest with vermic cambic rendzina from Padis (the Apuseni Mountains)

Species	Pigment	Length mm	Diameter mm	Fresh weight g	Ecologic category
D. alpina	reddish	40–50	2–3	0.02–0.07	epigeic
D. byblica	red	45–105	3–4	0.23–0.40	epigeic
D. clujensis	red	60–120	4–5	1.05–2.43	epi-endogeic
O. bihariensis	gray	126–240	4–5	4.80–9.05	endogeic
O. frivaldszkyi	gray	200–460	8–15	19.00–36.60	anecique

with the Padis beech forest. The yearly mean biomass of the community with the giant *Octodrilus frivaldszkyi* exceeds by more than 30 times that recorded for fir tree forests and by more than 20 times that for mixed beech-fir tree forests. The earthworm densities and biomass of these other communities are typical for the Carpathians (Pop 1987).

This enormous earthworm biomass, at least for Carpathian forests, implies extremely high earthworm activity in soil and, as will be shown in the next section, accounts for the conspicuous vermic characters of this soil.

The Role of Giant *Octodrilus* Species in Building Up Vermic Characters in Mountain Soils

The very large *Octodrilus* species imprint conspicuous vermic characters mainly in soils developed on limestone or dolomite, more rarely in neighboring acid soils. This activity is so intense that soils developed on different parent materials and usually classified into different classes exhibit quite similar structures and chemical properties in the upper horizons.

The term "vermic," introduced in soil systematics by the American "7th Approximation, 1960," indicates soils intensively processed by soil inverte-brates, especially by earthworms. According to the Romanian system of soil classification (1979), the vermic character designates soils which exhibit copro-lites (casts of earthworms or of other soil-inhabiting animals) and earthworm burrows (sometimes filled by soil material) in more than 50% of the volume of the A horizon and in more than 25% of the volume of the subsequent horizon.

Using this definition, the vermic character has been so far considered di-agnostic for only a few soil types, such as chernozems in the class of mollisols.

The definition can be misleading, because a normally developed soil must be vermic, i.e., developed by the participation of earthworms and other taxa of the

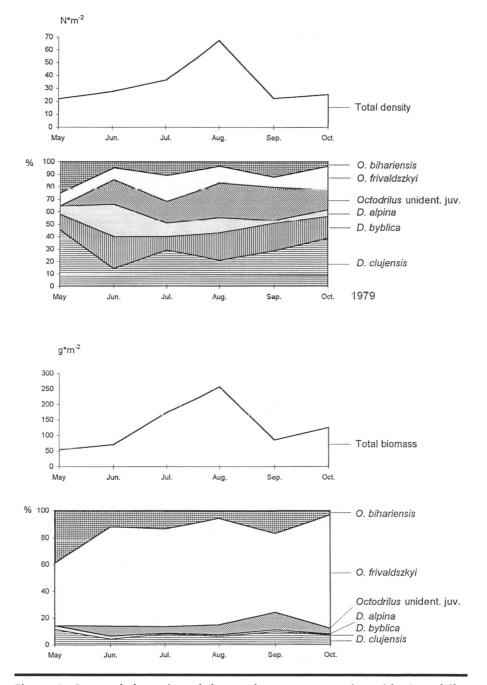

Figure 6. Seasonal dynamics of the earthworm community with *Octodrilus frivaldszkyi* in the vermic cambic rendzina from Padia (the Apuseni Mountains).

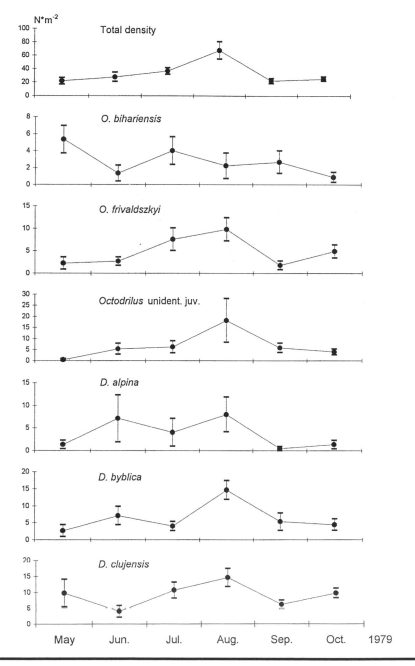

Figure 7. Seasonal dynamics of lumbricid density in the vermic cambic rendzina from Padis (the Apuseni Mountains).

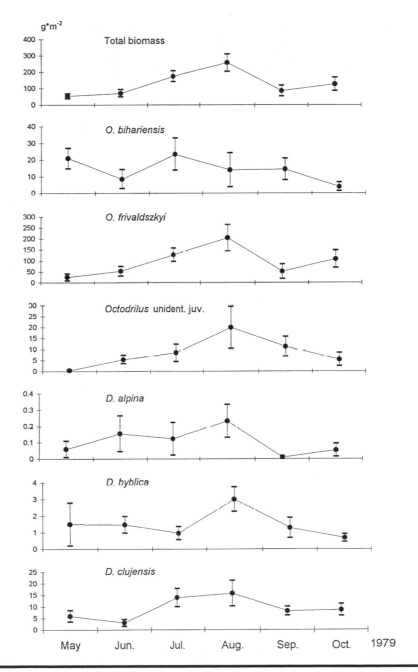

Figure 8. Seasonal dynamics of lumbricid biomass in the vermic cambic rendzina from Padis (the Apuseni Mountains).

Table 6. Yearly mean biomass with monthly mean range of earthworm communities in three forest ecosystems from the Apuseni Mountains (May–Oct 1979) (g/m² earthworms preserved in formalin)

Ecosystem	Species	Mean	Minimum	Maximum
Fir tree	D. alpina	2.38	0.29 (Oct)	4.96 (Jun)
Acid brown soil	D. clujensis	1.25	0.12 (Oct)	2.77 (Aug)
Călineasa	D. byblica	0.27	0.06 (Jun)	0.73 (Aug)
	Total	**3.90**	**0.34** (Oct)	**7.35** (Jun)
Mixed beech-fir	A. dacica	0.54	0.18 (Oct)	1.11 (Jun)
Brown forest soil	A. rosea	0.12	0.10 (May)	0.48 (Sep)
Pârâul Ponor	D. alpina	0.70	0.50 (May)	1.21 (Aug)
	D. byblica	1.93	1.10 (Oct)	2.91 (Jul)
	D. clujensis	2.39	0.15 (Oct)	7.12 (Aug)
	O. compromissus	0.39	0.08 (Oct)	1.54 (May)
	Total	**6.07**	**2.02** (Oct)	**11.14** (Aug)
Beech forest	D. alpina	0.10	0.01 (Sep)	0.23 (Aug)
Cambic rendzina	D. byblica	1.50	0.67 (Oct)	3.00 (Aug)
Padis	D. clujensis	9.29	3.03 (Jul)	15.79 (Aug)
	O. bihariensis	14.17	3.91 (Oct)	23.38 (Jul)
	O. frivaldszkyi	93.65	25.02 (May)	204.09 (Aug)
	Octodrilus (juv)	8.34	5.29 (Jul)	19.92 (Aug)
	Total	**127.0**	**53.60** (May)	**256.97** (Aug)

soil fauna. Kubiena (1953), when defining mull humus, states, "Practically all aggregates are earthworm casts or residues of them"; his statement should be extended because traces of the activity of soil fauna, especially of earthworms, can be shown micromorphologically throughout the entire profile of most soil types. So, in the opinion of Pop and Postolache (1987), the term vermic should be used only to indicate visible, macromorphologically stable, and lasting aggregates built up by soil fauna.

On this basis I have studied the morphology and chemical characters of soils inhabited by the giant *Octodrilus* species. Thus, the morphological and micromorphological features of a vermic cambic rendzina from the Padis karstic plateau were described (Pop and Postolache 1987).

Subsequent field research confirmed the occurrence of vermic characters in other soils, where the large *Octodrilus* species are present. Thus, vermic subtypes could be identified in rendzinas (Mollisols), eubasic, mesobasic, and argillic brown earth (Cambisols), and even in podzolic brown soils (Spodosols) (Pop and Vasu 1995).

Here, the vermic characters of three different soil types, a cambic rendzina, an eubasic brown earth, and a podzolic brown soil, are dealt with. They are soils developed under beech forests but on different parent material, and are classified into three different soil classes: mollisols, cambisols, and spodosols.

Site descriptions are as follows:

(i)   Padis, the Apuseni Mountains, 1,300 m alt., beech forest (As. *Phylitidi Fagetum*), vermic cambic rendzina on dolomitic limestone

(ii)   Buces Vulcan, the Apuseni Mountains, 550 m alt., beech forest (As. *Phylitidi Fagetum*) cambic brown earth on volcanic breccia with quartz, calcite, and andesite

(iii) Dealul Mare, Abrud, the Apuseni Mountains, 800 m alt., beech forest (As. *Symphyto cordati Fagetum*), vermic podzolic brown soil on orthogneiss and schists

The Earthworm Communities

In all three sites the same earthworm community pattern is found, but with different species combinations (Table 7). For additional information on the earthworm community in the rendzina see the previous section of this paper.

The three large *Octodrilus* species, *O. aporus, O. frivaldszkyi,* and *O. permagnus,* occur. All three are very large worms (Table 1). The highest biomass of 256 g/m^2 was recorded in the cambic rendzina, followed by the eubasic brown earth (200 g), and a much lower biomass of 98 g/m^2 in the podzolic brown soil.

Morphology and Micromorphology of Soil Profiles

The three soil types are rather shallow, with a depth of 50–60 cm in rendzina, podzolic brown soils, and 70–80 cm in eubasic brown earth. Coarse rocky fragments occur sparsely in the A horizon, up to 10–20% in the AB, and more than 40–50% in the B horizons (Figure 9) (Pop & Vasu 1995).

The most distinctive feature characteristic of these soils is the presence of a 4–6-cm-thick surface layer of discrete, stable, and large (2–4 cm in diameter) wormcasts. The earthworm cast layers, described as Am' (mollic) or Aou (ochric-umbric) horizons (Figure 8), consist of old, hardened, and rather rounded earthworm casts, not linked or united together, as well as fresh casts, mostly as conical heaps. Such a cast heap can weigh as much as 200–300 g (oven dried).

All of the species of cohabiting earthworms must influence soil formation, but the more evident and quite unusual traces or characters are produced by the giant species. The size of the structural elements in the soil (burrows and casts)

Table 7. Proportion of total density (D %) and biomass (B %) of lumbricid species in three soil types with vermic characters from the Carpathians

| | Soil, locality, date | | | | | |
| Species | Cambic rendzina Padis 16.08.79 | | Brown earth Buces Vulcan 6.06.72 | | Podzolic brown Abrud 12.06.92 | |
	D %	B %	D %	B %	D %	B %
Allolobophora dacica			26.5	2.2	13.9	1.7
Dendrobaena alpina	12.1	0.8				
D. byblica	22.7	1.2	4.4	0.4	25.0	1.5
D. clujensis	2.2	6.0			22.2	6.6
Lumbricus polyphemus			1.5	0.3		
Octolasion lacteum			2.9	0.6	5.6	0.4
Octodrilus aporus			48.5	92.5		
O. bihariensis	15.2	7.0				
O. compromissus			11.8	1.7		
O. exacystis			4.4	2.3		
O. frivaldszkyi	28.8	85.0				
O. permagnus					33.3	89.8
Total community/m²	66.0	257 g	34.0	200 g	18.0	98 g

depends on the size of the worms and is species specific. Experimental studies suggest that the stability or degradation of the surface earthworm casts is conditioned by the physio-chemical properties of the plasma and the texture of the soil, in which calcium plays an important role; in rendzina the vermic structure, induced by the same species, is more stable than in acid soils (Pop et al. 1992).

In the deeper horizons, the diameter of the wormcasts diminishes and the horizons appear more compact. The A horizon has a crumb structure, while the AB and B horizons have an angular blocky structure. Earthworm burrows with a diameter up to 1.5 cm occur in the entire soil profile. Micromorphological studies showed that the wormcast structure does not totally disappear even in the deeper horizons.

Reliable evidence of the strongly vermic character of these soils is shown in a series of structure photograms of the rendzina profile to the depth of 40 cm; the presence of hard rocks hindered us from sampling deeper (Figure 10).

In all structural photograms three types of wormcasts can be distinguished: wormcasts consisting of (i) *mineral* material brought up by worms from the deeper horizons; (ii) predominantly *organic* material, mainly plant remnants in

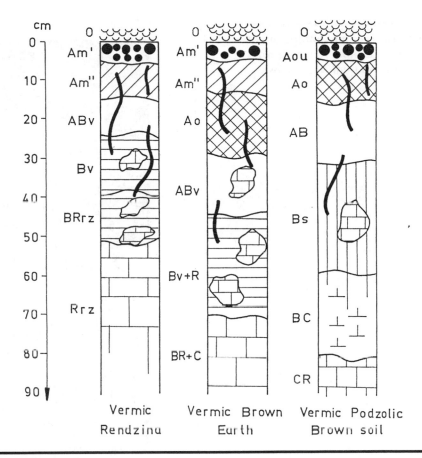

Figure 9. Profiles of three vermic soil subtypes from the Carpathians.

various breakdown stages, with casts or macroaggregates of mesofauna; and (iii) *organo-mineral* wormcasts from deeper soil material mixed with organic remnants of ingested food.

The series of structure photograms shows the well-aerated crumb, porous structure of the surface soil horizons, made up almost entirely of wormcasts with large spaces among them. In the deeper horizons, the casts are more and more pressed together and the pore spaces smaller.

In the upper soil horizons, a sponge-like microstructure dominates, due to the activity of the mesofauna. The earthworm castings, being rich in organic matter, provide a suitable medium for the development of smaller invertebrates.

Large amounts of soil material from the deeper soil horizons are brought to

Figure 10. Structure photogram of the vermic cambic rendzina from Padis (the Apuseni Mountains).

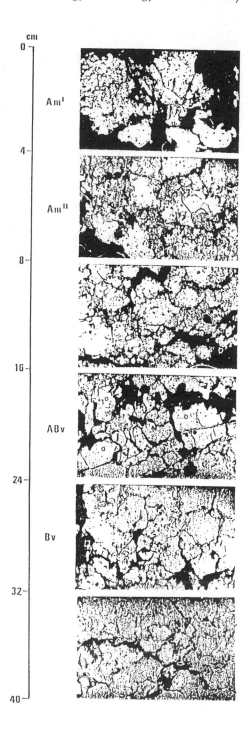

the surface and deposited as casts, thus burying former surface cast horizons. Their secondary and tertiary comminution is achieved by a series of smaller and smaller soil organisms (animals, fungi, and bacteria) as well as by physico-chemical weathering. The organic remnants brought into soil by earthworms, with an initial recognizable tissue structure, gradually turn into a "fine humus."

In the deeper horizons the diameter of earthworm casts is smaller than at the surface. The sponge-like microstructure caused by the mesofauna diminishes and the horizons appear more compact. However, the earthworm cast structure does not totally disappear even in the deeper horizons.

Physical and Chemical Properties of Vermic Soils

The physical and chemical properties of the three soils investigated are normal for their evolutionary stages and the pedoclimatic conditions. Thus, the particle size distribution, the humus content, pH, exchangeable bases, and total and mobile nutrient content are all within usual limits of "typic," non-vermic soils (Pop and Vasu 1995).

It seems that the giant earthworms have affected foremost the morphology of the soil profile. Nevertheless, their biochemical influences should not be neglected, even if it is not demonstrated by chemical analyses and is not entirely understood.

There are some peculiarities that are common to these very different soils, suggesting a somewhat convergent evolution, resulting from the unusually intense earthworm activity.

The very low bulk density, especially in the surface horizons (0.4–0.7 g/cm^3), has low resistance to penetration (1–6 kgf/cm^3) associated with a high permeability (290–1,280 mm/h), and a very high porosity (over 50–60%) provides the background to peculiar biochemical processes in these vermic soils.

The thermodynamic stability conditions evidenced by redox potential (Eh) values of 400–600 mV (that is 100–200 mV higher than in typical soils), associated with higher humidity than usual (Wi = 53–65%), indicate highly oxidative conditions, due to the highly aerated soil structure.

The humus content is very high, ranging between 4–11%. In all cases, the humification processes favor the formation of fulvic acids, a most unusual process in soils with high base saturation. This process is illustrated by the relatively high values of carbon contained in fulvic acids (CF = 300–600 mg/100 g soil) and especially by the ratio between humic and fulvic acid carbon, which is mainly below (0.5–0.9) or slightly above (1.1–1.4) unity.

The presence of ionic Al (2–80 ppm) and of ionizable SiO$_2$ (50–300 ppm) in the soil solution of the saturated soil ensures suitable conditions for the formation of Al-fulvate and Al-silicate gels. As our experiment pointed out, these are very efficient binding materials for soil aggregates. Differences in base content and in Al- and Fe-ion content, as well as in texture, account for differences in stability of soil aggregates in the three investigated soils.

In summary, the morphology, micromorphology, and physical and chemical properties of these soils allow the discrimination of new vermic subtypes in mountain rendzinas, brown eubasic earths, and podzolic brown soils, that result from the high pedogenetic activity of the soil fauna, dominated by giant earthworms of the genus *Octodrilus*.

Experimental Study of the Influence of Calcophilous Octodrilus Species on Soil

As discussed above, several of the endemic *Octodrilus* species may be regarded as calcophilous, their occurrence being confined to patchily distributed rendzinas and eubasic brown earths underlying beech or beech-hornbeam forests. These relatively small areas of soils developed on limestone are isolated from one another by soils developed on acid rocks. It was suggested (Pop 1994) that these acid soils could be regarded as barriers to the spreading of calcophilous earthworms, thereby promoting an accelerated insular-like speciation of the genus *Octodrilus*.

Some of these *Octodrilus* species, such as *O. frivaldszkyi, O. aporus, O. permagnus,* or *O. ophiomorphus*, are very large worms and, as shown above, are believed to have an important role in developing the most evident vermic features recorded so far in the soils of the northern temperate zone.

In a laboratory experiment, the relationship between *Octodrilus* species and calcium in the development of vermic structure in soil was investigated. Calcium is an important factor in stabilizing soil structure, and its concentration is also considered to be a key factor in determining the distribution of certain earthworms. The degree of stenobiontism towards calcium was also investigated by testing the tolerance of calcophilous earthworms to acid soils, presumed to act as barriers to their distribution (Pop et al. 1992).

Material and Methods—The activity of two calcophilous earthworm species, *Octodrilus frivaldszkyi* and *O. bihariensis,* in three different soils, with or without supplementary calcium carbonate, was investigated in subterranean laboratory conditions.

O. frivaldszkyi is a very large earthworm, (length 400–500 mm, dia 8–15 mm, weight 20–25 g), while *O. bihariensis* is a medium-sized earthworm (length 94–113 mm, dia 4–7 mm, weight 2–3 g).

Soil types used in the experiment were as follows: (i) a vermic cambic rendzina, from beech forest (1,100 m alt), Padis karstic area; (ii) an acid brown soil from fir tree forest (1,400 m alt), Baisoara, the Apuseni Mountains; and (iii) an albic luvisol from a mixed beech-oak forest (700 m alt) near Cluj-Napoca.

The rendzina represents the natural habitat of the two earthworm species studied, while the acid soils that separate the limestone areas in the Apuseni Mountains are considered a hostile environment.

Experimental cages were filled with soil material (passed through 2-mm mesh sieve) from the A horizon of the three soils. For each soil type, a variant with and without a supplementary calcium carbonate layer was designed. The earthworms were fed with dried beech leaves. Experiments were performed in a subterranean laboratory set up in a deep cellar, at an air humidity close to saturation and a temperature of 8–12°C, for 16 months (Nov. 1987–March 1988).

Results—The morphological traces of earthworm activity in soil can be explained tentatively by physico-chemical data, particularly by ionic equilibria in the soil solution.

Earthworm activity in the soil is evidently species specific, but it depends on soil type. Calcophilous species induce well-developed vermic characters in rendzina, which represents their natural habitat, but they do not when placed in acid soils, especially acid brown soil.

The size of structural elements in soil (casts and burrows) depends on the size of worms, but their stability and degradation are conditioned by differences between soil types, especially by the chemical and physico-chemical properties of plasma and texture. Thus, in rendzina, due to the existing chemical equilibria and physical properties, the vermic structure is more stable than in acid brown soil where the casts rapidly break down.

The nature of the cement of soil aggregates depends on the soil chemical composition, but differences detected in the cement composition of the casts of the two *Octodrilus* species show a specific or selective influence of the worms on soil structure.

The $CaCO_3$ treatment of soil leads to a marked improvement in soil structure in the conservation and stabilization degree of both discrete wormcasts and burrow layers.

Special neoformations with Ca, Fe, and Al have been observed in different parts of the soil profile. These include ferric and humic burrow linings in variants with acid soils that could be regarded as protecting the worms against adverse environmental conditions, and semicolloidal and semicrystalline gels whose role, for the time being, is unknown.

The alterations induced in soil by earthworms are sometimes so great that they affect not only the mobile ionic structure of the soil, but even the clay minerals, that is, its most stable constituents. If the bioaccumulation of K and the changes in clay mineral ratio detected in our experiment actually show an illitization, then this could be evidence that earthworms can produce much more rapid and profound changes in soils than believed hitherto. It is generally accepted that profound alterations in soils are very slow, taking hundreds or thousands of years. Our experiment lasted only 16 months, so this issue needs further investigation.

Conservation of the Endemic *Octodrilus* Species in the Carpathians

The endemic *Octodrilus* species, which have proved to be interesting for science and important for the stability of unique natural ecosystems from the Carpathians, are endangered by two common human activities, namely air-soil pollution and sylvicultural cutting, especially clear-felling of the forests.

Effect of Air Pollution on Earthworms

The largest part of the Romanian Carpathians is protected from or not affected by destructive air pollution. Nevertheless, over a limited area, air pollution does affect earthworms as well as the whole ecosystem.

I studied one of the most polluted areas in Romania, the Ampoiu Valley, in the Apuseni Mountains (V.V. Pop 1987). Here, sulphur dioxide and dust containing heavy metals are discharged into the air from metal-chemical works in Zlatna. Effects on the earthworm fauna were directly related to the distance from Zlatna.

In an old beech forest with well-developed tall trees near the immediate neighborhood of the pollution source, I found no earthworms. The vegetation and soil type, as well as a study of several unpolluted control forests, indicate that conditions would normally be suitable for an earthworm community with *Octodrilus frivaldszkyi, Allolobophora dugesi, A. rosea, Dendrobaena byblica,* and *D. clujensis* with an approximate density of 15–20 lumbricids per square meter and a biomass of 35–50 g/m^2.

Earthworms in the most polluted area, which includes the beech forest near the chemical works, were killed presumably either by the direct action of pollutants or by starvation induced by unpalatable food. It is also important to mention that other soil-inhabiting animals, such as *Acarina* and *Collembola,* are abundant in the litter. The accumulation on the soil surface of a thick undecomposed leaf litter layer is considered as evidence of the interruption of the organic matter and turnover food chain at the earthworm level.

Effect of Sylvicultural Cutting on Endemic Earthworms

Most of the Carpathians in Romania are covered by natural forests with large areas of secondary grassland following forest cutting. Agricultural fields are confined to near the rare villages at lower altitude. Substantial areas are nevertheless affected by sylvicultural cutting, which also jeopardizes the soil fauna, mostly on limestone where the shallow soils, without the protection of natural vegetation, are rapidly destroyed by erosion.

The giant endemic *Octodrilus* species which live on small patchily distributed areas are jeopardized most. It is considered that the disappearance of the giant endemic earthworms, after clear-cutting, endangers the restoration of the specific Carpathian beech forests of limestone areas (Pop 1982).

The conservation of endemic earthworms could be ensured only by protecting their environment, namely the islands of beech forests on limestone. In Romania, several projects aiming at the protection and conservation of floristic and faunistic elements of the Carpathians are in progress. The necessity to protect soil endemic organisms as a new aim of nature conservation in the Carpathians has been presented previously (Pop 1983). It is considered that endemic earthworm species are indicators of very particular edaphons, that can also be called "endemic edaphons."

The protection of the biotopes inhabited by the endemic *Octodrilus* species, besides the conservation of these species, may have theoretical value for the study of insular speciation in continental mountains.

REFERENCES CITED

Bouché, M.B. 1972. Lombriciens de France. Ecology et Systématique. Institut National de la Recherche Agronomique, Publ. 72.2, Paris.

Edwards, C.A., and J.R. Lofty. 1972. Biology of Earthworms. Chapman and Hall, London.

Lee, K.E. 1985. Earthworms. Their Ecology and Relationships with Soils and Land Use. Academic Press, Sydney.

Mayr, E. 1971. Populations, Species and Evolution. An Abridgment of Animal Species and Evolution. The Belkamp Press of Harvard University Press, Cambridge, Massachusetts.

Mayr, E., E.G. Linsley, and R.L. Usinger. 1953. Methods and Principles of Systematic Zoology. McGraw-Hill, New York.

Mršic, N. 1991. Monograph on earthworms (Lumbricidae) of the Balkans. Academia scientiarum et artium Slovenica, Historia Naturalis, Ljubljana, 31, I, II.

Omodeo, P. 1956. Contributo ala revisione dei Lumbricidae. Archivio Zoologico Italaliano, 41: 129–212.

Pop, V. 1941. Zur phylogenie und systematic der Lumbriciden. Zoologische Jahrbücher (Systematik), 74: 487–522.

Pop, V. 1948. Lumbricidele din România. Anal. Acad. Republicii Populare Romane, Sect. Stiinte Geologice, Geografice, Biologice. Ser. A, Mem., 9, 1: 383–506.

Pop, V. 1973. *Octolasium (Octodrilus) robustum* nouvelle espèce de Lumbricidae et ses affinités. Revue Roumaine de Biologie, Serie Zoologie, T.18, 4: 265–268.

Pop, V.V. 1980. The biogeographic significance of the earthworm fauna of the future National Park area in the Cerna Valley. Ocrotirea naturii si a mediului înconjurator, Bucuresti, t.24, 2: 157–164 (Romanian, English summary).

Pop, V.V. 1982. On the earthworm fauna of the Carpathian beech forests. In V. Preda and M. Boscaiu (eds.). Les Hetraies Carpatiques. Leur signification biohistorique et ecoprotective. Publ. Academiei R.S. România, Filiala Cluj-Napoca, Subcomsia. Protectia Naturii, 327–341 (Romanian, English summary).

Pop, V.V. 1983. The importance of the conservation of the endemic edaphobionts from the Romanian Carpathians. Ocrotirea naturii si a mediului înconjurator. Bucuresti, t.21, 1: 37–39 (Romanian, English summary).

Pop, V.V. 1985. Relationships between Lumbricide synusia and ecosystem types in the Apuseni Mountains (the Romanian Carpathians) in Actualitate si perspectiva in biologie. Structuri si functii in ecosisteme terestre si acvatice. Tipo Agronomia, Cluj-Napoca, 79–86 (Romanian, English summary).

Pop, V.V. 1987. Density and biomass of earthworm synusia in forest ecosystems of the Romanian Carpathians. In A.N. Bonvicini Pagliai and P. Omodeo (eds). On Earthworms. Selected Symposia and Monographs. U.Z.I., 2, Muchi, Modena, 183–190.

Pop, V.V. 1989. Studies on the genus *Octodrilus* Omodeo, 1956 (Oligochaeta, Lumbricidae) from the Apuseni Mountains (the Carpathians, Romania). I. Description of new taxa. Travaux du Museum d'Histoire Naturelle "Grigore Antipa," Bucarest, 30: 193–221.

Pop, V.V. 1991. Studies on the genus *Octodrilus* Omodeo, 1956 (Oligochaeata, Lumbricidae) from the Apuseni Mountains (the Carpathians, Romania). II. Variability of characters. Travaux du Museum d'Histoire Naturelle "Grigore Antipa," Bucarest, 31: 397–414.

Pop, V.V. 1994. On speciation in the genus *Octodrilus* Omodeo, 1956 (Oligochaeta, Lumbricidae). Mitteilungen aus dem Hamburgischen Zoologischen Museum und Institut, Band 89, Ergbd. 1: 37–46.

Pop, V.V. (in press). Earthworm—Vegetation—Soil Relationships in the Romanian Carpathians. Proceedings of the ISEE5, Columbus, Ohio, 1994. Soil Biology and Biochemistry.

Pop, V.V. and T. Postolache. 1987. Giant earthworms build up vermic mountain rendzinas. In A.N. Bonvicini Pagliai and P. Omodeo (eds.). On Earthworms. Selected Symposia and Monographs. U.Z.I., 2, Muchi, Modena, 141–150.

Pop, V.V., T. Postolache, A. Vasu, and C. Craciun. 1992. Calcophilous earthworm activity in soil: An experimental approach. Soil Biology and Biochemistry, 24(12): 483–1490.

Pop, V.V., and A.Vasu. 1995. Conspicuous vermic characters in mountain soils developed by large lumbricids (Oligochaeta). Acta Zoologica Fennica, 196: 83–86.

Satchell, J.E. 1967. Earthworms. In A. Burges and F. Raw (eds.). Soil Biology, pp. 259–322.

Sims, R.W. 1969. Outline of an application of computer technique to the problem of the classification of the Megascolecoid earthworms. Pedobiologia, 9: 35–41.

Zicsi, A. 1986. Über die taxonomischen Probleme der Gattung *Octodrilus* Omodeo, 1956 und *Octodriloides* gen. n. (Oligochaeta, Lumbricidae). Opuscula Zoologica, Budapest, 22: 103–112.

Zicsi, A., and V.V. Pop. 1984. Neue Regenwürmer aus Rumänien (Oligochaeta, Lumbricidae). Acta Zoologica Hungarica, 30(1–2): 241–248.

PRESENTATIONS IN THE SESSION ON EARTHWORM BIOLOGY, ECOLOGY, BEHAVIOR, AND PHYSIOLOGY, ISEE 5 COLUMBUS, OHIO, 1994

The session includes 27 rather heterogenous presentations (9 oral and 18 posters) which may be grouped under four main topics, namely, (i) methods, (ii) biology and behavior, (iii) ecology, and (iv) ecophysiology. The topics illustrate both the diversification and the narrowing of presented research.

Methods

Progress in a scientific field depends, to some extent, on the development of its appropriate methods of investigation. Earthworm scientists have readopted the old methods of hand-digging and expelling animals from soil with formalin to investigate the effect of local soil and climatical conditions (Callaham and Hendrix) as well as the diurnal rhythms of earthworms (Bough).

Nevertheless, modern methods are involved in analytical aspects, data processing, and as tools of synthesis of earthworm ecology.

Infra-red video recording has helped the study of reproductive behavior in *Lumbricus terrestris* (Nuutinen and Butt). Modeling the population dynamics of *Lumbricus rubellus* allows the identification of most sensitive parameters of life history as well as the assessment of the effects of environmental disturbance on these earthworms (Klok et al.). A graphic representation of entropy values for environmental factors leads to better definition of factors that affect the ecological behavior of earthworms (Sánchez et al.).

Biology and Behavior

Interesting and new data relate to the mating activity study of the most common earthworms. Using modern infra-red video recording, Nuutinen and Butt detected mutual burrow visits of *L. terrestris* preceding mating on the soil surface, hereby completing the known mating sequence ethogram.

An experimental study carried out by Meyer and Bouwman indicates a direct correlation between reproductive success and the mating time of *Eisenia fetida* as a function of sperm transfer, anisopary, or both.

Ecology

The structure of communities remains one of the major topics of earthworm ecology. New valuable quantitative data covered mostly natural forest and grassland ecosystems. In Central New York (North America), Shakir and Dindal recorded earthworm communities dominated by *Aporrectodea tuberculata, Octolasium tyrteum,* and *Lumbricus* species in a sequence of four ecosystems. In the Bieszczady Mountains (Poland) Kostecka investigated beech wood biotopes dominated by *Allolobophora cernosvitoviana* (Zicsi 1967). Grossi and Brun described earthworm communities and their relationships with the main environmental factors in the Alps. By analyzing the ecological preferences of 27 species as they relate to soil factors, Sanchez et al. found the factors that best define the ecological behavior of earthworms. The paper is a model of modern methods of processing ecological data. According to Muys and Granval, the structure of earthworm communities, as well as their biomass, could be useful in establishing the site quality of forest and forest site classifications. Bhawalker proposed a classification for ecological forms of earthworms.

The state of earthworm communities seems to be as expected for the given local conditions in most places, but several papers point out local decreases of earthworm populations, due to predators or parasites, mainly resulting from negative human impacts on the environment.

Thus, a special case of predation is reported by Blackshaw in Northern Ireland where the terrestrial planarian *Artioposthia triangulata* was found to reduce earthworm populations; these field observations have been confirmed by an experimental approach.

Field and pot experiments (Dalby et al.) showed that soil disturbance affected the populations of *Aporrectodea trapezoides, A. caliginosa,* and *A. rosea* negatively. Long periods of land disturbance, such as reported by Blanchard and Julka in South India, also produced alterations in earthworm communities. Some species, such as *Diplocardia mississippiensis*, are harvested for fish bait often with negative influences on soil properties (Hendrix et al.). An optimistic note to conclude this short summary of new achievements in earthworm ecology is provided by the reverse process, namely of natural or man-helped spreading or colonization of earthworms. *Dendrobaena octaedra* recently invaded aspen and pine forests in the Rocky Mountains through a natural process (Dymond et al.).

Introduction of earthworms in degraded or newly restored lands to promote soil improvement often fails due to adverse conditions or the high cost of the process. Kevin et al. propose a new method, the Earthworm Inoculation Unit, which seems to be successful.

Ecophysiology

Papers included in this symposium covered three topics, namely, basic physiology of earthworms, the influence of earthworm physiological processes on their environment, and the influence of xenobiotics on earthworms.

A comparative study of digestive enzymes in the gut of two tropical geophagous earthworms revealed new data on the controversial question of whether animal tissue can produce enzymes such as cellulase (Lattaud et al.). Laboratory experiments showed that in *Penthoscolex corethrurs* (Glossoscolecidae) the cellulase is produced by microorganisms ingested with soil, whereas in *Polypheretima elongata* (Magascolecidae) the cellulase seems to be the animal's own exoenzyme.

In an in vitro experiment carried out on the respiration of *Allolobophora molleri* and its casts, Trigo et al. confirm the activation of soil microflora by earthworms.

In the biotransformation processes of xenobiotics in earthworms, the glutathione transferases play an important role in the detoxification process. Burges et al. isolated and have characterized three major forms of GST in *Eisenia andrei*.

An anticancer (Huang et al.) and a spermatocidal earthworm extract which were reported at the symposium (Lattaud et al.) widen the applied aspects of earthworm studies.

My own research on the earthworms from the Carpathians covers diverse but related topics that might be considered a reflection on a regional scale of research development in earthworm ecology.

Presented at ISEE 5

Bhawalker, U.S. Ecological classification of earthworms.

Blackshaw, R.P. The life-cycle of the terrestrial planarian *Artioposthia triangulata* (Dendy) in Northern Ireland.

Blackshaw R.P. *Artioposthia triangulata* (Dendy) feeding on earthworms in soil columns.

Blanchard E., and J.M. Julka. Influence of forest disturbance on earthworm (Oligochaeta) communities in the Western Ghats (South India).

Bough, P.S. Diurnal and fleeing-activity of earthworms.

Borgeraas, J., K. Stepaniak, and J. Stenersen. Purification and characterisation of multiple forms of glutathione transferase from the genus *Eisenia*.

Butt, K.R., J. Frederickson, and R.M. Morris. The Earthworm Inoculation Unit (EIU) technique, an integrated system for cultivation and soil-inoculation of earthworms.

Callaham, M.A. Jr., and P.F. Hendrix. Comparison of hand-digging and formalin extraction as methods for the collection of earthworms (Lumbricidae and Megascolecidae) in forest soils on the Southern Appalachian Piedmont of Georgia, USA.

Cothrel, S.R., J.P. Vimmersedt, and D.A. Kost. In situ recycling of urban deciduous tree litter.

Curry, J. Factors affecting earthworm abundance in soil.

Dalby, P.R., G.H. Baker, and S.E. Smith. The effect of species interactions and soil disturbance on three lumbricid earthworms in a pasture soil.

Dymond, P., S. Scheu, and D. Parkinson. Abundance and distribution of *Dendrobaena octaedra*
(Lumbricidae) in an aspen and pine forest of the Canadian Rocky Mountains (Alberta).

Fuxia, Z., G. Baozhu, W. Huiyun, W. Xifa, and Y. Keping. The spermatocidal substances in
the earthworm tissues.

Fuzhen, H., Z. Shiwei, and Z. Yaling. Study on the anti-cancer effect of FNK, an extract from
earthworms.

Gould, E., and J. Kalmajin Ad. The electrical field of earthworms (*Lumbricus terrestris*).

Grossi, J.L., and J.J. Brun. Some aspects of the interactions between earthworm populations
and soil structure as well as its functioning in the Alps according to different plant
communities.

Hendrix, P.F., M.A. Callahan, Jr., and L. Kirn. Ecological relationships and effects of harvesting on *Diplocardia* (Oligochaeta) populations in Apalachicola Forest, Florida, USA.

Klok, C., A.M. de Roos, H.M. Baveco, J.C.Y. Marinissen, and W. Ma. Modeling population
dynamics of the earthworm *Lumbricus rubellus*. I. Identification of most sensitive life
history parameters.

Kostecka, J. Some notes on the ecology of *Allolobophora cernosvitoviana* (Zicsi 1967) a
species new to the Polish earthworm (Lumbricidae) fauna.

Lattaud, C., B.G. Zhang, S. Locati, C. Rouland, and P. Lavelle. Comparative study of digestive enzymes in the gut of two species of tropical geophagous earthworms *Pontoscolex
corethrurus* (Glossoscolecidae) and *Polypheretima elongata* (Megascolecidae).

Meyer, W.J., and H. Bouwman. Mating period and cocoon production of *Eisenia fetida*.

Muys, B., and P. Granval. Are earthworms useful for forest site classification? A case study
in temperate lowland forests (Flanders, Belgium).

Nuutinen, V., and K.R. Butt. The mating behaviour of the earthworm *Lumbricus terrestris* L.

Sánchez, E.G., G. Morales, J.B. Jesus, and D.J. Diaz-Cosin. Ecological preferences of some
earthworm species in SW Spain.

Shakir, S.H., and D.L. Dindal. Population density and biomass of earthworms in forest and
herbaceous microecosystems in central New York, North America.

Trigo, D., G. Almendros, and D.J. Diaz-Cosin. Soil respiratory activity in the presence of
Allolobophora molleri (Oligochaeta, Lumbricidae).

Valle, J.A., R.P. Moro, D. Trigo, and D.J. Diaz-Cosin. Annual study of a population of
Hormogaster elisae (Oligochaeta, Hormogastridae).

Influence of Earthworms on Soil Organic Matter Dynamics, Nutrient Dynamics, and Microbiological Ecology

III

Large-Scale Effects of Earthworms on Soil Organic Matter and Nutrient Dynamics

5

Patrick Lavelle,[1] Beto Pashanasi,[2]
Fabienne Charpentier,[1] Cécile Gilot,[1]
Jean-Pierre Rossi,[1] Laurent Derouard,[1] Jean Andre,[3]
Jean-François Ponge,[3] and Nicolas Bernier[3]
[1]*Laboratoire d'Ecologie des Sols Tropicaux, ORSTOM, 32 rue Henri Varagnat, 93143 Bondy Cedex, France;* [2]*Estacion Experimental San Ramon, INIAA, Yurimaguas, Loreto, Peru;* [3]*Université de Savoie, 73376-Le Bourget du Lac, France;* [4]*MNHN, 4 avenue du Petit Château, 91000 Brunoy, France*

After 30 years of unquestioned success, agriculture is now facing important problems. In developed countries, huge increases in productivity have accompanied a severe depletion of "soil quality" in terms of resistance to erosion, organic contents, and concentrations of heavy metals and pesticide residues. In developing countries, intensification has been less successful due to socio-economical limitations. Nonetheless, traditional practices do not conserve the quality of soils: stocks of organic matter are rapidly depleted and erosion pulls fine particles out of the surface horizons. In a context of increasing population pressure, this degradation of soils results in many social and environment problems (Eswaran 1994).

A common feature to all sorts of soil degradation is the significant decrease of organic reserves and a severe depletion of soil invertebrate communities, especially earthworms (Lavelle et al. 1994).

1-884015-74-3/98/$0.00/$.50

The contribution of earthworms to processes of soil fertility has been described in several hundred papers and books (Satchell 1983; Lee 1985). As a result, there is a growing expectation from soil users for methods that protect soil fertility through an enhancement of biological processes. Earthworms may be considered as a resource for the farming system, and the management of their communities is a promising field for progress in agriculture practices. Demand for techniques making optimal use of that resource is likely to increase, but basic research is still needed to support their development.

The relationships between earthworm activities and soil properties are not thoroughly understood, especially at large time scales of years to decades. Most results have been obtained in small-scale laboratory or field designs that exaggerate the process(es) under study and can by no means be extrapolated readily to larger scales of time and space.

This paper synthesizes information on effects of earthworms at scales larger than one year. Earthworm behaviors that may affect these processes are detailed.

EARTHWORMS AND SOIL FUNCTION: THE DRILOSPHERE CONCEPT

At the real scale of, for example, a small tropical holder's plot, earthworm activities are only one determinant of soil fertility, and their effects are likely to be determined by factors operating at larger scales of time and space, viz. climate, edaphic properties, and the quality and amount of organic inputs (Lavelle et al. 1993). Earthworms participate in the soil functions through the drilosphere system defined as earthworms, physical structures, and the whole microbial and invertebrate community. As a result of digestion processes and creation of structures, the composition, structure, and relative importance of the drilosphere system is clearly determined by climate, soil parameters, and quality of organic inputs. Earthworms in turn influence soil microbial communities, and hence have effects on microbial processes of soil organic matter (SOM) and nutrient dynamics. They also affect the activities of other invertebrates, either by modifying their environment or through competition for feeding resources (Figure 1).

Finally, earthworms are not a homogeneous entity. They comprise several functional groups which have clearly distinct ecologies and impacts on the environment (Bouché 1977). Current classifications based on earthworm location in the soil profile and feeding resources are still too general to describe the large diversity in functions. Classifications based on impact on soil parameters might be useful.

The effects of earthworms on soil function thus depend on their interactions

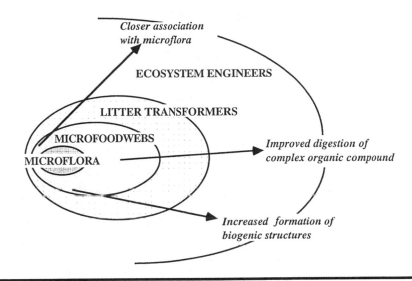

Figure 1. Relationships of earthworms and other soil "ecosystem engineers" with other soil biological components. Earthworms partly influence the occurrence and activity of other soil organisms since they create large structures that may persist over significant periods and affect the environment (Lavelle 1994).

with a wide range of identified abiotic and biotic factors that operate at rather different scales of time and space. Furthermore, the effects produced will affect structures of different sizes, and persist for highly variable periods of time, depending on the factor(s) with which they interact. For example, it is expected that physical structures created by earthworms, as a result of their interactions with soil components, will last much longer than the flush of activity of dormant microorganisms that they have activated in their guts (Figure 2).

Most studies have described processes at the scale of earthworm activities, typically in "microcosms," plots or small field enclosures. Results obtained in such conditions describe existing processes; however, they cannot be extrapolated directly to quantify and predict effects produced at the scale at which SOM dynamics and nutrient cycling are generally studied. One spectacular result of this approach is a huge discrepancy between the large importance that pedobiologists give to earthworms as regulators of soil physical structure and SOM dynamics, and the absence of any representation of earthworm activities in simulation models that describe SOM dynamics at scales of decades and hectares (Jenkinson and Rayner 1977; Molina et al. 1983; Parton et al. 1986).

A few papers have already described the effects of earthworms at the scale

PEDOGENESIS

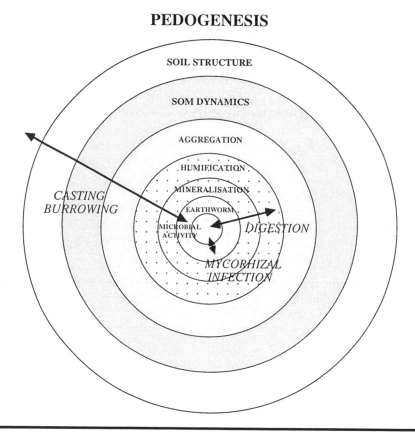

Figure 2. Effects of earthworm activities on soil processes operating at different scales.

of the different biotic and abiotic parameters with which they interact, viz. (1) selection of ingested particles and digestion processes at the scale of a gut transit (0.5–20 hours) (Lee 1985; Barois and Lavelle 1986); (2) immobilization-reorganization of nutrients in fresh casts (1–20 days) (Syers et al. 1979; Lavelle et al. 1992; Lopez-Hernandez et al. 1993); (3) evolution of SOM in aging casts (3–30 months) (Martin 1991; Lavelle and Martin 1992; Blair et al. 1994). Long-term evolution of SOM at the scale of the whole soil profile and pedogenesis during periods of years to centuries has been identified, although no information was currently available (Figure 3).

This paper describes effects of earthworms on SOM and nutrient dynamics observed in three-year field experiments, and details three sub-processes that

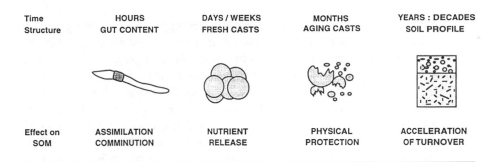

Time	HOURS	DAYS / WEEKS	MONTHS	YEARS : DECADES
Structure	GUT CONTENT	FRESH CASTS	AGING CASTS	SOIL PROFILE

Effect on	ASSIMILATION	NUTRIENT	PHYSICAL	ACCELERATION
SOM	COMMINUTION	RELEASE	PROTECTION	OF TURNOVER

Figure 3. Effects of earthworm activities on soil organic matter dynamics at different scales of time and space.

may determine the long-term effects of earthworms, i.e., feeding behaviors, patterns of horizontal distribution, and participation of earthworm activities in successional processes. Simulations of SOM dynamics, based on the CENTURY model (Parton et al. 1988), give some insight on effects to be observed at a time scale of 10–50 years.

EARTHWORM BEHAVIOR

Earthworm behavior may affect the soil function significantly. A major difference between short-scale experiments and the real world is that earthworms have limited opportunities to choose their food and move away in confined small experiments. This probably explains why they often lose weight or die in laboratory experiments. On the other hand, the introduction of unrealistically high earthworm populations to small enclosures in the field often creates concentrations of intense activity that would not normally have occurred in the field, or that only concern microsites that are either highly dispersed in nature or infrequently visited.

Selection of Particles

Earthworms are known to select the organic and mineral components that they ingest. As a result, their casts often have much higher contents of SOM and nutrients than the surrounding soil (Lee 1985). This is probably due to a preferential ingestion of plant residues (leaf and root litter debris) (Ferrière 1980; Piearce 1978; Kanyonyo 1984) and clay minerals. Barois and Patron (1994) demonstrated that the tropical peregrine species, *Pontoscolex corethrurus*, was able to select large organic debris and small mineral particles depending on soil type. Selection was made on aggregates rather than primary particles. There is evidence that some endogeic earthworms ingest only aggregates that do not exceed the diameter of their mouths, whereas other species may feed on large aggregates and split them into smaller aggregates (Blanchart 1990; Derouard 1993). The feeding behavior that allows such a selection has never been described in detail. The long-term consequences of that behavior, for dynamics of soil processes and SOM dynamics, have also not been directly addressed. Endogeic earthworms may deposit 20–200 t dry soil ha^{-1} surface casts that contain a significant proportion of SOM yearly. A much larger quantity of casts is deposited inside the soil and a volume of soil equivalent to the whole soil of the upper horizons may be passed through earthworm guts in a few years (Lavelle 1978). Nonetheless, the higher concentration of fine elements in casts than in the bulk soil suggests that earthworms may possibly reingest the same soil several times, while microsites with a relatively coarser texture may be avoided by earthworms.

Spatial Patterns of Horizontal Distribution

Several authors have pointed out the aggregative distribution of earthworm populations in such diverse ecosystems as an arable soil from Germany (Poier and Richter 1992), a deciduous forest of England (Phillipson et al. 1976), humid African (Lavelle 1978) and Colombian savannahs (Jimenez et al. unpub.), and an artificial pasture in southern Martinique (Rossi et al. in press). In some cases, the distribution was independent of basic soil parameters such as depth, clay, or carbon contents. Furthermore, different species tended to have different horizontal distributions (Poier and Richter 1992); in the case of an almost monospecific community of *Polypheretima elongata* in Martinique, Rossi et al. (in press) observed different distribution patterns for adults and juvenile worms. These observations suggest that some earthworm populations have patchy distributions with an average patch diameter of 20–40 m. Patches seem to be independent of soil parameters to some extent. The dynamics of earthworm populations in a patch are not synchronized with the populations of other patches. The occurrence of such patterns suggests that earthworm activities concentrate on patches probably for limited periods of time before becoming locally extinct. At Lamto, complementary patterns have been observed between large species that accumulate large casts and tend to compact the soil and smaller species that produce fine granular casts out of large casts of the first type of species that they ingest with root litter (Blanchart 1990). In that case, the observed patterns suggest a succession of patches made of "compacting" and "decompacting" species with complementary effects on soils (Blanchart et al. in press).

Compacting vs. Decompacting Species

The physical structure of earthworm casts is highly relevant to the dynamics of SOM at intermediate scales of months to years. Two different types of casts may be distinguished in this respect, viz. the globular casts of "compacting" species and the granular casts of "decompacting" species. Casts of the first category may be surrounded by a thin 10–20-mμ cortex made of clay minerals and organic particles which seem to reduce aeration and hence inhibit microbial activity at the scale of weeks to months (Blanchart et al. 1993; Martin 1991). Soils colonized by monospecific communities of such earthworm species are prone to compaction. In an experiment where the earthworm *Millsonia anomala* had been introduced into a yam and a maize culture, the proportion of large aggregates >2 mm increased significantly in soils that had been previously sieved, but no significant effect was observed in a soil that had kept its original structure (Table 1). Bulk density was increased significantly in both situations. Similar effects have been observed after inoculation of the peregrine, pantropical endogeic species *P. corethrurus* into a traditional cropping system of Peruvian Amazonia. After six successive crops, earthworms had increased the proportion of macro-aggregates (>2 mm) significantly from 25.4 to 31.2% at the expense of smaller (<0.5 mm) ones whose proportion had decreased from 35.4% to 27.4%. Changes in soil aggregation resulted in a slight increase of bulk density (significant during the first three cropping cycles) and a significant decrease of infiltration rates and sorptivity, the latter decreasing from 0.34 cm sec$^{-1/2}$ in non-inoculated treatments to 0.15 cm sec$^{-1/2}$ in treatments inoculated with 36 g m^{-2} fresh mass of

Table 1. Effects of inoculation of the earthworm *Millsonia anomala* into cropping systems on bulk density and aggregation of soil

	Crop				
	Bulk Density		% Aggregates >2 mm		
	Maize 0–10 cm	Maize 0–10 cm	Yam Mounds sieved soil	Maize 0–10 cm undisturbed soil	Maize 0–10 cm sieved soil
Time (months)	3	36	34	36	36
Inoculated	1.31	1.48	53.5	42.5	42.2
Non-inoc.	1.24	1.37	29.8	38.8	24.6
p	0.06	<0.001	<0.05	n.s.	<0.01

earthworms (Alegre et al. 1996). This transformation of soil physical properties eventually resulted in changes in the soil water regime, since soil tended to be drier during dry periods and wetter in periods of heavy rainfall than in the non-inoculated treatment.

Other endogeic earthworm species have opposite effects since they tend to break down large (>0.5 mm) aggregates and split them into smaller ones (Blanchart 1990; Derouard et al. in press). In Western African savannahs, for example, small species of the Eudrilidae family have such abilities, and it has been hypothesized that soil aggregation is regulated by the opposite effects of large "compacting" species like, for example, *Millsonia anomala* and "decompacting" species like the common eudrilid *Hyperiodrilus africanus*.

These results contrast with a rather broad set of results suggesting that earthworm activities improve aeration of soil and infiltration of water (review in Lee 1985). Three hypotheses may explain such discrepancies: (1) Most studies on relationships between earthworm activities and soil physical parameters have been on Lumbricidae. This family, unlike most tropical families, comprises a large proportion of species that dig semipermanent burrows which influence water infiltration significantly. (2) In natural ecosystems the association of compacting and decompacting species may regulate soil physical properties and, in the end, favor infiltration and aeration. It is important to consider that decompacting species may belong to other taxa like Enchytraeidae (Albrecht 1984; Didden 1990; Van Vliet et al. 1993) or millipedes (Tajovsky et al. 1991). (3) The effect of Lumbricidae could be a consequence of burial of large organic particles mixed with ingested soil, since it is commonly recognized that incorporation of litter into soil has significant effects on soil physical parameters (Aina 1984; Joschko et al. 1989; Kladivko et al. 1986; Kooistra 1991; Oades 1984; Shaw and Pawluk 1986; Springett 1983; Wolters 1991).

MEDIUM-TERM EFFECTS: EXPERIMENTS INOCULATING EARTHWORMS INTO CROPPING SYSTEMS OF THE HUMID TROPICS

Three-year experiments have been conducted at two tropical sites, Lamto (Côte d'Ivoire) and Yurimaguas (Peru). Annual cropping systems were inoculated with endogeic earthworms and the dynamics of the system compared to non-inoculated systems for six successive crops over three years (Pashanasi et al. 1996; Gilot 1994).

At Yurimaguas, the C and N contents of soil decreased significantly with time. After six cropping cycles, the C contents had decreased from 16.8 mg g^{-1}

to 1.36% and 1.51% respectively in systems inoculated with earthworms and the control (Figure 4). Although systems with earthworms tended to have less C from the fourth cropping cycle on, the observed difference was not significant at the end of the experiment. Changes in N content during the experiment showed similar trends: N concentration increased initially in both treatments, as a result of N inputs following burning and incorporation of ashes to the soil. During the first three cropping cycles, N contents were higher in the inoculated treatments. From the fourth harvest on, N contents were lower in the inoculated treatments but were not significant. Earthworms did not affect soil nutrient contents for the first five cropping cycles: Ca, Mg, K, and P contents first increased after burning and incorporation of ashes and then decreased steadily. At the last harvest, cation contents were slightly higher in the earthworm-inoculated treatments, but the difference was significant only for K contents. Similar trends were observed for pH and Al saturation.

At Lamto, similar results were obtained. After four cropping cycles of maize, the C contents in the upper 10 cm of soil had decreased from 13.37 mg g^{-1} at time 0 to 9.75 and 9.64 in control and earthworm-inoculated treatments respectively, the difference observed between the last two treatments being insignificant. In spite of these results, there seemed to exist some differences in the quality of organic matter. Physical fractionation of SOM using the Feller (1979) method showed some evidence of a protection of coarse organic particles in the inoculated treatments (Gilot 1994). Furthermore, laboratory respirometric tests showed a significant increase in soil respiration rate where earthworms had been active (Tsakala 1994).

Experiments by Gilot (1994) showed that the effect of earthworms in protecting coarse organic fractions was significant only in soils that had been sieved previously. In this case reaggregation of soil by earthworms had positive effects on SOM protection. In soils that had not been sieved, large aggregates resulting from earthworm activities in the natural soil were conserved in "no earthworm" treatment during the three years that the experiment lasted. Therefore, the effect of protection linked to aggregation was retained although no earthworms were present.

LONG-TERM EFFECTS OF EARTHWORMS: MODELING AND OBSERVATION OF SUCCESSIONAL PROCESSES

In the absence of long-term experiments, evidence for effects of earthworms at scales from 10 to 100 years or more has been sought from modeling and the observation of time sequences in successional processes.

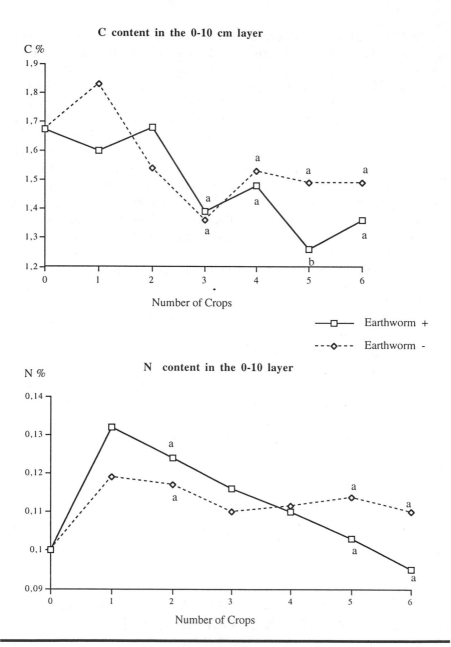

Figure 4. Changes in C and N contents in an ultisol of Peruvian Amazonia submitted to traditional slash and burn agriculture in the presence and absence of earthworms (*Pontoscolex corethrurus*) (Pashanasi et al. 1996). Pairs of data with different letters are significantly different.

Modeling

Current models that describe SOM dynamics do not take into account explicitly the effects of the soil fauna. Part of the effects of soil invertebrates may be implicit, either when describing initial conditions (for example through the C:N ratio that is influenced by their activities) or when choosing the decomposition rates of C pools that will actually include the overall effects of earthworms. An attempt was made to simulate the effect of earthworm activities on the three kinetically defined organic pools of the CENTURY model (Parton et al. 1988). This model, which simulates plant production and SOM dynamics in various agricultural and natural systems, considers three different SOM functional pools. A labile fraction (active SOM) has a rapid turnover and exists as live microbes and microbial products. The remaining fractions comprise SOM that is stabilized, either because it is physically protected (slow pool) or because it is chemically resistant (passive pool) to decomposition or both.

As a first step, the CENTURY model was used to simulate SOM dynamics and plant production in the savannah of Lamto (Martin and Parton unpub. data) and validated against observed values. Then the model was calibrated for this site and run to simulate C dynamics in earthworm casts and a control soil of the same savannah, sieved at 2 mm. Observations made by Martin (1991) during a 450-day incubation of earthworm casts and control soil sieved at 2 mm were used as a reference. In the case of sieved soil, the model outputs were close to the experimental results, provided that slow soil C decomposition rates increased. Conversely, it was necessary to decrease the rates for both slow and active decomposition rates of soil C to simulate the dynamics in casts. Earthworm removal was simulated by replacing the active and slow soil C decomposition rates of the model with those obtained by calibration with control soil. Under these assumptions, the CENTURY model indicated that SOM would decrease by ca. 10% in 30 years, the largest proportion being lost in the slow pool that includes physically protected organic matter (Figure 5). This suggests that the slow decomposition rate of soil C may be influenced significantly by earthworm activities. This pool would comprise organic matter that binds micro-aggregates into macro-aggregates (Elliott 1986) which is generally lost during cultivations. Earthworms may, therefore, play an important role in stabilizing SOM, hence maintaining the SOM stock and soil structure in agroecosystems in the long term.

Earthworm Activities and Successional Processes

Successional processes of vegetation dynamics such as those observed in natural forests may precede, or follow, significant changes in the organic status of soils.

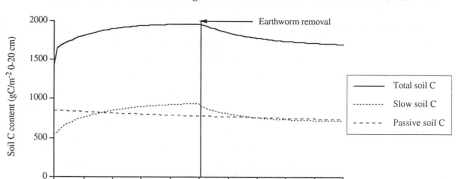

Figure 5. Changes of C contents in soils of a grass savanna at Lamto (Côte d'Ivoire) in the presence and absence of endogeic earthworms; results of a simulation using the CENTURY model (A. Martin and W.J. Parton unpub. data).

Several examples indicate that earthworm activities during these successions vary significantly (Miles 1985) and may be limited to periods when organic matter that they can digest is available.

Sampling of soil invertebrates in a diachronic series of hevea plantations in the Côte d'Ivoire showed great changes in soil faunal communities as plantations aged (Gilot et al. 1995). During the early stages of the succession, soil faunal communities were dominated by termites, especially xylophagous species. After a few years, the abundance of this group of termites declined and other groups dominated the termite communities. After 20 years, earthworms became dominant; mesohumic and endogeic categories prevailed. Finally, in a 30-year plantation, soil faunal abundance decreased steadily, as did the production of hevea. It has been suggested that these changes could reflect successions in soil fauna communities following changes of the quality and quantity of organic matter. When the plantations were created, woody material from the primary forest was left at the soil surface. Xylophagous termites were the first invertebrate group that used this resource. They transformed decaying wood into fecal pellets that may have been used by other groups of termites and surface-living earthworms. Eventually, fecal pellets of humivorous termites may have been incorporated into the soil and been used as food by endogeic mesohumic and oligohumic species of earthworms. Once organic matter from the wood had passed through this food chain and lost most of the energy stored as carbon compounds, the food resource base for soil faunal communities was reduced to the plant residues currently available in the hevea plantation and their populations decreased drastically. Interestingly, this sharp decrease in numbers coincided with a reduction in production of hevea. These observations suggest that soil fauna, and especially earthworms, may at some stages use carbon sources that had been previously stored in the ecosystem at different stages of natural or artificial successional processes. In case of the hevea plantation, it is hypothesized that soil faunal activities are sustained, at least partly, by the energy progressively released from the decaying logs, with positive effects on hevea production.

The hypothesis that earthworm activities may develop at a determined stage in plant successions is supported by observations of Bernier et al. (1993) in an alpine forest of France located at a 1550-m elevation. In a succession of forest patches from 10 to 190 years old, significant changes in earthworm communities were observed (Figure 6). In the early stages, earthworm density was high with a clear dominance of endogeic populations. Density decreased steadily during the following 20 years and, after 60 years, when the forest was mature, earthworm populations started to increase again, although their density was low. These population changes coincided with clear changes in the amounts and quality of organic matter stored in the humus layers. The proportion of organic matter bounded to minerals, i.e., organic matter that has been mixed into the soil by earthworm activities, was greatest at 10 years and then decreased steadily, being almost absent after 60 years (Figure 7). In the late stages of succession, bound organic matter resumed accumulation. The pattern of changes with time of unbound organic matter was exactly opposite to that of bound organic matter. The amount of unbound organic matter decreased when earthworms were abun-

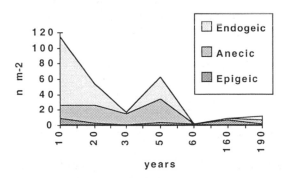

Figure 6. Changes in the abundance of earthworms of different ecological categories along a succession in an alpine spruce forest (Bernier et al. 1993).

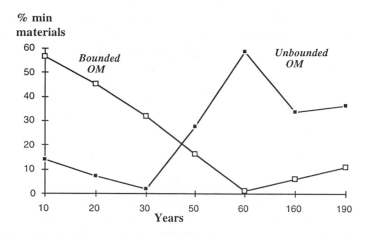

Figure 7. Changes in the abundance of organic matter bounded to soil minerals, and unbounded organic matter along a succession in an alpine spruce forest (Bernier et al. 1994).

dant, and increased when their populations were at low densities. This is evidence that during the cycle of growth, maturation, and senescence of the forest, humus type changed with a maximum development of a moder at 60 years and a mull at 10 years. It is hypothesized that a forest accumulates organic matter as litter and raw humus during the early phases of growth, when primary production is high. Then earthworm populations start to develop at the expense of these organic accumulations, and they progressively incorporate the non-digested part of this raw organic matter into organo-mineral complexes (Figure 7). This process results in the release of large amounts of nutrients and the creation of physical structures (macro-aggregates, macropores, and galleries) typical of a mull type humus. This medium is believed to be favorable for the establishment and growth of seedlings. Processes whereby earthworm populations establish and the reason why earthworms become able to live in what was previously an acid environment have not yet been identified.

DISCUSSION

The long-term effects of earthworms on SOM dynamics vary depending on the scale of time considered. When earthworms are introduced artificially into an ecosystem, they use part of the C resources for their activities. In the African savannahs of Lamto (Côte d'Ivoire), the amount of C mineralized directly through earthworm respiration was estimated as 1.2 t C ha^{-1} year^{-1} in a grass savannah, which is equivalent to about 5% of primary production (Lavelle 1978). The annual average population densities and biomass were 202 individuals and 39.7 g m^{-2} respectively, and this population ingested up to 1000–1250 t dry soil ha^{-1} year^{-1}. As part of this process, nutrients were released and made available to plants or microorganisms. In the same savannah, the overall amount of assimilable N released as ammonium in feces, or labile organic N in dead worms, and mucus has been estimated at 21.1 to 38.6 kg/ha/yr of NH_4-N in a population of *Millsonia anomala* that comprises 60% of the population biomass. The overall production of mineral-N for the earthworm community is therefore expected to range from 30 to 50 kg. In tropical pastures, with earthworm biomasses of 1–3 t ha^{-1} and soils with higher contents in organic nitrogen, the contribution of earthworms to N-mineralization may probably reach a few hundred kg mineral-N ha^{-1} year^{-1}. In temperate pastures, the flux of mineral-N from earthworms may be estimated at a few hundred kg ha^{-1} year^{-1} (Syers et al. 1979; Hameed et al. 1994). Similar processes have been observed regarding P, but no real estimates of amounts released ha^{-1} year^{-1} have been produced (Sharpley and Syers 1976; Lopez-Hernandez et al. 1993; Brossard et al. 1994). There is some evidence that plants may accumulate these nutrients but the exact proportion, especially on a yearly basis, is not known (Spain et al. 1992; Hameed et al. 1994).

Increased nutrient turnover from earthworm activities usually results in increased plant growth. Most experiments on the scale of one to six successive cropping cycles show significant effects of earthworm activities on plant production; these effects seem to be proportional to earthworm biomass, within a limited range of biomass (Lavelle 1994). Whether this increased production is sustained in the long term is not known. On the one hand, earthworms tend to feed on existing stocks of almost undecomposed organic matter and accelerate their decomposition. Once these stocks are depleted, earthworm activities may cease, and the system will return to lower levels of plant production. Observations made in rubber plantations of different ages in Côte d'Ivoire seem to support this hypothesis (Gilot et al. 1995). Observations of successional processes in an alpine spruce forest of France showed that earthworm activities seem to have been reduced by the accumulation of low-quality litter residues that they could not process, rather than by the exhaustion of available organic resources. In that case, spruce litter may have become palatable only after a long period of maturation during which fungal attacks progressively eliminated those toxic compounds present in fresh litter. The effect of litter quality on earthworm activities has already been stressed in studies on Finnish spruce forests where the input of high-quality litter allowed earthworm populations to increase significantly in an acid environment (Huhta 1979).

However, earthworms may participate in the accumulation of organic matter through (1) an increase of organic matter produced in the ecosystem and (2) the protection of SOM in structures of the drilosphere (Martin 1991). In the three-year experiment carried on at Yurimaguas and Lamto, the combination of C consumption by inoculated earthworms and increased capture of C by plants and protection of SOM in compact casts did not together result in significant changes in the abundance of C. Nevertheless, there were clear indications that the quality of organic matter estimated by either physical fractionation or respirometry was modified. Consequences of such long-term modifications are not predictable yet.

Physical effects resulting from earthworm activities seem to persist for long periods in soils. Blanchart et al. (1993) demonstrated that casts deposited by large earthworms (of the "compacting" category) had largely kept their structure 30 months after earthworms had disappeared. These casts tend to conserve organic matter, because little microbial activity is possible in these compact structures. Nonetheless, in natural conditions, such macro-aggregates cannot comprise more than 40% to 60% of soil. Despite their continuous production these aggregates do not accumulate beyond that limit, probably because earthworm populations that decompact soil regulate aggregation. These may be earthworms such as the small species of Eudrilidae at Lamto. They may also be species of Enchytraeidae, Myriapoda, or microarthropods. Therefore, the long-term efficiency of these processes of protection of aggregates in casts largely depends on (1) the maximum percentage of large aggregates that are present at a given site and (2) the lifetime of aggregates.

Spatial patterns of earthworm populations may be understood best in terms of their impact on soils. At Lamto, there was a significant negative correlation at some seasons between populations of compacting species that accumulate large compact casts in the upper 20 cm of soil, and decompacting species that produce fine granular-shaped casts out of soil macro-aggregates and the large casts produced by the former species (I.P. Rossi and P. Lavelle, unpub. after Lavelle 1978). This may indicate that earthworm sub-population experiments have successions inside a patch. Species that compact soils develop once those that decompact soils have produced small aggregates rich in the organic matter that the compacting species may ingest. Such patterns may also be determined by the local availability of assimilable organic matter. Studies in hevea plantations and spruce forests show clearly that the impact of earthworms becomes important when organic matter has been sufficiently prepared by a succession of termite and arthropod digestions in the first case and development of fungal attacks in the second one.

These results and hypotheses open several avenues for future research as follows:

(1) Testing the effect of earthworm activities on quality of soil organic matter (through physical fractionations and respirometry) in long-term experiments using natural ^{13}C labeling after, for example, a change from C3 to C4 vegetation;

(2) Establishment of carbon budgets to quantify the amount of C derived to earthworms and identify the pools in which this C is taken;

(3) Experiments on the effects of the addition of organic matter, of different physical and chemical qualities, on earthworm activities. This last research theme has clear practical implications, since what is envisaged is the improvement of earthworm activities in agricultural systems with a view to increasing crop production and soil sustainability.

REFERENCES CITED

Aina, P.O. 1984. Contribution of earthworms to porosity and water infiltration in a tropical soil under forest and long-term cultivation. Pedobiologia, 26, 131–136.

Albrecht, A. 1984. Role des Enchytraeidae dans l'agrégation et l'humification d'humus de type moder de l'Est de la France. Thèse de Doctorat. Nancy I.

Alegre, J., B. Pashanasi, and P. Lavelle. 1996. Dynamics of soil physical properties in a low input agricultural system inoculated with the earthworm *Pontoscolex corethrurus* in Peruvian Amazonia. Soil Science Society of America Journal, 60, 1522–1529.

Anderson, J.M. 1994. Functional attributes of biodiversity in land use systems. In Soil Resilience and Sustainable Land Use (eds. J. Greenland and I. Szabolcs), CAB International, Wallingford, U.K., pp. 267–290.

Barois, I., and P. Lavelle. 1986. Changes in respiration rate and some physicochemical properties of a tropical soil during transit through *Pontoscolex corethrurus* (Glossoscolecidae, Oligochaeta). Soil Biology and Biochemistry, 18, 539–541.

Barois, I., and C. Patron. 1994. Short scale effects of tropical endogeic species: Selection of particles by *Pontoscolex corethrurus*. In CCE/STD Project No. ERBTS3*CT920128, pp. 33–37.

Barois, I., B. Verdier, P. Kaiser, A. Mariotti, P. Rangel, and P. Lavelle. 1987. Influence of the tropical earthworm *Pontoscolex corethrurus* (Glossoscoleciae) on the fixation and mineralization of nitrogen. In On Earthworms (eds. A.M. Bonvicini and P. Omodeo), Mucchi, Bologna, Italy, pp. 151–158.

Bernier, N., J.F. Ponge, and J. Andre. 1993. Comparative study of soil organic layers in two bilberry spruce forest stands (Vaccinio-Picetea). Relation to forest dynamics. Geoderma, 59, 89–108.

Blair, J.M., R.W. Parmelee, and P. Lavelle. 1994. Influence of earthworms on biogeochemistry in North American ecosystems. In Earthworm Ecology in Forest Rangeland and Crop Ecosystems in North America (ed. P.F. Hendrix), Lewis Publishers, Chelsea, MI, pp. 1–44.

Blanchart, E. 1990. Rôle des vers de terre dans la formation et la conservation de la structure des sols de la savane de Lamto (Côte d'Ivoire). Thèse de l'Université. Rennes I.

Blanchart, E., A. Bruand, and P. Lavelle. 1993. The physical structure of casts of Millsonia anomala (Oligochaeta:Megascolecidae) in shrub savannah soils (Côte d'Ivoire). Geoderma, 56, 119–132.

Blanchart, E., P. Lavelle, E. Braudeau, Y. Le Bissonais, and C. Valentin. 1996. Regulation of soil structure by geophagous earthworm activities in humid savannahs of Cote d'Ivoire. Soil Biology and Biochemistry, in press.

Bouché, M.B. 1977. Stratégies lombriciennes. In Soil Organism as Components of Ecosystems (eds. T. Persson and U. Lohm), Ecological Bulletins (Stockolm), 25, 122–132.

Brossard, M., P. Lavelle, and J.Y. Laurent. 1996. Digestion of a vertisol by an endogeic earthworm (*Polypheretima elongata*, Megascolecidae) increases soil phosphate extractibility. European Journal of Soil Biology, 32, 107–111.

Derouard, L. 1993. Effets comparés de trois espèces de vers de terre sur la structure physique d'un sol de la savane de Lamto (Côte d'Ivoire). Mémoire de DESS "Gestion des Systèmes Agro-Sylvo-Pastoraux," Paris XII.

Derouard, L., J. Tondoh, Vilcosqui, and P. Lavelle. 1997. Species-specific effects in the response of tropical annual crops to the inoculation of earthworms. Short-scale experiments at Lamto (Côte d'Ivoire). Soil Biology and Biochemistry, in press.

Didden. W.A.M. 1990. Involvement of Enchytraeidae (Oligochaeta) in soil structure evolution in agricultural fields. Biology and Fertility of Soils, 9, 152–158.

Elliott, E.T. 1986. Aggregate structure and carbon, nitrogen, and phosphorus in native and cultivated soils. Soil Science Society of America Journal, 50, 627–633.

Eswaran, H. 1994. Soil resilience and sustainable land management in the context of AGENDA 21. In Soil Resilience and Sustainable Land Use (eds. D.J. Greenland and I. Szabolcs), CAB International, Wallingford, U.K.

Feller, C. 1979. Une méthode de fractionnement granulométrique de la matière organique des sols: Application aux sols tropicaux à texture grossière, trés pauvres en humus. Cahiers de l'O.R.S.T.O.M., Série Pédologie, XVII(4), 339–346.

Ferrière, G. 1980. Fonctions des Lombriciens. VII. Une méthode d'analyse de la matière organique végétale ingérée. Pedobiologia, 20, 263–273.

Gilot, C. 1994. Effets de l'introduction du ver géophage tropical Millsonia anomala Omodeo en systèmes cultivés sur les caractéristiques des sols et la production végétale en moyenne Côte d'Ivoire. Doctoral thesis. University of Paris VI/INAPG.

Gilot, C., P. Lavelle, Ph. Kouassi, and G. Guillaume. 1995. Biological activity of soils in Hevea stands of different ages in Côte d'Ivoire. Acta Zoologica Fennicii, 196, 186–190.

Hameed, R., M.B. Bouche, and J. Cortez. 1994. Etudes in situ des transferts d'azote d'origine lombricienne (*Lumbricus terrestris* L.) vers les plantes. Soil Biology and Biochemistry, 26, 495–501.

Huhta, V. 1979. Effects of liming and deciduous litter on earthworm (Lumbricidae) populations of a spruce forest, with an inoculation experiment on *Allolobophora caliginosa*. Pedobiologia, 19, 340–345.

Jenkinson, D.S., and J.H. Rayner. 1977. The turnover of soil organic matter in some of the Rothamsted classical experiments. Soil Science, 123, 298–305.

Joschko, M., H. Diestel, and O. Larink. 1989. Assessment of earthworm burrowing efficiency in compacted soil with a combination of morphological and soil physical measurements. Biology and Fertility of Soils, 8, 191–196.

Kanyonyo ka Kajondo, J.B. 1984. Ecologie alimentaire du ver de terre detritivore *Millsonia lamtoiana* (Acanthdrilidae, Oligochètes) dans la savane de Lamto (Côte d'Ivoire). Thèse 3è cycle. Paris VI.

Kladivko, E.J., A.D. Mackay, and J.M. Bradford. 1986. Earthworms as a factor in the reduction of soil crusting. Soil Science Society of America Journal, 50, 191–196.

Kooistra, M.J. 1991. A micromorphological approach to the interactions between soil structure and soil biota. Agriculture, Ecosystems and Environment, 34, 315–328.

Lavelle, P. 1978. Les Vers de Terre de la savane de Lamto (Côte d'Ivoire): Peuplements, populations, et fonctions dans l'écosystème. Publications du Laboratoire de Zoologie de l'ENS n° 12, Paris.

Lavelle, P. 1997. Faunal activities and soil processes: Adaptive strategies that determine ecosystem function. Advances in Ecological Soil Research, 27, 93–132.

Lavelle, P., and A. Martin. 1992. Small-scale and large-scale effects of endogeic earthworms on soil organic matter dynamics in soils of the humid tropics. Soil Biology and Biochemistry, 24, 1491–1498.

Lavelle, P., G. Melendez, B. Pashanasi, and R. Schaefer. 1992. Nitrogen mineralization and reorganisation in casts of the geophagous tropical earthworm *Pontoscolex corethurus* (Glossoscolecidae). Biology and Fertility of Soils, 14, 49–53.

Lavelle, P., E. Blanchart, A. Martin, S. Martin, I. Barois, F. Toutain, A. Spain, and R. Schaefer. 1993. A hierarchical model for decomposition in terrestrial ecosystems. Application to soils in the humid tropics. Biotropica, 25, 130–150.

Lavelle, P., M. Dangerfield, C. Fragoso, V. Eschenbrenner, D. Lopez-Hernandez, B. Pashanasi, and L. Brussaard. 1994. The relationship between soil macrofauna and tropical soil fertility. In The Biological Management of Tropical Soil (eds. M.J. Swift and P. Woomer), John Wiley-Sayce, New York, pp. 137–169.

Lee, K.E. 1985. Earthworms: Their Ecology and Relationships with Soils and Land Use. Academic Press, New York.

Lopez-Hernandez, D., J.C. Fardeau, and P. Lavelle. 1993. Phosphorus transformations in two P-sorption contrasting tropical soils during transit through *Pontoscolex corethrurus* (Glossoscolecidae, Oligochaeta). Soil Biology and Biochemistry, 25, 789–792.

Martin, A. 1991. Short- and long-term effects of the endogeic earthworm *Millsonia anomala* (Omodeo) (Megascolecidae, Oligochaeta) of tropical savannas on soil organic matter. Biology and Fertility of Soils, 11, 234–238.

Miles, J. 1985. Soil in the ecosystem. In Ecological Interactions in Soil; Plants, Microbes and Animals (eds. D. Atkinson, A.H. Fitter, D.J. Read, and M.B. Usher), Blackwell Scientific Publications, Oxford, Great Britain, pp. 407–427.

Molina, J.A.E., C.E. Clapp, M.J. Shaffer, F.W. Chichester, and W.E. Larson. 1983. NCSOIL, a model of C and N transformations in soils: Description, calibration and behaviour. Soil Science Society of America Journal, 47, 85–91.

Oades, J.M. 1984. Soil organic matter and structural stability: Mechanisms and implication for management. Plant and Soil, 76, 319–337.

Parton, W.J., D.W. Anderson, C.V. Cole, and J.W.B. Stewart. 1983. Simulation of soil organic matter formation and mineralization in semiarid agroecosystems. In Nutrient Cycling in Agricultural Ecosystems (eds. R.R. Lowrance, R.L. Todd, L.E. Asmussen, and R.A. Leonard), Special Publication No. 23 of the Georgia Experimental Station, Athens, Georgia.

Parton, W.J., J.W.B. Stewart, and C.V. Cole. 1988. Dynamics of C, N, P and S in grasslands soils: A model. Biogeochemistry, 5, 109–131.

Pashanasi, B., P. Lavelle, and J. Alegre. 1996. Effect of inoculation with the endogeic earthworm *Pontocolex corethrurus* on soil chemical characteristics and plant growth in a low-input agricultural system of Peruvian Amazonia. Soil Biology and Biochemistry, 28, 801–810.

Phillipson, J., R. Abel, J. Steel, and S.R. Woodell. 1976. Earthworms and the factors that govern their distribution. Oecologia, 33, 291–309.

Piearce, T.G. 1978. Gut contents of some lumbricid earthworms. Pedobiologia, 18, 3–157.

Poier, K.R., and J. Richter. 1992. Spatial distribution of earthworms and soil properties in an arable loess soil. Soil Biology and Biochemistry, 24, 1601–1608.

Rossi, J.P., P. Lavelle, and A. Albrecht. 1997. Relationships between spatial pattern of the endogeic earthworm *Polypheretima elongata* and soil heterogeneity in a tropical pasture of Martinique (French West Indies). Soil Biology and Biochemistry, in press.

Sharpley, A.N., and J.K. Syers. 1976. Potential role of earthworm casts for the phosphorus enrichment of run-off waters. Soil Biology and Biochemistry, 8, 341–346.

Shaw, C., and S. Pawluk. 1986. The development of soil structure by *Octolasion tyrtaeum, Aporrectodea turgida* and *Lumbricus terrestris* in parent materials belonging to different textural classes. Pedobiologia, 29, 327–339.

Spain, A.V., P. Lavelle, and A. Mariotti. 1992. Stimulation of plant growth by tropical earthworms. Soil Biology and Biochemistry, 24, 1629–1634.

Springett, J.A. 1983. Effect of five species of earthworm on some soil properties. Journal of Applied Ecology, 20, 865–872.

Syers, J.K., A.N. Sharpley, and D.R. Keeney. 1979. Cycling of nitrogen by surface-casting earthworms in a pasture ecosystem. Soil Biology and Biochemistry, 11, 181–185.

Tajovsky, K., G. Villemin, and F. Toutain. 1991. Microstructural and ultrastructural changes of the oak leaf litter consumed by millipede *Glomeris hexasticha* (Diplopoda). Revue d'Ecologie et de Biologie du Sol, 28, 287–302.

Tsakala, R. 1994. Evolution spatio-temporelle de la minéralisation du carbne et de l'azote dans les sols de deux parcelles à Lamto (Côte d'Ivoire). Mémoire DESS, Université Paris XII, 58 pp.

Van Vliet, P.C.J., L.T. West, P.F. Hendrix, and D.C. Coleman. 1993. The influence of Enchytraeidae (Oligochaeta) on the soil porosity of small microcosms. Geoderma, 56, 287–299.

Wolters, V. 1991. Soil invertebrates—effects on nutrient turnover and soil structure—a review. Z. Pflanzenernähr Bodenk, 154, 389–402.

Earthworms and Nutrient Cycling Processes: Integrating Across the Ecological Hierarchy

6

Robert W. Parmelee,[1] Patrick J. Bohlen,[2] and John M. Blair[3]

[1]Department of Entomology, Ohio State University, Columbus, Ohio 43210, U.S.A.; [2]Institute of Ecosystem Studies, Millbrook, New York 12545, U.S.A.; [3]Division of Biology, Ackert Hall, Kansas State University, Manhattan, Kansas 66506, U.S.A.

Over the past 10 years, there has been an exponential increase in research addressing the impact of earthworms on terrestrial nutrient cycling processes. Earthworms have been shown to affect key soil properties and processes such as microbial biomass and activity, organic matter dynamics, nutrient availability, plant uptake and production, and soil structure significantly. Although the majority of these studies have been conducted in laboratory microcosms and/or agroecosystems, there is sufficient evidence to conclude that earthworms should be considered keystone organisms in regulating nutrient cycling processes in many ecosystems. Through their impact on nutrient cycling processes, earthworms may alter the balance between ecosystem conservation and loss of nutrients, particularly C and N. We are now in a position to formulate models that integrate the effects of earthworms on soil biological, chemical, and physical properties. Both mechanistic and system-level models should lead to new predictions and hypotheses on how earthworms influence soil processes and fluxes of nutrients in ecosystems. Realistic models will depend upon studies at all levels of the ecological hierarchy to produce an integrated understanding of the roles of earthworms in biogeochemical cycles.

OVERVIEW

We will concentrate on research that integrates soil biology, chemistry, and physics and that demonstrates how earthworms affect multiple soil nutrient cycling processes. We also highlight potentially fruitful new areas of research.

A few general points about current research should be noted. First, with a single exception (e.g., Steinberg et al. 1997), all of the research presented at this symposium was conducted in agricultural soils and systems. The absence of research in other ecosystems, such as forests and grasslands, points to a major shortcoming in current research programs, which leaves substantial gaps in our understanding of the effects of earthworms on nutrient cycling processes. There is clearly a strong need to increase research in natural, undisturbed ecosystems (Blair et al. 1995a). Secondly, the majority of studies examined the effects of exotic invaders of ecosystems and over 50% of the presenters studied exotic species of earthworms. This observation was due largely to the number of studies focused on exotic lumbricids in North America. Native communities of earthworms often inhabit ecosystems less highly disturbed by humans and represent a rich area for future research. Finally, over two thirds of the presentations focused on the effects of species of the family Lumbricidae on nutrient cycling. However, because of increased interest in the roles of earthworms in the tropics, we are beginning to see evidence of the importance of other earthworm families, such as the Megascolecidae and Glossoscolecidae.

Lavelle et al. (Chapter 5) highlighted the importance of spatial and temporal scale in addressing the roles of earthworms in nutrient cycling processes. The majority of studies have used laboratory microcosms or small field enclosures that typically span short periods of days to months and, occasionally, to years. The problem of expanding from small spatial and short temporal scales to long-term effects at the field or landscape level is a major barrier to overcome in our understanding of how earthworms affect nutrient cycles (Blair et al. 1995a).

Lavelle et al. (Chapter 5) focused on three sub-processes, based on three-year field experiments, that may help to determine the long-term effects of earthworms on nutrient cycling processes. They considered feeding behaviors, horizontal distribution, and the change in earthworm communities during ecological succession. They stressed the need to determine the quality and quantity of soil organic matter ingested by earthworms because earthworms may alter the ratio of labile to recalcitrant organic matter and influence long-term storage of soil C and N. Lavelle et al. also summarized some very interesting studies that have examined how the horizontal distribution of earthworms can affect nutrient cycles. Earthworms exist in patches 20–40 m in diameter that are not synchronized with the population dynamics of other patches (i.e., juveniles and adults have different distribution patterns) and can be composed of different species. The patch dynamics of earthworms results in areas of high activity, followed by possible local extinction and a cessation of activity, or increased activity of species occupying different ecological niches. Some species produce large casts that lead to compaction of the soil (increased bulk density), while others ingest the larger casts and root fragments to create smaller casts that lessen compaction of the soil (i.e., decrease bulk density). This dynamic patchiness of earthworm communities may have important consequences for soil structure and nutrient cycling processes.

Examining changes in the structure and function of earthworm communities through ecosystem succession provides another approach to study the longer-term role of earthworms. This approach has demonstrated that earthworm communities respond to changes in soil organic matter stocks as succession proceeds. We also have the opportunity to examine changes in soil properties as earthworms colonize new soil. Invasion of earthworms into previously uncolonized soil altered microbial biomass pool size, plant biomass, and leaching of nutrients (Scheu and Parkinson 1994a,b), as well as soil C content and soil profile development (Alban and Berry 1994). Simulation models can be useful for understanding the longer-term effects of earthworms on soil organic matter dynamics. Using the CENTURY carbon model, Lavelle et al. considered that earthworms can promote stabilization of soil organic matter and maintain organic pools and soil structure in the long term (10–50 years).

Gilot (1997) presented more specific aspects of the research of Lavelle's group. The study was field-based in the tropics and extended for several years. Gilot (1997) reported on the effects of earthworms on yam production and soil characteristics in Africa. Earthworms altered soil structure by decreasing the percentage of small aggregates and increasing the percentage of larger ones. These larger aggregates, primarily aging casts, may have contributed to the protection of soil C, as indicated by a decrease of 5% in C mineralization after three years. Additionally, the presence of earthworms generally enhanced crop production.

Devliegher and Verstraete (1997) introduced the concepts of "nutrient enrichment process" (NEP) and "gut associated process" (GAP). They recognized that earthworms are performing two different functions that may have contrasting effects on soil microbiology, chemistry, and plant growth. Earthworms, such as *Lumbricus terrestris*, incorporate and mix surface organic matter with soil and increase biological activity and nutrient availability (NEP). However, they also assimilate nutrients from soil and organic matter as these materials pass through the gut (GAP). Devliegher and Verstraete established three treatments to factor out the influences of NEP and GAP on soil properties. Their three treatments were (1) earthworms plus lettuce on the soil surface, (2) lettuce manually mixed into the soil with no earthworms, and (3) lettuce left on the surface without earthworms. Differences between the first two treatments were attributed to GAP and differences between the two treatments without earthworms were attributed to NEP. They concluded that GAP reduced microbial biomass and activity, soil nitrate, and total N content of the crop. However, when NEP was factored in, most of the decreases attributed to GAP were counteracted and led to an increase in biological activity and nutrient availability in the presence of *L. terrestris*. A criticism of Devliegher and Verstraete's research is that manually mixing in the lettuce may not adequately simulate the effects of earthworm incorporation of organic material. Nonetheless, the authors' experiment illustrates the complexity of how earthworms affect soil processes and has provided us with a useful framework for conducting future research. It is likely that the relative importance of GAP and NEP will vary among earthworm species and in soils with different levels of fertility. Indeed, Blair et al. (1995a) noted that stimulatory effects of earthworms on soil biological and chemical activity appeared to be greater in soils lower in C and N content.

Our soil ecology group at Ohio State University has been conducting experiments involving large-scale field manipulations of earthworms in agroecosystems. We have manipulated earthworm populations by electroshocking the soil to reduce their numbers or by adding earthworms to increase their numbers (Blair et al. 1995b; Bohlen et al. 1995a). We have focused initially on the effects of earthworms on soil biological, chemical, and physical processes.

Blair et al. (1997) suggested a possible mechanism whereby earthworm-microbial interactions can influence soil N availability. In plots where earthworm populations were reduced by 70%, microbial biomass N was significantly higher than in plots with ambient populations. Microcosm studies yielded similar results; microcosms with earthworms had less microbial biomass N compared to controls without earthworms (Bohlen and Edwards 1995). In plots where earthworms were increased above ambient levels by additions, soil nitrate levels increased in systems fertilized with inorganic fertilizer. Together, these results indicate that earthworms can increase N availability by reducing microbial immobilization and enhancing mineralization.

Other contributors also focused on how earthworms influence N availability. Bouche et al. (1997) used ^{15}N to develop models to quantify the direct role of earthworms in the N cycle. Steinberg et al. (1997) examined the importance of earthworms in increasing the availability of N in forests. They found that earthworms can increase potential net N-mineralization rates in both urban and rural oak forests. From the studies discussed above, it is apparent that a major result of earthworm activity is to accelerate the transformations of N, often increasing N availability.

At the ecosystem level, the fate of the N made more available by earthworms is of interest. Some of this N is available for plant uptake (Devliegher and Verstraete 1997). However, the Ohio field studies indicate that at least some of this N leaches below the rooting zone. Blair et al. (1997) found increased concentrations of soil nitrate deeper in the soil (30–45 cm) in earthworm addition treatments. In a similar study, Subler et al. (1997) found that there were higher volumes of leachate at 45 cm in earthworm addition plots, and that the leachate had much higher concentrations of dissolved organic nitrogen (DON) compared to control plots. The effects of earthworms on soil DON provide another previously unexplored avenue for research. In both studies, increased macropore formation due to earthworm burrows (e.g., Lachnicht et al. 1997) could have increased preferential flow pathways, which could explain the increased movement of N through the soil profile.

More evidence was presented on the importance of earthworms in soil respiration and organic matter dynamics. For instance, Hendriksen (1997) found that earthworms increased microbial respiration beneath cow dung pats. To understand the mechanisms of this process, he developed a simple model and applied pathway analysis. This analysis suggested that earthworms enhanced microbial respiration beyond simply incorporating dung and increasing soil C and water content. Development of such models will be important subcomponents for the type of simulation models proposed below.

While earthworms are known to increase the decomposition rates of surface applied litter (e.g., Tian et al. 1997), little is known about the fate of this material once it is incorporated into the soil. McCartney et al. (1997), using the earthworm manipulation plots in Ohio, observed strong seasonal effects of earthworms on coarse and intermediate size classes of soil organic matter with amounts being greater in earthworm reduction plots than in control plots. This is an important new area of earthworm research particularly because there is evidence that different size classes of soil organic matter have different rates of mineralization.

CONCEPTUAL MODELS

With the information available in the literature and the new data presented at the symposium, we can begin to develop mechanistic simulation models and ecosystem-level nutrient budget models to explore the roles of earthworms in biogeochemical cycles. The simulation models should investigate how earthworms, by their own respiration and excretion of C and N and through their effects on microbial turnover, processing of organic matter, and aggregate formation, affect the production of CO_2 and the availability of N. The nutrient budget models will help to determine whether earthworms contribute to sustainability or degradation of ecosystems by examining the processes that lead to storage of C and N within the system or to loss of C and N from the system. As discussed by Lavelle et al., both types of models need to incorporate spatial and temporal patterns and abiotic constraints.

We have developed a series of conceptual models as an initial step towards the development of more sophisticated simulation and system-level models. Our conceptual models provide a basis for exploring fundamental questions about the influence of earthworms on biogeochemical flux.

Mechanistic Models

The first conceptual model explores mechanisms by which earthworms affect the system-level flux of C (Figure 1). The model is based on five major components whereby earthworms can affect soil respiration: earthworm respiration and mucus production, microbial turnover, processing of litter and soil organic matter, and soil aggregate formation. With the exception of earthworm respiration and mucus production, the other three factors are largely co-dependent.

Although the direct contribution of earthworm respiration to system flux of C is generally a small proportion of the total heterotrophic respiration, e.g., 5–6% (Lee 1985), when earthworm populations are large the direct contribution of earthworms to system respiration can be substantial, e.g., 30% (Hendrix et al. 1987). The data base on this subject is inadequate, and we need to determine the

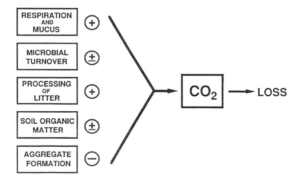

Figure 1. Conceptual model to examine the mechanisms through which earthworms can affect system-level flux of C. Note: + indicates an increase in CO_2 flux due to earthworms, − indicates a decrease in output, and ± indicates that the effect of earthworms on CO_2 output can vary.

contribution of earthworms to overall system respiration in the field under a variety of environmental conditions. Similarly, there is very little information on rates of C excretion in earthworm mucus, which can be a particularly labile form of C. Using ^{14}C, Scheu (1991) demonstrated that production of mucus was a significant pathway of C loss from earthworms and exceeded the losses though respiration.

A critical component of the model is the interaction between earthworms and microbial activity. Much of the available data comes from microbiological studies of fresh casts and laboratory studies. Earthworm casts typically have higher microbial biomass and respiration rate than bulk soil (Scheu 1987; Lavelle et al. 1992). However, the situation is more complex, since earthworms also seem to increase microbial turnover. Scheu (1987) observed a simultaneous decrease in microbial biomass and increase in microbial respiration in casts after 2 weeks. Similarly, Wolters and Joergensen (1992) observed a lower microbial biomass but higher microbial activity per unit biomass in soils after 21 days of earthworm activity. The simultaneous increase in respiration and decreases in microbial biomass suggest that earthworm-worked soil may contain a smaller, but more metabolically active, microbial community than soil without earthworms. While the short-term dynamics of microbial activity in casts are becoming better documented, there is very little information on respiration of older casts (Martin 1991). Investigations need to be initiated on how earthworms influence microbial respiration and turnover under field conditions over longer periods of time.

It is well known that earthworms increase the disappearance rate of surface litter, but less is known about how this process affects soil respiration rates. Burial of litter increases its decomposition rate because the litter becomes fragmented and is in a more favorable environmental condition for microbial activity (e.g., Beare et al. 1992). Mixing of litter with soil by earthworms may create an even more favorable environment because of the high moisture content and availability of nutrients found in fresh casts. It is possible that earthworms may enhance microbial activity beyond that due strictly to the input of litter C (Hendriksen 1997). Bohlen et al. (1997) found that litter associated with *L. terrestris* middens had higher microbial biomass and microbial activity than litter not associated with middens. The movement of litter into organic soil matter pools and the effects of earthworms on various pools are also of great interest. Whether earthworms feed on labile or recalcitrant soil organic matter pools can have important implications for the long-term storage of C and N. The available evidence suggests that earthworms do selectively ingest different pools of soil C (Parmelee et al. 1990; Martin 1992a,b; McCartney et al. 1997), but we need further data to predict the effect of selective feeding on ecosystem-level flux of C realistically.

A final component of the model is the effect of earthworms on soil aggregate formation. While the overall effect of earthworms on other components of the model is to increase system flux of C, the formation of soil aggregates by earthworms may reduce the availability of C and protect it from mineralization (e.g., Gilot 1997). However, few studies have examined this. The results of Martin (1991) were consistent with other research that reported increased short-term mineralization of organic matter in casts. Long-term studies revealed that respiration rates were lower in casts than in surrounding soil, indicating increased protection of organic matter in the stable soil aggregates created by earthworm casting. The extent and timing of this protection needs to be investigated further.

A similar mechanistic model can be developed for quantifying the effects of earthworms on N availability (Figure 2). Generally, the same components that are incorporated into the carbon model are also part of the nitrogen model. An important distinction is the earthworm excretion compartment. While the contribution of earthworms to system respiration is often considered to be small, estimates of earthworm excretion of N indicate that this can be quite large (18–50 kg N ha^{-1}; Lee 1983). For microbial turnover, burial of litter, and aggregate formation, the state of knowledge and need for further research are the same as for carbon. The fate of N in the N model differs from that of C in the C model.

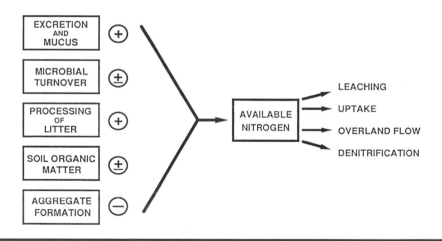

Figure 2. Conceptual model to examine the mechanisms through which earthworms can affect system-level availability and fate of N. Note: + indicates that earthworms increase the availability of N, − indicates a decrease in availability, and ± indicates that the effect of earthworms on N availability can vary.

While C is eventually lost from the system, mainly as CO_2, increased concentrations of available N can lead to a loss of N from the system through leaching, overland flow, and gaseous flux or retention in the system by microbial or plant uptake.

Each component of the models, with the exception of earthworm respiration, interacts strongly with the other components. It is the interaction between microbial activity, excretion of mucus, processing of organic matter, and protection of C and N from microbial attack in stable aggregates that determines the overall role of earthworms in ecosystem fluxes of C and N. Experiments that address more than one component will provide a greater understanding of the mechanisms by which earthworms affect the cycling of C and N than single-component studies.

Ecosystem Budget Models

We have incorporated concepts from our mechanistic models into conceptual ecosystem models that compare nutrient fluxes in the presence (Figure 3) and absence (Figure 4) of earthworms in an agroecosystem. These models emphasize the major pathways by which earthworms alter the retention and loss of C and N, incorporating the effects of earthworms on soil biological, chemical, and physical processes. In order to determine the role of earthworms in agroecosystem sustainability, we must focus on the processes affected by earthworms that lead to storage or loss of nutrients. Quantification of these nutrient budget models can provide data essential for reaching this goal and help to determine if earthworms are always beneficial organisms.

When earthworms are present in the system, there are dramatic changes in the size of various nutrient pools and fluxes of C and N (Figure 3). Earthworms reduce pool sizes of surface litter (Bohlen et al. 1997), coarse and particulate soil organic matter (Parmelee et al. 1990; McCartney et al. 1997), and microbial biomass (Blair et al. 1997). As discussed previously (Figure 1), through interactions with the microbial community and the processing of organic matter, earthworms can increase the system flux of C (gaseous loss). These same interactions, coupled with earthworm excretion, can also lead to increased availability of N. In our system, the increase in available N resulted in increased concentrations of nitrate (Blair et al. 1997). Available N can be retained within the system by microbial or plant uptake (we have not observed increased plant uptake in our Ohio system; Stinner et al. 1997 but see also Devliegher and Verstraete 1997). There is also the potential for this N to be lost from the system through leaching. We have observed increased nitrate levels deeper in the soil (Blair et al. 1997) and increased leachate volume and dissolved organic N con-

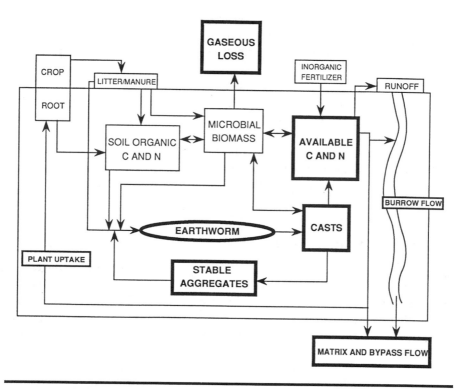

Figure 3. Ecosystem budget model to examine pools and fluxes of C and N in the presence of earthworms. Note: Bold boxes indicate pools and fluxes where earthworms are predicted to have a particularly significant impact.

centrations in earthworm addition plots (Subler et al. 1997). The increased movement of N through the soil profile may be due to a greater density of earthworm burrows (Lachnicht et al. 1997) and greater bypass flow. Earthworm cast production may also play an important role in system-level fluxes of C and N. Earthworm casts are microsites rich in available C and N, and may be anaerobic, conditions that are favorable for denitrification (Svensson et al. 1986). Elliott et al. (1990, 1991) compared the denitrification rates in earthworm casts and bulk soil and found consistently higher rates in casts, and Knight et al. (1992) estimated that surface casts could contribute from 12 to 26% of total denitrification in English pastures. While denitrification from casts contributes to loss of N from the system, formation of stable soil aggregates from casts could lead to longer-term protection of C and N.

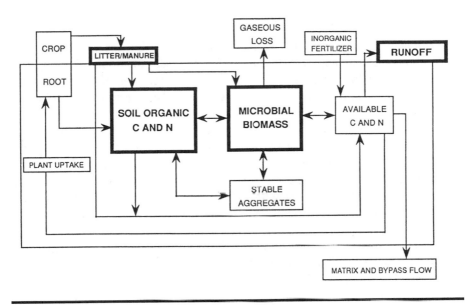

Figure 4. Ecosystem budget model to examine pools and fluxes of C and N in the absence of earthworms. Note: Bold boxes indicate pools and fluxes that will be particularly affected by the absence of earthworms.

In the system without earthworms (Figure 4), surface litter and soil organic C and N pools are larger than when earthworms are present. The microbial biomass C and N pool is also larger but with a predicted slower turnover of nutrients. The increase in size of these pools, coupled with longer residence times, would lead to a decrease in available C and N pools. As a consequence, there would be less loss of C and N in gaseous and leaching fluxes. Leaching, in general, would be expected to be lower because of the absence of earthworm burrows and their contribution to bypass flow. However, the absence of earthworm burrows which open to the soil surface could lead to increased overland flow and associated loss of nutrients. The role of earthworms in affecting overland flow of nutrients has rarely been investigated. Sharpley et al. (1979) reported that, in pastures without earthworms (treated with carbaryl), there was increased loss of N and P in surface run-off compared to pastures where earthworms were present. Before we can determine whether earthworms contribute to a net gain or loss of nutrients from the system, we need to further quantify how earthworms influence different nutrient pool sizes and fluxes.

Future Experiments

To provide data to validate the simulation and nutrient budget models, we suggest an experimental approach that is field-based, uses manipulated earthworm communities, stable isotopes (^{13}C and ^{15}N), and, when possible, extends for several years. Lavelle et al. echo these sentiments. To investigate the effects of earthworms on microbial activity and turnover, microbial biomass could be labeled with ^{13}C glucose and ^{15}N ammonium sulphate in the field in plots with different densities of earthworms. To examine how earthworms influence the redistribution and lability of surface and soil organic matter, double-labeling of plants with ^{13}C and ^{15}N holds much promise. Over time, the soil could be analyzed for organic fractions with different mineralization kinetics. Surface casting estimates are not difficult, but creative methodologies need to be developed to quantify belowground cast production in the field. The use of fluorescent dyes may be a suitable approach. Equally important is to determine the length of time over which casts maintain their structural integrity, and how C and N cycling processes change as casts age. Finally, more information is required on how earthworms contribute to gaseous, leaching, and overland flow fluxes of nutrients.

HIERARCHICAL APPROACH

Determining the role of earthworms in nutrient cycling processes can unify different approaches to investigating the biology and ecology of earthworms. Studies that operate at all levels of the ecological hierarchy can provide information that can be used to better understand how earthworms influence biogeochemical cycles (Figure 5).

Individuals

Information on the physiological ecology of earthworms will help in understanding the type and amounts of organic matter earthworms consume. Fundamental to the understanding of the biology of any soil-inhabiting organism is knowledge of its efficiency of assimilation of C and N. Quantification of C and N assimilation efficiencies is important because this could allow for estimates of the amount and type of C that must be consumed by earthworms to support their populations. Very little information is available on C and N assimilation efficiencies of earthworms, and there is no data for a wide range of common species. Carbon assimilation efficiency is assumed to be quite low, e.g., 2–6%

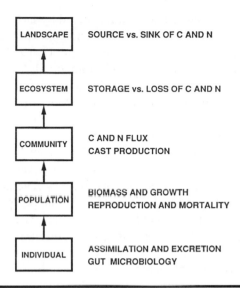

Figure 5. Hierarchical approach to investigate the effects of earthworms on nutrient cycling processes.

(Bolton and Phillipson 1976), but this remains to be determined for organic matter of different quality and for different earthworm species.

There is a strong need to determine the N assimilation efficiencies of earthworms because they may be particularly important in the N cycle. With few exceptions (e.g., Binet and Trehen 1992), N assimilation efficiencies of earthworms are unknown. While there is certainly enough N in the soil to satisfy the demand by earthworms for N, much of it is considered to be unavailable. Nevertheless, earthworms excrete copious amounts of N in urine and mucus, and N turnover appears to be quite rapid (Ferriere and Bouche 1985; Barois et al. 1987; Binet and Trehen 1992). Therefore, earthworms do not appear to be conservative of N. This suggests that either they are very selective in their food preference and choose materials with high N content, or that they have very high N assimilation efficiencies. Using a budget approach with ^{15}N, Binet and Trehen (1992) calculated an N assimilation efficiency of 27%, much higher than estimates for C assimilation efficiencies. There is intriguing evidence from field studies that earthworms may ingest organic material with a low C:N ratio (Bohlen 1997; Ketterings et al. 1997). As with C, assimilation rates of N need to be determined for a wide range of earthworm species occupying different ecological habitats and for food resources of different quality. It is likely that the absence of research in these critical areas has been hampered by lack of suitable methodologies, but the use of stable isotopes has considerable promise for quantifying C and N assimilation efficiencies (e.g., Binet and Trehen 1992).

Earthworm excretion of nitrogenous compounds in urine and mucus may provide a particularly labile N source for soil microbes. Earthworm urine is composed primarily of ammonium and urea. Mucus is composed of mucoproteins with a low C:N ratio of 3.8 (Scheu 1991). There are few realistic estimates of rates of urine or mucus excretion by earthworms. To date, nearly all estimates of urine and mucus excretion rates are based on the method of Needham (1957), who placed earthworms in a small volume of water and analyzed the water for N content after 24 hours. Whether or not estimates generated by this method are realistic remains to be confirmed. Nonetheless, it appears that the amounts of N excreted in urine and mucus could be substantial (Lee 1983; Dash and Patra 1979). Again, use of stable isotopes may be useful in overcoming methodological problems in determining earthworm excretion rates (Curry et al. 1995).

Another particularly intriguing area of research is the gut microbiology of earthworms. Microbial gut processes of earthworms may be of great importance in increasing the assimilation efficiencies of C and N. Barois and Lavelle (1986) first proposed the hypothesis that earthworms and soil microflora have developed a mutualistic relationship in order to exploit soil organic matter reserves. As soil enters the gut, earthworm moisture levels, pH, and water-soluble C content increase. The soil is then mixed in the gizzard, followed by a significant increase in microbial activity. Water and solutes are reabsorbed in the hindgut, and soil is egested with a reduced C content by as much as 19%. The "priming" of the microbial community with mucus leads to a more complete and efficient extraction of nutrients. The commonly observed initial burst of biological activity in fresh casts may merely be an after-effect of earthworm gut processes. While there is increasing evidence that this hypothesis is correct for both temperate and tropical earthworms, research in gut microbiology will continue to provide valuable information on how earthworms affect nutrient cycling processes. Similarly, the microbiology and nutrient dynamics of casts for different species of earthworms will also be a fruitful research area.

Populations

Earthworm population size, growth, reproduction, and mortality all have significant consequences for C and N cycling. Estimations of population density and biomass remain one of the most important areas of research. While there have been a multitude of studies gathering data for a variety of ecosystems, many of these studies have shortfalls. Factors causing this include inadequate sampling frequency and qualitative sampling techniques. However, the most serious problem with many studies is the improper determination of earthworm population biomass. The vast majority of studies report biomass as fresh or dry weight, often with no indication of whether gut contents are included in the reported values. Therefore, it becomes very difficult to compare studies or extract useful information. The correct way to express earthworm population biomass is to determine g ash-free dry weight (AFDW—earthworms ashed at 500°C for 4 hours) per unit area. It is also appropriate to express biomass as g C per unit area. As part of a continued effort to quantify earthworm biomass, we also need to develop long-term data sets to be able to evaluate temporal variability in population size. And, as Lavelle et al. suggest, greater attention needs to be paid to spatial or "patch" dynamics of earthworm populations.

Earthworm population growth and reproduction rates are key components in determining the amount of C and N that flows directly through earthworm tissue. Unfortunately, growth rates are unknown for many species and those that have been studied are often based on laboratory studies under optimum conditions. Growth rates need to be determined under field conditions for a variety of earthworm species. Similarly, very little is known about cocoon production in the field. While cocoon biomass may only be a small fraction of total earthworm biomass, knowledge of cocoon production can provide information about earthworm reproductive rates and can signal periods of high earthworm activity and potential rapid turnover of earthworm tissue.

Earthworms ingest organic matter of relatively wide C:N ratios and convert it to earthworm tissue of lower C:N ratio (Syers and Springett 1984). In effect, this accelerates the cycling of nutrients in soil, particularly N. While some of the earthworm N is excreted in urine and mucus, significant amounts also are returned to the soil in dead tissue. Because earthworm tissue is a highly labile form of N, dead earthworms can be an important input of N into the soil. Satchell (1967) reported that over 70% of the N in dead earthworm tissue was mineralized in less than 20 days, and that 60–70 kg of N ha^{-1} was returned to the soil annually. Christensen (1988) also reported high seasonal inputs of N from dead earthworms. Studies on earthworm population mortality rates in the field are very difficult, but results of the few estimates indicate that future research is warranted.

Communities

Much of the information gathered at lower levels in the ecological hierarchy can be integrated at the level of the earthworm community. Estimates of earthworm community secondary production can quantify the direct role of earthworms in the C and N cycle (Parmelee and Crossley 1988). Secondary production estimates the C and N flux through earthworm tissue as the sum of the production of new earthworm tissue and the loss through mortality.

Secondary production for earthworms during any given time interval is calculated as the growth rate times the change in biomass $\{P = IGR \times [(B_f + B_i)/2] \times t$; where P equals production, IGR is the instantaneous growth rate, and B_f and B_i are the final and initial standing stock biomasses (g AFDW m^{-2}) observed over a time interval (t) measured in days (Romanovsky and Polishchuk 1982)}. The values for all time intervals are then summed to calculate annual secondary production. To obtain an estimate of the C or N flux through earthworm biomass, the annual earthworm community secondary production estimate is multiplied by the average percentage C or N in earthworm tissue. Using this method in a no-tillage agroecosystem, we estimated that there was a 40-kg ha^{-1} yr^{-1} flux of N through earthworms (Parmelee and Crossley 1988). When estimates of N excreted in urine and mucus were included, the total N flux through earthworms increased to 63 kg N ha^{-1} yr^{-1}. We concluded that this N flux was significant for the no-tillage system, and earthworms could process 50% of the N input from plant residues accounting for 38% of the N uptake by plants. Furthermore, the N flux through earthworm biomass exceeded the loss from the system by denitrification and leaching. While this example illustrates the direct importance of earthworms in C and N cycles, it may be inadequate because it relies on laboratory growth rates and Needham's (1957) estimates of urine and mucus production. Furthermore, studies of this type are rare and further research on earthworm community secondary production with communities composed of different species in a variety of ecosystems needs to be initiated.

As discussed previously, reliable estimates of aboveground earthworm cast production exist, but aboveground casting may constitute only a small proportion of the total cast production. Studies that quantify belowground casting rates for earthworm communities are needed urgently.

Ecosystems

The effects of earthworms on nutrient cycling processes at the individual, population, and community levels of the hierarchy are fully integrated at the ecosystem level. Much of the research needed at the ecosystem level has been discussed previously in our discussion of ecosystem budget models (Figures 3 and 4). The main questions of interest concern how earthworms affect the balance between processes that lead to conservation or storage versus loss of nutrients from the system. Processes that lead to storage of C and N include plant uptake and protection in stable soil aggregates formed by casts. Another possible mechanism, as discussed by Lavelle et al., may involve the type of organic material earthworms choose to ingest. From our field studies in Ohio, we have observed that earthworms ingest organic material that has a low C:N ratio selectively (Bohlen et al. 1997; Ketterings et al. 1997). Consequently, the remaining organic material has a higher C:N ratio with the potential for slower decay and greater immobilization of nutrients. Loss pathways include a more rapid turnover of microbial biomass and greater production of CO_2, denitrification, leaching, and run-off.

LANDSCAPES

The effects of earthworms on nutrient cycling processes at the landscape level have yet to be fully explored. Lavelle et al. present the intriguing concept of earthworm patch dynamics in which patches of different species and different size classes of earthworms move through the soil, altering soil structure and nutrient cycling processes and contributing to soil heterogeneity. The spatial distribution of earthworms in an agroecosystem was examined by Poier and Richter (1992). They identified patch sizes of 20–50 m, and found correlations among earthworm abundance and soil carbon and aggregate density. Hendrix et al. (1992) examined the abundance and distribution of earthworms in relation to landscape factors in the southeastern U.S. They concluded that earthworm abundance was related to soil textural properties, quantity and quality of plant inputs, and standing stocks of soil organic matter. Similarly, Bohlen et al. (1995b) found that earthworm community structure in seven different watersheds was influenced by cropping patterns, geographic location, and tillage. More of these types of studies are needed, and the next step should be to tie spatial distribution patterns to the effects of earthworms on nutrient cycling properties. The ultimate goal of landscape-level research should be to identify the major source versus sink relationships for C and N. For example, the influence of earthworms on erosion and surface run-off may also influence loss or retention of nutrients from landscape units (Sharpley et al. 1979). As landscape-level studies progress, it may become possible to assess the roles of earthworms in biogeochemical cycles at regional or even global scales.

CONCLUSIONS

Research presented at this symposium and in existing literature indicates that earthworms play a major role in soil nutrient cycling processes. Studies are increasingly interdisciplinary, combining various aspects of the effects of earthworms on soil biological, chemical, and physical processes. Earthworm ecologists need to continue to expand this type of research. All researchers of earthworm ecology, no matter what level of the ecological hierarchy is their focus, can contribute to our understanding. Without a holistic approach, that integrates data from different levels of the hierarchy, it will be impossible to quantify the roles of earthworms in nutrient cycling processes at the ecosystem level. We have produced enough data to suggest that earthworms may be keystone organisms in regulating ecosystem nutrient dynamics. The challenge now is to move from laboratory microcosm studies to field-based studies and to the development of mechanistic and nutrient budget models that explore larger spatial and temporal scales.

ACKNOWLEDGMENTS

Mike Allen, Scott Subler, and Joann Whalen provided helpful comments on earlier versions of this manuscript. Many of the ideas presented in the paper were developed through interactions with Mike Allen, Clive Edwards, Dave McCartney, Ben Stinner, and Scott Subler. Our research has been supported by grants from the National Science Foundation (DEB-9020461) and the United States Department of Agriculture (NRI-9402520).

REFERENCES CITED

Alban, D.H., and E.C. Berry. 1994. Effects of earthworm invasion on morphology, carbon, and nitrogen of a forest soil. Applied Soil Ecology 1: 243–249.

Barois, I., and P. Lavelle. 1986. Changes in respiration rate and some physicochemical properties of a tropical soil during transit through *Pontoscolex corethrurus* (Glossoscolecidae, Oligochaeta). Soil Biology and Biochemistry 18: 539–541.

Barois, I., B. Verdier, P. Kaiser, A. Mariotti, P. Rangel, and P. Lavelle. 1987. Influence of the tropical earthworm *Pontoscolex corethrurus* (Glossoscolecidae) on the fixation and mineralization of nitrogen. In: On Earthworms. A.M. Bonvicini Pagliai and P. Omodeo (eds.). Selected Symposia and Monographs U.Z.I., 2, Mucchi, Modena.

Beare, M.H., R.W. Parmelee, P.F. Hendrix, W. Cheng, D.C. Coleman, and D.A. Crossley, Jr. 1992. Microbial and faunal interactions and effects on litter nitrogen and decomposition in agroecosystems. Ecological Monographs 62: 569–591.

Binet, F., and P. Trehen. 1992. Experimental microcosm study of the role of *Lumbricus terrestris* (Oligochaeta: Lumbricidae) on nitrogen dynamics in cultivated soils. Soil Biology and Biochemistry 24: 1501–1506.

Blair, J.M., R.W. Parmelee, and P. Lavelle. 1995a. Influences of earthworms on biogeochemistry. pp. 127–158. In: Earthworm Ecology and Biogeography in North America. P.F. Hendrix (ed.). Lewis Publishers, Boca Raton, FL.

Blair, J.M., P.J. Bohlen, C.A. Edwards, B.R. Stinner, D.A. McCartney, and M.F. Allen. 1995b. Manipulation of earthworm populations in field experiments in agroecosystems. Acta Zoologica Fennica 196: 48–51.

Blair, J.M., R.W. Parmelee, M.F. Allen, D.A. McCartney, and B.R. Stinner. 1997. Changes in soil N pools in response to earthworm population manipulations in agroecosystems with different N sources. Soil Biology and Biochemistry 29, 361–367.

Bohlen, P.J., and C.A. Edwards. 1995. Earthworms effects on N dynamics and soil respiration in microcosms receiving organic and inorganic nutrients. Soil Biology and Biochemistry 27: 341–348.

Bohlen, P.J., R.W. Parmelee, J.M. Blair, C.A. Edwards, and B.R. Stinner. 1995a. Efficacy of methods for manipulating earthworm populations in large-scale field experiments in agroecosystems. Soil Biology and Biochemistry 27: 993–999.

Bohlen, P.J., W.M. Edwards, and C.A. Edwards. 1995b. Earthworm community structure and diversity in experimental agricultural watersheds in Northeastern Ohio. Plant and soil. In: The Significance and Regulation of Soil Biodiversity. H.P. Collins, G.P. Robertson, and M.J. Klug (eds.). Kluwer Academic Publishers, Netherlands.

Bohlen, P.J., R.W. Parmelee, D.A. McCartney, and C.A. Edwards. 1997. Earthworm effects on carbon and nitrogen dynamics of surface litter in corn agroecosystems. Ecological Applications (in press).

Bolton, P.J., and J. Phillipson. 1976. Burrowing, feeding, egestion and energy budgets of *Allolobophora rosea* (Savigny) (Lumbricidae). Oecologia (Berlin) 23: 225–245.

Bouche, M.B., F. Al-Addan, J. Cortez, R. Hameed, J.C. Heidet, G. Ferriere, D. Mazaud, and M. Samih. 1997. Role of earthworms in N cycle: A falsifiable assessment. Soil Biology and Biochemistry 29: 375–380.

Christensen, O. 1988. The direct effects of earthworms on nitrogen turnover in cultivated soils. Ecological Bulletins (Copenhagen) 39: 41–44.

Curry, J.P., D. Byrne, and K.E. Boyle. 1995. The earthworm population of a winter cereal field and its effects on soil and nitrogen turnover. Biology and Fertility of Soils 19: 166–172.

Dash, M.C., and U.C. Patra. 1979. Wormcast production and nitrogen contribution to soil by a tropical earthworm population from grassland site in Orissa, India. Revue Ecologie et Biologie du Sol 16: 79–83.

Devliegher, W., and W. Verstraete. 1997. The effect of *Lumbricus terrestris* on soil in relation to plant growth: Effects of nutrient-enrichment processes (NEP) and gut-associated processes (GAP). Soil Biology and Biochemistry 29: 341–346.

Elliott, P.W., D. Knight, and J.M. Anderson. 1990. Denitrification in earthworm casts and soil from pasture under different fertilizer and drainage regimes. Soil Biology and Biochemistry 22: 601–605.

Elliott, P.W., D. Knight, and J.M. Anderson. 1991. Variables controlling denitrification from earthworm casts and soil in permanent pasture. Biology and Fertility of Soils 11: 24–29.

Ferriere, G., and M.B. Bouche. 1985. Premiere mesure ecophysiologique d'un debit d'azote de *Nicodrilus longus* (Ude) (Lumbricidae Oligochaeta) dans la prairie de Citeaux. CR Academy Science 301: 789–794.

Gilot, C. 1997. Effects of a tropical geophagous earthworm, *M. anomala* (Megascolecidae), on soil characteristics and production of a yam crop in Cote d'Ivoire. Soil Biology and Biochemistry 29: 353–359.

Hendriksen, N.B. 1997. Earthworm effects on respiratory activity in a dung-soil system. Soil Biology and Biochemistry 29: 347–351.

Hendrix, P.F., D.A. Crossley, Jr., D.C. Coleman, R.W. Parmelee, and M.H. Beare. 1987. Carbon dynamics in soil microbes and fauna in conventional and no-tillage agroecosystems. INTECOL Bulletin 15: 59–63.

Hendrix, P.F., B.R. Mueller, R.R. Bruce, G.W. Langdale, and R.W. Parmelee. 1992. Abundance and distribution of earthworms in relation to landscape factors on the Georgia piedmont, U.S.A. Soil Biology and Biochemistry 24: 1357–1361.

Ketterings, Q.M., J.M. Blair, and J.C.Y. Marinissen. 1997. Effects of earthworms on soil aggregate stability and carbon and nitrogen storage in a legume cover crop agroecosystem. Soil Biology and Biochemistry 29: 401–408.

Knight, D., P.W. Elliott, J.M. Anderson, and D. Scholefield. 1992. The role of earthworms in managed, permanent pastures in Devon, England. Soil Biology and Biochemistry 24: 1511–1518.

Lachnicht, S.L., R.W. Parmelee, D. McCartney, and M. Allen. 1997. Characteristics of macroporosity in a reduced tillage agroecosystem with manipulated earthworm populations: Implications for infiltration and nutrient transport. Soil Biology and Biochemistry 29: 493–498.

Lavelle, P., G. Melendez, B. Pashanasi, and R. Schaefer. 1992. Nitrogen mineralization and reorganization in casts of the geophagous tropical earthworm *Pontoscolex corethrurus* (Glossoscolecidae). Biology and Fertility of Soils 14: 49–53.

Lee, K.E. 1983. The influence of earthworms and termites on soil nitrogen cycling. In: New Trends in Soil Biology. Ph. Lebrun et al. (eds.). Proceedings of the VIII International Colloquium of Soil Zoology. Louvain-la-Neuve, Belgium.

Lee, K.E. 1985. Earthworms, Their Ecology and Relationships with Soils and Land Use. Academic Press, Sydney.

Martin, A. 1991. Short- and long-term effects of the endogeic earthworm *Millsonia anomala* (Omodeo) (Megascolecidae, Oligochaeta) of tropical savannas, on soil organic matter. Biology and Fertility of Soils 11: 234–238.

Martin, A., A. Mariotti, J. Balesdent, and P. Lavelle. 1992a. Soil organic matter assimilation by a geophagous tropical earthworm based on delta ^{13}C measurements. Ecology 73: 118–128.

Martin, A., J. Balesdent, and A. Mariotti. 1992b. Earthworm diet related to soil organic matter dynamics through ^{13}C measurement. Oecologia 91: 23–29.

McCartney, D.A., B.R. Stinner, and P.J. Bohlen. 1997. Organic matter dynamics in maize agroecosystems as affected by earthworm manipulations and fertility source. Soil Biology and Biochemistry 29: 397–400.

Needham, A.E. 1957. Components of nitrogenous excreta in the earthworm *Lumbricus terrestris* L. and *Eisenia foetida* (Savigny). Experimental Biology 34: 425–446.

Parmelee, R.W., and D.A. Crossley, Jr. 1988. Earthworm production and role in the nitrogen cycle of a no-tillage agroecosystem on the Georgia Piedmont. Pedobiologia 32: 353–361.

Parmelee, R.W., M.H. Beare, W. Cheng, P.F. Hendrix, D.A. Crossley, Jr., and D.C. Coleman. 1990. Earthworms and enchytraeids in conventional and no-tillage agroecosystems: A biocide approach to assess their role in organic matter breakdown. Biology and Fertility of Soils 10: 1–10.

Poier, K.R., and J. Richter. 1992. Spatial distribution of earthworms and soil properties in an arable loess soil. Soil Biology and Biochemistry 24: 1601–1608.

Romanovsky, Y.E., and V. Polishchuk. 1982. A theoretical approach to calculation of secondary production at the population level. Int. Rev. Gesamten Hydrobiol. 67: 341–359.

Satchell, J.E. 1967. Lumbricidae. In: Soil Biology. A. Burges and F. Raw (eds.). Academic Press, New York.

Scheu, S. 1987. Microbial activity and nutrient dynamics in earthworm casts (Lumbricidae). Biology and Fertility of Soils 5: 230–234.

Scheu, S. 1991. Mucus excretion and carbon turnover of endogeic earthworms. Biology and Fertility of Soils 12: 217–220.

Scheu, S., and D. Parkinson. 1994a. Effects of earthworms on nutrient dynamics, carbon turnover and microorganisms in soils from cool temperate forests of the Canadian Rocky Mountains—laboratory studies. Applied Soil Ecology 1: 113–125.

Scheu, S., and D. Parkinson. 1994b. Effects of invasion of an aspen forest (Canada) by *Dendrobaena octaedra* (Lumbricidae) on plant growth. Ecology 75: 2348–2361.

Sharpley, A.N., J.K. Syers, and J.A. Springett. 1979. Effect of surface-casting earthworms on the transport of phosphorus and nitrogen in surface runoff from pasture. Soil Biology and Biochemistry 11: 459–462.

Steinberg, D.A., R.V. Pouyat, R.W. Parmelee, and P.M. Groffman. 1997. Earthworm abundance and nitrogen mineralization rates along an urban-rural land use gradient. Soil Biology and Biochemistry 29: 427–430.

Stinner, B.R., D.A. McCartney, J.M. Blair, R.W. Parmelee, and M.F. Allen. 1997. Earthworm effects on crop and weed biomass, and N content in organic and inorganic fertilized agroecosystems. Soil Biology and Biochemistry 29: 423–426.

Subler, S., C.M. Baranski, and C.A. Edwards. 1997. Earthworm additions increased short-term nitrogen availability and leaching in two grain-crop agroecosystems. Soil Biology and Biochemistry 29: 413–421.

Svensson, B.H., U. Bostrom, and L. Klemedtson. 1986. Potential for higher rates of denitrification in earthworm casts than in the surrounding soil. Biology and Fertility of Soil 2: 147–149.

Syers, J.K., and J.A. Springett. 1984. Earthworms and soil fertility. Plant and Soil 76: 93–104.

Tian, G., B.T. Kang, and L. Brussaard. 1997. Effect of mulch quality on earthworm activity and nutrient supply in the humid tropics. Soil Biology and Biochemistry 29: 369–373.

Wolters, V., and R.G. Joergensen. 1992. Microbial carbon turnover in beech forest soils worked by *Aporrectodea caliginosa* (Savigny) (Oligochacta: Lumbricidae). Soil Biology and Biochemistry 24: 171–177.

Effects of Earthworms on Soil Physical Properties and Function

IV

Consequences of Earthworms in Agricultural Soils: Aggregation and Porosity

7

W.M. Edwards and M.J. Shipitalo

Soil Scientists, USDA-ARS, at the North Appalachian Experimental Watershed, Coshocton, OH 43812-0488

In agricultural ecosystems, the soil serves as the framework for the physical, chemical, and biological processes that make conditions suitable for crop production. We manage soil properties and processes with tillage, irrigation, drainage, nutrients, and pesticides to increase profitability and to protect long-term productivity and the local environment.

Within the wide range of soils and climates, farmers use many management options to influence such measurable soil properties as density, aggregation, pore size distribution, water and organic matter contents, chemical distributions, and the rate that chemical transformations take place. In trying to make field soils more favorable for crop production, we often inadvertently make the managed soil more or less favorable for soil invertebrates. Therefore, the resulting agronomic responses to management may be due partially to unmeasured changes in populations and activity of many different soil organisms.

Earthworms, because of their size, abundance, and activity, can make visible and easily measured changes in soil properties. In high numbers, earthworms can have notable effects on soil structure and porosity. Therefore, we must consider not only the direct effects of management on soil properties and processes, but also their effects on earthworm populations.

1-884015-74-3/98/$0.00/$.50

AGGREGATION

Soil structure and the consequences of its variation are hard to quantify. Although many physical and chemical factors that influence soil structure have been documented (Allison 1968; Greenland 1981; Hamblin and Davies 1977; McKeague et al. 1987; Oades 1984, 1993), it is difficult to relate improvements in aggregation or aggregate stability to enhanced crop growth. Similarly, Logsdon and Linden (1992) noted that few reliable field studies have documented improved root and plant growth due to the effects of earthworms on soil structure.

Especially in humid regions, earthworms and other soil fauna usually have positive effects on soils (Dindal 1985; Edwards and Lofty 1977; Hole 1981; Lee 1985; Lee and Foster 1991). Shaw and Pawluk (1986), however, noted that earthworms can also have negative effects on soil physical condition, depending on the species of earthworms and/or the nature of the soil.

Although earthworms generally increase the size and stability of aggregates, primarily in the uppermost soil horizons, exceptions have been reported (Hopp and Hopkins 1946; MacKay and Kladivko 1985; Blanchart et al. 1989; Brussaard et al. 1990). Kladivko et al. (1986) showed that *Lumbricus rubellus* (Hoff.) increased both the mean weight diameter and stability of aggregates which had a favorable effect on reducing crusting and enhancing crop emergence. Hamilton and Dindal (1989) noted that one species, *Lumbricus terrestris* (L), improved aggregation in sludge-amended plots whereas another species, *Eisenia fetida* (Sav.), had no effect. This is not surprising since *E. fetida* is not a soil species.

The stability of fresh earthworm casts, which eventually become components of soil structure, can vary tremendously depending upon moisture status and age (Shipitalo and Protz 1988; Marinissen and Dexter 1990) and the earthworm's diet (Shipitalo et al. 1988). Shaw and Pawluk (1986) found that the production of more desirable soil fabrics made by earthworms was correlated with increased concentrations of a clay-bound carbohydrate. The proliferation of fungal hyphae on the surface has also been related to increased stabilization of casts with age (Marinissen and Dexter 1990).

At the microfabric scale, earthworms affect soils by thoroughly mixing organic and mineral components as they are passed through the earthworm gut. In this process the existing soil structure is destroyed, and some organic components are liberated while others may be protected by the formation of new casts and aggregates (Shipitalo and Protz 1988, 1989; Barois et al. 1993).

Characteristics of the resultant casts, whether deposited on the surface or below, vary among earthworm species and are affected by soil and vegetation factors (Tomlin et al. 1995). The most compact casts of the tropical geophagous earthworm, *Millsonia anomala* (Omodeo), are so dense that carbon mineralization in the casts is reduced compared to that in sieved soil (Martin 1991). The slower movement of air and water in these casts inhibits biochemical reactions (Blanchart et al. 1993), effectively blocking mineralization for months and even years in the compact structure of aged casts (Lavelle and Martin 1992). In a cold, Canadian soil, fecal pellets of earthworms were so dense that the smaller units within were strongly fused and their structural integrity was frequently lost (Juma 1991). Altemüller and Joschko (1992) developed a fluorescent staining technique that aided identification and diagnostic interpretation of earthworm casts in complex cast/aggregate mixtures. Martin and Marinissen (1993) more thoroughly discussed effects of earthworms on processes that influence stability, nutrient release, and decomposition of faunal excrements.

It is not surprising that science has not clearly defined all of the effects of earthworms on soil structure. There is general agreement, however, that most earthworms burrow, cast, and mix mineral and organic components of the soil, and high earthworm numbers have more effect on soil properties than sparse populations. Blanchart (1992) directly assessed earthworm effects on restructuring of a Savanna soil by measuring the aggregate distribution of undisturbed soil columns by sieving the material before replacing it in the field without invertebrates, with native soil invertebrates, or with added earthworms (*M. anomala*). Thirty months later the columns were excavated again. The proportion of >2.0-mm aggregates was nearly four times greater with native soil fauna and nearly five times greater with *M. anomala* than in the soil without any fauna.

As was reported by Tomlin et al. (1995), the organic component of the earthworms' diet may be as much as 25 Mg/ha/yr of cow dung (Guild 1955) or 3 Mg/ha of deciduous leaf fall in approximately three months (Satchell 1967). Where a limited supply of palatable organic matter or harsh soil surface conditions limited earthworm activity, the addition of manure consistently increased earthworm numbers (Berry and Karlen 1993). As food supply limits populations, it also controls cast production which can range from almost nil to >2,500 Mg/ha/yr in the tropics (Watanabe and Ruaysoongnern 1984).

In temperate climates, where most earthworm activity is concentrated in the spring and autumn months, the stability of casts and their conversion into stable aggregates may depend on when they are produced. The vegetation supply will differ between spring and autumn, and the weather conditions following casting, which influence drying, may differ greatly. Even within the spring or autumn casting periods, the fate of a surface or near-surface cast will be very different if it is produced immediately before a 5-cm rain storm or a two-week drought. Similarly, in the tropics where casting rates are commonly high (Lee 1985; Lavelle et al. 1989), the stability of casts produced at the beginning of a rainy season and their subsequent contribution to soil aggregation may be quite different from those produced at the beginning of the dry season.

In addition to the physical, temporal, climatic, and species differential effects on earthworm casts and aggregation, measurement strategies also add to variability. Worms interact with many other soil organisms, and measuring the effects of only part of the complex mixture often results in less than perfect understanding of the direct and indirect causes of the observed results.

Research on factors affecting the stability of earthworm casts has been reviewed thoroughly by Oades (1993) and Tomlin et al. (1995). The physical nature of casts has a major influence on organic matter and nitrogen transformations (Tisdall and Oades 1982; Van Veen and Kuikman 1990). Further evidence of the complexity of earthworm effects on soil structure was presented by Hamilton et al. (1988), who studied earthworm interactions in soil microcosms that had received sludge amendments, and by Hartenstein (1986), who reviewed and interpreted global earthworm biotechnology.

POROSITY AND INFILTRATION

Field Studies

The activity of most burrowing soil organisms tends to increase soil porosity, pore size, and the variability of porosity. These changes affect many soil processes. For instance, Knight et al. (1992) showed that earthworms increased soil macroporosity and tripled the amount of leaching from pastures in England. Because of the continuity of many biopores, especially earthworm burrows (Bouché 1971; Edwards et al. 1988b; Schrader 1993), a single biopore can dominate water movement under some conditions as measured by traditional soil physical methods. Smettem and Collis-George (1985b) showed that a single, continuous 0.3-mm-diameter macropore can conduct more water than the rest of a 100-mm-diameter soil sample.

L. terrestris burrows are easily recognized, vertically continuous biopores that have been implicated in "short-circuiting" water and solutes in soils (Bouma et al. 1981; Steenhuis et al. 1990; Wildenschild et al. 1994). This phenomenon is also termed "by-pass flow" and can be characterized by early breakthrough of chemical tracers (Bouma et al. 1983; Bouma 1991). Colored dyes and other tracers have been used by numerous investigators to confirm that flow can occur in these burrows and other preferential flow paths (Ehlers 1975; Linden and Dixon 1976; Douglas et al. 1980; Bouma 1981; Tyler and Thomas 1981; Germann et al. 1984; Smettem and Collis-George 1985a; Smith et al. 1985; Zachmann et al. 1987; Everts et al. 1989; Andreini and Steenhuis 1990).

Lee (1985) and Smettem (1992) reviewed research documenting high infiltration rates in soils containing earthworms (Hopp and Slater 1948; Teotia et al.

1950; Scharpenseel and Gewehr 1960; Stockdill 1966; Carter et al. 1982) and into individual earthworm burrows (Ehlers 1975) or burrow systems (Bouché 1971). Just as the introduction of earthworms has been shown to increase infiltration (Stockdill 1966; Kladivko et al. 1986; Joschko et al. 1992), the elimination of earthworms by repeated insecticide applications has reduced infiltration rates (Clements 1982; Sharpley et al. 1979).

Urbánek and Dolezal (1992) surveyed the abundance and hydraulic efficiency of earthworm channels in Czechoslovakian soils and reported that burrows can increase infiltration and speed drainage to the deep tile level. However, Ela et al. (1992) concluded from pot experiments using soils from the northern Corn Belt of the United States that the addition of *Aporrectodea tuberculata* did not increase simulated rainfall infiltration. Their burrows did not go deep into the soil, and the soil surface quickly sealed any openings to the burrows. It may be that *L. terrestris* contribute to surface scaling or crusting by removing protective residue from parts of the soil surface as they create middens.

Two potentially important consequences of infiltration in earthworm burrows involve reduced surface runoff and the possibility for increased percolation through the soil profile. In most agricultural situations, reducing runoff and the overland transport of sediments and chemicals is desired. An unwanted increase of chemical movement through the root zone, however, may accompany increased infiltration (Zachmann et al. 1987; Isensee et al. 1990; Shipitalo et al. 1990; Steenhuis et al. 1990; Trojan and Linden 1992; Propes et al. 1993). In some parts of the eastern United States, where no-tillage has replaced conventional moldboard plowing of sloping fields for row-crop production, runoff and erosion have been greatly reduced while infiltration and populations of the vertically-burrowing *L. terrestris* have increased (Edwards 1991; Bohlen et al. 1995).

Because *L. terrestris* numbers usually increase under no-tillage and the lack of disruptive tillage allows old burrows to persist, the number of burrows per unit area can increase with years of continuous no-tillage production. With more water infiltrating into the non-tilled fields each year and with the increased number of *L. terrestris* burrows in these soils, the opportunity for preferential flow that bypasses the soil matrix increases. Additionally, annual chemical inputs required for continuous no-tillage row crop production may be much greater than those used previously when the crop rotation needed for erosion control included several years of meadow. Therefore, much of the recent hydrologic research in sloping, humid areas, where no-tillage is an important management practice, has involved identifying factors and conditions under which nutrients and herbicides used in row-crop production may move down in *L. terrestris* burrows.

In one study, the number of biopores >0.4 mm in diameter was determined at four depth intervals within the top 30 cm of a long-term no-till corn watershed using image analyses of field photos (Edwards et al. 1988a). These silt loam surface horizons averaged >14,500 such pores per m^2, 160 of which were *L. terrestris* burrows >5 mm in diameter. Mean pore diameter ranged between 1 and 2 mm, and the number of pores was inversely proportional to pore diameter. The >0.4-mm-diameter pores comprised <1.5 % of the area at four measured depths, but tracer studies showed that surface water could infiltrate rapidly through the larger pores, possibly contributing to a reduction in runoff from the gauged watershed (Germann et al. 1984).

Buried samplers were installed to intercept and characterize water infiltrating in *L. terrestris* burrows near gauged watersheds (Edwards et al. 1989) and in farmer-owned fields (Shipitalo et al. 1994). Water infiltrating through burrows averaged 4% of the rainfall in 12 summer storms that were big enough to cause burrow flow; however, burrow flow accounted for 10% of the rain in a brief, high-intensity storm that fell under very dry antecedent surface conditions. Both studies showed that downward movement of chemicals in the burrows was small, approximately 5% of the total NO_3-N, Br and Sr transport as determined from pan lysimeter measurements (Shipitalo et al. 1994).

Laboratory Studies

The field studies documented that water infiltrated frequently in *L. terrestris* burrows, as a result of natural storms falling on no-till fields. They also showed that rainfall intensity, antecedent soil moisture, and time between surface application of the chemicals and subsequent rainfall events influenced the concentration and downward transport of chemicals. Van Ommen et al. (1989) reached similar conclusions after studying infiltration with solutes and dye in field plots in the Netherlands.

Dependency on natural storms made field evaluation of specific factors that might affect chemical transport in burrow flow difficult. Therefore, a system was developed at the USDA hydrologic experiment station, Coshocton, Ohio, that enabled the drip-application of water at controlled intensity to the surface of 30-by-30-by-30-cm blocks of undisturbed soil collected from no-till fields (Shipitalo et al. 1990). The location of ≥2.0-mm-diameter biopores at the bottom surface of each block was recorded with respect to a 64-compartment grid that supported the block under a rainfall simulator. During each simulated storm, water infiltrated through each of the 64 grid cells could be measured, sampled, and related to macroporosity in individual cells.

Shipitalo et al. (1990) used this simulator to show that if a small, low-intensity storm fell on a residue-covered surface shortly after atrazine application, concentration and transport of the herbicide in *L. terrestris* burrows in a subsequent average-sized storm was half as great as when the average storm occurred without the preceding small one. The small simulated storm caused no flow through the test blocks, but by wetting and possibly leaching herbicide from the residue into the surface soil, it effectively reduced transport of herbicides in burrow flow in subsequent storms. Repeated storms on the same soil blocks that did not receive additional herbicide treatments showed that the concentration of atrazine in burrow flow decreased in successive events, regardless of intensity and amount of water in preceding storms. Propes et al. (1993) also reported that a low-volume pretreatment storm caused more atrazine to be retained by the soil matrix as compared to samples that did not receive the pretreatment storm.

The results of the study by Shipitalo et al. (1990) also indicated that near-surface water content also affected chemical flow in the burrows. As noted by Germann et al. (1984), White (1985), and Edwards et al. (1989), the residue-covered surface of nontilled soil appears to be somewhat hydrophobic under dry antecedent conditions, limiting infiltration into the soil matrix for a few minutes at the onset of storms. Chan (1992) investigated this condition and attributed the initial water repellency at the surface of direct drilled fields to the growth of fungal hyphae under slow drying conditions, the absence of soil disturbance, and the presence of a permanent layer of organic matter. Bisdom et al. (1993) concluded that water repellency of sandy soils was caused by organic components in micro-aggregates, plant fragments, and coatings on sand grains and could be influenced by soil biota such as earthworms. Bond (1969) reviewed several factors that influence water repellency of soils and its potential effect on infiltration.

The rainfall simulator in Ohio was used in a subsequent study to evaluate the effect of storm intensity on the movement of water and herbicides in earthworm burrows. Relatively dry blocks (15% v/v), partially covered with corn residue from previous crops, received 30 mm of simulated rain at intensities of 120, 60, or 15 mm/hr (Edwards et al. 1992a). The results supported the conclusions from the field studies that more of the *L. terrestris* burrows produced flow and more of the applied water passed through burrows in the blocks as storm intensity increased. Although the concentration of surface-applied atrazine in the burrow flow was not affected by rainfall intensity, total transport of atrazine in burrow flow increased with intensity because the volume of burrow flow increased. Trojan and Linden (1992) reported that burrows of *A. tuberculata* also transported more water when subjected to higher simulated rainfall intensities.

The block studies of Edwards et al. (1992a) also showed that the dry surface of the blocks allowed water to enter the *L. terrestris* burrows soon after the onset of rainfall and run through the 30-cm-deep blocks almost immediately. At the 120-mm/hr intensity, free water dripped out of some burrows within two minutes of the rainfall start, after <4.5 mm of water had been applied to the surface.

At lower application intensities, flow through the blocks began later and fewer of the burrows were involved in the rapid transport of water.

Field watershed and plot studies have shown that the first storm following surface application of chemicals, especially if it occurs soon after application, usually contains the highest concentrations of those chemicals in surface runoff water (Baker and Laflen 1983; Owens et al. 1984). To determine if time between pesticide application and the onset of the first subsequent storm had a similar effect on chemical transport in subsurface flow, three blocks received a simulated storm either one hour, one day, one week, two weeks, or six weeks after atrazine was applied to the residue-covered surface (Edwards et al. 1993). No rain fell on the blocks during the first two weeks of the experiment, other than the 30-mm simulated storms. Transport of atrazine in burrow flow, through the blocks that received the storm one hour after herbicide application, was three times greater than that through the blocks that received similar storms two weeks later. Four small natural storms fell on the final three blocks before they were brought in from the field to the simulator. Due to the extra time following chemical application, and to the four small storms that preceded the simulated rain, transport of atrazine in burrow flow on the six-week blocks averaged 2% of that from the blocks treated one hour before the simulated storm (Edwards et al. 1993).

The observed flow in *L. terrestris* burrows at 30 cm depth, as early as two minutes after the onset of rain, indicates that the entry of water into the burrows must take place very near the soil surface. It also indicates that the water that drains freely from burrows at the bottom of the blocks soon after the onset of rain could not have infiltrated into the fine pore matrix of the soil where it would be held under high tension. Therefore, the first water to accumulate in depressions on the soil surface may pick up atrazine, which was sprayed on the surface, and transport it down in the earthworm burrows without interaction with the antecedent soil water.

We evaluated the range of likely concentrations of atrazine that would be available to infiltrate in earthworm burrows in treated fields (Edwards et al. 1996). One day after atrazine was sprayed on the surface of corn fields, we used syringes to collect 10-mL samples of the first water to accumulate in small surface depressions after onset of simulated rainfall. With continued application of water from the simulator, subsequent samples of water from the same depression were collected at 5-minute intervals for 30 minutes. The experiment consisted of five replications of this sampling sequence on days 1, 2, 4, 8, 16, and 32 following herbicide application on three corn fields: no-till with manure, no-till without manure, and moldboard plowing without manure. The simulator was moved to a new location in each field for each sampling.

In every case, the concentration of atrazine was highest in the first sample collected from a depression and was from 50 to 90% lower in water from that depression 30 minutes later. The first samples from the plowed field contained atrazine concentrations as much as 200% higher than those from the mulch-covered fields. The pattern of decreasing atrazine concentration during the 30-minute simulated rain continued through all sampling days with the final concentrations on day 32 being approximately 1% of the initial concentrations on day 1.

Burrow Linings

Chemical transport through earthworm burrows may differ from that through similar size macropores of non-biological origin (Turner and Steele 1988; Trojan and Linden 1992). The species *L. terrestris* casts within its burrow so that the lining, or drilosphere, is rich in organic matter, microorganisms, and available plant nutrients, providing a channel ideal for root growth (Edwards and Lofty 1980; Pawluk and Bal 1985; Mouat and Keogh 1987). Mucus secreted through the earthworm's cuticle and often noted on burrow walls has been shown to neutralize the pH of the drilosphere, by either raising or lowering pH when the surrounding conditions are too acid or alkaline, respectively (Schrader 1991, 1993).

Edwards et al. (1992b) poured herbicide-laden water into *L. terrestris* burrows and found much lower concentrations in the water intercepted 50 cm below, only seconds later. Stehouwer et al. (1993, 1994) investigated the characteristics of burrow linings at several depths as compared to those of the surrounding bulk soil. They showed that *L. terrestris* burrow linings were enriched in organic C, relative to the soil matrix, and that the C enrichment was correlated with enhanced sorption of atrazine on the burrow linings (Stehouwer et al. 1993). They also poured water containing several herbicides through *L. terrestris* burrows and similar-sized man-made holes in blocks of no-till soil. Sorption of the more strongly sorbed herbicides was enhanced by a factor of three on the burrow lining, relative to the bulk soil, while there was little difference in retention of two weakly sorbed herbicides as they passed through both the burrows and the man-made holes (Stehouwer et al. 1994).

SUMMARY

Numerous studies have been conducted to quantify the effects of earthworms on soil aggregation and porosity of agricultural soils. Most results indicate that earthworms, through their burrowing activities and their search for food, can ingest large quantities of soil and organic matter. Passage of this material through the earthworm gut disrupts preexisting aggregates, but results in the intimate mixing of mineral and organic matter. Reformation of stable aggregates in the casted material depends on a number of factors, including the nature and relative amounts of mineral and organic matter ingested, where and when casts are deposited, and species of earthworm.

The burrows formed by earthworms can serve as preferential pathways for root growth, water movement, and chemical transport. Continuity and persistence of burrows are influenced directly by tillage practices. Entry of water and chemicals into the earthworm-formed macropores is dependent on weather-related factors (such as rainfall amount, intensity, and timing), soil moisture content, chemical characteristics, and method of application.

Despite much research, answers to some fundamental questions remain elusive. We still do not know how important earthworm activity is to maintaining aggregation and productivity of agroecosystems in general. Likewise, the conditions under which chemical transport through earthworm burrows ultimately affects groundwater contamination are still uncertain.

REFERENCES CITED

Allison, F.E. 1968. Soil aggregation—Some facts and fallacies as seen by a microbiologist. Soil Sci. 106:136–143.

Altemüller, H.J., and M. Joschko. 1992. Fluorescent staining of earthworm casts for thin section microscopy. Soil Biol. Biochem. 24:1577–1582.

Andreini, M.S., and T.S. Steenhuis. 1990. Preferential paths of flow under conventional and conservation tillage. Geoderma 46:85–102.

Baker, J.L., and J.M. Laflen. 1983. Water quality consequences of conservation tillage. J. Soil Water Conserv. 38:186–193.

Barois, I., G. Villemin, P. Lavelle, and F. Toutain. 1993. Transformation of the soil structure through *Pontoscolex corethrurus* (Oligochaeta) intestinal tract. Geoderma 56:57–66.

Berry, E.C., and D.L. Karlen. 1993. Comparison of alternative farming systems. II. Earthworm population density and species diversity. Amer. J. Alt. Agric. 8:21–26.

Bisdom, E.B.A., L.W. Dekker, and J.F.Th. Schoute. 1993. Water repellency of sieve fractions from sandy soils and relationships with organic material and soil structure. Geoderma 56:105–118.

Blanchart, E. 1992. Restoration by earthworms (Megascolecidae) of the macroaggregate structure of a destructured savanna soil under field conditions. Soil Biol. Biochem. 24: 1587–1594.

Blanchart, E., P. Lavelle, and A.V. Spain. 1989. Effects of two species of tropical earthworms (Oligochaeta: Eudrilidae) on the size of aggregates in an African soil. Revue d'Ecologie et de Biologie du Sol 26:417–425.

Blanchart E., A. Bruand, and P. Lavelle. 1993. The physical structure of casts of *Millsonia anomala* (Oligochaeta: Megascolecidae) in shrub savanna soil (Côte d'Ivoire). Geoderma 56:119–132.

Bohlen, P.J., W.M. Edwards, and C.A. Edwards. 1995. Earthworm community structure and diversity in experimental agricultural watersheds in northeastern Ohio. Plant Soil 170: 233–239.

Bond, R.D. 1969. Factors responsible for water repellence of soils. pp. 259–264. In L.F. De Bano and J. Letey (eds.). Proc. Symp. on Water Repellent Soils. University of California, Riverside.

Bouché, M.B. 1971. Relations entre les structures spatiales et fonctionelles des écosystemes, illustrées par le rôle pédobiologique des vers de terre. pp. 189–209. In C. Delamere Deboutteville (ed.). La Vie dans les Sols. Gauthiers Villars, Paris.

Bouma, J. 1981. Soil morphology and preferential flow along macropores. Agric. Water Mgt. 3:235–250.

Bouma, J. 1991. Influence of soil macroporosity on environmental quality. Advances in Agronomy, 46. Academic Press, San Diego, CA, pp. 1–37.

Bouma, J., C. Belmans, L.W. Dekker, and W.J.M. Jeurissen. 1983. Assessing the suitability of soils with macropores for subsurface liquid waste disposal. J. Environ. Qual. 12: 305–311.

Bouma, J., L.W. Dekker, and C.J. Muilwijk. 1981. A field method for measuring short-circuiting in clay soils. J. Hydrol. 52:347–354.

Brussaard, L., D.C. Coleman, D.A. Crossley, Jr., W.A.M. Didden, P.F. Hendrix, and J.C.Y. Marinissen. 1990. Impacts of earthworms on soil aggregate stability. Transactions of the 14th International Congress of Soil Science, Kyoto, Japan, III:100–105.

Carter, A., J. Heinonen, and J. de Vries. 1982. Earthworms and water movement. Pedobiologia 23:395–397.

Chan, K.Y. 1992. Development of seasonal water repellence under direct drilling. Soil Sci. Soc. Am. J. 56:326–329.

Clements, R.O. 1982. Some consequences of large and frequent pesticide applications to grassland. pp. 393–396. In K.E. Lee (ed.). Proc. 3rd Australasian Conf. Grass. Invert. Ecol. S. Aust. Gov. Printer, Adelaide.

Dindal, D.L. 1985. Soil animals and soil fabric production: Facts and perceptions. Quaestiones Entomologicae 12:587–594.

Douglas, J.T., J.J. Gross, and D. Hill. 1980. Measurements of pore characteristics in a clay soil under ploughing and direct drilling, including the use of a radioactive tracer (^{144}Ce) technique. Soil Tillage Res. 1:11–18.

Edwards, C.A., and J.R. Lofty. 1977. Biology of Earthworms. Chapman and Hall, London, England. 333 pp.

Edwards, C.A., and J.R. Lofty. 1980. Effects of earthworm inoculation upon the root growth of direct drilled cereals. J. Appl. Ecol. 17:533–543.

Edwards, W.M. 1991. Soil structure: Processes and management. pp. 7–14. In R. Lal and F.J. Pierce (eds.). Soil Management for Sustainability. Soil and Water Conservation Society, Ankeny, IA.

Edwards, W.M., L.D. Norton, and C.E. Redmond. 1988a. Characterizing macropores that affect infiltration into non-tilled soil. Soil Sci. Soc. Am. J. 52:483–487.

Edwards, W.M., M.J. Shipitalo, and L.D. Norton. 1988b. Contribution of macroporosity to infiltration into a continuous corn no-tilled watershed: Implications for contaminant movement. J. Contamin. Hydrol. 3:193–205.

Edwards, W.M., M.J. Shipitalo, L.B. Owens, and L.D. Norton. 1989. Water and nitrate movement in earthworm burrows within long-term no-till cornfields. J. Soil Water Conserv. 44:240–243.

Edwards, W.M., M.J. Shipitalo, W.A. Dick, and L.B. Owens. 1992a. Rainfall intensity affects transport of water and chemicals through macropores in no-till soil. Soil Sci. Soc. Am. J. 56:52–58.

Edwards, W.M., M.J. Shipitalo, S.J. Traina, C.A. Edwards, and L.B. Owens. 1992b. Role of *Lumbricus terrestris* (L.) burrows on quality of infiltrating water. Soil Biol. Biochem. 24:1555–1561.

Edwards, W.M., M.J. Shipitalo, L.B. Owens, and W.A. Dick. 1993. Factors affecting preferential flow of water and atrazine through earthworm burrows under continuous no-till corn. J. Environ. Qual. 22:453–457.

Edwards, W.M., M.J. Shipitalo, R. Lal, and L.B. Owens. 1996. Rapid changes in concentration of herbicides in corn field surface depressions. J. Soil Water Conserv. (in press).

Ehlers, W. 1975. Observations on earthworm channels and infiltration on tilled and untilled loess soil. Soil Sci. 119:242–249.

Ela, S.D., S.C. Gupta, and W.J. Rawls. 1992. Macropore and surface seal interactions affecting water infiltration into soil. Soil Sci. Soc. Am. J. 56:714–721.

Everts, C.J., R.S. Kanwar, E.C. Alexander, Jr., and S.C. Alexander. 1989. Comparison of tracer mobilities under laboratory and field conditions. J. Environ. Qual. 18:491–498.

Germann, P.F., W.M. Edwards, and L.B. Owens. 1984. Profiles of bromide and increased soil moisture after infiltration into soils with macropores. Soil Sci. Soc. Am. J. 48:237–244.

Greenland, D.J. 1981. Soil management and soil degradation. J. Soil Sci. 32:301–322.

Guild, W.J.McL. 1955. Earthworms and soil structure. pp. 83–98. In D.K.McE. Kevan (ed.). Soil Zoology. Butterworths, London.

Hamblin, A.P., and D.B. Davies. 1977. Influence of organic matter on the physical properties of some East Anglian soils of high silt content. J. Soil Sci. 28:11–22.

Hamilton, W.E., and D.L. Dindal. 1989. Impact of landspread sewage sludge and earthworm introduction on established earthworms and soil structure. Biol. Fert. Soils 8:160–165.

Hamilton, W.E., D.L. Dindal, D.M. Parkinson, and J.J. Mitchell. 1988. Interaction of earthworm species in sewage sludge-amended soil microcosms: *Lumbricus terrestris* and *Eisenia fetida*. J. Appl. Ecol. 25:847–852.

Hartenstein, R. 1986. Earthworm biotechnology and global biogeochemistry. Adv. Ecol. Res. 15:379–409.

Hole, F.D. 1981. Effects of animals on soil. Geoderma 25:75–112.

Hopp, H., and H.T. Hopkins. 1946. Earthworms as a factor in the formation of water-stable aggregates. J. Soil Water Conserv. 1:11–13.

Hopp, H., and C.S. Slater. 1948. Influence of earthworms on soil productivity. Soil Sci. 66:421–428.

Isensee, A.R., R.G. Nash, and C.S. Helling. 1990. Effect of conventional vs. no-tillage on pesticide leaching to shallow groundwater. J. Environ. Qual. 19:434–440.

Joschko, M., W. Söchtig, and O. Larink. 1992. Functional relationship between earthworm burrows and soil water movement in column experiments. Soil Biol. Biochem. 24: 1545–1547.

Juma, N.G. 1991. Interrelationships between soil structure, soil biota and primary plant production. Abstract #80 of International Workshop on Methods of Research on Soil Structure/Soil Biota Interrelationships. IAC, Wageningen.

Kladivko, E.J., A.D. Mackay, and J.M. Bradford. 1986. Earthworms as a factor in the reduction of soil crusting. Soil Sci. Soc. Am. J. 50:191–196.

Knight, D., P.W. Elliot, J.M. Anderson, and P. Scholefield. 1992. The role of earthworms in managed, permanent pastures in Devon, England. Soil Biol. Biochem. 24:1511–1517.

Lavelle, P., and A. Martin. 1992. Small-scale and large-scale effects of endogeic earthworms on soil organic matter dynamics in soils of the humid tropics. Soil Biol. Biochem. 24:1491–1498.

Lavelle, P., R. Schaefer, and Z. Zaidi. 1989. Soil ingestion and growth in *Millsonia anomala*, a tropical earthworm, as influenced by the quality of the organic matter ingested. Pedobiologia 33:379–388.

Lee, K.E. 1985. Earthworms—Their Ecology and Relationships with Soils and Land Use. Academic Press, New York. 411 pp.

Lee, K.E., and R.C. Foster. 1991. Soil fauna and soil structure. Aust. J. Soil Res. 29:745–775.

Linden, D.R., and R.M. Dixon. 1976. Soil air pressure effects on route and rate of infiltration. Soil Sci. Soc. Am. J. 40:963–965.

Logsdon, S.D., and D.R. Linden. 1992. Interactions of earthworms with soil physical conditions influencing plant growth. Soil Sci. 154:330–337.

Mackay, A.D., and E.J. Kladivko. 1985. Earthworms and the rate of breakdown of soybean and maize residues in soil. Soil Biol. Biochem. 17:851–857.

Marinissen, J.Y.C., and A.R. Dexter. 1990. Mechanisms of stabilization of earthworm casts and artificial casts. Biol. Fert. Soils 9:163–167.

Martin, A. 1991. Short- and long-term effects of the endogeic earthworm *Millsonia anomala* (Omodeo) (Megascolecidae, Oligochaeta) of tropical savannas, on soil organic matter. Biol. Fert. Soils 11:234–238.

Martin, A., and J.C.Y. Marinissen. 1993. Biological and physico-chemical processes in excrements of soil animals. Geoderma 56:331–347.

McKeague, J.A., C.A. Fox, J.A. Stone, and R. Protz. 1987. Effects of cropping system on structure of Brookston clay loam in long-term experimental plots at Woodslee, Ontario. Can. J. Soil Sci. 67:571–584.

Mouat, M.C.H., and R.G. Keogh. 1987. Absorption by soil of water-soluble phosphate from earthworm casts. Plant Soil 97:223–231.

Oades, J.M. 1984. Soil organic matter and structural stability: Mechanisms and implications for management. Plant Soil 76:319–337.

Oades, J.M. 1993. The role of biology in the formation, stabilization and degradation of soil structure. Geoderma 56:377–400.

Owens, L.B., W.M. Edwards, and R.W. Van Keuren. 1984. Peak NO_3-N values in runoff from fertilized pastures. J. Environ. Qual. 13:310–312.

Pawluk, S., and L. Bal. 1985. Micromorphology of selected mollic epipedons, pp. 63–83. In L.A. Douglas and M.L. Thompson (eds.). Soil Micromorphology and Soil Classification. SSSA Spec. Publ. 15. Soil Sci. Soc. Am., Madison, WI.

Propes, K.L., F.W. Simmons, G.K. Sims, and C.W. Boast. 1993. Herbicide movement into and through earthworm induced soil macropores. North Central Weed Sci. Soc. Proc. 48:49–50.

Satchell, J.E. 1967. Lumbricidae. pp. 259–322. In A. Burges and F. Raw (eds.). Soil Biology. Academic Press, London. 532 pp.

Scharpenseel, H.W., and H. Gewehr. 1960. Studien zur Wasserbewegung im Boden mit Tritium-Wasser. Z. Pflanzenernährung u. Düngung 88:35–49.

Schrader, S. 1991. Darstellung des Einflusses von Regenwürmern auf Redoxpotential und Ph-Wert mit Indicatoren. Mitt. Dtsch. Bodenkdl. Ges. 66:577–580.

Schrader, S. 1993. Semi-automatic image analysis of earthworm activity in 2D soil sections. Geoderma 56:257–264.

Sharpley, A.N., J.K. Syers, and J.A. Springett. 1979. Effect of surface-casting earthworms on the transport of phosphorus and nitrogen in surface runoff from pasture. Soil Biol. Biochem. 11:459–462.

Shaw, C., and S. Pawluk. 1986. The development of soil structure by *Octolasion tyrtaeum, Aporrectodea turgida* and *Lumbricus terrestris* in parent materials belonging to different textural classes. Pedobiologia 29:327–339.

Shipitalo, M.J., and R. Protz. 1988. Factors influencing the dispersibility of clay in worm casts. Soil Sci. Soc. Am. J. 52:764–769.

Shipitalo, M.J., and R. Protz. 1989. Chemistry and micromorphology of aggregation in earthworm casts. Geoderma 45:357–374.

Shipitalo, M.J., W.M. Edwards, W.A. Dick, and L.B. Owens. 1990. Initial storm effects on macropore transport of surface-applied chemicals in no-till soil. Soil Sci. Soc. Am. J. 54:1530–1536.

Shipitalo, M.J., W.M. Edwards, and C.E. Redmond. 1994. Comparison of water movement and quality in earthworm burrows and pan lysimeters. J. Environ. Qual. 23:1345–1351.

Shipitalo, M.J., R. Protz, and A.D. Tomlin. 1988. Effect of diet on the feeding and casting activity of *Lumbricus terrestris* and *L. rubellus* in laboratory culture. Soil Biol. Biochem. 20:233–237.

Smettem, K.R.J. 1992. The relation of earthworms to soil hydraulic properties. Soil Biol. Biochem. 24:1539–1543.

Smettem, K.R.J., and N. Collis-George. 1985a. Statistical characterization of soil biopores using a soil peel method. Geoderma 36:27–36.

Smettem, K.R.J., and N. Collis-George. 1985b. The influence of cylindrical macropores on steady-state infiltration in a soil under pasture. J. Hydrol. 52:107–114.

Smith, M.S., G.W. Thomas, R.E. White, and D. Ritonga. 1985. Transport of *Escherichia coli* through intact and disturbed soil columns. J. Environ. Qual. 14:87–91.

Steenhuis, T.S., W. Staubitz, M.S. Andreini, J. Surface, T.L. Richard, R. Paulsen, N.B. Pickering, J.R. Hagerman, and L.D. Geohring. 1990. Preferential movement of pesticides and tracers in agricultural soils. J. Irrig. Drain. Eng. 116:50–66.

Stehouwer, R.C., W.A. Dick, and S.J. Traina. 1993. Characteristics of earthworm burrow lining affecting atrazine sorption. J. Environ. Qual. 22:181–185.

Stehouwer, R.C., W.A. Dick, and S.J. Traina. 1994. Sorption and retention of herbicides in vertically oriented earthworm and artificial burrows. J. Environ. Qual. 23:286–292.

Stockdill, S.M.J. 1966. The effect of earthworms on pastures. Proc. N.Z. Ecol. Soc. 13: 68–75.

Teotia, S.P., F.L. Duley, and T.M. McCalla. 1950. Effect of stubble mulching on number and activity of earthworms. Nebraska Agric. Exp. Sta. Bull. No. 165. 20 pp.

Tisdall, J.M., and J.M. Oades. 1982. Organic matter and water stable aggregates in soils. J. Soil Sci. 33:141–163.

Tomlin, A.D., M.J. Shipitalo, W.M. Edwards, and R. Protz. 1995. Earthworms and their influence on soil structure and infiltration. pp. 159–183. In P.F. Hendrix (ed.). Earthworm Ecology and Biogeography in North America. Lewis Publishers, Boca Raton, FL.

Trojan, M.D., and D.R. Linden. 1992. Microrelief and rainfall effects on water and solute movement in earthworm burrows. Soil Sci. Soc. Am. J. 56:727–733.

Turner, R.R., and K.F. Steele. 1988. Cadmium and manganese sorption by soil macropore linings and fillings. Soil Sci. 145:79–86.

Tyler, D.D., and G.W. Thomas. 1981. Chloride movement in undisturbed soil columns. Soil Sci. Soc. Am. J. 45:459–461.

Urbánek, J., and F. Dolezal. 1992. Review of some case studies on the abundance and on the hydraulic efficiency of earthworm channels in Czechoslovak soils, with reference to the subsurface pipe drainage. Soil Biol. Biochem. 24:1563–1571.

Van Ommen, H.C., R. Dijksma, J.M.H. Hendrickx, L.W. Dekker, J. Hulshof, and M. Van den Heuvel. 1989. Experimental assessment of preferential flow paths in a field soil. J. Hydrol. 105:253–262.

Van Veen, J.A., and P.J. Kuikman. 1990. Soil structural aspects of decomposition of organic matter by micro-organisms. Biogeochemistry 11:213–233.

Watanabe, H., and S. Ruaysoongnern. 1984. Cast production by the Megascolecid earthworm *Pheretima* sp. in northeastern Thailand. Pedobiologia 26:37–44.

White, R.E. 1985. The influence of macropores on the transport of dissolved and suspended matter through soil. Adv. Soil Sci. 3:95–120.

Wildenschild, D., K.J. Jensen, K. Villholth, and T.J. Illangasekare. 1994. A laboratory analysis of the effect of macropores on solute transport. Ground Water 32:381–389.

Zachmann, J.E., D.R. Linden, and C.E. Clapp. 1987. Macroporous infiltration and redistribution as affected by earthworms, tillage and residue. Soil Sci. Soc. Am. J. 51:1580–1586.

Earthworm Interactions with Soil Organization

8

André Kretzschmar

INRA–Zoologie, Site Agroparc, 84914 Avignon Cedex 9 (France)

E arthworm activity and behavior and earthworm-originated structures, on one hand, and physical and biological soil properties and soil structure, on the other, result from non-independent interactions. In this chapter, examples of such interactions are given and used to show how the observation of interactions avoids the "chicken and egg" dispute; additionally, some technical measures are used to address the question of the spatial stability of the interactions.

EARTHWORMS AND SOIL ORGANIZATION: EFFECTS OF INTERACTION?

Earthworm-Originated Soil Porosity

Endogeic earthworms contribute to soil porosity by burrowing and ingesting soil. The former action creates large pore systems with complex structures that reflect the animal behavior and adaptations responding to the fluctuations of soil environmental conditions (Lamparsky 1987; Kretzschmar 1982, 1992). Soil ingestion leads to structures of smaller size, mainly related to casts, deposited either on the soil surface or within the soil profile, and also to cast aggregation properties. The microporosity of casts results from the content and evolution of bound or free organic compounds after casting (Blanchard 1992); cast pore properties spread to the soil matrix and contribute partially to the soil matrix porosity characteristics that interfere with macropores.

The two types of structures described below belong to the two main categories of soil pores: macropores (roughly defined as >to 0.5 mm) and matrix

1-884015-74-3/98/$0.00/$.50

porosity. Macropores are created either by physical processes (clay swelling, freezing, etc.) or biological processes (roots, mesofauna, earthworms, etc.). Matrix pores are considered to be the basic fabric that defines the soil as a porous medium.

The Expected Role of Earthworm-Originated Soil Structures

Macropores formed as earthworm burrows are expected to improve mass transfers in soil at the profile scale. The extent of this improvement is based on connectivity and tortuosity of the burrows themselves, on the one hand (Kretzschmar 1987; Joschko et al. 1989; Edwards et al. 1992), and connections between burrow walls and the matrix porosity at the vicinity of these macropores, on the other (Kretzschmar 1987; Babel and Kretzschmar 1994). Earthworm burrows are not the main source of soil macropores; a burrow system could range from 1 to 2% of the total porosity. The importance of earthworm burrow in mass transfer relies on two main facts.

First, because they are constructed roughly cylindrically, with lightly compacted walls and/or with at least several coatings of mucopolysaccharides (Kretzschmar 1985), earthworm burrows are consolidated structures; they stay open even when soil moisture is at higher levels (i.e., when the soil matrix porosity is saturated with water, as are also the macropores created by roots) and when clay swelling has closed down most of the large cracks. At this stage, air-filled porosity is at its lowest (Monnier 1992); the burrows might represent about 20% of air-filled porosity.

Second, in temperate climates, a noticeable proportion of the burrow systems made by earthworm populations shows strong anisotropic orientation marked by a vertical direction. Earthworm burrows are then regarded as preferential vertical paths for gravitic mass transfer (water and partial solutes) (Ehlers 1975; Shipitalo et al. 1990; Edwards et al. 1992; Smettem 1992).

Earthworm burrows are also expected to influence the spatial distribution of other living organisms, such as roots and microorganisms. Root distribution can be affected by the presence of burrows. The density of roots in the vicinity of pores (cracks and burrows) is not the same as farther away (Krebs et al. 1994); nevertheless, no evidence has shown experimentally that roots grew preferentially towards burrows or entered holes filled with earthworm cast (Hirth et al., in press). The distribution of microorganisms dependent on earthworm burrows is due partially to the organic carbon source transferred through the burrow system—mechanical transport of organic debris from the surface litter, mucus deposition along the burrow walls, infillings of old burrows with casts—and the distribution of microorganisms is also due to transfer of microorganisms through the gut transit and the dispersion of microorganisms with water flowing through the large burrows. Evidence of microorganism dispersion has been shown in experimental conditions (Reddell and Spain 1991; Stephens et al. 1994).

Is There a Specific Effect of Earthworm Burrows on the Soil Function or Structures?

The effect of earthworm burrows on soil structures and soil functions cannot be regarded as a simple causal relationship. When transport properties are measured in soils where earthworm burrows exist, it is questionable whether the burrow systems in these soils are so extensive because they provides suitable conditions for development of earthworm populations, or if earthworms develop a burrow system that improves mass transfer properties in this soil and then respond to soil environmental limitations. Observations of the development of earthworm burrow systems in new agricultural soils, previously deprived of any earthworm populations (for example, pastures at Manatuke Experimental Station, Gisborne, New Zealand, personal observations), show interesting strategies of soil colonization: it is not possible to find any earthworm burrows (mainly due to *Aporrectodea caliginosa*) below the depth reached by plant roots. On the other hand, the burrow systems observed in pasture in north France (Kretzschmar 1982) showed a high density of burrows at a depth where very few roots were present.

In these two cases, it is difficult to state whether the mechanism having the primary effect on soil structure is the effect of existing root system on the development of earthworm burrows or the contrary. The answer is almost certainly that roots and earthworm develop together and adapt their own strategies to suit the pedological environment.

When studying the possible effect of the presence of burrows opening at the soil surface on the pattern of surface cracks in experimental conditions (Chadoeuf et al. 1994), the best we could prove was that there is spatial interaction between the distribution of burrows and the distribution of cracks; none was assessed as the prime factor, and the conclusion was that the density of burrows in the vicinity of cracks (distance less than 2.5 cm) was greater than the density that would be predicted if the burrow had been distributed following a stationary Poisson pattern. It was not possible to decide whether the burrows opened closer to the cracks or if the cracks developed closer to the burrows (experimental conditions could be changed without solving the dilemma).

This "chicken and egg" type of question demonstrates the limit of searching for causal relationships between earthworm activities and soil physical and biological properties, where the former would cause the variations in the latter.

Soil-Structure-Dependent Effect of Burrows

In temperate zones, soils with "natural good structure," "high fertility," and "no earthworms" are known in North America and New Zealand (as well as tropical soils). It is then questionable how one should define an improvement of soil physical properties in those types of soil after earthworms are introduced, since the introduction of earthworms is often made at the same time as the introduction of new soil management. The improvement of pasture productivity in New Zealand following the monitored introduction of a north European species of earthworm brought remarkable and stable increases in dry matter production (Springett 1985) in pastures which were then managed (i.e., fertilized and grazed) in the same way as northern European pastures. Earthworm populations developing in the pastures of South Australia have the advantage of lime applications for pH control (Baker et al. 1992).

Experimental evidence can be given for the conditions under which earthworm activities in soil bring significant modifications in soil properties. When a soil's air-filled porosity is in the median values (i.e., 15% soil volume), the development of a burrow system does not bring significant improvement of gas diffusion compared to soil with 25% air-filled porosity; conversely, when air-filled porosity is down to about 10%, conditions at which gas diffusion is severely limited (Glinski and Stepniewski 1985), a single burrow can dramatically change the gas diffusion and its effect (Kretzschmar and Monestiez 1992; Kretzschmar and Ladd 1993). If the presence of earthworm burrows could be simulated as a short-circuit in the mass transfer pathways in the soil matrix, the efficiency of this short-circuit depends entirely on the connectivity associated with the burrows; furthermore, the connectivity must be looked at from different views. In the profile, the short-circuit could join two zones of equal permeability crossing a less permeable zone; at the scale of the soil matrix in the burrow vicinity, the connectivity of burrow volume with the pore space of the matrix through the wall will govern the extent of influence of burrows. These two types of interaction have been described as axial and radial effect in the case of gas diffusion (Arah and Ball 1994).

Earthworm Behavior Is Not Stable

Earthworm species change their behavior greatly when they are transferred from one environment to another, despite apparently similar environmental conditions. It seems that there is no specific behavior pattern at the level of species or even at the level of "ecological" group, as defined by Lee (1959, 1985), Bouché (1977), and Lavelle (1983). *Aporrectodea caligonosa*, a strictly endogeic species making short disconnected burrows in the Northern Hemisphere, makes long vertical burrows in the temperate soils of the Southern Hemisphere, a burrow shape reported by the previous authors to characterize "anecic" species. Similar observations can be made about *Octolasium cyaneum*, the burrow patterns of which have been observed as being very different in pre-alpine pastures in Switzerland and in forested hills north of Adelaide, South Australia (personal observations). *Lumbricus terrestris,* which is considered to be a species with a strong potential for development in orchard soils (Daniel 1992), is observed to be unable to spread in similar soil type and cultivation conditions (brown soil, orchards in organic farming system) in New Zealand (Springett, personal communication, and personal observations).

Interestingly, preliminary findings about the burrow patterns of earthworm species introduced into homogenized soil plots set in field conditions seem to show that *A. longa* and *A. caliginosa* exhibit the expected burrow patterns (i.e., similar to the burrow patterns they develop in their natural native environment (Springett, personal communication).

Although the apparent similarity of the soil conditions might be due mainly to the lack of suitable parameters to describe the functional difference, such a large variation in behavior depicts the ecological plasticity of the species that can be used to respond to local soil conditions. Moreover, the best examples of this behavioral plasticity are observed in these northern European species introduced into temperate America or into the temperate Southern Hemisphere. Introduced species have to face soil conditions that result from interactions between natural local soil evolution and introduced soil management. Such interactions could develop a soil organization that one might regard as deeply different compared to the soil conditions of places where the introduced species originated.

It is noteworthy to observe that, almost without exception, the northern European species perform well when introduced at the same time new agricultural management is developed, despite variations of soil type and climate. The question is whether the northern European earthworm species, which resist or adapt themselves to northern European soil management, are, at the same time, those species which have the best aptitude to colonize new areas.

A simple experiment is needed to confirm the ecological significance of behavioral plasticity of earthworms: for example, the intentional introduction of Southern Hemisphere earthworm species into northern European areas. What would be the population success of *Microscolex dubius*, well-established in the temperate area of Australia, if it was introduced into polders in the Netherlands?

INTERACTIONS BETWEEN BURROWS AND SOIL PROPERTIES

Interaction of Burrows with Other Soil Pores

There are a large variety of structures that develop at the interface of the soil matrix and earthworm burrows. Essentially, one can observe lined walls, cracked walls in empty burrows, and burrows filled partially or completely with casts. Graff (1970) described the lining of the burrow walls with organic material by *Lumbricus terrestris*. *Lumbricus terrestris* pulls leaves and large fragments of organic debris into its burrows; the black lining observed by Graff resulted from the decomposition of this organic material.

In many other species, a fine black layer is visible on the burrow walls. Reused burrows are lined by a layer of mucus from the accumulation of a mucus deposit about 10–15 µ thick each time an earthworm passes. Older burrows, which can be considered as abandoned, present cracks that connect burrows to porosity in the soil matrix (Kretzschmar 1985). Typical cracking patterns of compacted layers around the burrows have been observed for the burrows of *Megascolides australis* (Babel and Kretzschmar 1994). These different patterns govern the contribution of burrow systems to soil transfer, whether they are connected to the surface or not. The presence of macropores and their connections with the surrounding soil porosity create heterogeneous patterns of connectivity. It has been shown in simulated burrow systems that the mean length of the burrows plays a role in the transfer properties at the scale of the soil profile, while the average distance between burrow (governed by the burrow number) controls the mass transfer at the local scale of a given horizon (Kretzschmar 1988).

The patterns of distribution of cracks around earthworm burrows have been described by Krebs et al. (1994). It is nevertheless still difficult to quantify interactions between these two components of the soil pore systems.

Nevertheless, a similar interaction has been estimated in the case of the distribution of burrows open at the surface and the surface cracks during the drying phase, under experimental conditions (Chadoeuf et al. 1994). The density of surface open burrows at a distance of less than 2.5 cm from cracks is greater than one would expect if the distribution of burrows and cracks were independent. The possibility of observing such "attraction-like" interactions within the soil profile, between cracks and burrows, depends on the soil structural context, mainly on the presence of roots. More interestingly, the intensity of this interaction could summarize the history of the use of burrows both by earthworms and by water transfer.

Interaction Between Earthworm Burrows and Mass Transfer

The presence of high numbers of earthworms has been correlated with high soil hydraulic conductivity (Ehlers 1975); this observation has been confirmed many times with earthworms introduced into pastures or in differently cultivated plots (Springett et al. 1992), in experimental compacted columns (Joschko et al. 1992), and even in situations where earthworms are not expected. (Clothier and Vogeler [1994] report improvements in conductivity which range from 0.3 $\mu m.s^{-1}$ to 1.2 $\mu m.s^{-1}$ under disc permeameters with salt solution, due to earthworms being attracted to or repelled from the surface by salt solution.)

The contribution of macropores to hydraulic conductivity is also shown by theoretical considerations (Smettem 1992). Nevertheless, the effect of earthworm burrows depends on the type of connectivity they attain, within the burrow system itself or between the burrow system and the pore space. Francis et al. (1994) reported the differential effects of *A. caliginosa* and *O. cyaneum* in opening, respectively, top soil and sub-soil burrows. Despite the fact that the total porosity was the same in both cases, the effect of the latter was much greater (Ksat = 573 mm h^{-1} with *O. cyaneum* compared to 103 with no earthworms) than the effect of the former (Ksat = 729 mm h^{-1} with *A. caligonosa* compared to 439 with no earthworms). The gas diffusivity is improved in the presence of earthworm burrows, only when air-filled porosity is below a threshold (Kretzschmar and Monestiez 1992).

It is then inappropriate to attempt to measure the effect of burrows on mass transfer, because experiments tend to make this measurement in conditions where they are visible, or obvious; in essence, the absence of visible effects of burrows could be governed by opposite interactions: the burrow volume is totally connected to the matrix pores and the burrow volume is totally isolated from the matrix pores because of the impermeable walls.

The global contribution of burrows to mass transfer does not describe the way they interact with the soil structure; the effectiveness of short-circuits due to earthworm burrows is shown poorly by the increase of gas diffusion coefficient. This effectiveness is clearly pointed out when the evolution of tracer gas concentrations with time is compared to the theory of diffusion following the non-steady-state equation (= second Fick's law). In homogeneous soil cores, data fit perfectly with the theoretical diffusion calculations. When macropores were present in the cores, the "distance" between observed data and theory showed the effect of macropores. Diffusion in the presence of macropores did not follow the Fickian diffusion process anymore (unpublished data). Modeling and simulations of specific diffusion due to macropores, associated with basic diffusion due to the matrix, are not yet available.

Interactions Between Burrows and Other Biological Components

The interactions between roots and macropores, especially earthworm burrows, are easy to observe in soil profile; nevertheless, it is not so easy when an attempt is made to follow this interaction in experimental conditions (Hirth et al., in press). Observations on the soil profile have led to overestimations of the presence of roots in burrows, because, while roots in burrows are easy to see, almost the whole root system is concealed in the soil matrix. Statistical estimations of a spatial interaction between roots and fine cracks have been attempted on polished blocks of soil, i.e., in two dimensions (Krebs et al. 1994). There is a large variability of these estimations within the same horizon and for the same plant species; moreover, it is shown neatly that the interaction between roots and fine cracks is specific for each plant species, even when they are mixed in a pasture. A three-dimensional estimation of the probability of crossing between earthworm burrow systems and root systems is not available. Burrows have been said to pave the way for roots; however it is more realistic to expect that roots have a scouting function in exploring soil depth and that earthworms follow the way and stabilize and develop the root-originated structures. The actual soil organization observed in an aged soil structure depicts an equilibrium that is reached through roots' and earthworms' joint development, both interacting with the other soil conditions.

Interactions between burrow and microbial activity have also been described either by counting the microbial biomass in the vicinity of burrow walls (Loquet et al. 1977) or by showing the CO_2 release associated with the presence of burrows. The chemical and organic properties of burrow walls are responsible for the development of microbial activities together with the interactions of burrows with mass transfer between the soil surface and soil matrix through burrow systems. Water, solutes, and gas content or concentration gradients are higher in the macropores than in the soil matrix, and the dynamics of microbial activities are closely related to the dynamics of these gradients.

The observed effect of earthworms on CO_2 release is dependent on the interaction of macropores with the surrounding porosity (Kretzschmar and Ladd 1993). CO_2 release results from the combined effect of macropores on gas diffusion due to their connection to the matrix pore and to the surface, and the enrichment of organic material along the burrow walls.

The microbial population distribution interacts with the burrow system by way of active and passive transport. Microorganisms are washed down and along the burrows walls when water flows intensively in vertical burrows; they are also transported into the gut of earthworms and deposited at the place where earthworms cast.

OBSERVATION OF SOIL INTERACTIONS INVOLVING EARTHWORMS: METHODOLOGICAL CONSIDERATIONS

From Two to Three Dimensions

Most of the distribution data on earthworm burrows are available in two dimensions (from the pioneer work of Ehlers [1975] to the latest CAT scan observations). As connectivity and tortuosity have been reported to be the primary characteristics of the way burrows will interact with mass transfer properties, three-dimensional reconstruction is a necessary step to studying burrow systems. Several attempts to do this have been made and new developments use X-ray CAT scan (see review in Daniel and Kretzschmar). Although three-dimensional reconstruction views the burrow system structure for the first time, it also raises two essential issues:

- What can be said about the similarity of two burrow system patterns? What are the pattern characteristics which describe the burrow system at a given site, and which characteristics can be associated with soil physical properties as mass transfer or with biological activities as root distribution?
- The three-dimensional reconstruction of burrow systems does not give evidence of the distribution in three-dimensional connectivity of this system with the soil matrix. The spatial interaction between biological components (root, earthworms, microbes...) requires that any of these components' distribution be described in three dimensions; as they develop at different scales, description methods should be compatible.

Topology and Functional Problems When Comparing Burrow Patterns

Topological and stereological analyses (Kretzschmar 1988) seem to be insufficient to describe the specificity of burrow system patterns. The simplest case has been described for *Lumbricus* species (Lamparsky et al. 1987) where individual earthworms lived in a single burrow and developed few branches around it. The necessity to describe the whole burrow is the major difficulty to be faced in this case. It has been shown that complex and continuous burrow patterns could be developed by single individual *Megascolides australis* (Kretzschmar and Aries 1992).

When the burrow system results from the activity of a monospecific population (without the possibility of identifying individual earthworm territory) or from multispecific earthworm populations where even the territory and pattern specificity of burrows do not make it possible to distinguish each species, comparison of burrow system pattern requires that the topological and functional characteristics would rely not only on geometrical distribution but also take into account the behavior that governs such patterns. Behavioral studies on earthworm movements and related functions in natural conditions are, currently, extremely rare and should be one of the priorities for the development of understanding the development of earthworm populations in soils.

Scale Problems

As biological organisms interact with each other and with soil physical properties (mainly soil pore systems), it is necessary to describe the spatial distribution of each of them and to establish if their specific distributions can be considered independently. Functional links between living organisms and pore systems occur at any scale to such an extent that it is not possible not to consider, at any place in the soil profile, the whole range of scales at which these interactions take place, from centimeters to microns. Observation techniques are unable to deal with such a range; it is then necessary to develop a technical series where, on the same sample, soil organization can be observed in such a way that the different scale levels can be related to each other. It is possible to take large undisturbed soil cores (Ø ≈ 150–200 mm) and describe them with a CAT scanner with a resolution of 1 mm (Joschko et al. 1991; Daniel and Kretzschmar, in review). The same core could be impregnated and cut into 2-mm slices from which X-ray images are taken with a resolution of 500 to 300 µm. Finally, the faces of these slices, once polished, could be observed under a microscope at a resolution of 50 to 30 µm (Vogel and Kretzschmar 1996). At any scale, specific models are to be designed for the analysis of the pore system properties and their interactions with distributions of living organisms and activities (Monestiez et al. 1993; Krebs et al. 1994; Vogel and Kretzschmar 1996).

CONCLUSIONS

Interactions Between Earthworms and Soil Formation

As biological functions and physical properties interact with the distribution and the seasonal variations in burrow distributions, we see burrows as a part of the development of soil organization, which is a characteristic of soils under given climatic, relief, and parent-rock conditions (Dokuchaev 1883). Dokuchaev's definition of soil genesis fixed the context of soil typology. The scientific literature has been generous in books and articles on soil-forming factors without any definite improvements of Dokuchaev's statement. From the interactions of factors soil "organization" is derived as a concept for soil geometrical, functional, and topological properties.

A recent paper from Babel et al. (1995) proposed an interesting definition of soil fabrics that is based on soil morphological features. Soils are described by three characteristics: place, pathways, and boundaries. These characteristics are attached to each object or function and are valid on any scale. It is probable that these characteristics would fit the description of interactions we addressed here perfectly. Soil-forming factors would be replaced by "soil-forming interactions," for which places, pathways, and boundaries would be attached to geometrical, functional, and topological properties of these interactions respectively.

Monitoring Earthworm Introductions

The rationale of intentional introduction of earthworms is based on the assumption of a beneficial effect of earthworms on soil fertility. However, transplanted species cannot be expected to behave as they did in their original habitat. Earthworm activities should be regarded as "soil organization dependent" in the same way that one describes the "density dependence" of predator-prey relationships. In other words, these activities could not be understood without being able to identify the specific interactions which take place in a given location (native habitat or introduction area).

The question of soil organization reactions to earthworm introduction should be regarded in terms of dynamics equilibrium: Are introduced earthworms able to change the characteristics of the actual organization of soils where they are introduced to such an extent that they bring a new equilibrium, i.e., a new state of organization involving and relying on a new set of interactions? The success of earthworm introductions (when both expected soil properties are obtained and introduced earthworm populations reach the expected and stable level of density) results from the conflict, or the synergy, of both soil and earthworm behavior plasticity.

REFERENCES CITED

Arah, J.R.M., and B.C. Ball. 1994. A functional model of soil porosity used to interpret measurements of gas diffusion. Eur. J. Soil Sci., 45, 135–144.

Babel, U., and A. Kretzschmar. 1994. Micromorphological observations of casts and burrow walls of the Gippsland giant earthworm (*Megascolides australis* McCoy 1878). 9th International Working Meeting on Soil Micromorphology, Townsville (AUS), 1992/07.

In Soil Micromorphology: Studies in Management and Genesis (A.J. Ringrose-Voase and G.S. Humphreys, eds.). Elsevier, Amsterdam, 451–457.

Babel, U., H. Vogel, M. Krebs, G. Leithold, and C. Hemmann. 1995. Morphological investigations on genesis and functions of soil fabric—places, pathways, boundaries. In Soil Structure. Its Development and Function (K.H. Hartge and B.A. Stewart, eds.). Adv. Soil Sci. Lewis Publishers, Boca Raton, FL, 11–30.

Baker, G., J. Buckerfield., R. Grey-Gardner, R. Merry, and B. Doube. 1992. The abundance and diversity of earthworm in pasture soils in the Fleurie Peninsula, South Australia. 4th International Symposium on Earthworm Ecology (A. Kretzschmar, ed.). Soil Biology and Biochemistry 24, 12, 1539–1544.

Blanchard, E. 1992. Restoration by earthworms (Megascolecidae) of the macroaggregate structure of a destructured savanna soil under field conditions. 4th International Symposium on Earthworm Ecology (A. Kretzschmar, ed.). Soil Biology and Biochemistry 24, 12, 1587–1594.

Bouché, M. 1977. Statrégies lombriciennes. In Soil Organisms as Components of Ecosystems (U. Lohm and T. Persson, eds.). Ecological Bulletin 25, 122–132.

Chadoeuf, J., A. Kretzschmar, M. Goulard, and K.R.J. Smettem. 1994. Description of the spatial interaction between earthworms burrows and cracks at the soil surface. 9th International Working Meeting on Soil Micromorphology, Townsville (AUS), 1992/07. In Soil Micromorphology: Studies in Management and Genesis (A.J. Ringrose-Voase and G.S. Humphreys, eds.). Elsevier, Amsterdam, 521–530.

Clothier, B., and I. Vogeler. 1994. Soil physics under pressure (still a can of worms!). WISPAS, Hortresearch 58, 4.

Daniel, O. 1992. Population dynamics of *Lumbricus terrestris* L. (Oligochaeta : Lumbricidae) in a meadow. 4th International Symposium on Earthworm Ecology (A. Kretzschmar, ed.). Soil Biology and Biochemistry 24, 12, 1425–1431.

Daniel, O., and A. Kretzschmar. (in review). Application of CAT-scanning to investigate earthworm-related soil macropores in a pre-alpine meadow.

Dokuchaev, V.V. 1883. Russian Chernozem. St Petersburg.

Edwards, W.M., M.J. Shipiltalo, S.J. Traina, C.A. Edwards, and L.B. Owens. 1992. Role of *Lumbricus terrestris* (L.) burrows on quality of infiltrating water. 4th International Symposium on Earthworm Ecology (A. Kretzschmar, ed.). Soil Biology and Biochemistry 24, 12, 1555–1562.

Ehlers, W. 1975. Observations on earthworm channels and infiltration on tilled and untilled loess soils. Soil Science 119, 242–249.

Francis, G., T. Fraser, and W. Jian. 1994. The worms that turned.... WISPAS, Hortresearch 58, 3–4.

Glinski, J., and W. Stepniewski. 1985. Soil Aeration and Its Role for Plants. CRC Press, Boca Raton, FL, 229.

Graff, O. 1970. Effect of different mulching materials on the nutrient content of earthworm tunnels in the subsoil. Pedobiologia 10, 305–319.

Hirth, J.R., B.M. McKenzie, and J.M. Tisdall. (in press). Do ryegrass roots grow to biopores filled with earthworm casts? 5th International Symposium on Earthworm Ecology (C.A. Edwards, ed.). Soil Biology and Biochemistry.

Joschko, M., H. Diestel, and O. Larink. 1989. Assessment of earthworm burrowing efficiency in compacted soil with a combination of morphological and soil physical measurements. Biology and Fertility of Soils 8, 191–196.

Joschko, M., O. Graff, P.C. Müller, K. Kotzke, P. Linder, D.P. Pretschner, and O. Larink. 1991. A non-destructive method for the morphological assessment of earthworm burrow systems in three dimensions by X-ray computed tomography. Biol. Fert. Soils 11, 88–92.

Joschko, M., W. Söchtig, and O. Laring. 1992. Functional relationships between earthworm burrows and soil water movement in column experiments. 4th International Symposium on Earthworm Ecology (A. Kretzschmar, ed.). Soil Biology and Biochemistry 24, 12, 1545–1548.

Krebs, M., A. Kretzschmar, U. Babel, J. Chadoeuf, and M. Goulard. 1994. Investigations on distribution patterns in soil: basic and relative distributions of roots, channels and cracks. 9th International Working Meeting on Soil Micromorphology, Townsville (AUS), 1992/ 07. In Soil Micromorphology: Studies in Management and Genesis (A.J. Ringrose-Voase and G.S. Humphreys, eds.). Elsevier, Amsterdam, 437–449.

Kretzschmar, A. 1982. Description des galeries de vers de terre et variations saisonnières des réseaux (observations en conditions naturelles). Revue d'Écologie et de Biologie du Sol 19, 579–591.

Kretzschmar, A. 1987. Caractéristiques micromorphologiques de l'activité des lombriciens. In 7th International Workshop on Soil Micromorphology (N. Fedorov, ed.). AFES, Paris, 325–330.

Kretzschmar, A. 1988. Structural parameters and functional patterns of simulated earthworm burrow systems. Biology and Fertility of Soils 6, 252–261.

Kretzschmar, A., and F. Aries. 1992. Analysis of the structure of the burrow system of the giant Gippsland earthworm *Megascolides australis,* McCoy (1878) using 3D-images. Soil Biology and Biochemistry 24, 12, 1583–1586.

Kretzschmar, A., and J.N. Ladd. 1993. Decomposition of 14C-labelled plant material in soil: the influence of substrate location, soil compaction and earthworm number. Soil Biology and Biochemistry 25, 6, 803–809

Kretzschmar, A., and P. Monestiez. 1992. Physical control of soil biological properties due to endogeic earthworm behaviours. 4th International Symposium on Earthworm Ecology (A. Kretzschmar, ed.). Soil Biology and Biochemistry 24, 12, 1609–1614.

Lamparsky F., A. Kobel-Lamparsky, and R. Kaffenberger. 1987. The burrow of *Lumbricus badensis* and *Lumbricus polyphemus.* In On earthworms (A.M. Bonvicini and P. Omodeo, eds.). Mucchi, Modena, 131–140.

Lavelle, P., 1983. The structure of earthworm communities. In Earthworm Ecology (J.E. Satchell, ed.). Chapmann & Hall, London, 449–466.

Lee, K.E. 1959. The earthworm fauna of New Zealand. NZ Dept. Sci. Industr. Res. Bull., 130.

Lee, K.E. 1985. Earthworms. Their Ecology and Relationships with Soils and Land Uses. Academic Press, Sydney.

Loquet, M., T. Bhatnagar, M. Bouché, and J. Rouelle. 1977. Essai d'estimation de l'influence écologique des lombriciens sur les micro-organismes. Pedologia 17, 400–417.

Monestiez, P., A. Kretzschmar, and J. Chadoeuf. 1993. Modeling natural burrow systems in soil by fibre process: Monte-Carlo test on independence of fibre characteristics. Acta Stereologica (YUG) 12, 2, 237–242

Monnier, G., 1992. L'activité des vers de terre du point de vue de la physique du sol. 4th International Symposium on Earthworm Ecology (A. Kretzschmar, ed.). Soil Biology and Biochemistry 24, 12, 1197–1200.

Reddell, P.R., and A.V. Spain. 1991. Earthworms as vectors of viable propagules of mycorrhizal fungi. Soil Biology and Biochemistry 23, 767–774.

Shipitalo M.J., W.M. Edwards, W.A. Dick, and L.B. Owens. 1990. Initial storm effects on macropore transport of surface-applied chemicals in no-till soil. Soil Sci. Soc. Am. J. 54, 1530–1536.

Smettem, K.R.J. 1992. The relation of earthworms to soil hydraulic properties. 4th International Symposium on Earthworm Ecology (A. Kretzschmar, ed.). Soil Biology and Biochemistry 24, 12, 1539–1544.

Springett, J.A. 1985. Effect of introducing *Allobophora longa* (Ude) on root distribution and some soil properties in New Zealand pastures. In Ecological Interactions in Soils: Plants, Microbes and Animals (A.H. Fitter et al., eds.). Blackwell, Oxford, 399–405.

Springett, J.A., R.A.J. Gray, and J.B. Reid. 1992. Effect of introducing earthworms into horticultural land previously denuded of earthworms. 4th International Symposium on Earthworm Ecology (A. Kretzschmar, ed.). Soil Biology and Biochemistry 24, 12, 1615–1622.

Stephens, P.M., C.W. Davoren, B.M. Doube, and M.H. Ryder. 1994. Ability of the earthworm *Aporrectodea rosea* and *Aporrectodea trapezoides* to reduce take-all under greenhouse and field conditions. Soil Biology and Biochemistry 26, 1291–1297.

Vogel, H., and A. Kretzschmar. 1996. Topological characterisation of pore space in soil—sample preparation and digital image processing. Geoderma 73, 23–38.

Interactions of Earthworms with Microorganisms, Invertebrates, and Plants

V

Life in a Complex Community: Functional Interactions Between Earthworms, Organic Matter, Microorganisms, and Plants

9

Bernard M. Doube[1] and George G. Brown[2]

[1]CSIRO Division of Soils and the CRC for Soil and Land Management, Glen Osmond, Australia; [2]Instituto de Ecologia, Xalapa, Mexico

From the moment a seed germinates, it comes into contact with soil micro organisms and the two-way plant–microbe interactions that follow have profound effects on the growth and development of both the plant and the soil microbial communities. These processes can be modified strongly by interactions with soil micro-, meso-, and macrofauna and may, over extended periods of time, significantly affect the floral and faunal diversity both above and below ground (Brown 1995), as well as the productivity of the ecosystem in which they occur. The intensity of the spatial and functional interactions in subterranean food webs (Anderson 1988) (depicted in Figure 1) is influenced strongly by the daily, seasonal, and annual patterns of rainfall and temperature. These interactions occur in a number of key biological locations which are foci of intense microbial activity associated with the decomposition of organic residues. These include the rhizosphere (roots), the detritusphere (surface detritus), the drilosphere (earthworms), and the termitosphere (termites) (Lavelle et al. 1992; Beare et al. 1995).

The spatial scales at which soil organisms act are determined mainly by their size and mode of operation. Swift et al. (1979) recognized three spatial scales

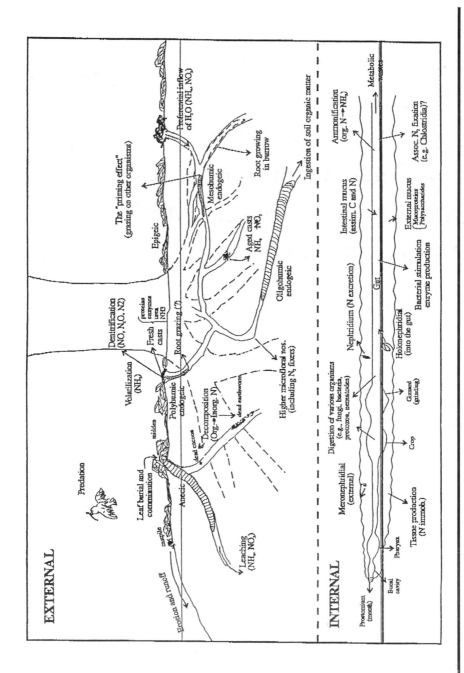

Figure 1. Schematic representation of the functional relationships between earthworms and their internal and external environment. (Drawing by G.G. Brown.)

based on animal size: micro, meso, and macro. At the microscale there are algae and bacteria (which are unable to move large distances except if carried by water or larger soil organisms) and fungi (in which hyphal growth provides the capacity to colonize new soil); these three are crucial to primary decomposition, nutrient cycling processes, soil aggregation, and root health.

Meanwhile, still at a microscale but increasing in size and spatial influence, the microfood web comprises microfauna, such as nematodes, protozoa, rotifers, and other organisms that feed primarily on the microflora and are important in regulating nutrient cycling, particularly in the rhizosphere (e.g., Clarholm 1985; Ingham et al. 1985).

At the mesoscale there are larger organisms such as enchytraeids and microarthropods that feed on litter, microflora, and microfauna, and are important in accelerating nutrient cycling and small-scale dispersal of microorganisms (Hassal et al. 1987).

Finally at the macroscale, there are larger bodied organisms such as earthworms, termites, macroarthropods, and ants—the ecosystem engineers (Lavelle 1994), which disperse microorganisms, produce important physical structures (mounds, burrows, casts, pellets) that may occupy or modify a great portion of the soil volume (and the microbial communities found therein), and therefore regulate many soil processes.

Not only must these interactions be observed at different scales, but also in many directions. Typically, earthworm interaction studies have focused on one-way interactions, commonly disregarding the possibility of multiple interactions. For instance, the one-way effects of earthworms on plant growth have been investigated intensively (Lee 1985; Haimi et al. 1992; Spain et al. 1992), but there may be other interactions (e.g., between earthworms and root pathogens or beneficial soil microorganisms [Doube et al. 1994a,b]) which also affect plant growth. Further, the corresponding effects of plants and microbial processes on earthworms are rarely considered in the same studies.

In this review we are concerned primarily with the interactions amongst the soil biota and their effects on plants, in temperate and subtropical agricultural systems, with emphasis on cropped soils. We shall consider the interactions between earthworms, soil microorganisms (bacteria, fungi, algae, and protozoa), and plants (roots, seeds, and aboveground parts), while examining them at three different spatial scales: micro (gut, burrows, and casts), meso (whole soil), and macro (a field), although there are few data on some topics, particularly interactions at larger scales, and comparative data concerning different life strategies of earthworms. At each scale we shall address the two-way interactions between earthworms and other organisms or processes and attempt to reach some conclusions about the functional significance of these interactions.

Our theme is that the composition and activity of the microbial communities which are responsible for the decomposition of organic substrates in soil can be significantly affected by the activity of the soil macrofauna, especially earthworms, which can therefore play a vital role in regulating the microbial processes that maintain the biological health of soils.

ORGANIC MATTER AND MICROBIAL COMMUNITIES

In this section, we consider the amount and types of organic materials which enter soil systems and their distribution, and the succession of microorganisms that are responsible for their decomposition. These inputs and microbial processes are the basis of the soil food webs which support and are modified by earthworms (Lavelle et al. 1993; Brown 1995; Killham 1994).

Annual Organic Inputs and Decomposition Processes

Organic residues that enter soil are derived primarily from dead animals and three plant sources: surface plant residues (which may be incorporated by tillage or biotic processes), dead roots and sloughed cells, and exudates leaked into the rhizosphere from living roots (Lynch and Whipps 1990). The succession of microorganisms associated with the decomposition of each of these different types of residue is similar in many respects, but also has unique features which are dependent upon their origin (e.g., leaf tissue is buried with phyloplane species) and composition (e.g., all root exudates leaked into the rhizosphere are readily assimilable).

Annual inputs of surface organic residues in cropping systems can be as high as 40 t ha^{-1} (e.g., in sugar cane), although the mass of surface residues is commonly much less than that amount (e.g., ca. 2–6 tons ha^{-1} in temperate cereal production). In agricultural systems, aboveground and subsurface plant residue inputs are commonly of a similar order of magnitude with between 35% and 80% of the net photosynthate being transferred to the roots of plants and entering the soil as roots or root exudates (Swartz et al. 1994). During the first year in the soil, between 60% and 75% of the introduced carbon is respired and so lost to the pool of soil organic matter (Jenkinson and Ladd 1981), with the remainder persisting in organic-soil associations and living tissue. The living tissue, making up the soil food web, comprises autotrophic algae and a vast array of heterotrophic primary and secondary decomposers.

The primary decomposers (largely bacteria, 30–90% by weight, and fungi, 5–70% by weight) are grazed by a variety of secondary decomposers (e.g., protozoans and earthworms which make up 0.6–6.0% and 0–14% respectively of the total biomass) (Brussaard et al. 1990). The microbial biomass (bacteria, fungi, algae, rotifers, protozoa) in soil in temperate and subtropical regions occupies <1% of the surface soil volume and is commonly in the order of 0.5–3 tonnes biomass ha^{-1}, while that of the macrofauna is commonly much lower (Brussaard et al. 1990; Coleman et al. 1994) although higher values have been recorded. For example, Doube et al. (1994c) measured 1.15 t ha^{-1} biomass of the earthworm *A. trapezoides* in soil under a canola crop. The amount of carbon in the soil biota comprises only a few percent (<0.5–3.0%) of the total organic carbon in soil (Haines and Uren 1990; Gupta 1994; Sparling et al. 1994). The remaining organic carbon is bound in non-living associations in soil.

The microbial agents responsible for decomposition of organic residues vary with region, location, and management practice. For example, at Lovinkhoeve in the Netherlands, Brussaard et al. (1990) found that bacteria constituted by far the greatest portion of the microbial biomass (93–95%), with fungi representing only about 5%. Similarly, at Horseshoe Bend in Georgia, USA, Hendrix et al. (1986, 1987) found that bacteria predominated (60–76% biomass), with fungi making up only 17–22% of the microbial biomass. In contrast, Andren et al. (1988, 1990) found that at Kjetteslinge, Sweden, fungi dominated in a barley soil (64–69% of microbial biomass) and bacteria made up only about 30% of the biomass. In forest soil in Canada, bacterial:fungal ratios were 0.1–0.2 in the surface layers of soil (Scheu and Parkinson 1994).

In the surface soils (where some species of earthworms are active) in agroecosystems, both bacteria and fungi appear to be more abundant under reduced tillage than under conventional cultivation (Hendrix et al. 1986; Brussaard et al. 1990; Coleman et al. 1994), but no-tillage management appears to increase the importance of fungi relative to bacteria as primary decomposers, and hence the resource base for the food web. The corresponding consequence is that the fungal-consuming nematodes and earthworms are also more abundant (Coleman et al. 1994). These latter increases in biomass appear to be a response to the increases in the biomass of specific resource base (e.g., fungi), but the degree to which the composition of the microbial community is influenced by the corresponding increase in predatory organisms (e.g., earthworms) is not known.

Vertical Carbon Gradients, Patchiness, and Quality of Residues in Soil

There are strong vertical gradients in the concentrations of organic matter and microbial biomass in the upper soil layers. These gradients are strongest in the absence of tillage, which redistributes organic residues through the soil profile.

Some species of earthworms bury surface plant residues and are more common in direct drilled (DD) or no-till (NT) fields than in conventionally cultivated (CC) fields (Lee 1985). Despite this, soil carbon gradients are commonly, but not always (e.g., Brussaard et al. 1990), steeper in DD/NT than in CC cereal fields (Hendrix et al. 1986; Haines and Uren 1990), suggesting that tillage is more effective than are biological processes in redistributing surface residues through soil.

The patchiness of the distribution of the organic matter residues through the topsoil varies with the spatial scale that is examined (Robertson 1994). Patchiness is extremely high at a small spatial scale (e.g., that of a root, a fragment of buried organic matter, or an earthworm cast) but decreases as the spatial scale increases and the microsite differences become integrated into a relatively homogeneous pattern of organic matter distribution, e.g., at the paddock scale. The degree to which earthworm activity alters this pattern is understood poorly, but clearly fresh earthworm casts are foci of new, high microbial activity.

The quality of organic inputs into soil, which vary with the type of vegetation and management practices, has an important bearing on the composition and functioning of microbial communities. For example, the leaves and stalks of cereal crops contain large amounts of cellulose, hemicellulose, and lignin and have high C:N ratios, whereas in the rhizosphere the inputs from roots are soluble carbohydrates and amino acids with few recalcitrant residues (Bowen and Harper 1989; Moody 1993; Lynch and Whipps 1990).

Succession of Microorganisms During the Decomposition Processes

There is a clear succession of microorganisms associated with the decomposition of fragments of organic residue in litter and soil (Ponge 1991; Moody 1993; Robinson et al. 1993) and in the rhizosphere (Bowen and Rovira 1976; Rovira 1978; Gilbert et al. 1993; Swartz et al. 1994). The species composition of the microbial communities is determined by the nature of the substrate and the colonists (which include phylloplane species i.e., those introduced to soil with plant residues) and soil residents found near the organic residue.

The initial colonists of decomposing organic residues (e.g., cereal straw) are microbial species which exploit soluble organic compounds (carbohydrates, organic acids, amino acids) and are dominated by fungi such as *Mucor, Pythium,* and *Penicillium* (Harper and Lynch 1985; Bowen and Harper 1989; Moody 1993, 1995) and bacteria such as *Pseudomonas*. The second successional phase in the decomposition of organic residues is dominated by fungi such as *Trichoderma, Fusarium,* and *Chaetomium* and bacteria such as *Bacillus,* which have the capacity to decompose cellulose and hemicellulose (Garnett 1981; Moody 1993), although much still remains undecomposed at the end of this phase. The third phase of decomposition is associated with the slow metabolism of recalcitrant organic residues with high lignin or polyphenol contents. Fungi such as white rot fungi (Lavelle et al. 1993) and basidiomycetes commonly dominate this phase of the successional process, although cellulolytic fungi which can decompose delignified polysaccharides (e.g., *Fusarium* and *Trichoderma* spp.) may also occur at this stage (Bowen 1990; Bowen and Harper 1990; Moody 1993).

This flush of primary decomposers induces corresponding increases in the abundance of secondary decomposers (protozoa, bacterivorous and fungivorous nematodes) (Anderson 1993; Zwart et al. 1994). In the rhizosphere, similar biological processes occur in response to root exudation and sloughed dead root cells (Zwart et al. 1994). Rhizosphere populations of bacteria and protozoans may be many times higher than in bulk soil but fungi often show a proportionately smaller increase, or no increase, in relation to bulk soil (Newman 1985; Gilbert et al. 1993; Zwart et al. 1994; Gupta 1994).

Feeding Behavior of Earthworms

Three ecological strategies for earthworms have been recognized (Lee 1985; Lavelle et al. 1993). Epigeic species are litter-dwelling, active primarily in the detritusphere, feeding on fresh organic materials and important in comminution of litter and its decomposition. Endogeic species, which live in the soil (from the top few cm down to >2-m depths) and consume large quantities of soil and organic residues and some surface litter, are responsible for pronounced changes in the soil physical structure. Anecic species live in all strata of soil, normally in permanent vertical burrows which open to the soil surface. Here they feed on and bury surface litter and hence are important in modifying soil gaseous and water regimes (Lavelle et al. 1989; Edwards et al. 1990). Obviously the consequences of the interactions between earthworms and microbial communities vary substantially with the ecological category to which the earthworms belong.

INTERACTIONS BETWEEN EARTHWORMS AND MICROBIAL COMMUNITIES

Here we examine the interactions between earthworms and microbial communities at three spatial scales. At a microscale (that of the burrow lining or casts: the drilosphere), we examine the food preferences of earthworms, the fate of microorganisms in the intestine of earthworms, and the chemical and biological composition of casts and successional processes within them. At a mesoscale, which integrates the drilosphere with the surrounding soil, we consider the ways in which earthworm activity influences whole soil characteristics and functions such as the distribution of microorganisms, soil respiration, microbial biomass, bacterial:fungal ratios, and the way these effects alter soil fertility and the incidence and severity of root diseases. These can be analyzed using microcosms or in small-scale field trials.

At a macroscale (e.g., that of a field), few data are available, but earthworm-induced changes in microbial function have the potential to influence broad-scale processes such as soil structure (affecting water infiltration and erosion), microbial biodiversity, patterns of plant abundance, soil productivity, and crop yield. Conversely, at the latter two spatial scales, the composition of the microbial community has the capacity to affect the distribution and abundance of earthworm communities.

The Drilosphere: Microscale Interactions

The soil volume influenced directly or indirectly by earthworm activities has been termed the drilosphere by Lavelle (1988) and includes the gut of the earthworm (internal processes), burrows, and casts (external processes).

Food Preferences and Dietary Requirements

Many species of earthworms consume a mixture of soil and organic matter. For example, Doube et al. (1995) showed that species from all functional groups (the epigeic *Lumbricus rubellus*, the endogeic *Aporrectodea caliginosa*, and the anecic species *Lumbricus terrestris* and *Aporrectodea longa*) preferred a mixture of soil and organic matter over pure organic matter. Further, the observation that levels of organic carbon in the casts were higher than those of the average bulk soil in which the earthworms had been living (Figure 2) indicates that earthworms feed selectively on patches of soil which are relatively rich in organic matter (Lee 1985; Mulongoy and Berodet 1989; Zhang and Schraeder 1993; Doube et al. 1994d). Judas (1992) confirmed this by direct observation of earthworm gut contents. However, most earthworms have minimal capacity to digest organic residues and obtain nutrition by digestion of the microorganisms which are associated with ingested organic matter (Edwards and Fletcher 1988; Brown 1995; Lavelle et al. 1994).

 Fungi have been shown to be an important source of food for many earthworms (Dash et al. 1979, 1986; Edwards and Fletcher 1988), and it is possible

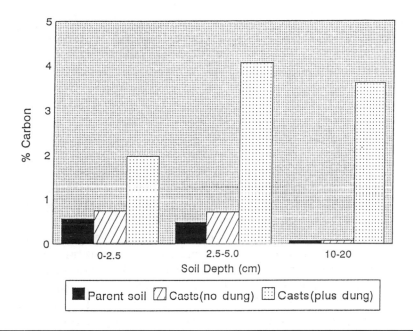

Figure 2. Organic carbon levels in parent soil from three sampling depths and in the casts of *A. trapezoides* maintained in those soils in the presence and absence of added sheep dung. The sandy soil was taken from three depths (0–5 cm, 5.0–10.0 cm, and 20–30 cm) in a field near Monato, South Australia (from Doube et al. 1994d).

that dietary reliance on fungi may be particularly strong for epigeic and anecic earthworm species that feed on litter and other materials which are extensively colonized by fungi. More work, especially on endogeic species, is required.

During passage through the earthworm gut, most fungal hyphae (except those protected inside root fragments [Reddell and Spain 1991a]) are digested preferentially, whereas many (but not all) types of fungal spores pass through unharmed. This has important consequences for soil resilience and microbial processes in soil. Reddell and Spain (1991a,b) demonstrated that spores of an actinomycete, *Frankia* sp., and spores of >20 mycorrhizal fungal species/groups remained intact after passage through the gut of *Pontoscolex corethrurus,* and most remained viable. Morgan (1988) studied the food value (for the epigeic *Eisenia fetida*) of pure cultures of a range of fungi. Earthworms gained or maintained weight when fed six of the eight fungi tested, and died when fed the other two. Several other species of fungi (primarily toxin- or antibiotic-producing fungi such as *Aspergillus* spp., *Fusarium* spp., and *Penicillium* spp.) appear to be detrimental to earthworms (Edwards and Fletcher 1988; Morgan 1988).

Fungal hyphae may be the preferred fungal food source of some earthworms. For example, Cooke and Luxton (1980) showed that *L. terrestris* fed preferentially on cellulose discs inoculated with two fungal species (*Mucor* spp. and *Penicillium* spp.) but did not recognize the presence of a bacterium (*P. fluorescens*). Moody (1993, 1995) studied the feeding behavior of two earthworm species (*L. terrestris* and *A. longa*) in relation to six species of saprophytic fungi that decompose cereal straw. For both earthworm species, the cellulolytic fungal species and those which consumed soluble carbohydrate (e.g., *Fusarium* and *Trichoderma*) were eaten in preference to lignolytic fungal species (e.g., basidiomycetes) that appeared later in the succession of microbial decomposers. Further, she examined survival of spores of these fungi during passage through the earthworm intestine and found that no viable spores of one species (*Fusarium lateritium*) survived passage through the gut of either earthworm species, while spores of another species (*Mucor hiemalis*) were more severely affected by passage through the gut of *L. terrestris* than through that of *A. longa* (10% and 28% survival respectively). Survival of spores of yet another fungal species (*Chaetomium globosum*) was unaffected by passage though guts of either earthworm species.

Spores of other species, such as *Ulocladium botrytis,* appear to have low (fungistasis) germination rates in earthworm casts (Striganova et al. 1989a), while still others (e.g., *Pithomyces chartarum*) do not germinate at all (fungicidal effect) (Keogh and Christensen 1976) after passage through earthworm guts. Fungal digestion in the gut appears to show a gradient in which most of the fungi are digested in the anterior and middle gut regions, with little digestion occurring in the hindgut (Gonzalez 1990; Tiwari et al. 1990). A similar pattern of digestion on passage through the gut has been observed with protozoa (Piearce and Phillips 1980).

Some species of free-living soil protozoa may be important dietary elements for some earthworm species. For example, *E. fetida* was able to grow to maturity in sterilized soil recolonized by soil bacteria and fungi only after the addition of protozoa (Miles 1962). Flack and Hartenstein (1984) recorded large weight gains in earthworms after adding protozoa to their food. Bonkowski and Schaefer (in press) showed that the endogeic earthworm *A. caliginosa* accumulated in soils containing high densities of amoebae, and that earthworm growth rates were increased by the addition of amoebae to soil. Similarly, Doube and Gupta (unpublished data) have shown that *Aporrectodea trapezoides* and *E. fetida* preferentially ate soil containing flagellate and cilliate protozoans and both earthworm species responded positively to the fluid in which the protozoa had been living, indicating that the earthworms responded to the products of protozoan activity, possibly small molecular weight compounds, as well as to protozoa. Protozoan protoplasm is highly assimilable, and non-encysted (trophozoite) protozoa are digested preferentially, while encysted forms seem to readily survive gut passage (Piearce and Phillips 1980; Rouelle 1983; Barois 1987; Gupta and Doube, unpublished data). However, not all protozoa are beneficial: Morgan (1988) found that two species of protozoa (*Tetrahymena pyriformis* and *Proterioochromonas minuta*) killed *E. fetida* within three days in a restricted culture environment.

The role of bacteria in the diet of earthworms and the extent of species-specific feeding patterns and digestion are largely unknown. In the case of the compost earthworm *E. fetida*, nineteen species of bacteria were digested in the gut and this dietary addition significantly increased the earthworm's growth rate (Flack and Hartenstein 1984; Hand et al. 1988). However, Morgan (1988) found that only two of twelve bacterial species tested allowed *E. fetida* to maintain weight, while the earthworms either lost weight or died when fed other species. Thorpe et al. (1993) showed that the bacterium *P. fluorescens* could proliferate in the gut of *L. terrestris* in the absence of competition from other gut microorganisms. Doube et al. (1994a,e) showed that rhizobia and *Pseudomonas corrugata* survived passage through the intestines of *A. trapezoides* and *Aporrectodea rosea*.

Different earthworm species may affect the same bacteria in different ways. For example, Schmidt (1994) fed the same concentration of an inoculum of *P. corrugata* to four species of lumbricid, but the density of *P. corrugata* found in the fresh casts of *A. longa* was 10-fold higher than those in fresh casts of *L. rubellus*, *A. caliginosa*, and *L. terrestris*. On the other hand, bacteria such as *Enterobacter aerogenes* have been shown to infect and kill the tropical earthworm *Hoplochaetella suctoria* (Rao et al. 1983), while other species, such as *Pseudomonas* spp., *Streptomyces* spp., and *Flavobacterium* spp., that produce antimicrobial substances have led to death in cultures of the earthworm *E. fetida* (Hand et al. 1988).

The role of algae in earthworm diets is still not clear, since earthworms can be common in soils which contain a low biomass of algae (e.g., in Mediterranean climate regions), but laboratory trials suggest that algae can play an important role in the nutrition of some species (e.g., *E. fetida* [Atlavinyte and Pociene 1973; Piearce 1978]).

The Fate of Microorganisms in the Intestine of Earthworms

In the earthworm gut, various enzymes of microbial and earthworm origin are secreted, as well as intestinal mucus (a readily assimilable C source), $CaCO_3$ (if calciferous glands are present), and bacteriostatic and microbicidal substances (including antibiotics of microbial origin and bacteriolysins, peroxidases, and phagocytoses of earthworm origin). All of these influence the ability of a particular ingested organism to survive passage through the earthworm gut (Brown 1995). Hence, different species of bacteria, fungi, protozoa, and algae are affected in different ways, depending on the species of earthworm and the particular conditions created in its gut, and the ability of these organisms to take advantage of, or resist, the gut conditions. The survivors (largely fungal and protozoan spores and resistant bacteria) provide the inocula for microbial colonization of the casts (Dash et al. 1986; Spiers et al. 1986; Brown 1995).

The microbial composition of the intestine contents has been considered to reflect that of the soil or ingested plant remains (Morgan 1988; Brown 1995) but the studies of Lavelle and others on several tropical and temperate earthworm species have also demonstrated the presence of a mutualistic digestive system (Barois and Lavelle, 1986; Barois 1987, 1992; Martin et al. 1987; Trigo and Lavelle 1993; Lavelle et al. 1994). In this, soluble organic C, in the form of a low molecular weight mucus, is added in large quantities (5–42% of the dry weight of soil, depending on the species) into the foregut. The foregut has a near-neutral pH which, combined with the intimate mixture of organic residues and high water content, promotes the development of a microflora which can digest cellulose and other recalcitrant substances (which earthworms cannot digest by themselves) (Barois and Lavelle 1986; Lavelle and Gilot 1994). Most metabolites are reabsorbed in the hindgut.

The extent to which similar mutualistic systems occur in other species of earthworms is not known. Litter-feeding epigeic species feed on higher quality, less recalcitrant materials (litter, fresh organic materials) and may not need to stimulate the microflora with mucus secretions to be able to digest their food. Additionally, epigeic species have a more complete enzyme system (including cellulase) than do endogeic species (Urbasek and Pizl 1991). A comprehensive description of the digestive system and the origin of different gut enzymes has so far been made for only two species, both endogeic: *Pontoscolex corethrurus* and *Polypheretim elongata* (Zhang et al. 1993; Lattaud et al. in press).

Ingested actinomycetes may inhibit the growth of other organisms (particularly fungi and Gram-positive bacteria) in the gut by releasing antibiotics, leading to a predominance of antibiotic-resistant Gram-negative bacteria and other actinomycetes in earthworm guts (Kristufek et al. 1993). However, the activity of these antibiotics has been tested only *in vitro* with specific test microorganisms (Ravasz et al. 1986; Kristufek et al. 1993) and has not yet been tested *in vivo*. Hence the extent to which this inhibition actually occurs in earthworm guts is still unknown. Finally, in the microaerophilic guts of some earthworm species (e.g., *P. corethrurus* and *A. caliginosa*), free-living *Clostridia* spp. may fix N_2

(Striganova et al. 1989b; Barois et al. 1987), although this contribution to the N budget in casts is relatively small.

Transit time through the earthworm gut may also be an important factor determining the fate of ingested organisms in earthworm intestines (Brown 1995). This is highly variable between species and, furthermore, depends on the quality of ingested materials (Hendriksen 1991) and on temperature (Barois and Lavelle 1986). Gut transit times range between 1 and 3 hours for *Millsonia anomala* (Martin et al. 1987), *A. rosea* (Bolton and Phillipson 1986), *E. fetida* (Hartenstein et al. 1981), *A. caliginosa* and *Octolasion lacteum* (Scheu 1992), and may be >8 hours for *L. terrestris* (Parle 1963a; Hartenstein and Amico 1983), *L. festivus* (Hendriksen 1991), and *L. rubellus* (Daniel and Anderson 1992). In a short transit time there is little potential for microbial multiplication (although there may be a large increase in activity), but with longer gut transit times there may be sufficient time for microbial multiplication, particularly since many *Lumbricus* species tend to feed on litter or organic-rich materials, which already contain substantial microbial populations.

Microbiological Composition and Activity in Burrows and Casts

When an earthworm ingests microorganisms, or burrows through or casts soil containing the dormant microorganisms, the latter become activated (the bacterial "priming effect" of Lavelle et al. [1994]). In casts of *A. caliginosa,* Scheu (1987) reported an approximately 90% increase in microbial respiration over a four-week incubation period. Decomposition rates of litter and organic matter (including lignin) arc often higher in worm-worked soils under laboratory (Mackay and Kladivko 1985; Scheu 1993) and field (van Rhee 1963) conditions. However, Martin (1991) observed lower decomposition rates in the casts of *M. anomala*, an earthworm from the Lamto (Ivory Coast) savannas, due to their compact physical structure "protecting" C from microbial attack. Nonetheless, in the drilosphere, increased decomposition rates and enhanced microbial activity have been shown to increase nutrient mineralization rates significantly, releasing greater quantities of plant-available N and P (e.g., Satchell and Martin 1984; Lavelle et al. 1992b; Lopez-Hernandez et al. 1992). Therefore, in terms of nutrients, earthworm casts and also their burrows, lined with carbon and protein-rich mucus, constitute very favorable microenvironments for microbial (both beneficial and harmful) and invertebrate activity and plant root growth. As a consequence, not only microfloral and microfaunal activity, but also populations of organisms, may be higher in burrows and casts than in unaltered soil (Brown 1995).

In a temperate grassland with a complex earthworm community, burrow walls supported up to 42% of the total soil aerobic N_2-fixing bacteria, 13% of anaerobic N_2 fixers, and 16% of denitrifying bacteria and had higher numbers of ammonifiers, denitrifiers, free-living aerobic and anaerobic nitrogen fixers, and proteolytic bacteria (Bhatnagar 1975). Earthworm casts had higher numbers of cellulolytic aerobes and hemicellulolytic, amylolytic, nitrifying, and denitrifying bacteria than the soil in which they lived (Bhatnagar 1975; Loquet et al. 1977). Therefore, earthworm casts (and possibly burrows) may be important microsites for denitrification (Elliott et al. 1990) since they possess higher numbers of denitrifiers and higher levels of soluble C, NO_3, and water than the surrounding soil.

Several species of fungi grow rapidly in earthworm casts (Parle 1963b)—inocula are derived from spores which survived gut passage (see earlier) or from the surrounding soil. Algae also appear to be able to take advantage of the high nutritional value of worm casts. Of nineteen species of algae found in the casts of an unidentified earthworm species (probably a lumbricid), six had higher growth rates in casts than in uningested soil (Shtina et al. 1981). Protozoa (live and encysted) that survive passage through the earthworm gut may also feed on the increased numbers of bacteria and fungi found in worm casts and multiply rapidly so that their numbers are higher than in uningested soil (Shaw and Pawluk 1986).

Earthworms have high consumption rates and low assimilation efficiencies of organic matter, and their feeding results in both physical (comminution, re-structuring, movement from one location to another in soil) and chemical (quality) modification of large amounts of organic matter in the casts and mucus (Brown 1995). Assimilation efficiencies range from about 1% of the ingested carbon for the temperate species *A. rosea* (Bolton and Phillipson 1976) to about 3–10% for the tropical earthworm *M. anomola* (Martin and Lavelle 1992).

Successional Processes within Earthworm Casts

Passage through the earthworm intestine results in the removal of the active stages of most species of protozoa and fungal hyphae and some (less resistant) bacteria. Some earthworm species may have a proliferation of specialized bacteria in the intestine (Lavelle et al. 1994a) but these bacteria are killed in the hindgut and the nutrients absorbed by the earthworm. In either case, the casts contain bacteria, fungal spores, protozoan cysts, and relatively high levels of soluble nutrients (those not absorbed by the earthworm gut). These resistant stages, together with the microbial species found in the burrow walls, provide the inocula for colonization of the newly formed casts.

The microbial successional processes in casts have been studied little, and, although a number of authors have detailed the type and abundance of micro-organisms found in casts (Brown 1995), there has been little reference to changing patterns of relative abundance over time following deposition. Unpublished data (Gupta and Doube) on the composition of casts of *A. trapezoides* have shown that fresh casts contain numerous bacteria but no active protozoa or fungal hyphae. During the four weeks following cast deposition, a succession of fungal and protozoan species appeared in the casts.

Conclusion

From the above discussion, it is clear that earthworm nutrition is provided by their ingesting and digesting microorganisms that are associated with the decomposition of organic residues, whether in litter or in soil. Fungi, protozoa, and algae appear to provide the major source of such nutrition. Bacteria, although abundant in the earthworm gut, appear to provide some, but limited, nutrition. Data on the value of individual microbial species and species groups are sparse, somewhat contradictory, and based primarily on two earthworm species: *L. terrestris* and *E. fetida*.

Further, earthworms feed on a mixture of microbial species, and so studies based on pure microbial cultures are of limited relevance to natural environments. Nevertheless, we suggest that the microbial species composition, metabolic activity, and microbial successional processes in casts differ substantially from those in the parent soil. As a consequence, in situations in which earthworms process substantial amounts of soil or organic matter, earthworm activity can have a major influence on the form and scale of microbial processes in soil.

Mesoscale Interactions Between Earthworms and Microorganisms

Under this heading we consider the ways in which the activity of earthworms influences the average composition and functioning of microbial communities in small patches of soil, and the possibility that the composition of microbial communities at this scale influences earthworm populations. These effects are commonly studied using microcosms or small-scale field trials.

In studies designed to understand the complex soil changes associated with the invasion of the Canadian Rocky Mountains by earthworms, Scheu and Parkinson (1994) showed, using uniform soil in microcosms, that the earthworm *Dendrobaena octaedra* decreased the microbial biomass (measured by substrate-induced respiration, SIR), whereas in layered soil the activity of both *D. octaedra* and *Octolasion lacteum* redistributed organic residues into the deeper soil layers, resulting in increased microbial biomass at these depths. In contrast, in the presence of both earthworm species there was a decrease (ca. 40% after 12 weeks) in the microbial biomass of the organic-rich surface material and, in most situations, there was a marked increase in the bacterial:fungal ratios (bacteria increased to make up 20–27% of the biomass compared with 10–17% in controls).

In the same study (Scheu and Parkinson 1994), earthworm activity induced only minor immediate changes in the composition (species dominance) of the fungal community after 8 weeks, but such changes, if compounded over several years, would result in major changes in community composition. In the deepest soil layer after 8 and 12 weeks, bacterial:fungal ratios increased in the presence of earthworms, with bacteria making up 60–70% of the biomass compared with 50–55% in the worm-free soil. Similar earthworm-induced increases in bacterial:fungal ratios in soil have been demonstrated for several species by Parle (1963b) and Ausmus (1977) and for *A. caliginosa* by Wolters et al. (1989) and Kollmannsperger (1952) (both papers in German, cited by Scheu and Parkinson 1994). Scheu and Parkinson's own experiments were conducted in microcosms and were limited to 12 weeks. Nevertheless, over time the colonization of forest soils by these two species of earthworm may have profound effects on the composition and functioning of the soil microbial community. These effects would be achieved primarily through redistribution of organic surface residues, reduction in microbial biomass, and favoring of bacteria over fungi, and could result in the formation of a mull soil with an A_H layer rich in humus covered by a thin layer of fragmented material.

Other studies have shown that the microbial species that are favored by earthworm activity vary with circumstances. For example, feeding by *O. lacteum* on partly decomposed organic matter in peat-humus forests in Russia appears to benefit spore-forming bacteria (e.g., *Bacillus* spp. which decompose recalcitrant substances) to the detriment of fluorescing bacteria, which generally use fresh and easily decomposed organic matter (Kozlovskaya and Zdannikova 1961). In contrast, when *L. rubellus* was feeding on fresh substrates, fluorescing bacteria were favored over *Bacillus* spp. Yet, in podzolized soils *O. lacteum* had the same effect on microbial development as did *L. rubellus*, since in these soils *O. lacteum* rose to the surface and fed on newer materials. In the peat-humus soils later in the season (summer), the absence of fresh residues caused *L. rubellus* to feed on older residues and have an effect similar to that of *O. lacteum* in the same soil (Kozlovskaya and Zdannikova 1961).

Microbial and invertebrate successions on decomposing plant debris and other substrates are modified by earthworm-induced changes in the quality (physico-chemical nature) of these resources. This occurs through the earthworms' ingestion and comminution of organic residues, by creating heterogeneous microsites within the soil (e.g., middens) and by selectively grazing on and dispersing particular organisms. For instance, in apple orchards (Raw 1962) and temperate deciduous forests (Knollenberg et al. 1985) *L. terrestris* buried >90% of the annual litterfall. Thus, in apple orchards up to 22 species of fungi and 5 species of insects inhabiting this litter were buried and their populations reduced (Mills 1976; Niklas and Kennel 1981; Laing et al. 1986; Kennel 1990). Under these conditions, distinct changes in microfloral successions are also likely, not only because some species are buried and reduced, but also because the comminution of litter by anecic earthworms (and also by epigeic species and some surface-feeding endogeic species) favors the development of r-selected (fast-growing) fungi such as Phycomycetes (e.g., *Mortierella* and *Mucor* spp.), Ascomycetes, and Deuteromycetes (e.g., *Phoma* and *Trichoderma* spp.) capable of rapid exploitation of the easily assimilable materials found in earthworm casts (Visser 1985).

Nevertheless, selective grazing (or burial) of fungi by earthworms (Moody 1993, 1995) may reduce their competitive ability and allow slower growing (k-selected) fungi such as Basidiomycetes to gain a competitive advantage. For instance, Scheu (1992) found that lignin-decomposing fungi (which occur late in succession) decomposed lignin in earthworm feces only after a lag phase of three months, and, in a later experiment, Scheu (1993) observed an overall increase in lignin mineralization by a factor of 1.1 for columns with *Octolasion lacteum* and 1.2 for those with *L. castaneus*. Selective grazing may also lead to an increase in populations of the selected microbial species in earthworm structures and, occasionally, in total fungal diversity as well (Tiwari and Mishra 1993). Similar processes may also exist for algae and protozoa. Gupta and Doube (unpublished data) recovered over 30 species of protozoa from the casts of field-collected *A. trapezoides*, a substantially increased level of diversity compared with bulk soil on a g/g basis.

In a mesocosm study, using a simulated forest floor and a combination of various soil invertebrates (including earthworms), Huhta et al. (1991) reported more N mineralization in the presence of *L. rubellus* than with a complex fauna in the absence of earthworms. Similarly in lysimeters with different combinations of animals, Anderson et al. (1983) observed increased losses of Na, K, Ca, and mineral N from oak-leaf litter and up to 60 times greater NH_4 losses in the presence of *L. rubellus* than in their absence. These responses are presumed to be caused by earthworm-induced changes in microbial activity, although the organisms responsible have not been characterized.

Earthworm activity has also been shown to influence the distribution and activity of bacteria, fungi, and protozoa. In laboratory trials, the earthworm *A.*

trapezoides was fed sheep manure, containing *Rhizobium trifolii,* in pots in which subterranean clover was growing (Doube et al. 1994e). The earthworm activity dispersed the surface-applied rhizobia through the soil, resulting in a five-fold increase in the total number of root nodules on the clover and a four- to six-fold increase in the number of nodules on the primary roots 2–8 cm below the surface. Stephens et al. (1994) showed that both *A. trapezoides* and *Microscolex dubius* could disperse *Rhizobium meliloti* through soil, and root colonization of alfalfa by this species was increased >100-fold in the presence of *A. trapezoides.* However, survival of *R. meliloti* in soil in pots was related inversely to earthworm density and, at the highest density tested, was reduced by 99% after 40 days in the presence of *A. trapezoides.* The reasons for this are unclear and these results need to be confirmed in the field before we can have confidence that such processes occur in natural environments.

The majority of root diseases of agricultural crops are caused by soil-borne fungi, and the possibility that earthworm-dispersed biological control agents (bacteria and fungi) can enhance control of these fungal diseases has prompted a number of recent investigations (Doube et al. 1994a,b). One such study concerns the bacterium *P. corrugata,* which has been shown to contol take-all, a serious fungal root disease of wheat plants. Using cylinders of soil, Doube et al. (1995) showed that both *A. trapezoides* and *A. rosea* dispersed *P. corrugata* up to 20 cm in 8 days and that large numbers (ca. log 6 g^{-1}) were recovered from both the casts and the tunnel walls. This work was followed by other experiments by Stephens et al. (1993b), who placed straw pellets (inoculated with *P. corrugata*) on the soil surface in the presence and absence of *A. trapezoides.* In the presence of the earthworm, the bacteria was dispersed through the soil (>log 4 g^{-1} soil at 9 cm soil depth after 9 days) and there was a substantial increase in the level of colonization of the roots of seedling wheat plants by the bacteria. However, attempts to evaluate experimentally the capacity of this earthworm-dispersed inoculum to control take-all have been frustrated because the earthworm presence alone controlled the disease (Doube et al. 1994a).

Stephens et al. (1994b,c) thoroughly examined this interaction in a series of greenhouse and field studies using the earthworms *A. trapezoides* and *A. rosea,* the two most common species in the cropping soils of southern Australia. Both species caused a significant reduction in the severity of the disease symptoms (root lesions) in both laboratory and field trials. These effects were also observed in two soils of contrasting texture (a red-brown earth and a calcareous sandy loam). Reduced severity of disease was associated with a corresponding increase in plant growth but in some cases the earthworm activity had no effect on plant growth. In pot trials, the level of disease control increased with increased earthworm density, but in the field trials the level of disease control (30–

40% reduction in lesions) with the equivalent of 100 earthworms m^{-2} was not increased by tripling the earthworm density (300 m^{-2}).

Similar results have been obtained for the effects of the activity of the earthworm *A. trapezoides* on the root disease caused by *Rhizoctonia solani*, the causal agent of bare patch disease in wheat (Stephens et al. 1993a, 1994b). Laboratory and field trials have demonstrated reduced severity of root lesions (20–40% reduction) by earthworms and, by inference, in the activity of *Rhizoctonia* in soil. Once again, earthworm densities of 100 m^{-2} and 300 m^{-2} gave similar levels of disease suppression. Why additional earthworms failed to increase the level of control of root disease is not known. Although the earthworm densities used in these experiments were greater than those commonly encountered in cropping soils in southern Australia, it seems likely that earthworms have the potential to help control root diseases of crops in some situations. For example, Doube et al. (1994c) found *A. trapezoides* at densities of 410 m^{-2} and 140 m^{-2} in soil under canola and wheat respectively in NSW, Australia. Moreover, from these findings it seems probable that earthworm activity can modify the microenvironment in soils in such a manner that its suitability for root-associated fungi (including pathogens) is affected. This has important consequences for the composition of the microbial community and for plant productivity (Brown 1995).

Clearly, earthworm activity influences microbial communities but, conversely, the microorganisms also influence earthworm behavior and abundance, although the evidence is somewhat circumstantial. For example, endogeic earthworms are more abundant in the root zones of wheat plants (Rovira et al. 1987), corn plants (Binet et al. in press), and sugar cane (Spain et al. 1990) than in adjacent soil. Bates (1933) demonstrated a positive association between the distributions of earthworms and white clover. Doube (unpublished data) found a density of about 100 earthworms m^{-2} (a mixture of *A. trapezoides, A. rosea,* and *M. dubius*) amongst the roots of *Salvia verbenaca* while none was recovered from *Salvia*-free soil 1 m away.

Root herbivory by the anecic earthworm *L. terrestris* has been inferred from pulse labeling experiments (Cortez and Bouche 1992), from direct observation (Carpenter 1985; Shumway and Koide 1994), and indirectly by assessment of the presence of root fragments in earthworm guts or casts. For example, Reddell and Spain (1991a) observed root fragments in fresh casts of *P. corethrurus*.

Similarly, Bayliss et al. (1986) suggest that earthworms graze on living clover roots. In contrast, studies on endogeic species in a rhizotron (Gunn and Cheritt 1993) and on *A. trapezoides* (Figure 3) suggest that they consume the rhizosphere soil (possibly containing root hairs) but do not eat the root itself. In both cases, the rhizosphere microorganisms will form at least part of the earthworm's diet, and so earthworm activity has the potential to influence rhizo-

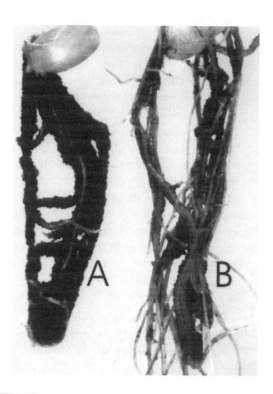

Figure 3. Grazing by *A. trapezoides* on rhizosphere soil surrounding the roots of seedling wheat plants. (A) Controls showing ungrazed rhizosphere soil attached to the root. (B) Bare roots exposed following removal of rhizosphere soil by earthworm feeding. (Photo J. Coppi.)

sphere function. Endogeic earthworms also tend to accumulate in soil patches with higher levels of organic matter (Hughes et al. 1994). Since plant roots and organic residues are localities of relatively high levels of microbial activity, and earthworms recognize and selectively consume some microorganisms, it seems probable that endogeic earthworms aggregate in such regions in response to microbial activity. Whether such behavior enhances their reproductive performance (and corresponding abundance) has not been demonstrated, but the positive links between organic residues, microbial activity, and earthworm food make such an association very likely.

Plant seeds are preferentially ingested by earthworms (Shumway and Koide 1994) with seed selection based on variations in size, shape, and surface texture. Many seeds survive passage through the earthworms and are redistributed through the soil (Piearce 1994; Shumway and Koide 1994; Thompson et al. 1994) with corresponding consequences for the soil seed bank and plant successional patterns.

Macro-Scale Interactions Between Earthworms and Microorganisms

When conventionally cultivated cropping soils (CC) are converted to no-till (NT) or direct-drill (DD) fields, a change in the composition of the soil microbial communities occurs, increasing fungal:bacterial ratios (Brussard et al. 1990; Coleman et al. 1994). Earthworms are also more abundant under NT (DD) than under CC (Lee 1985), and this has been attributed in part to shifts in the composition of the decomposer community. While such causal relationships can be inferred readily from observed changes in community composition, experimental field evidence which supports such conclusions is scarce. However, Blair et al. (in press), in large-scale field plots in the USA, demonstrated an association between the experimental reduction in the density of earthworms and a corresponding increase in microbial biomass-N, providing some of the first experimental evidence that earthworm activity can influence microbial biomass in the field.

There is much evidence indicating the involvement of earthworm activity in cycling of C, N, and P in soils (Hendrix et al. 1987; Böstrom and Lofs-Holmin 1988; Parmelee et al. 1990; Scheu 1990; Lavelle and Martin 1992; Marinissen and de Ruiter 1993) which, by implication, suggests that earthworms also modify soil microbial function. For instance, as much as 60% of the C losses from earthworms during their life span can be in the form of mucus excretions (soluble organic C) (Scheu 1991) and as much as 1 t ha^{-1} yr^{-1} of mucus was added by *P. corethrurus* to a Mexican pasture (Lavelle et al. 1983). Carbon losses due to earthworm respiration are generally not large, but can be as much as 29% of the total heterotrophic respiration in DD systems (Hendrix et al. 1987). In an extensive study of the role of earthworms in C-cycling in a Swedish alfalfa field, Bostrom and Lofs-Holmin (1988) found that C flow through a population of *A. caliginosa* (with a biomass of 33 kg C ha^{-1}) in one year totaled 3.9 t C ha^{-1} in consumption, 3.8 t C ha^{-1} in fecal egestion (casts), 47 kg C ha^{-1} lost in respiration, 41 kg C ha^{-1} in dead tissue, 10 kg C ha^{-1} in cocoon production, and 40 kg C ha^{-1} in tissue production. Mucus production was not assessed.

Nitrogen flows through earthworm populations have been estimated by several authors for various systems (Marinissen and de Ruiter 1993), and in a study by Bostrom and Lofs-Holmin (1988) were as much as 516 kg N ha^{-1} yr^{-1}, with 10 kg N ha^{-1} in tissue production, 2 kg ha^{-1} in excretions (mostly in plant-assimilable N forms), and 504 kg ha^{-1} in cast production in the same alfalfa field. Additionally, the priming effects and indirectly increased N cycling (due to consumption and activation of microorganisms and invertebrates) are important but difficult to assess. Finally, other factors, such as earthworm effects on denitrification and N-leaching losses from soils, are important.

Although earthworms have very little direct effect on P cycling in soils (only trace quantities of P are excreted in liquid wastes [Bahl 1947]), they may have substantial indirect effects due to enhanced phosphatase (acid and alkaline) activity in casts, burrows, and gut; increased availability of P (organic and inorganic) in casts; reduction in Al-binding of P; and increased incorporation of surface-applied fertilizer and plant litter in the soil (Sharpley and Syers 1977; Mansell et al. 1981; Mackay et al. 1982; Satchell and Martin 1984; Alter and Mitchell 1992). Thus, as much as 9–13 kg ha^{-1} of organic plus inorganic P can be accumulated in earthworm casts in one year in New Zealand pastures (Sharpley and Syers 1977). These casts, containing more P than the nearby soil, form microsites rich in P that enhance microbial activity and root growth, particularly in soils poor in phosphorus.

The size and composition of earthworm populations, even within one locality, vary widely with soil type and management practice (e.g., cultivation or liming) (Lee 1985; Robinson et al. 1992) and it is possible that such population differences may reflect differences in the composition and abundance of the microbial communities which form the basis of the food web in soil. For example, it is widely recognized that microbial populations are strongly influenced by soil pH (Gupta 1994) and earthworms are sensitive to soil pH, being more abundant in neutral to slightly acid soil (Lofs-Holmin 1986). However, the relationship between such changes in microbial populations and the reproductive success of earthworms is still not known.

The type of plant community and the corresponding litter–soil–rhizosphere conditions also have broad-scale effects on earthworm abundance. For instance, Boettcher and Kalisz (1991) found changes in the earthworm community structure (abundance and species composition) in a vegetation sequence involving hemlock, rhododendron, and yellow poplar, with one earthworm species (*Bimastos parvus*) largely replacing another (*Komarekiona eatoni*) along the sequence. Similarly, in agroecosystems earthworms appear to be more abundant in soils under certain crops (e.g., clover) (Westernacher and Graff 1987) or under certain grasses in meadows (Babel et al. 1992).

The possibility that earthworms may be used to introduce and disperse beneficial microorganisms through soil has been reviewed by Doube et al. (1994b). They examined the possibility of using pellets of a mixture of earthworm food and beneficial microorganisms (rhizobia for root nodulation, pseudomonads for biological control of take-all, and *Metarhizium* for biological control of root-feeding scarab larvae). These microorganisms would be applied to the field and dispersed through soil as a consequence of the feeding activities of earthworms. The success of this process relies on developing a food that is attractive to earthworms, on survival of the microorganisms in the food pellet and during passage through the earthworm gut, and on effective earthworm dispersal through the soil.

Although only in the early stages of development, a number of these constraints have been examined in laboratory experiments and Doube et al. (1994b) considered that this novel mechanism showed considerable promise, especially for dispersal of *Metarhizium*. Success would require that earthworm activity alter the composition and functioning of microbial communities on a broad scale.

SUMMARY AND CONCLUSIONS

Microbial decomposition of organic residues in soil provides the energy and nutrients which promote and sustain the biological fertility of soils. Surface crop residue inputs into agricultural systems in temperate and subtropical regions are commonly in the order of 2–10 tons ha^{-1} yr^{-1} and similar or much greater amounts enter the soil as roots or root exudates. Between 60% and 75% of the introduced carbon is lost through respiration during the first year in the soil. The microbial biomass in these systems is commonly of the order of 0.5–5.0 tons ha^{-1} and this comprises only 1–2% of the total soil carbon pool.

The microalgae and the primary decomposers (bacteria, actinomycetes, fungi) provide the basis of the food web in soils and provide the food for a wide diversity of secondary consumers (predators), including protozoa and earthworms. Earthworms also feed selectively on soil rich in organic materials (organic fragments and the rhizosphere) and gain their nutrition by digesting microorganisms which are associated with the decomposition of these materials. Furthermore, earthworms selectively consume some species and digest fungal hyphae, trophozoite protozoa, algae, and some bacteria, and disperse the survivors (spores and resistant structures) throughout the soil. Survivors shown to be dispersed include bacteria (pseudomonads and rhizobia), fungi, and protozoa.

Earthworms create (through selective feeding, casting, and burying organic residues) zones of high microbial activity (e.g., in plant roots and residue patches) and aggregate in these zones. In addition, their activity has been shown to reduce the severity of plant root disease. Because of these various activities, earthworms, if present in moderate biomass, are likely to have a substantial influence on the distribution, composition, and activity of the microbial communities which are responsible for decomposition of organic residues and play a key role in regulating the biological processes which maintain soil health.

REFERENCES CITED

Alter, D., and A. Mitchell. 1992. Use of vermicompost extract as an aluminum inhibitor in aqueous solutions. Communications in Soil Science and Plant Analysis 23: 231–239.

Anderson, J.M. 1988. Spatiotemporal effects of invertebrates on soil processes. Biology and Fertility of Soils 6: 216–227.

Anderson, J.M. 1994. Functional attributes of biodiversity in land use systems. pp. 267–290. In D.J. Greenland and I. Szabolcs (eds.). Soil resilience and sustainable land use. CAB International, Wallingford, U.K.

Anderson, J.M., P. Ineson, and S.A. Huish. 1983. The effects of animal feeding activities on element release from deciduous forest litter and soil organic matter. pp. 87–100. In Ph. Lebrun, H.M. André, A. De Medts, C. Grégoire-Wibo, and G. Wauthy (eds.). New trends in soil biology. Dieu-Brichart, Louvain-la-Neuve, Belgium.

Andren, O., T. Lindberg, K. Paustian, and T. Rosswall. 1990. Ecology of arable land: Organisms, carbon and nitrogen cycling. Munksgaard, Copenhagen. Vol. 40.

Andren, O., K. Paustian, and T. Rosswall. 1988. Soil biotic interactions in the functioning of agroecosystems. Agriculture Ecosystems and Environment 24: 57–65.

Atlavinyte, O., and C. Pociene. 1973. The effect of earthworms and their activity on the amount of algae in the soil. Pedobiologia 13: 445–455.

Ausmus, B.S. 1977. Regulation of wood decomposition rates by arthropod and annelid populations. pp. 180–192. In U. Lohm and T. Persson (eds.). Soil organisms as components of ecosystems. Ecological Bulletins, Stockholm. Vol. 25.

Bahl, K.N. 1947. Excretion in the Oligochaeta. Biological Reviews of the Cambridge Philosophical Society 22: 109–147.

Barois, I. 1987. Interactions entre les Vers de Terre (Oligochaeta) tropicaux géophages et la microflore pour l'exploitation de la matière organique du sol. Travaux des Chercheurs de la Station de Lamto. Vol. 7. Publication of the Laboratoire de Zoologie de l'ENS, Paris. 152 pp.

Barois, I. 1992. Mucus production and microbial activity in the gut of two species of *Amynthas* (Megascolecidae) from cold and warm tropical climates. Soil Biology and Biochemistry 24: 1507–1510.

Barois, I., and P. Lavelle. 1986. Changes in respiration rate and some physicochemical properties of a tropical soil during transit through *Pontoscolex corethrurus* (Glossoscolecidae, Oligochaeta). Soil Biology and Biochemistry 18: 539–541.

Barois, I., B. Verdier, P. Kaiser, A. Mariotti, P. Rangel, and P. Lavelle. 1987. Influence of the tropical earthworms *Pontoscolex corethrurus* (Glossoscolecidae) on the fixation and mineralization of nitrogen. pp. 151–158. In A.M.B. Pagliai and P. Omodeo (eds.). On earthworms. Mucchi Editore, Modena, Italy.

Bates, G.H. 1933. The distribution of wild white clover (*Trifolium repens*) in relation to the activity of earthworms (Lumbricidae). The Welsh Journal of Agriculture 9: 195–208.

Baylis, J.B., J.M. Cherrett, and J.B. Ford. 1986. A survey of invertebrates feeding on living clover roots (*Trifolium repens* L.) using 32P as a radiotracer. Pedobiologia 29: 201–208.

Beare, M.H., D.C. Coleman, D.A. Crossley, Jr., P.F. Hendrix, and E.P. Odum. 1995. A hierarchical approach to evaluating the significance of soil biodiversity to biogeochemical cycling. Plant and Soil 170: 5–22.

Bhatnagar, T. 1975. Lombriciens et humification: Un aspect noveau de l'incorporation microbienne d'azote induite par les vers de terre. pp. 169–182. In G. Kilbertius, O. Reisinger, A. Mourey, and J.A.C. da Fonseca (eds.). Humification et biodegradation. Pierron, Sarreguemines, France.

Binet, F., V. Hallaire, and P. Curmi. (in press). Effects of agricultural practices on the spatial distribution of earthworms in maize fields. Relationships between earthworm abundance, maize plants and soil compactness. Soil Biology and Biochemistry.

Blair, J.M., R.W. Parmelee, M.F. Allen, D.A. McCartney, and B.R. Stinner. (in press). Changes in N pools in response to earthworm population manipulations in agroecosystems with different N sources. Soil Biology and Biochemistry.

Blakemore, R.J. (in press). Earthworms of South-East Queensland and their agronomic potential in brigalow soils. Soil Biology and Biochemistry.

Boettcher, S.E., and P.J. Kalisz. 1991. Single-tree influence on earthworms in forest soils in eastern Kentucky. Soil Science Society of America Journal 55: 882–865.

Bolton, P.J., and J. Phillipson. 1976. Burrowing, feeding, egestion, and energy budget of *Allolobophora rosea* (Savigny) (Lumbricidae). Oecologia (Berlin) 23: 225–245.

Bonkowski, M., and M. Schaefer. (in press). Interactions between earthworms and soil protozoa—a new component in the soil food web. Soil Biology and Biochemistry.

Boström, U., and A. Lofs-Holmin. 1988. Earthworm population dynamics and flows of carbon and nitrogen through *Aporrectodea caliginosa* (Lumbricidae) in four cropping systems. In Ecology of earthworms in arable land: Population dynamics and activity in four cropping systems. Institutionen for ekologi och miljovard, Report no. 34. Swedish University of Agricultural Sciences, Uppsala.

Bowen, R.M. 1990. Decomposition of wheat straw by mixed cultures of fungi isolated from arable soils. Soil Biology and Biochemistry 22: 401–406.

Bowen, R.M., and S.H.T. Harper. 1989. Fungal populations on wheat straw decomposing in arable soils. Mycological Research 93: 47–54.

Bowen, R.M., and S.H.T. Harper. 1990. Decomposition of wheat straw and related compounds by fungi isolated from straw in arable soils. Soil Biology and Biochemistry 22: 393–399.

Brown, G.G. 1995. How do earthworms affect microfloral and faunal community diversity? Plant and Soil 170: 209–231.

Brussaard, L., L.A. Bouwman, M. Geurs, J. Hassink, and K.B. Zwart. 1990. Biomass, composition and temporal dynamics of soil organisms of a silt loam soil under conventional and integrated management. Netherlands Journal of Agricultural Science 38: 283–302.

Carpenter, A. 1985. Studies on invertebrates in a grassland soil. Ph.D. thesis, University of Wales.

Clarholm, M. 1985. Possible roles for roots, bacteria, protozoa and fungi in supplying nitrogen to plants. pp. 355–365. In A.H. Fitter, D. Atkinson, D.J. Read, and M.B. Usher (eds.). Ecological interactions in soil: Plants, microbes, and animals. Blackwell Scientific Publications, Oxford, Great Britain.

Coleman, D.C., P.F. Hendrix, M.H. Beare, D.A. Crossley, Jr., S. Hu, and P.C.J. Van Vliet. 1994. The impacts of management and biota on nutrient dynamics and soil structure in sub-tropical agroecosystems: Impacts on detritus food webs. pp. 133–143. In C.E. Pankhurst, B.M. Doube, V.V.S.R. Gupta, and P.R. Grace (eds.). Soil biota: Management in sustainable farming systems. CSIRO, East Melbourne, Australia.

Cooke, A., and M. Luxton. 1980. Effects of microbes on food selection by *Lumbricus terrestris* L. Revue d'Ecologie et Biologie du Sol 17: 365–370.

Cortez, J., and M.B. Bouché. 1992. Do earthworms eat living roots? Soil Biology and Biochemistry 24: 913–915.

Daniel, O., and J.M. Anderson. 1992. Microbial biomass and activity in contrasting soil materials after passage through the gut of the earthworm *Lumbricus rubellus* Hoffmeister. Soil Biology and Biochemistry 24: 465–470.

Dash, H.K., B.N. Beura, and M.C. Dash. 1986. Gut load, transit time, gut microflora, and turnover of soil, plant, and fungal material by some tropical earthworms. Pedobiologia 29: 13–20.

Dash, M.C., P.C. Mishra, and N. Behera. 1979. Fungal feeding by a tropical earthworm. Tropical Ecology 20: 10–12.

Doube, B.M., P.M. Stephens, C.W. Davoren, and M.H. Ryder. 1994a. Interactions between earthworms, beneficial soil microorganisms and root pathogens. Applied Soil Ecology 1: 3–10.

Doube, B.M., P.M. Stephens, C.W. Davoren, and M.H. Ryder. 1994b. Earthworms and the introduction and management of beneficial soil microorganisms. pp. 32–41. In C.E. Pankhurst, B.M. Doube, V.V.S.R. Gupta, and P.R. Grace (eds.). Soil biota: Management in sustainable farming systems. CSIRO, East Melbourne, Australia.

Doube, B.M., J.C. Buckerfield, and J.A. Kirkegaard. 1994c. Short-term effects of tillage and stubble management on earthworm populations in cropping systems in southern New South Wales. Australian Journal of Agricultural Research 45: 1587–1600.

Doube, B.M., C.W. Davoren, R. Hindell, N. Long, and A. Cass. 1994d. Surface cast production by the earthworm *Aporrectodea trapezoides* and the influence of organic matter on cast structural stability. pp. 123–125. In C.E. Pankhurst (ed.). Soil biota: Management in sustainable farming systems (Poster Papers). CSIRO, East Melbourne, Australia.

Doube, B.M., M.H. Ryder, C.W. Davoren, and P.M. Stephens. 1994e. Enhanced root nodulation of subterranean clover (*Trifolium subterraneum*) by *Rhizobium leguminosarium* biovar *trifolii* in the presence of the earthworm *Aporrectodea trapezoides* (Lumbricidae). Biology and Fertility of Soils (in press).

Doube, B.M., M.H. Ryder, C.W. Davoren, and T. Meyer. 1995. Earthworms: A down-under delivery service for biocontrol agents of root disease. Acta Zoologica Fennica 196: 219–223.

Doube, B.M., O. Schmidt, and Killham. (in press.) A choice chamber to evaluate the food preferences of earthworms. Soil Biology and Biochemistry.

Edwards, C.A., and K.E. Fletcher. 1988. Interactions between earthworms and microorganisms in organic-matter breakdown. Agriculture Ecosystems and Environment 24: 235–247.

Edwards, W.M., M.J. Shipitalo, L.B. Owens, and L.D. Norton. 1990. Effects of *Lumbricus terrestris* L. burrows on hydrology of continuous no-till corn fields. Geoderma 46: 73–84.

Elliott, P.W., D. Knight, and J.M. Anderson. 1990. Denitrification in earthworm casts and soil from pasture under different fertilizer and drainage regimes. Soil Biology and Biochemistry 22: 601–605.

Flack, F.M., and R. Hartenstein. 1984. Growth of the earthworm *Eisenia foetida* on microorganisms and cellulose. Soil Biology and Biochemistry 16: 491–495.

Garrett, S.D. 1981. Soil fungi and soil fertility. An introduction to soil mycology. Second edition. Pergamon Press, London.

Gonzalez, C.L. 1990. Determinación de la influencia de *Pontoscolex corethrurus* (Oligochaeta) sobre las poblaciones microbianas presentes en un sembradio de maiz de la region de Gomez Farias, Tamaulipas. Thesis, Universidad Nacional Autonoma de Mexico Los Reyes Iztacala, Mexico. 108 pp.

Grant, J.D. 1983. The activities of earthworms and the fates of seeds. pp. 107–122. In J.E. Satchell (ed.). Earthworm ecology: From Darwin to vermiculture. Chapman and Hall, London.

Gunn, A., and Cherritt, J.M. 1993 The exploitation of food resourses by soil meso and macro invertebrates. Pedobiologia 37: 303 320.

Gupta, V.V.S.R. 1994. The impact of soil and crop management practices on the dynamics of soil microfauna and mesofauna. pp. 107–124. In C.E. Pankhurst, B.M. Doube, V.V.S.R. Gupta, and P.R. Grace (eds.). Soil biota: Management in sustainable farming systems. CSIRO, East Melbourne, Australia.

Haimi, J., V. Huhta, and M. Boucelham. 1992. Growth increase of birch seedlings under the influence of earthworms—a laboratory study. Soil Biology and Biochemistry 24: 1525–1528.

Haines, P.J., and N.C. Uren. 1990. Effect of conservation tillage farming on soil microbial biomass, organic matter and earthworm populations, in north-eastern Victoria. Australian Journal of Experimental Agriculture 30: 365–371.

Hand, P., W.A. Hayes, J.E. Satchell, and J.C. Frankland. 1988. The vermicomposting of cow slurry. pp. 49–63. In C.A. Edwards and E.F. Neuhauser (eds.). Earthworms in waste and environmental management. SPB Academic Publishing, The Hague, The Netherlands.

Harper, S.H.T., and J.M. Lynch. 1985. Colonisation and decomposition of straw by fungi. Transactions of the Royal Mycological Society 85: 655–661.

Hartenstein, F., E. Hartenstein, and R. Hartenstein. 1981. Gut load and transit time in the earthworm *Eisenia foetida*. Pedobiologia 22: 5–20.

Hartenstein, R., and L. Amico. 1983. Production and carrying capacity for the earthworm *Lumbricus terrestris* in culture. Soil Biology and Biochemistry 15: 51–54.

Hassal, L., J.G. Turner, and M.R.W. Rands. 1987. Effects of terrestrial isopods on the decomposition of woodland leaf litter. Oecologia 72. 23–36.

Hendriksen, N.B. 1991. Gut load and food-retention in the earthworms *Lumbricus festivus* and *L. castaneus*: a field study. Biology and Fertility of Soils 11: 170–173.

Hendrix, P.F., D.A. Crossley, Jr., D.C. Coleman, R.W. Parmelee, and M.H. Beare. 1987. Carbon dynamics in soil microbes and fauna in conventional and no-tillage agroecosystems. INTECOL Bulletin 15: 59–63.

Hendrix, P.F., R.W. Parmelee, D.A. Crossley, Jr., D.C. Coleman, E.P. Odum, and P.M. Groffman. 1986. Detritus food webs in conventional and no-tillage agroecosystems. BioScience 36: 374–380.

Hoogerkamp, M. 1987. Effect of earthworms on the productivity of grassland: An evaluation. pp. 485–495. In A.M.B. Pagliai and P. Omodeo (eds.). On earthworms. Mucchi Editore, Modena, Italy.

Hughes, M.S., C.M. Bull, and B.M. Doube. 1994. The use of resource patches by earthworms. Biology and Fertility of Soils 18: 241–344.

Huhta, V., J. Haimi, and H. Setala. 1991. Role of fauna in soil processes: Techniques using simulated forest floor. Agriculture Ecosystems and Environment 34: 223–229.

Ingham, R.E., J.A. Trophymow, R.E. Ingham, and D.C. Coleman. 1985. Interactions of bacteria, fungi and their nematode grazers: Effects on nutrient cycling and plant growth. Ecological Monographs 55: 119–140.

Jenkinson, D.S., and J.N. Ladd. 1981. Microbial biomass in soil: Measurement and turnover. pp. 415–471. In E.A. Paul and J.N. Ladd (eds.). Soil biochemistry. Vol. 5. Marcel Dekker, New York.

Judas, M. 1992. Gut content analysis of earthworms (Lumbricidae) in a beechwood. Soil Biology and Biochemistry 24: 1413–1418.

Kennel, W. 1990. The role of the earthworm *Lumbricus terrestris* in integrated fruit production. Acta Horticulturae 285: 149–156.

Keogh, R.G., and M.J. Christensen. 1976. Influence of passage through *Lumbricus rubellus* Hoffmeister earthworms on viability of *Pithomyces chartarum* (Berk. and Curt.) M.B. Ellis spores. New Zealand Journal of Agricultural Research 19: 255–256.

Killham, K. 1994. Soil ecology. Cambridge University Press, Cambridge, U.K.

Kladivko, E.J., A.D. Mackay, and J.M. Bradford. 1986. Earthworms as a factor in the reduction of soil crusting. Soil Science Society of America Journal 50: 191–196.

Knollenberg, W.G., R.W Merritt, and D.L. Lawson. 1985. Consumption of leaf litter by *Lumbricus terrestris* (Oligochaeta) on a Michigan woodland floodplain. American Midland Naturalist 113: 1–6.

Kozlovskaya, L.S., and E.N. Zhdannikova. 1961. The combined activity of earthworms and the microflora in forest soils. Doklady Akademii Nauk, SSSR 139: 574–576.

Kristufek, V., K. Ravasz, and V. Pizl. 1993. Actinomycete communities in earthworm guts and surrounding soil. Pedobiologia 37: 379–384.

Laing, J.E., J.M. Heraty, and J.E. Corrigan. 1986. Leaf burial by the earthworm, *Lumbricus terrestris* (Oligochaeta: Lumbricidae), as a major factor in the population dynamics of *Phyllonorycter blancardella* (Lepidoptera: Gracillariidae) and its parasites. Environmental Entomology 15: 321–326.

Lattaud, C., B.G. Zang, S. Locati, C. Rouland, and P. Lavelle. (in press). Activities of the digestive enzymes in the gut and in tissue culture of a tropical geophagous earthworm, *Polypheretima elongata* (Megascolicidae). Soil Biology and Biochemistry.

Lavelle, P. 1988. Earthworms activities and the soil system. Biology and Fertility of Soils 6: 237–251.

Lavelle, P. 1994. Faunal activities and soil processes: Adaptive strategies that determine ecosystem function. pp. 189–220. In Transactions of the 15th World Congress of Soil Science. ISSS, Acapulco, Mexico.

Lavelle, P., and C. Gilot. 1994. Priming effects of macroorganisms on microflora: A key process for soil function? In K. Ritz, J. Dighton, and K. Giller (eds.). Beyond the biomass. Wiley-Sayce, London.

Lavelle, P., and A. Martin. 1992. Small-scale and large-scale effects of endogeic earthworms on soil organic matter dynamics in soils of the humid tropics. Soil Biology and Biochemistry 24: 1491–1498.

Lavelle, P., P. Rangel, and J. Kanyonyo. 1983. Intestinal mucus production by two species of tropical earthworms: *Millsonia lamtoiana* (Megascolecidae) and *Pontoscolex corethrurus* (Glossoscolecidae). pp. 405–410. In Ph. Lebrun, H.M. André, A. De Medts,

C. Grégoire-Wibo, and G. Wauthy (eds.). New trends in soil biology. Dieu-Brichart, Louvain-la-Neuve, Belgium.

Lavelle, P., I. Barois, A. Martin, Z. Zaidi, and R. Schaefer. 1989. Management of earthworms populations in agroecosystems: A possible way to maintain soil quality? pp. 109–122. In M. Clarholm and L. Bergström (eds.). Ecology of arable land: Perspectives and challenges. Kluwer Academic Publishers, Dordrecht, Netherlands.

Lavelle, P., G. Melendez, B. Pashanasi, and R. Schaefer. 1992a. Nitrogen mineralization and reorganization in casts of the geophagous tropical earthworm *Pontoscolex corethurus* (Glossoscolecidae). Biology and Fertility of Soils 14: 49–53.

Lavelle, P., A.V. Spain, E. Blanchart, A. Martin, and S. Martin. 1992b. Impact of soil fauna on the properties of soils in the humid tropics. pp. 157–185. In P.A. Sanchez and R. Lal (eds.). Myths and science of soils in the tropics. ASA, Madison, WI. Special Publication no. 29.

Lavelle, P., E. Blanchart, A. Martin, S. Martin, A.V. Spain, F. Toutain, I. Barois, and R. Schaefer. 1993. A hierarchical model for decomposition in terrestrial ecosystems: Application to soils of the humid tropics. Biotropica 25: 130–150.

Lavelle, P., C. Lattaud, D. Trigo, and I. Barois. 1995. Mutualism and biodiversity in soils. Plant and Soil 170: 23–33.

Lee, K.E. 1985. Earthworms: Their ecology and relationships with soils and land use. Academic Press, Sydney. 411 pp.

Lee, K.E., and R.C. Foster. 1991. Soil fauna and soil structure. Australian Journal of Soil Research 29: 745–775.

Lofs-Holmin, A. 1986. Occurrence of eleven earthworm species (Lumbricidae) in permanent pastures in relation to soil-pH. Swedish Journal of Agricultural Research 16: 161–165.

Lopez-Hernandez, D., J.C. Fardeau, and P. Lavelle. 1992. Phosphorus transformations in two P-sorption contrasting tropical soils during transit through *Pontoscolex corethrurus* (Glossoscolecidae, Oligochaeta). Soil Biology and Biochemistry 25: 789–792.

Loquet, M., T. Bhatnagar, M.B. Bouche, and J. Rouelle. 1977. Essai d'estimation de l'influence ecologique des lombrices sur les microorganismes. Pedobiologia 17: 400–417.

Lynch, J.M., and J.M. Whipps. 1990. Substance flow in the rhizosphere. Plant and Soil 129: 1–10.

Mackay, A.D., and E.J. Kladivko. 1985. Earthworms and the rate of breakdown of soybean and maize residues in soil. Soil Biology and Biochemistry 17: 851–857.

Mackay, A.D., J.K. Syers, J.A. Springett, and P.E.H. Gregg. 1982. Plant availability of phosphorus in superphosphate and phosphate rock as influenced by earthworms. Soil Biology and Biochemistry 14: 281–287.

Mansell, G.P., J.K. Syers, and P.E.H. Gregg. 1981. Plant availability of phosphorus in dead herbage ingested by surface casting earthworms. Soil Biology and Biochemistry 13: 163–167.

Marinissen, J.C.Y., and P.C. de Ruiter. 1993. Contribution of earthworms to carbon and nitrogen cycling in agro-ecosystems. Agriculture Ecosystems and Environment 47: 59–74.

Martin, A. 1991. Short-term and long-term effect of the endogeic earthworm *Millsonia anomala* (Omodeo) (Megascolecidae, Oligochaeta) of tropical savannas, on soil organic matter. Biology and Fertility of Soils 11: 234–238.

Martin, A., and P. Lavelle. 1992. Effect of soil organic matter quality on its assimilation by

Millsonia anomala, a tropical geophagous earthworm. Soil Biology and Biochemistry 24: 1535–1538.

Martin, A., J. Cortez, I. Barois, and P. Lavelle. 1987. Les mucus intestinaux de Ver de Terre, moteur de leurs interactions avec la microflore. Revue d'Ecologie et de Biologie du Sol 24: 549–558.

McRill, M., and G.R. Sagar. 1973. Earthworms and seeds. Nature 243: 482.

Miles, H.B. 1962. Soil protozoa and earthworm nutrition. Soil Science 95: 407–409.

Mills, J.T. 1976. Interrelationships between microorganisms, nematodes, insects, and other invertebrates affecting their role as pests. pp. 20–32. In Integrated control of soil pests. WPRS Bulletin no. 3, Wageningen, The Netherlands.

Moody, S.A. 1993. Dispersal of wheat straw fungi by earthworms and springtails. Ph.D. thesis, Lancaster University, U.K.

Moody, S.A. 1993. Selective consumption of decomposing wheat straw by earthworms. Soil Biology and Biochemistry 27: 1209–1213.

Morgan, M.H. 1988. The role of microorganisms in the nutrition of *Eisenia foetida*. pp. 71–82. In C.A. Edwards and E.F. Neuhauser (eds.). Earthworms in waste and environmental management. SPB Academic Publishing, The Hague.

Mulongoy, K., and A. Bedoret. 1989. Properties of worm casts and surface soils under various plant covers in the humid tropics. Soil Biology and Biochemistry 21: 197–203.

Niklas, J., and W. Kennel. 1981. The role of the earthworm, *Lumbricus terrestris* (L.) in removing sources of phytopathogenic fungi in orchards. Gartenbauwissenchaft 46: 138–142.

Parle, J.N. 1963a. Micro-organisms in the intestines of earthworms. Journal of General Microbiology 31: 1–11.

Parle, J.N. 1963b. A microbiological study of earthworm casts. Journal of General Microbiology 31: 13–22.

Piearce, T.G. 1978. Gut contents of some lumbricid earthworms. Pedobiologia 18: 3–157.

Piearce, T.G., and M.J. Phillips. 1980. The fate of ciliates in the earthworm gut: An in vitro study. Microbial Ecology 5: 313–319.

Piearce, T.G., N. Roggero, and R. Tipping. 1994. Earthworms and seeds. Journal of Biological Education 28: 195–202.

Ponge, J.F. 1991. Succession of fungi and fauna during decomposition of needles in a small area of Scots pine litter. Plant and Soil 138: 90–113.

Rao, B.R., I.K. Sagar, and J.V. Bhat. 1983. *Enterobacter aerogenses* infection of *Haplochaetella suctoria*. pp. 383–391. In J.E. Satchell (ed.). Earthworm ecology: From Darwin to vermiculture. Chapman and Hall, London.

Ravasz, K., A. Zicsi, E. Contreras, V. Széll, and I.M. Szabo. 1986. Über die Darmaktinomyceten-Gemeinschaften einiger Regenwurm-Arten. Opuscula Zoologica Budapest 22: 85–102.

Raw, F. 1962. Studies of earthworm populations in orchards. I: Leaf burial in apple orchards. Annals of Applied Biology 50: 389–404.

Reddell, P., and A.V. Spain. 1991a. Earthworms as vectors of viable propagules of mycorrhizal fungi. Soil Biology and Biochemistry 23: 767–774.

Reddell, P., and A.V. Spain. 1991b. Transmission of infective *Frankia* (Actinomycetales) propagules in casts of the endogeic earthworm *Pontoscolex corethrurus* (Oligochaeta: Glossoscolecidae). Soil Biology and Biochemistry 23: 775–778.

Robertson, G.P. 1994. The impact of soil and crop management practices on soil spatial heterogeneity. pp. 156–161. In C.E. Pankhurst, B.M. Doube, V.V.S.R. Gupta, and P.R. Grace (eds.). Soil biota: Management in sustainable farming systems. CSIRO, East Melbourne, Australia.

Robinson, C.H., T.G. Piearce, P. Ineson, D.A. Dickson, and C. Nys. 1992. Earthworm communities of limed coniferous soils: Field observations and implications for management. Forest Ecology and Management 55: 117–134.

Robinson, C.H., J. Dighton, and J.C. Frankland. 1993. Resource capture by interacting fungal colonisers of straw. Mycological Research 97: 547–588.

Rouelle, J. 1983. Introduction of amoebae and *Rhizobium japonicum* into the gut of *Eisenia foetida* (Sav.) and *Lumbricus terrestris* L. pp. 375–381. In J.E. Satchell (ed.). Earthworm ecology: From Darwin to vermiculture. Chapman and Hall, London.

Rovira, A.D., K.R.J. Smettem, and K.E. Lee. 1987. Effects of rotation and conservation tillage on earthworms in a red-brown earth under wheat. Australian Journal of Experimental Agriculture 31: 509–513.

Samedov, P.A. 1988. Significance of soil invertebrates in decomposition of plant remains and humus formation in meadow sierozem soils. Soviet Soil Science 20: 54–60.

Satchell, J.E., and K. Martin. 1984. Phosphatase activity in earthworm faeces. Soil Biology and Biochemistry 16: 191–194.

Scheu, S. 1987. Microbial activity and nutrient dynamics in earthworm casts (Lumbricidae). Biology and Fertility of Soils 5: 230–234.

Scheu, S. 1990. Changes in microbial nutrient status during secondary succession and its modification by earthworms. Oecologia 84: 351–358.

Scheu, S. 1991. Mucus excretion and carbon turnover of endogeic earthworms. Biology and Fertility of Soils 12: 217–220.

Scheu, S. 1992. Decomposition of lignin in soil microcompartments: A methodological study with three different ^{14}C labelled lignin substrates. Biology and Fertility of Soils 13: 160–164.

Scheu, S. 1993. Litter microflora-soil macrofauna interactions in lignin decomposition: A laboratory experiment with ^{14}C-labelled lignin. Soil Biology and Biochemistry 25: 1703–1711.

Scheu, S., and D. Parkinson. 1994. Effects of earthworms on nutrient dynamics, carbon turnover and microorganisms in soil from cool temperate forests on the Canadian Rocky Mountains—laboratory studies. Journal of Applied Soil Ecology 1: 113–125.

Schmidt, O. 1994. Investigations of earthworms (Lumbricidae) for delivery of *Pseudomonas corrugata,* a biocontrol agent of wheat take-all. M.Sc. thesis, Aberdeen University, U.K.

Sharpley, A.N., and J.K. Syers. 1977. Seasonal variation in casting activity and in the amounts and release to solution of phosphorus forms in earthworm casts. Soil Biology and Biochemistry 9: 227–231.

Shaw, C., and S. Pawluk. 1986. Faecal microbiology of *Octolasium tyrtaeum, Apporectodea turgida* and *Lumbricus terrestris* and its relation to the carbon budgets of three artificial soils. Pedobiologia 29: 377–389.

Shipitalo, M.J., and R. Protz. 1988. Factors influencing the dispersibility of clay in worm casts. Soil Science Society of America Journal 52: 764–769.

Shtina, E.A., L.S. Kozlovskaya, and K.A. Nekrasova. 1981. Relations of soil oligochaetes and algae. Soviet Journal of Ecology 12: 44–48.

Shumway, D.L., and R.T. Koide. 1994. Seed preferences of *Lumbricus terrestris* L. Journal of Applied Soil Ecology 1: 11–16.

Spain, A.V., P. Lavelle, and A. Mariotti. 1992. Stimulation of plant growth by tropical earthworms. Soil Biology and Biochemistry 24: 1629–1633.

Spain, A.V., P.G. Safigna, and A.W. Wood. 1990. Tissue carbon sources for *Pontoscolex corethrurus* (Oligochaeta, Glossoscolecidae) in a sugarcane ecosystem. Soil Biology and Biochemistry 22: 703–706.

Sparling, G.P., P.B.S. Hart, J.A. August, and D.M. Leslie. 1994. A comparison of soil and microbial carbon, nitrogen, and phosphorus contents, and macroaggregate stability of a soil under native forest and after clearance for pasture and plantation forest. Biology and Fertility of Soils 17: 91–100.

Spiers, G.A., D. Gagnon, G.E. Nason, E.C. Packee, and J.D. Louiser. 1986. Effects and importance of indigenous earthworms on decomposition and nutrient cycling in coastal forest ecosystems. Canadian Journal of Forest Research 16: 983–989.

Springett, J.A., 1985. Effect of introducing *Allolobophora longa* Ude on root distribution and some soil properties in New Zealand pastures.

Stephens, P.M., C.W. Davoren, M.H. Ryder, and B.M. Doube. 1993a. Influence of the lumbricid earthworm *Aporrectodea trapezoides* on the colonization of wheat roots by *Pseudomonas corrugata* strain 2140R in soil. Soil Biology and Biochemistry 25: 1719–1724.

Stephens, P.M., C.W. Davoren, B.M. Doube, M.H. Ryder, A.M. Benger, and S.M. Neate. 1993b. Reduced severity of *Rhizoctonia solani* disease on wheat seedlings associated with the presence of the earthworm *Aporrectodea trapezoides* (Lumbricidae). Soil Biology and Biochemistry 25: 1477–1484.

Stephens, P.M., C.W. Davoren, M.H. Ryder, and B.M. Doube. 1994a. Influence of the earthworm *Aporrectodea trapezoides* (Lumbricidae) on the colonization of alfalfa (*Medicago sativa* L.) roots by *Rhizobium meliloti* strain L5-30R and the survival of *Rhizobium meliloti* L5-30R in soil. Biology and Fertility of Soils 18: 63–70.

Stephens, P.M., C.W. Davoren, M.H. Ryder, and B.M. Doube. 1994b. Field experiments demonstrating the ability of earthworms to reduce the disease severity of *Rhizoctonia* on wheat. pp. 19–20. In C.E. Pankhurst (ed.). Soil biota: Management in sustainable farming systems (Poster Papers). CSIRO, East Melbourne, Australia.

Stephens, P.M., C.W. Davoren, M.H. Ryder, and B.M. Doube. 1994c. Greenhouse and field experiments demonstrating the ability of earthworms to reduce the disease severity of Take-all on wheat. pp. 19–20. In C.E. Pankhurst (ed.). Soil biota: Management in sustainable farming systems (Poster Papers). CSIRO, East Melbourne, Australia.

Stockdill, S.M.J. 1982. Effects of introduced earthworms on the productivity of New Zealand pastures. Pedobiologia 24: 29–35.

Striganova, B.R., O.E. Marfenina, and V.A. Ponomarenko. 1989a. Some aspects of the effect of earthworms on soil fungi. Biological Bulletin of the Academy of Sciences of the USSR 15: 460–463.

Striganova, B.R., T.D. Pantos-Derimova, G.P. Mazantseva, and A.V. Tiunov. 1989b. Effects of earthworms on biological nitrogen fixation in the soil. Biological Bulletin of the Academy of Sciences of the USSR 15: 560–565.

Swartz, K.B., P.J. Kiukman, and J.A. van Veen. 1994. Rhizosphere protozoa: Their significance in nutrient dynamics. pp. 93–122. In J.F. Darbyshire (ed.). Soil protozoa. CAB International, Wallingford, U.K.

Swift, M.J., O.W. Heal, and J.M. Anderson. 1979. Decomposition in terrestrial ecosystems. Blackwell Scientific, London.

Thompson, L., C.D. Thomas, J.M.A. Radley, S. Williamson, and J.H. Lawton. 1993. The effect of earthworms and snails in a simple plant community. Oecologia 95: 171–178.

Thompson, K., A. Green, and A.M. Jewels. 1994. Seeds in soil and worm casts from a neutral grassland. Functional Ecology 8: 29–35.

Thorpe, I.S., K. Killham, J.I. Prosser, and L.A. Glover. 1993. Novel method for the study of the population dynamics of a genetically modified microorganism in the gut of the earthworm *Lumbricus terrestris*. Biology and Fertility of Soils 15: 55–59.

Tiwari, S.C., and R.R. Mishra. 1993. Fungal abundance and diversity in earthworm casts and in uningested soil. Biology and Fertility of Soils 16: 131–134.

Tiwari, S.C., B.K. Tiwari, and R.R. Mishra. 1990. Microfungal species associated with the gut content and casts of *Drawida assamensis* Gates. Proceedings of the Indian Academy of Sciences (Plant Sciences) 100: 379–382.

Trigo, D., and P. Lavelle. 1993. Changes in respiration rate and some physico-chemical properties of soil during gut transit through *Allolobophora molleri* (Lumbricidae). Biology and Fertility of Soils 15: 185–188.

Urbasek, F., and V. Pizl. 1991. Activity of digestive enzymes in the gut of five earthworm species (Oligochaeta; Lumbricidae). Revue d'Ecologie et de Biologie du Sol 28: 461–468.

Van der Reest, P.J., and H. Rogaar. 1988. The effect of earthworm activity on the vertical distribution of plant seeds in newly reclaimed polder soils in the Netherlands. Pedobiologia 31: 211–218.

Van Rhee, J.A. 1963. Earthworm activities and breakdown of organic matter in agricultural soils. pp. 55–59. In J. Doeksen and J. van der Drift (eds.). Soil organisms. North Holland Publishing Company, Amsterdam.

Visser, S. 1985. Role of the soil invertebrates in determining the composition of soil microbial communities. pp. 297–317. In A.H. Fitter, D. Atkinson, D.J. Read, and M.B. Usher (eds.). Ecological interactions in soil: Plants, microbes and animals. Blackwell Scientific Publications, Oxford, Great Britain.

Westernacher, E., and O. Graff. 1987. Orientation behavior of earthworms (Lumbricidae) towards different crops. Biology and Fertility of Soils 3: 131–133.

Zhang, B.G., C. Rouland, C. Lattaud, and P. Lavelle. 1993. Origin and activity of enzymes found in the gut content of the tropical earthworm *Pontoscolex corethrurus* Müller. European Journal of Soil Biology 29: 7–11.

Zhang, H., and S. Schraeder. 1993. Earthworm effects on selected physical and chemical properties of soil aggregates. Biology and Fertility of Soils 15: 229–234.

Impacts of Earthworms on the Community Structure of Other Biota in Forest Soils

10

Dennis Parkinson and Mary Ann McLean

Department of Biological Sciences, University of Calgary, Calgary, Alberta, Canada

Interactions of the soil fauna, between both different faunal groups and soil microorganisms, are considered to be important in affecting soil processes (e.g., organic matter decomposition and nutrient cycling) and in influencing the community composition of various groups of the soil biota (Seastedt 1984; Visser 1985). The ways in which these functional and community structure effects are achieved are by (a) comminution of and channelling in organic debris, and mixing of organic debris and mineral soil; (b) grazing on microbial tissues; and (c) dispersal of microbial propagules (Visser 1985).

Earthworms form an important group of the soil fauna, and while they show different ecological strategies (see Doube and Brown, this volume), all facets of their life in organic and mineral soil layers can potentially have major impacts on other groups of soil organisms. These have been discussed, with particular reference to earthworm effects in temperate and subtropical agricultural systems, by Doube and Brown (this volume).

The aim of this chapter is to provide information and comments on earthworm influences on the structure of microbial and faunal communities in forest soils, particularly in the organic layers of temperate coniferous forests. At the outset it must be admitted that, while substantial data are available on earthworm effects on various soil processes and on microbial biomass dynamics, relevant detailed data on their effects on other soil biota are fragmentary at best.

1-884015-74-3/98/$0.00/$.50

EFFECTS OF CHANNELING, COMMINUTION, AND MIXING

While earthworm species differ in size and behavior, their activities have great consequences for the physical and chemical characteristics of organic and mineral soil (Lee and Foster 1991). These activities include ingestion of soil and organic material (plus comminution of organic matter) and the intermixing of these materials, ejection of gut contents as casts, and the formation of burrow systems (Guild 1955).

Burrowing activities vary from species (epigeic worms) inhabiting surface organic layers and producing no well-defined burrows to species (endogeic worms) that produce deep vertical burrows into the mineral soil with branches near the soil surface. These activities have great consequences for the physical and chemical nature of the soil (Lee 1985; Kretzschmar 1992) and therefore may have impacts on microbial and faunal communities.

Around earthworm burrows is the drilosphere soil zone (Bouché 1975). This zone has been described by Doube and Brown (this volume), and it is generally richer in nitrogen, phosphorus, and humified organic matter than is the surrounding soil (Beare et al. 1994). However, the detailed conditions in the drilosphere depend on the ecological group of the burrowing species. Doube and Brown (this volume) have noted that substantial percentages of the total soil numbers of various types of nitrogen transforming bacteria are located in the drilosphere (Bhatnagar 1975), together with increased enzyme activities and CO_2 efflux (Loquet 1978).

Warcup (1965), using direct observation of arable soil blocks, observed fungal sporulation in tunnels of *Eisenia rosea* and *Allolobophora caliginosa* on substrates such as remains of other soil invertebrates (e.g., animal parasites such as *Beauveria, Conidiobolus,* and *Entomophthora* and saprotrophs such as various Mucorales, *Penicillium, Aspergillus,* and *Verticillium*), worm casts (fructifications of *Dictyostelium mucoroides*), and mineral particles (several cleistothecial Ascomycetes and some aphyllophoraceous Basidiomycetes). Also, he observed sporulation of some fungi being confined to organic fragments which abutted the drilosphere; the fungi observed were *Dinemasporium, Chaetomium, Periconia, Trichoderma, Gonytrichum, Brachysporiella,* and *Endophragmia*. Apart from fungi, actinomycetes were seen in the tunnels growing on plant and animal debris, on fungal hyphae, and on humus particles. This rarely quoted work represents probably the most detailed account to date of the substrate relationships of soil fungi in earthworm tunnels and the drilosphere.

Apart from burrowing, earthworms can have other significant effects on the fabric of mineral soil and of surface organic layers. Kubiena (1955) showed that, in mineral soils possessing sufficient water-stable binding substances, earthworms can create a "spongy fabric" (i.e., aggregates bond together producing a porous internal structure). This fabric, which has good aeration and water status, enhances the development of aerobic bacteria, actinomycetes, and fungi. Also, the soil spaces allow the development of a wide range of species of soil fauna. However, in some tundra soils the upper mineral layers show a "spongy fabric" that has developed from processes other than faunal activity (Pawluk 1985).

In compact soil fabrics, root development (with subsequent decomposition) and earthworm activity may allow the development of "channel fabrics." Again, these effects on soil structure can enhance microbial and faunal development and it could be hypothesized that this would include increases in their species diversity.

Another major impact of earthworm activities is the incorporation of organic debris from the soil surface into subsurface mineral soil layers. As Doube and Brown (this volume) have stated, the subsequent increase in the organic matter content in these mineral soil layers may allow changed soil structure, increased microbial biomass and activity, and changed patterns of saprotrophic microorganisms on the decomposing organic matter. However, once again, detailed data on effects of organic matter/mineral soil mixing on community structures for the different groups of the soil biota are lacking. The importance of worm casts in adding "processed" organic materials to mineral soil, and thus affecting other soil biota, will be considered in a subsequent section in this chapter.

Earthworms in Temperate Forest Ecosystems

While much of the information cited above has been drawn from studies of agricultural or pasture soils, a similar situation regarding our knowledge of earthworm effects on other groups of the soil biota exists for their effects in forest ecosystems. Certainly substantial data, mainly gained from laboratory studies, are available on earthworm impacts on soil processes and on biomass dynamics of some major groups of the soil biota (e.g., Haimi and Huhta 1990; Haimi and Boucelham 1991; Scheu and Parkinson 1994); however, there is a lack of detailed information about effects of earthworm activities on soil microbial and faunal community structures.

Roles of Biota in Development of Forest Humus Forms

In forest ecosystems the importance of soil fauna, frequently with emphasis on the roles of earthworms, in the development and maintenance of soil structure has been recognized for over a hundred years. In temperate forests organic matter ("humus" in the broad sense) frequently accumulates on the soil surface and there may be an organic-enriched upper mineral horizon. In classifying forest and heathland humus forms, Müller (1878) introduced the terms "mull" and "mor," and Ramann (1911) added the term "moder." Green et al. (1993) gave an account of the tortuous subsequent history of the development of terminology for humus forms and provided a proposal for their classification. In the present paper a simplified view is taken, and only mor, mull, and moder forms will be considered.

The mor form is one where organic matter accumulates on the soil surface, in which definable L, F, and H layers can be distinguished. There is very little or no mixing of organic materials with the upper mineral soil.

In the mull form, there is little accumulation of organic matter on the soil surface because there is incorporation of this material into the upper mineral soil. This humus form is generally found in forests on base-rich soils and in grasslands.

In forests with the moder humus form, there is accumulation of organic materials on the soil surface, but the distinction between F and H layers is frequently unclear and in these layers there may be incorporation of mineral particles. Also, there may be limited infiltration of humus material into the uppermost mineral soil layer. Moders have been considered intermediate in the complex gradient from mor to mull humus forms (Green et al. 1993).

The type of humus form in a particular ecosystem will be determined by a range of climatic, edaphic, and vegetation factors. However, it is well known that the biota play important, interactive roles in the development and maintenance of specific humus forms (e.g., Rusek 1985).

In the low pH, base-poor, high C/N conditions in mor humus forms there is high fungal biomass with frequent production of hyphal mats and hyphal strands, high arthropod and nematode populations, and rarity or absence of earthworms; therefore, mixing of the organic layers or mixing of organic matter into the mineral soil does not occur. The L, F, and H layers formed in mor "humus" represent a chronosequence in litter decomposition. Consequently numerous studies of fungal "succession" during this process have been made (see Kjøller and Struwe 1982; Widden 1986; Hansen 1989). Similarly there have been numerous studies of arthropod communities in this humus type (Petersen 1982; Hågvar and Abrahamsen 1980; Kaneko 1985; Seastedt et al. 1989), including studies of the feeding preferences of various species (Dash and Cragg 1972; Moore et al. 1987; Klironomos et al. 1992; Shaw 1988) and of their interactions with the litter fungi. As stated earlier, earthworms are generally rare in mor humus, but data on their occurrence in this humus form have been given by Huhta and Koskenniemi (1975), Muys and Lust (1992), and Piearce (1972).

In the mull humus forms, with higher pH, base-rich, and lower C/N conditions, fungal biomass is considered to be lower and bacterial biomass higher than in mor humus forms. Arthropod numbers are low and earthworm populations are high. The activities of anecic and endogeic worms are major factors in removing organic materials from the soil surface and in maintaining the mixing of these materials into the mineral soil with subsequent, stimulatory effects on soil microorganisms.

The nature of the moder humus form results, at least in part, from the activities of epigeic earthworms (Rusek 1985). These activities, which cause mixing of organic materials and incorporation of casts, create major changes in the surface organic layers which may have considerable effects on the communities of other litter-inhabiting fauna and microorganisms. Up to now, no details are available on these effects.

From the foregoing comments and those in Doube and Brown (this volume), it can be seen that earthworms affect significantly the physical and chemical conditions in soil and different humus forms which may affect the structure of the communities of other soil organisms. Studies of these biological effects are rare because of experimental difficulties.

Experimental Approaches

Just as in many grassland and agricultural ecosystems, in mull and moder forests earthworms have been present and active over long time periods. As a result, the total complex litter/soil biota has evolved in co-existence with earthworms. Consequently there appear to be a relatively small number of laboratory and field approaches possible for assessing earthworm impacts on other groups of soil organisms.

Laboratory Studies

The laboratory approach involves the use of systems (micro- or mesocosms) of varying degrees of complexity which allow experiments to be carried out under controlled temperature and moisture conditions. Thus the variable field conditions of microclimate, etc., are evaded. However, if laboratory experiments are oversimplified, it is difficult to interpret them in terms of actual field situations.

In work on the effects of earthworms in soil processes and soil communities, serious attempts have been made to use laboratory systems that reflect the realities of field situations. Nevertheless, it would seem very difficult to use this approach for studies of litter/soil systems taken from locations in which worms have been active for some time and have already had their effects on soil structure, processes, and the rest of the soil biota.

In a laboratory study of the litter/soil profile of an aspen forest in the early stages of colonization by an epigeic earthworm species (*Dendrobaena octaedra*), Scheu and Parkinson (1994) showed that the presence of these worms caused a decrease in microbial biomass in the L/F layer but increased microbial biomass in the H and A_h layers. In the L/F and A_h layers there was an increase in the bacterial contribution to the total microbial biomass. Wolters et al. (1989) had previously found the same phenomenon resulting from activities of an endogeic worm species (*Aporrectodea caliginosa*) in beech leaf litter.

Also, Scheu and Parkinson (1994) showed that while there were slight changes in species dominance, there was little if any change in the fungal community of L/F litter resulting from activities of *D. octaedra* over 54 days. However, this very restricted study can only be considered preliminary at best and much more detailed investigations are required to elucidate these earthworm effects.

Field Studies

There are two major field approaches for studying earthworm impacts on other soil biota. One of these major approaches involves the partial or, preferably, total elimination of worms from replicate study plots, for subsequent comparisons with plots where no worm elimination has occurred. There are a number of types of area where this situation can be studied, for example, areas where partial or total elimination of worms is normally a chronic, unplanned side effect of human activities and areas where worm elimination is a direct, acute result of planned human activity.

Examples of the former case can be seen in areas subjected to various agricultural practices or to various forms of soil pollution. However, in many of these examples there can be severe difficulties in experimental design and data interpretation; for example, it is frequently difficult to establish appropriate, analogous unimpacted control areas, and frequently it is difficult to determine the real cause of observed changes in the soil biota (earthworm absence or physical/chemical impacts of disturbance itself).

Another example of the former case is areas where land-use changes have been or are being made. Yeates (1988) showed that, with the change in land use from grassland to *Pinus radiata* plantations of different densities, earthworm populations disappeared under high tree densities. Yeates (1991) has reviewed the effects of historical land-use changes on the soil fauna in New Zealand. Muys et al. (1992) showed, as part of a larger study, that 18 years after changing a pasture to a *Quercus palustris* plantation there was a fall in earthworm biomass. Neither the study by Yeates (1988) nor that of Muys et al. (1992) aimed to investigate the effects of changed earthworm densities on other groups of the soil biota.

In all the foregoing examples, there is the problem of timing of the experiments on the effects of earthworm density decline or elimination. Lavelle (1988) posed the question, "When earthworms disappear, how long does it take before significant changes, if any, occur in soil structure and nutrient cycling?" This may well be extended to include changes in the communities of other soil organisms.

In the latter case of planned, acute elimination of worms, two approaches have been taken: application of biocides and electroshocking. Bohlen et al. (1995) have briefly reviewed these, and to avoid problems in the use of biocides (e.g., their impacts on non-target organisms, etc.), they used electroshocking. However, if this type of approach is to be effective in soil community studies, then it must be one of long term to allow the soil to "equilibrate" in a zero earthworm state. Thus, once again timing of studies becomes important.

The second major field approach is to study hitherto earthworm-free soils into which earthworms have been purposely introduced or into which unplanned colonization is occurring.

Stockdill (1982) showed that lumbricid worms (*Aporrectodea caliginosa*) introduced into New Zealand pastures improved their soil qualities. Yeates (1981) showed that the introduction of these worms into pasture soils led to a 50% reduction in soil nematodes as well as a significant change from bacterial- to fungal-feeding species. Any impact of this change on microbial community structure is not known.

Hoogerkamp et al. (1983) showed beneficial changes following the introduction of various mixtures of earthworm species into pastures developing on reclaimed polder soils. While they did not study the impacts of these earthworm introductions on other soil biota, Marinissen and Bok (1988) showed that earthworm effects on the structure of polder soils allowed increased size, abundance, and distribution of collembola in those soils.

Fortunately, there are areas that have been worm-free for centuries and where colonization of worms is beginning, presumably as an indirect result of human activities. Recently earthworm invasion of forests in the Kananaskis Valley (southern Alberta, Canada) has begun (Scheu and McLean 1993; Dymond et al., in press), and similar invasions are being observed in other forest regions in south and central Alberta. The major earthworm species involved is the epigeic *Dendrobaena octaedra*. Studies of several *Pinus contorta* forest sites in the Kananaskis Valley have shown that, since 1990, significant populations of *D. octaedra* have developed or are developing in these forests and that there is great variation in worm numbers between sites and within individual sites. In one site the average maximum number, over three years, has been 1080 ± 430 worms m^{-2}, while in another site over a 100-m transect numbers ranged from 0 to 3200 worms m^{-2}. In all areas numbers are strongly correlated with the moisture contents of the organic layers.

These forests appear to present excellent sites for studying the impacts of earthworms both on soil processes and soil communities. This is particularly the case because detailed data are available on organic matter, nitrogen, and phosphorus dynamics; on fungal and arthropod community structures; and on microbial biomass dynamics in these forest litter/soil systems when earthworms were absent (much of this work is summarized in Parkinson 1988).

In the *P. contorta* forests, the organic layer on the forest floor is of the mor type with marked, unmixed L, F, and H layers. Effectively these layers represent a chronosequence of litter decomposition in which the fungi comprise a high percentage (c. 80%) of the total microbial biomass (max. 21,000 µg microbial biomass C g^{-1}).

The sequence of fungi involved in pine litter decomposition is very different from that described (Doube and Brown, this volume) for organic residues in agricultural and grassland soil. In the early stages of pine litter decomposition (L and F layers) dematiaceous hyphomycetes, coelomycetes, and sterile forms appear frequently and represent c. 85% of the fungal hyphae in these layers. Basidiomycete mycelia increase in frequency of occurrence with increasing litter decomposition, and in the H layer, hyaline fungi such as species of *Mortierella, Penicillium,* and *Trichoderma* appear with increased frequency. The F and H organic layers are permeated with fine ectomycorrhizal roots of pine and with VA mycorrhizal roots of such shrub species as *Shepherdia canadensis* (which also has root nodules of *Frankia*).

In areas where substantial invasion by *D. octaedra* has occurred, there is the beginning of moder development. Indeed, in areas of high earthworm density the F and H layers are thoroughly mixed and replaced by worm casts together with more mineral soil than is seen in worm-free areas.

Some of the repercussions of these invasions on soil processes have been given by Scheu and Parkinson (1994a,b), and detailed studies of their impacts on fungal and arthropod communities are currently underway. It is hypothesized that the "homogenizing" effects of worms in the F and H layers, with resulting loss in diversity of microsites for microbial and faunal activities, will cause a reduction in species diversity of these groups of soil organisms.

GRAZING ON MICROBIAL TISSUES

It is considered likely that fungi may be a primary food source for many earthworm species (see Brown [1995] and Doube and Brown [this volume] for reviews on this matter). However, particularly for coniferous forest ecosystems, there is little if any information on the impacts of grazing on the soil fungal community structure.

In coniferous forests, briefly described earlier, the organic layers contain large amounts of diverse hyphae, mycelial strands, rhizomorphs and other fungal structures together with ectomycorrhizal associations with tree roots (e.g., fungal mantles on fine root tips, etc.) and VAM structures associated with shrub and herbaceous plant roots. These fungi represent a large, potential food resource for the epigeic worms colonizing these environments. However, to date, there are a number of open questions regarding the impacts of earthworm feeding on these different types of fungi in the forest litter layers. For example:

a. There is evidence, from fungal feeding preference studies, that some other members of the forest soil fauna, particularly collemboles and mites, frequently prefer dark-pigmented fungi. Does the same situation hold for epigeic earthworms such as *D. octaedra*? Up to now no feeding preference studies using fungi from the L, F, and H layers of the forest floor have been attempted.

b. While fungal feeding preference studies, particularly when allied with studies of growth rates and fecundity, provide interesting data, they may not be indicators of the potential impacts of the soil fauna on the fungal community in complex environments such as coniferous forest floors. Certainly data have been provided showing that grazing by individual species of microarthropods, in litter/soil microcosms inoculated with at most a small number of fungal species, can affect the structure of these simple fungal communities.

However, data are emerging (McLean et al. 1996) that indicate that microarthropod grazing does not have significant effects on the structure of the natural, complex fungal communities on/in decomposing L layer *P. contorta* litter. It may be that the potentially far more dramatic actions of epigeic worms (e.g., *D. octaedra*), described earlier, will provide different information.

c. Since both saprotrophic and mycorrhizal basidiomycete fungi are abundant in coniferous forest litter layers, are any of these palatable for epigeic worms? If so, is there preferential grazing on the different types of mycorrhizal root tips, and what is the impact of this on the frequency of different mycorrhizal types?

d. Since VA mycorrhizal plants are components of many coniferous forests, is their community structure affected by the grazing activities of epigeic earthworms? As for fungi, the impacts of earthworm feeding on soil actinomycetes and bacteria have been reviewed by Brown (1995) and Doube and Brown (this volume). However, once again, the impacts of this activity by epigeic worms in coniferous forest litter are currently unknown.

The importance of the production of worm casts in determining the physical/chemical structure of coniferous forest organic layers has been discussed earlier. Apart from these effects, the casts themselves are sites for microbial development resulting from propagules which have retained viability during passage through the worm gut and from microorganisms already active in the forest organic layers and which colonize the casts. Brown (1995) and Doube and Brown (this volume) have reviewed work on some general microbial characteristics of worm casts (e.g., microbial biomass-C and the relative contributions of bacteria and fungi to this biomass) and also the small amount of information on the types of bacteria and fungi associated with casts.

With respect to the microbial community status of casts of *D. octaedra* in coniferous forests, no substantial information is available. A very restricted, preliminary study of H layer samples, from *P. contorta* forest floor, with and without the presence of *D. octaedra*, indicated that there was a higher frequency of occurrence of *Penicillium* spp. and *Mortierella* spp. in worm-free samples, while *Oidiodendron* was more frequent in worm-processed H layer material. Widden and Parkinson (1973) found *Oidiodendron* spp. to be frequent in the mineral horizons of *P. contorta* forest soils, and its occurrence in these H layer samples may have been the result of worms ingesting mineral soil containing this fungus and then moving into the H layer and depositing casts containing the fungus in a viable state.

Obviously, more detailed studies of actinomycetes, bacteria, and fungi in earthworm casts are needed to allow assessment of their community structures.

Apart from casts, worms contribute other materials into mineral soil and organic layers. Mucus, urine, and, ultimately, worm bodies are some of these materials. The impacts of these materials on microbial communities await elucidation.

DISPERSAL OF MICROORGANISMS

The importance of earthworms in the dispersal of beneficial and harmful soil microorganisms has been reviewed by Doube et al. (1994), Brown (1995), and Doube and Brown (this volume). A very high percentage of these microorganisms are dispersed in worm casts, with few being dispersed while adhering to worm body surfaces.

While the vast majority of the information given in these reviews has been drawn from studies of non-forested areas, it does allow consideration of earthworm roles in microbial dispersal in coniferous forest soils. For example:

a. Given that VA mycorrhizal plants occur commonly in *P. contorta* forests in W. Canada, and given that earthworms can be important agents for dispersal of VAM fungal spores in non-forest ecosystems, does *D. octaedra* play such a role in coniferous forests?

b. Since it has been reported (Reddell and Spain 1991) that the earthworm *Pontoscolex corethrurus* disperses the *Casuarina* nodule-forming actinomycete (*Frankia* sp.), can *D. octaedra* act in the same way in *P. contorta* forests which contain several species of actinorrhizal shrubs?

c. Following on the foregoing comments on worm casts, what is the role of these casts in the dispersal of saprotrophic microorganisms in coniferous forest soils?

CONCLUDING COMMENTS

Doube et al. (1994) commented that "evidence demonstrating that earthworms influence the overall size and impact of populations of microorganisms in soil at a larger scale is scarce, although such effects are implicit in the literature (Brown 1995)." This is a potentially dangerous assumption and explicit information on these effects is sorely needed. Unfortunately this chapter has done little to satisfy this need, since mainly it has emphasized the lacunae in our knowledge of the impacts of earthworm activities on communities of microorganisms and fauna in coniferous forest soils. While this is regrettable, particularly since there is such interest in various aspects of both ecosystem functioning and biodiversity of soil organisms, perhaps it is understandable for a variety of reasons.

One reason is that the methods for analyzing species diversity of the various groups of soil organisms differ in their efficiency. For example, methods exist to allow efficient extraction and accurate determinations of the communities of the different groups of the soil fauna, whereas currently it is considered extremely difficult to obtain complete information on the total fungal species complement in litter/soil samples.

Another problem is caused by the fact that the various groups of organisms in the litter layers of forests show high spatial heterogeneity. This means that large numbers of litter samples must be taken to achieve understanding of this heterogeneity and consequently a very high, sometimes unrealistic, research time commitment.

Many groups of soil organisms present significant problems for their identification and the recognition and diagnosis of new taxa. Therefore real taxonomic expertise must be developed prior to embarking on community structure studies of any major group of soil organisms. Regrettably, the number of recognized experts, essential for identification confirmation, on numerous groups of soil organisms is declining steadily and this will cause major future problems for soil ecologists.

REFERENCES CITED

Beare, M.H., D.C. Coleman, D.A. Crossley, Jr., P.F. Hendrix, and E.P. Odum. 1994. A hierarchical approach to evaluating the significance of soil biodiversity to biogeochemical cycling. Plant and Soil, 170: 5–22.

Bhatnagar, T. 1975. Lombriciens et humification: un aspect nouveau de l'incorporation microbienne d'azote induite par les vers de terre. In K. Gilbertus, O. Reisinger, A. Mourey, and J.A. Cancela da Fonseca (eds.), Biodégradation et Humification. Pierron, Sarruguemines, pp. 169–182.

Bohlen, P.J., R.W. Parmelee, J.M. Blair, C.A. Edwards, and B.R. Stinner. 1995. Efficacy of methods for manipulating earthworm populations in large-scale field experiments. Soil Biol. Biochem., 27: 993–999.

Bouché, M. 1975. Action de la faune sur les états de la matière organique dans les écosystèmes. In K. Gilbertus, O. Reisinger, A. Mourey, and J.A. Cancela da Fonseca (eds.), Biodégradation et Humification. Pierron, Sarruguemines, pp. 157–168.

Brown, G.G. 1995. How do earthworms affect microfloral and faunal community diversity? Plant and Soil, 170: 209–231.

Dash, M.C., and Cragg, J.B. 1972. Selection of microfungi by Enchytraeidae (Oligochaeta) and other members of the soil fauna. Pedobiologia, 12: 282–286.

Doube, B.M., and Brown, G.G. 1998. Life in a complex community: functional interactions between earthworms, organic matter, microorganisms, and plants (this volume).

Doube, B.M., P.M. Stephens, C.W. Davoren, and M.H. Ryder. 1994. Interactions between earthworms, beneficial soil microorganisms and root pathogens. Appl. Soil Ecol., 1: 3–10.

Dymond, P., S. Scheu, and D. Parkinson. (in press). Density and distribution of *Dendrobaena octaedra* (Lumbricidae) in an aspen and pine forest in the Canadian Rocky Mountains (Alberta). Soil Biol. Biochem.

Green, R.N., R.L. Trowbridge, and K. Klimka. 1993. Towards a taxonomic classification of humus forms. For. Sci. Monog. 29. Soc. Am. For., Bethesda, MD.

Guild, W.J.McL. 1955. Earthworms and soil structure. In D.K.McE. Kevan (ed.), Soil Zoology. Butterworths Scientific Publications, London, pp. 83–98.

Hågvar, S., and G. Abrahamsen. 1980. Colonisation by Enchytraeidae, Collembola and Acari in sterile soil samples with adjusted pH levels. Oikos, 34: 245–258.

Haimi, J., and M. Boucelham. 1991. Influence of a litter feeding earthworm, *Lumbricus rubellus*, on soil processes in a simulated coniferous forest floor. Pedobiologia, 35: 247–256.

Haimi, J., and V. Huhta. 1990. Effects of earthworms on decomposition processes in raw humus soil: a microcosm study. Biol. Fertil. Soils, 10: 178–183.

Hansen, P.A. 1989. Species response curves along a mull/mor gradient in Swedish beech forests. Vegetatio, 82: 69–78.

Hoogerkamp, M., H. Rogaar, and H.J.P. Eijsackers. 1983. Effect of earthworms on grasslands on recently reclaimed polder soils in the Netherlands. In J.E. Satchell (ed.), Earthworm Ecology, From Darwin to Vermiculture. Chapman & Hall, London, pp. 85–105.

Huhta, V., and A. Koskenniemi. 1975. Numbers, biomass and community respiration of soil invertebrates in spruce forests at two latitudes in Finland. Ann. Zool. Fennici, 12: 164–182.

Kaneko, N. 1985. A comparison of oribatid mite communities in two different soil types in a cool temperate forest in Japan. Pedobiologia, 28: 255–264.

Kjøller, A., and S. Struwe. 1982. Microfungi in ecosystems: fungal occurrence and activity in litter and soil. Oikos, 39: 389–422.

Klironomos, J., P. Widden, and I. Deslandes. 1992. Feeding preferences of the collembolan *Folsomia candida* in relation to microfungal successions on decaying letter. Soil Biol. Biochem., 24: 685–692.

Kretzschmar, A. 1992. Special Editor, 4th International Symposium on Earthworm Ecology. Soil Biol. Biochem., 24.

Kubiena, W.L. 1955. Animal activity as a decisive factor in establishment of humus forms. In D.K.McE. Kevan (ed.), Soil Zoology. Butterworths Scientific Publications, London, pp. 73–82.

Lavelle, P. 1988. Earthworm activities and the soil system. Biol. Fertil. Soils, 6: 237–251.

Lee, K.E. 1985. Earthworms, Their Ecology and Relationships with Soils and Land Use. Academic Press, North Ryde, N.S.W. Australia.

Lee, K.E. and R.C. Foster. 1991. Soil fauna and soil structure. Aust. J. Soil Res., 29: 745–775.

Loquet, M. 1978. The study of respiratory and enzymatic activities of earthworm-made pedological structures in a grassland soil at Citeaux, France. Scientific Proc. R. Dublin Soc. Ser., A6: 207–214.

Marinissen, J.C.Y., and J. Bok. 1988. Earthworm-amended soil structure: its influence on Collembola populations in grassland. Pedobiologia, 32: 243–252.

McLean, M.A., N. Kaneko, and D. Parkinson. 1996. Does selective grazing by mites and Collembola affect litter fungal community structure? Pedobiologia, 40: 97–105.

Moore, J.C., E.R. Ingham, and D.C. Coleman. 1987. Inter- and intra-specific feeding selectivity of *Folsomia candida* (Willem) (Collembola, Isotomidae) on fungi. Biol. Fertil. Soils, 5: 6–12.

Müller, P.E. 1878. Studier over Skovjord. Tidskr. Skovbrug, 3: 1–124.

Muys, B., and N. Lust. 1992. Inventory of the earthworm communities and the state of litter decomposition in the forests of Flanders, Belgium, and its implications for forest management. Soil Biol. Biochem., 24: 1677–1681.

Muys, B., N. Lust, and Ph. Granval. 1992. Effects of grassland afforestation with different tree species on earthworm communities, litter decomposition and nutrient status. Soil Biol. Biochem., 24: 1459–1466.

Parkinson, D. 1988. Linkages between resource availability, microorganisms and soil invertebrates. Agric. Ecosystems Environ., 24: 21–32.

Pawluk, S. 1985. Soil micromorphology and soil fauna: problems and importance. Quaestiones Entomologicae, 21: 473–496.

Petersen, H. 1982. Structure and size of soil animal populations. Oikos, 39: 306–329.

Piearce, T.G. 1972. Acid intolerant and ubiquitous Lumbricidae in selected habitats in North Wales. J. Anim. Ecol., 41: 397–410.

Ramann, E. 1911. Bodenkunde. Ed. 3. Julius Springer, Berlin.

Reddell, P., and A.V. Spain. 1991. Transmission of infective *Frankia* (Actinomycetales) propagules in casts of the endogeic earthworm *Pontoscolex corethrurus* (Oligochaeta: Glossoscolecidae). Soil Biol. Biochem., 23: 775–778.

Rusek, J. 1985. Soil microstructures—contributions on specific soil organisms. Quaestiones Entomologicae, 21: 497–514.

Scheu, S., and M.A. McLean. 1993. The earthworm (Lumbricidae) distribution in Alberta (Canada). Megadrilogica, 4: 175–180.

Scheu, S., and D. Parkinson. 1994a. Effects of earthworms on nutrient dynamics, carbon turnover and microorganisms in soils from cool temperate forests of the Canadian Rocky Mountains—laboratory studies. Appl. Soil Ecol., 1: 113–125.

Scheu, S., and D. Parkinson. 1994b. Effects of an invasion of an aspen forest (Canada) by *Dendrobaena octaedra* (Lumbicidae) on plant growth. Ecology, 75: 2348–2361.

Seastedt, T.R. 1984. The role of microarthropods in decomposition and mineralization processes. Ann. Rev. Entomol., 29: 25–46.

Seastedt, T.R., M.V. Reddy, and S.P. Cline. 1989. Microarthropods in decaying wood from temperate coniferous and deciduous forests. Pedobiologia, 33: 69–77.

Shaw, P.J.A. 1988. A consistent hierarchy of fungal feeding preferences of the Collembola *Onychiurus armatus*. Pedobiologia, 31: 179–187.

Stockdill, S.M.J. 1982. Effects of introduced earthworms on the productivity of New Zealand pastures. Pedobiologia, 24: 29–35.

Visser, S. 1985. Role of invertebrates in determining the composition of soil microbial communities. In A.H. Fitter, D. Atkinson, D.J. Read, and M.B. Usher (eds.), Ecological Interactions in Soil: Plants, Microbes and Animals. Blackwell Scientific Publications, Oxford, pp. 297–317.

Warcup, J.H. 1965. Growth and reproduction of soil microorganisms in relation to substrate. In K.F. Baker and W.C. Snyder (eds), Ecology of Soil-Borne Plant Pathogens, Prelude to Biological Control. University of California Press, Berkeley, pp. 52–68.

Widden, P. 1986. Microfungal community structure from forest soils in southern Quebec, using discriminant function and factor analysis. Can. J. Bot., 64: 1402–1412.

Widden, P., and D. Parkinson. 1973. Fungi from Canadian coniferous forest soils. Can. J. Bot., 51: 2275–2290.

Wolters, V., T. Sprengel, M. Vanselow, and S. Scheu. 1989. Bodentiere als Steuergrößen für die Zusammensetzung und Leistunsfähigkeit der Zersetzergemeinschaft von Waldökosystemen Perspektiven für einen integrierten Forschungsansatz. Berichte Forschungszentrum Waldökosysteme, A 49: 153–157.

Yeates, G.W. 1981. Soil nematode populations depressed in the presence of earthworms. Pedobiologia, 22: 191–195.

Yeates, G.W. 1988. Earthworm and enchytraeid populations in a 13 year old agroforestry system. New Zealand J. For. Sci., 18: 304–310.

Yeates, G.W. 1991. Impact of historical changes in land use on the soil fauna. New Zealand J. Ecol., 15: 99–106.

Earthworms in Agroecosystems

The Ecology, Management, and Benefits of Earthworms in Agricultural Soils, with Particular Reference to Southern Australia

11

G.H. Baker

Division of Entomology, CSIRO and Cooperative Research Centre for Soil and Land Management, Glen Osmond, South Australia

T he earthworm fauna of agricultural soils in southern Australia is similar to that of several other countries with temperate or mediterranean climates. The fauna is dominated by introduced Lumbricidae from Europe, in particular *Aporrectodea caliginosa, A. trapezoides, and A. rosea.* Population numbers and species richness are usually low (e.g., mean density for permanent pastures in southeastern Australia = 141 worms m^{-2}, mean species richness per pasture = 2.9). The geographic distributions of the most common species are patchy. Earthworm abundance is correlated with a number of climatic and edaphic variables, most notably rainfall and soil nitrogen and carbon. The common species are active in the top 10 cm of soil for four to seven months of the year (winter–spring) when the soil water suction potential is less than approximately 150 kPa. Deep-burrowing (anecic) species are rare.

Several Australian studies have shown that earthworms can improve soil properties and increase agricultural production. Particular attention is given in this chapter to the abilities of earthworms to enhance the burial of surface-

1-884015-74-3/98/$0.00/$.50
©1998 by CRC Press LLC

applied lime and organic matter and to increase pasture and cereal growth. Differences in performance between earthworm species are highlighted. *Aporrectodea longa* and *A. trapezoides* are shown to be more beneficial than other species. In particular, *A. longa* buried lime to 10–15 cm depth within five minutes in field experiments and increased pasture growth by up to 60%.

Agricultural management practices can markedly influence earthworm numbers and biomass. Examples are given of the effects of tillage, crop rotation, drainage, irrigation, lime and fertilizer application, stocking rates, machinery compaction, and pesticide use. Earthworm numbers and biomass may be improved by the introduction of earthworms to habitats lacking them. *A. longa,* which is restricted in its Australian distribution to Tasmania, is being introduced into pastures in South Australia and Victoria to increase its distribution. The potential for further introductions of exotic species and alternative strains is also discussed.

The use of earthworms as biological indicators of the sustainability of agricultural practices is considered briefly. Comparisons are made between the results of earthworm research in Australia and other studies in similar climatic regions of the world.

INTRODUCTION

In recent years, there has been a significant increase in research aimed at improving the management of earthworms as a resource in agricultural soils in southeastern Australia (Baker et al. 1994; Temple-Smith and Pinkard 1996). Several factors have encouraged this expansion in earthworm research. Increased on-farm costs (fuel, labor, machinery), reduced values in agricultural products, and a greater awareness of soil structural decline have encouraged farmers to adopt reduced cultivation techniques. Under such practices, the abundance of earthworms is enhanced (Rovira et al. 1987), and their presence in optimal numbers is needed to replace some of the benefits previously brought by the plow. In addition, the increasing costs of fertilizers, as well as the pollution problems they bring (e.g., through leaching and erosion into waterways), has stimulated thought on more efficient and safer means of transfer of nutrients to plants. Studies in other countries, which have shown the potential for earthworms to increase plant production significantly and offset soil degradation (e.g., improved lime burial and reduction in soil acidity, improved water infiltration and rates of breakdown of surface litter, leading to reduced runoff of phosphorus and nitrogen) (Sharpley et al. 1979; Stockdill 1982; Springett 1983; Hoogerkamp et al. 1983; Curry and Boyle 1987), have also heightened interest in introducing such benefits to Australia.

Research in southern Australia has been aimed primarily at determining the distribution and abundance of the earthworm fauna in agricultural soils, measuring the effects of the most common species on soil properties and plant production, and recognizing means by which the beneficial role of earthworms can be enhanced (e.g., optimal farm management practices, introduction of new taxa) (Baker 1992; Baker et al. 1994). This paper presents new data and reviews progress on these topics. The research is set in a broader context by comparing the findings in Australia with related research elsewhere in the world. Because the climate of southern Australia is temperate or mediterranean, discussion is confined to earthworms in agricultural systems in similar climatic zones elsewhere. Earthworms have been suggested as potential indicators of sustainable agricultural practices in Australia (Oades and Walters 1994; Buckerfield and Auhl 1994). The suitability of earthworms as indicators of soil health is briefly discussed.

THE EARTHWORM FAUNA

Extensive surveys have been made of the abundance and species composition of earthworm populations in agricultural soils used for pastures and pasture-cereal rotations in South Australia and western Victoria (Baker 1994) (Figure 1). The soils of these regions are typically duplex with coarse-textured sands over clay, fine textured red-brown earths and deep, coarse-textured sands and sandy loams (Rovira 1992). The densities of earthworms (all species combined) found in the surveys varied between 0–1262 m ^{2}. Few sites had high numbers of earthworms. For example, less than 10% of permanent pastures and no pasture-cereal rotations had >400 worms m^{-2} (Figure 2). The average densities of earthworms were 140.8 and 40.2 m^{-2} in permanent pastures and pasture-cereal rotations respectively. Introduced species (mostly Lumbricidae from Europe) predominated, with native species rare or absent on most farms, especially in pasture-cereal rotations (native species comprised 18.0 and 0.9% of the populations in permanent pastures and pasture-cereal rotations respectively) (Figure 3). Up to six species were recorded site^{-1}, but species richness was generally low with an overall average of 2.5 species site^{-1} (2.9 for permanent pastures and 1.1 for pasture-cereal rotations).

The dominant species differed between geographical regions within south-eastern Australia. For example, in permanent pastures in the Mt. Lofty Ranges, South Australia (see Figure 1), *Aporrectodea trapezoides* was most abundant (Figure 3), occurring at 95% of sites. Its abundance varied from 0–509 m^{-2} (mean = 95.8). The next most abundant species were *A. rosea* (38% of sites, mean density = 26.0 m^{-2}) and *A. caliginosa* (36% of sites, mean density = 23.9

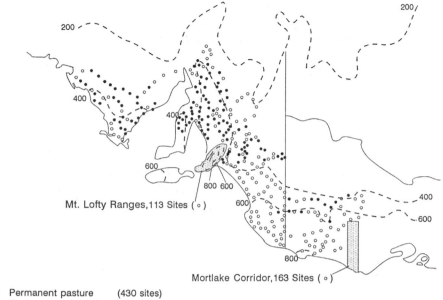

O Permanent pasture   (430 sites)
● Pasture-cereal rotation (126 sites)

Figure 1. Distribution of 556 pastures surveyed for earthworms in southeastern Australia during mid-winter to early spring from 1989–92. Note: The pastures were either permanent (o) or grown in rotation with cereals (•). Shaded areas indicate regions of intensive sampling. Isohyets are included (- - - - -). See Baker (1992) and Baker et al. (1992) for further sampling details.

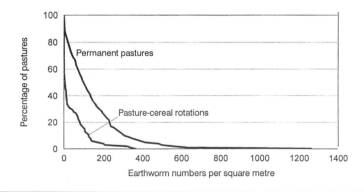

Figure 2. Percentage of pastures in South Australia and western Victoria with a given number of earthworms or more m^{-2}.

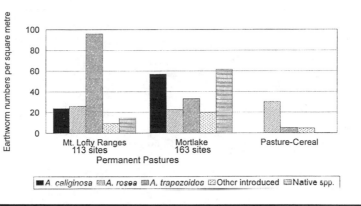

Figure 3. Average abundance of earthworms (m⁻²) in permanent pastures and pasture-cereal rotations in South Australia and western Victoria.

m^{-2}). *Microscolex dubius* was widespread (61% of sites) but much less abundant than the *Aporrectodea* species (mean density = 6.3 m^{-2}). In the Mortlake corridor, Victoria (see Figure 1), *A. caliginosa* was the most abundant species in permanent pastures (52% of sites, mean density = 57.0 m^{-2}), but *A. trapezoides* was found at most sites (81%, mean density = 33.1 m^{-2}) (Figure 3). A native species, *Spenceriella* sp. (Megascolecidae), was also very common (65% of sites, mean density = 54.6 m^{-2}). *A. rosea* was found at 21% of sites with a mean density = 22.5 m^{-2}. In contrast, *A. rosea* was generally much more abundant than any other species in the pasture-cereal rotations (Figure 3). It occurred at 45% of sites and its abundance varied from 0–358 m^{-2} (mean = 31.4). Three other introduced species, *A. trapezoides*, *M. dubius,* and *Microscolex phosphoreus* (Acanthodrilidae), occurred at 13–29% of sites at mean densities of 2.2–5.0 m^{-2}. The abundance of *A. trapezoides*, *M. dubius,* or *M. phosphoreus* exceeded that of *A. rosea* on only four occasions (1, 1, and 2 respectively).

The distributions of earthworm species were often very patchy within geographical regions in southeastern Australia. For example, introduced species predominated towards the south and native species towards the north of the Mortlake corridor (see Figure 4 for examples of species distributions). If the data are partitioned north and south of Mortlake, then the dominant species in the north was *Spenceriella* (90% of sites, mean density = 80.9 m^{-2}). *A. trapezoides* (78% of sites, mean density = 35.1 m^{-2}) and the native megascolecid, *Gemascolex octothecatus* (61% of sites, mean density = 8.5 m^{-2}), were also common. South of Mortlake, *A. caliginosa* predominated (91% of sites, mean density = 171.6 m^{-2}), with the next most common species being *A. rosea* (59%, 67.3 m^{-2}),

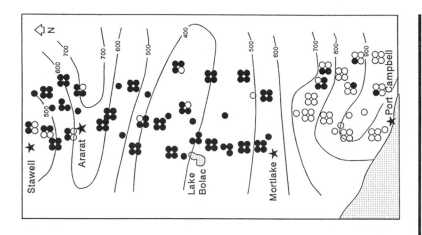

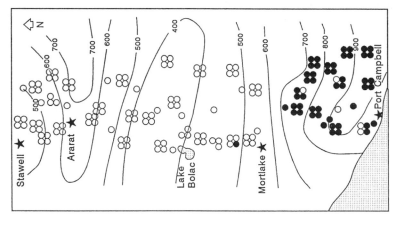

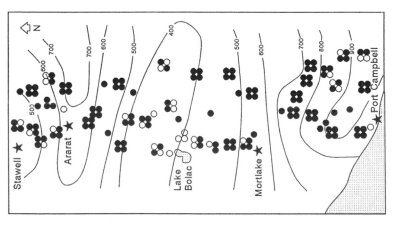

Figure 4. Distribution of the introduced (left) *Aporrectodea trapezoides* and (middle) *Lumbricus rubellus* (Lumbricidae) and the native (right) *Spenceriella* sp. (Megascolecidae) in 163 pastures near Mortlake, Victoria. Note: Presence at a site is indicated by (•). Rainfall isohyets are included in the maps.

Lumbricus rubellus (93%, 48.3 m^{-2}), and *A. trapezoides* (87%, 28.9 m^{-2}). Only 14 *A. caliginosa*, 18 *A. rosea,* and 1 *L. rubellus* were found north and 50 *Spenceriella* sp. and no *G. octothecatus* were found south of Mortlake (means all <2 m^{-2}; six soil samples were taken at each site, each 0.1 m^2 in area × 10 cm deep).

Several significant (p < 0.05), but weak, correlations were obtained between the numbers of earthworms and a range of environmental variables measured at each survey site throughout South Australia and western Victoria (annual rainfall, summer maximum temperature, soil particle size, soil pH, and the concentrations of several elements in the soil of agricultural importance, such as N, C, P, K, S, and Al). Highest correlations with populations of individual earthworm species were obtained for rainfall (*A. caliginosa* = 0.44, *A. trapezoides* = 0.35, *L. rubellus* = 0.35), % N (*A. caliginosa* = 0.36, *A. trapezoides* = 0.30, *L. rubellus* = 0.34), and % C (*A. caliginosa* = 0.27, *A. trapezoides* = 0.20, *L. rubellus* = 0.25). Stepwise multiple regressions were computed for earthworm numbers against these environmental variables. The results suggested that rainfall, which varied between 230–1150 mm throughout the survey area, explained more of the variance in earthworm numbers than any other variable (r^2 = 24.52 for all species combined; r^2 = 29.18 if % N added into the regression). Similar results were obtained when earthworm weights were substituted for numbers. If the data were split to eliminate areas with low rainfall, then other environmental variables emerged as important statistical regressors. For example, in the Mt. Lofty Ranges, S.A., where rainfall varies between 550–1150 mm, clay content was the most significant regressor and explained 29.8% of the variance in total earthworm numbers. Such partitioning of the data can be further expanded to determine the most important environmental variables for particular regions or habitat types. For some species, scatter plots of earthworm numbers and environmental variables are instructive, in that thresholds are indicated, below which some species are rarely found (e.g., 600 mm annual rainfall for *A. caliginosa*) (Figure 5). Strongest correlations (p < 0.05) between the abundance of individual species were obtained for the introduced *A. caliginosa* and *L. rubellus* (+0.54) and the native *Spenceriella* sp. and *G. octothecatus* (+0.44). There was a significant, although very weak, negative correlation between the total abundances of introduced and native species (–0.10).

The distributions of earthworms north and south of Mortlake (Figure 4) are particularly intriguing. There is a strong positive association between most of the introduced species and rainfall (*A. trapezoides* appears to be an exception) and a negative association for native species. However, several other factors vary with the rainfall patterns in this region. For example, south of Mortlake most pastures are used for dairy production. The land was heavily forested

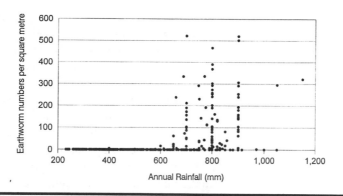

Figure 5. Abundance of *Aporrectodea caliginosa* (m⁻²) at 556 pasture sites in South Australia and western Victoria in relation to annual rainfall (mm).

before being cleared for agriculture. North of Mortlake, sheep production predominates. The land there was originally a savannah of native grasses. It is tempting to question if the distributions of the various earthworm species reflect these differences in original habitat and current agricultural practice. However, why are some introduced species, such as *A. rosea* (which is common elsewhere in regions with 400–600 mm annual rainfall), so rare north of Mortlake? What was the original distribution of native species such as *G. octothecatus* and *Spenceriella* sp. prior to invasion by exotic species? Can the current distributions of native species be explained (in part) by competition with introduced species? These questions remain to be resolved.

Other surveys for earthworms in agricultural soils in southern Australia (Abbott and Parker 1980; Kingston and Temple-Smith 1989; Mele 1991) have reported similar findings to those given above, with some minor variations in dominant species between regions. Baker et al. (1997a) made a national survey of earthworms, mostly in urban gardens but also in agricultural habitats. They found that introduced lumbricids predominated throughout southern Australia, but north of the Tropic of Capricorn these species were rare and replaced by other introduced species such as *Pontoscolex corethrurus* (Glossoscolecidae).

Introduced lumbricid earthworms from Europe are also very common in agricultural habitats in other countries with temperate or mediterranean climates (e.g., Reinecke and Visser 1980; Fender 1985; Springett 1992). The species that are most common in southern Australia (e.g., *A. caliginosa*, *A. trapezoides*, *A. rosea*) also predominate elsewhere. Lee (1985) has suggested that many of these peregrine lumbricid species have several features (e.g., parthenogenesis, polyploidy, broad environmental tolerances) that contribute to their success as colonists.

EFFECTS OF EARTHWORMS ON SOIL PROPERTIES AND PLANT PRODUCTION

There is a great variety of ways in which earthworms can influence soil properties and plant production (Lee 1985; Lavelle 1988; Curry 1994). Several studies have been made of the influence of the most common earthworm species in agricultural soils in southern Australia on soil structure (e.g., Barley 1959c; Hindell et al. 1994; Hirth et al. 1994), nutrient availability (Barley and Jennings 1959), burial of surface organic matter and lime (Barley 1959b; Baker et al. 1993e, 1995), distribution of beneficial microorganisms (Stephens et al. 1993b; Doube et al. 1994), reduction of root diseases (Stephens et al. 1993a, 1995), and plant yield and quality (Abbott and Parker 1981; Temple-Smith et al. 1993; Garnsey 1994; Stephens et al. 1994; Baker et al. 1997b). Two of these topics will be addressed here in more detail: the burial of surface-applied lime and organic matter by earthworms and the influence of earthworms on pasture and cereal production.

As in many other countries, soil acidity is a major environmental problem in high rainfall regions of Australia (Coventry 1985; Chartres et al. 1992). The use of ammonium-based nitrogen fertilizers and nitrogen fixing legumes has contributed significantly to soil acidification. Lime is applied to the surface of the soil to offset acidity but it is generally slow to be incorporated into the root zone where it is needed (Helyar 1991). It is often too costly or inappropriate to incorporate lime mechanically using tillage (e.g., in permanent pastures on steep slopes). Research in New Zealand (Stockdill and Cossens 1966; Springett 1983, 1985) has shown that some species of earthworms have the potential to bury lime and increase soil pH. Similar experiments have recently been conducted in South Australia to determine the species most likely to be useful in reducing soil acidity in this way. Earthworms have been caged in the field in PVC cylinders (30 cm diam., 20 cm long), driven into the soil using a vibrating plate compactor. The cylinders, and the undisturbed soil enclosed within them, were covered top and bottom with nylon mesh to prevent earthworm escape/invasion. Lime was added to the soil surface as required and the pH of the soil was measured down the profile inside the cages after four or five months exposure to different earthworm species. Controls were established by securing the mesh on the bottoms of the cages in summer, when most earthworms had retreated deep into the soil to aestivate below the depth of the PVC.

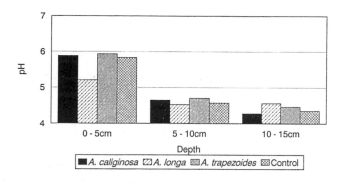

Figure 6. Average soil pH (in 0.01 *M* CaCl₂) at different depths within PVC cages in a pasture at Springmount, South Australia. Note: Soil samples were taken five months after adding lime (4 t ha⁻¹) and different earthworm species (460 m⁻²) to the soil surface. A control treatment is included. The soil pH in the absence of lime was 4.7 (0–5 cm), 4.3 (5–10 cm), and 4.3 (10–15 cm).

The results for one experiment on lime incorporation in a ryegrass/subclover pasture growing on an acid, duplex yellow clay soil (Palexeralf) in South Australia are given in Figure 6. The data suggest that *A. longa* buries lime more effectively than *A. caliginosa* and *A. trapezoides*. After liming, soil pH was lower near the soil surface (0–5 cm depth) in the presence of *A. longa* compared with the other species and a control (F = 5.83, p < 0.01). In contrast, soil pH was higher at 10–15 cm depth in the presence of *A. longa* compared with the other treatments (F = 8.72, p < 0.001). Visually, the soil surface was far more disturbed by *A. longa* than by the other two species.

Baker et al. (1993e, 1995) also studied lime incorporation by earthworms in pastures and cereal crops in South Australia, but on a finer scale (2-cm-depth intervals). They demonstrated that *A. trapezoides* could increase soil pH by up to a unit at 2–4 cm depth after four months. In contrast, *A. rosea* had a negligible effect on lime burial. Baker et al. (1993e, 1995) explained the difference in influence of these two species in terms of their relative surface activities. *A. trapezoides* is more surface-active and creates a greater number of surface-venting pores than *A. rosea*, down which lime particles can be washed by rainwater.

Large amounts of cattle and sheep dung accumulate on the surface of Australian pastures (Waterhouse 1974). As well as fouling pasture growth and increasing fly numbers, this dung represents an inefficient return of plant nutrients to the soil. Many species of exotic dung beetles have been introduced to Australia to encourage the burial of cattle dung (Tyndale-Biscoe 1990), but the role of earthworms in this process has largely been ignored (Ferrar 1975). Holter (1979) showed that *A. longa*, working in concert with dung beetles, was particularly effective in burying cattle dung in a Danish pasture, and Martin and Charles (1979) demonstrated that *A. caliginosa* and *L. rubellus* buried large amounts of both cattle and sheep dung in New Zealand pastures. The influence of earthworms on the burial of sheep dung has been measured in southern Australia in cages as described above. A known volume of dung was applied to the soil surface and the amount left after five months of earthworm activity was assessed. *A. longa* was clearly very efficient at burying sheep dung, more so than several other species (Figure 7).

In Australian cereal fields, farmers are now encouraged to reduce tillage and retain their stubbles after harvest (Rovira 1992). It is desirable that this source of organic matter is buried to improve soil structure and nutrient return. In a soil used for grain production, *A. trapezoides* reduced the amount of surface pea straw by an extra 52% compared with controls, while *A. rosea* had no effect (Baker et al. 1995).

Glasshouse experiments have demonstrated the potential for some earthworm species to increase cereal and pasture production. For example, Baker et al. (1997b) have shown that *A. trapezoides* can increase wheat and subclover

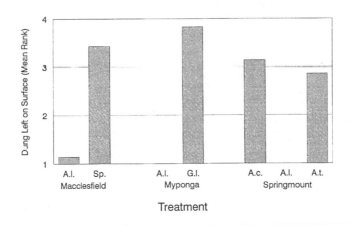

Figure 7. Visual ranking (mean of seven replicates) of the amount of sheep dung remaining on the soil surface within PVC cages in three pastures in South Australia. Note: Observations were made approx. five months after adding the dung (276 g cage^{-1}) and earthworms (30 cage^{-1} or 460 m^{-2}). Rank 1 = 0–25% of dung remaining, 2 = 26–50%, 3 = 51–75%, and 4 = 76–100%. A.l. = *Aporrectodea longa*, Sp. = *Spenceriella* sp., G.l. = *Gemascolex lateralis*, A.c. = *Aporrectodea caliginosa*, and A.t. = *Aporrectodea trapezoides*.

plant biomass by 39% and 21% respectively, grain yield by 35%, and N content of the grain by 14%. *A. rosea*, on the other hand, had limited influence, increasing wheat plant biomass by 13% but having no effect on the other production indices. McColl et al. (1982) have also shown that *A. caliginosa* can greatly enhance nutrient uptake and early growth of perennial ryegrass in pots.

A few field experiments have demonstrated the potential for earthworms to increase plant production in southern Australia. T.A. McCredie and C.A. Parker (pers. comm.) have attributed a 62% increase in wheat yield (grain) to the introduction of *A. trapezoides* in field cages in Western Australia. Temple-Smith et al. (1993) reported increases in pasture production of up to 75% due to *A. caliginosa* and *A. longa* in Tasmania. Manipulations of earthworm populations in PVC cages, in established pastures in South Australia and Victoria, have demonstrated that some earthworm species, most notably *A. longa*, can increase pasture production significantly (up to 60%) within just five months of introduction (F = 5.28, p < 0.001) (Figure 8). How sustainable such increases are likely to be through time has yet to be determined, but it is encouraging to note that significant increases in pasture production have been maintained for many years following the introductions of appropriate earthworms elsewhere in the world, e.g., New Zealand (Stockdill 1982). Further examples of earthworm introductions leading to increased plant production in countries other than Australia are given later (see *Introductions of New Taxa*).

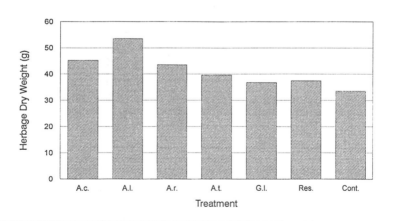

Figure 8. Average pasture yield (cage⁻¹) in response to earthworm introductions at Myponga, South Australia. Note: Herbage cuts were taken on three occasions over five months following earthworm introduction (460 worms m⁻²). A.c. = *Aporrectodea caliginosa*, A.l. = *Aporrectodea longa*, A.r. = *Aporrectodea rosea*, A.t. = *Aporrectodea trapezoides*, G.l. = *Gemascolex lateralis*, Res. = residents, and Cont. = control (no worms).

INFLUENCE OF MANAGEMENT PRACTICES
ON EARTHWORM ABUNDANCE

Agricultural management practices such as tillage, crop rotation, stubble retention, drainage, irrigation, lime, fertilizer and slurry application, pesticide use and
stocking rate can influence earthworm numbers and biomass (Lee 1985; Lavelle
et al. 1989; Curry 1994; Fraser 1994). Rovira et al. (1987) demonstrated that the
abundance of earthworms in a red-brown earth soil in South Australia was
doubled by direct drilling of cereals compared with conventional cultivation
(soil disturbed several times by machinery prior to sowing). Fewer earthworms
were found under a lupin-wheat rotation than under a pasture-wheat rotation.
Rovira et al. (1987) identified the earthworms in their plots as *A. caliginosa*, but
since this species has never been recorded at the site since, nor in surveys
throughout neighboring farms (Buckerfield 1993a; Baker et al. 1993c, 1995), it
is more likely that Rovira et al. were counting *A. rosea*, possibly with some *A.
trapezoides* and *M. dubius* as well. Haines and Uren (1990) and Buckerfield
(1993a, 1994) have provided supportive evidence that tillage reduces earthworm
numbers in Australia and that pastures in rotation with cereals and retention of
stubble can increase abundance. Numerous studies in other countries have demonstrated the negative effect of tillage and the positive influence of adding plant
residues on earthworm numbers (Barnes and Ellis 1979; Jensen 1985; Springett
et al. 1992). Tillage can reduce earthworm numbers in a variety of ways. Earthworms may be damaged directly by machinery, exposed to predation or adverse
weather, their burrow systems may be disrupted, or the availability of suitable
food may be reduced (Edwards and Lofty 1982a; Springett 1983; Lee 1985;
Dalby 1996).

Water-logging of soils is a significant problem in high rainfall zones of
southeastern Australia (Reed and Cocks 1982). Underground drainage is expensive to install, but can significantly increase lucerne (alfalfa) production (Chin
1990). The influence of drainage on earthworm numbers was investigated in
Chin's lucerne plots (Figure 9). The abundance of *A. caliginosa*, the most common species at the site, was increased greatly by drainage (F = 12.84, p < 0.001).
Such increases in earthworm numbers may contribute, at least in part, to the
observed increases in plant production under drainage. In Ireland, Baker (1983)
found soil moisture levels in a grassland on reclaimed peat bog explained patchiness in the distributions of several species of earthworm (and color morphs
within *Allolobophora chlorotica*).

Without irrigation, pasture growth usually ceases during the hot, dry summer in South Australia and no earthworms are active in the root zone (Baker
et al. 1992, 1993c,d). Baker et al. (1993c) suggested that earthworm activity

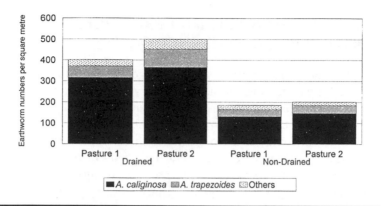

Figure 9. Average abundance of earthworms in drained and undrained soil beneath lucerne at the Pastoral and Veterinary Institute, Hamilton, Victoria.

ceases in soils above approximately 150 kPa water suction potential. With irrigation, several species remain active during summer (e.g., *A. trapezoides*, *A. caliginosa*, *A. rosea*). Pastures that have been irrigated are dominated by *A. caliginosa* during the cool, wet winter (Figure 10). *A. trapezoides* is most common in dryland pastures in winter. *L. rubellus* occurs in small numbers in irrigated pastures, but has never been found in dryland fields. Increases in the abundance of *A. caliginosa* and *L. rubellus* with irrigation are to be expected, given their apparent restrictions to moist habitats in their national distributions (see earlier comments and Baker et al. 1997a). *L. rubellus* is also regarded as

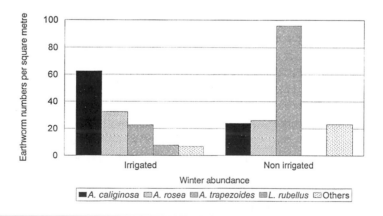

Figure 10. Average abundance of earthworms in irrigated and non-irrigated pastures in the Mt. Lofty Ranges, S.A., during winter.

an epigeic species and therefore particularly susceptible to surface aridity (Fraser 1994). The decline in the abundance of *A. trapezoides* associated with irrigation is intriguing. Possibly this poorer performance by *A. trapezoides* is related to increased competition for limited resources with other species, such as *A. caliginosa*, in moister soils.

Elsewhere in southern Australia, Noble and Mills (1974) have reported that the numbers of *A. caliginosa* increased with irrigation, but began to decline over time at the heaviest irrigation rate. They explained this population decline as due to increased surface activity and greater predation by birds. In Tasmania, Kingston (1989) and Lobry de Bruyn (1993) recorded decreases in the abundance of *A. caliginosa* with irrigation, but increases in numbers of *L. rubellus*. The authors have explained their results in terms of trampling-induced mortality for both species (see below) and increased parasitism by Diptera, overcome for *L. rubellus* by greatly enhanced summer survival and reproduction.

Several authors (see Edwards and Lofty 1977) have shown that liming an acid soil can increase earthworm abundance. Springett and Syers (1984) argued that the change in pH per se influences earthworms, rather than the availability of calcium. Edwards and Lofty (1977) concluded that population responses to lime are not likely to occur if the initial pH of the soil is >4.5–5, above which most species are insensitive. Mixed results have been recorded in response to liming pastures in southeastern Australia. Baker (1992) found that liming a pasture on a clay loam soil in western Victoria had no overall impact on total earthworm numbers nine years later (rates of 0–10 t ha^{-1}, pH range 4.5–5.6 at the time of earthworm sampling), but at the species level there were increases in abundance with increased pH (*Octolasion cyaneum* and *M. dubius*), decreases (*Heteroporodrilus* sp. and *Spenceriella* sp.), and no significant changes (*A. trapezoides* and *A. rosea*). In contrast, Buckerfield (1994) reported that liming a pasture in South Australia and increasing soil pH over a similar range to that of Baker (1992) increased the abundance of *A. trapezoides*. In field cages in South Australia, the addition of 4 t lime ha^{-1} had no influence on the establishment of *A. longa* after five months, in a range of soil types (initial pH 4.3–5.2), but reduced the survival of *Spenceriella* sp. at some sites (Baker, unpubl. data). Garnsey (1994) reported that the addition of lime (5 t ha^{-1}) increased the abundance of *A. trapezoides*, *L. rubellus,* and *A. longa* in one Tasmanian pasture after one or two years (initial pH = 5.9), but had no influence in another (initial pH = 6.0). Garnsey (1994) attributed the earthworm response he did get to an indirect effect mediated through increased clover production and hence improved food quality for the worms. The numerical responses of earthworms to liming seem likely to vary according to the soil type, earthworm species present, and the range of pH involved.

Barley (1959a) showed that the numbers and weights of earthworms (probably mostly *A. rosea* and *A. trapezoides*) increased with the addition of superphosphate to a pasture in South Australia. Barley argued this was due to an increase in plant production and hence available food (as decomposing plant material). Similarly, Fraser et al. (1994) found that earthworm numbers (mostly *A. caliginosa* and *L. rubellus*) increased with superphosphate use and plant production in a New Zealand pasture. However, such associations are not always evident. Baker et al. (1993a,b) were unable to demonstrate changes in earthworm densities following superphosphate applications to pastures in Victoria. Food supply was possibly not limiting for earthworms in these latter situations. Lee (1985) indicated that some fertilizers can acidify soils and hence reduce earthworm abundance. The additions of nitrogenous fertilizers and moderate amounts of manures and slurries increase earthworm numbers (Gerard and Hay 1979; Edwards and Lofty 1982b; Curry 1994). However, excessive amounts of the latter may reduce abundance.

Trampling by agricultural animal stock is likely to squash earthworms that live near the soil surface, compact the soil, and return organic matter and nutrients in a different form (dung and urine) and spatial distribution than occurs with senescent plants. Stock therefore have the potential to influence earthworm populations. However, there has been surprisingly little data published on the interactions between stocking rates and earthworm abundance. Lobry de Bruyn (1993) excluded dairy cattle from pastures in Tasmania and demonstrated that trampling reduced the abundance of both *A. caliginosa* (19%) and *L. rubellus* (25%). As well as the difference due to trampling per se, pasture growth was reduced in the untrampled plots and species composition also changed (more weeds). The mechanism driving the change in earthworm populations was therefore not clear. Nevertheless, both Kingston (1989) and Lobry de Bruyn (1993) have suggested that mortality of *A. caliginosa* and *L. rubellus* in irrigated dairy pastures in Tasmania is due, at least in part, to direct trampling effects, exacerbated by greater surface activity in moist soils, and to compaction of the soil which renders it unsuitable for earthworm survival.

With smaller animal stock, Hutchinson and King (1980) observed that earthworm populations were highest at a stocking rate of 20 sheep ha^{-1} in pastures in northern New South Wales. This stocking rate corresponded with maximum primary productivity. On the other hand, Baker et al. (1993a,b) could show no consistent pattern between earthworm abundance and the stocking rate of sheep (range 5–23 ha^{-1}) in several pastures in western Victoria.

Pizl (1992) and Sochtig and Larink (1992) have demonstrated significant declines in earthworm numbers following compaction from machinery traffic in orchards and cereal fields in Czechoslovakia and Germany, respectively. The only comparable Australian study is that of T. Ellis in South Australia (pers. comm.), who demonstrated a reduction of earthworm numbers beneath wheel tracks in a controlled-traffic, cereal production trial.

Lee (1985), Edwards and Bohlen (1992), and Curry (1994) have provided detailed discussions of the effects of various pesticides on earthworm abundance. It is generally accepted that most herbicides are not directly toxic to earthworms, but they may influence numbers indirectly by changing plant production, food supply, and microclimate. Some fungicides, such as benomyl, can be very toxic to earthworms and influence them indirectly by altering their food supply. Buckerfield (1993b) showed that the use of fungicides can alter species composition of earthworm populations in South Australian pastures. Fumigants such as methyl bromide and many insecticides (e.g., organochlorines and carbamates) also kill earthworms. A worrying trend in southern Australia is the increased use of methiocarb baits to control introduced helicid snails in pastures and crops (Baker 1989). These snails are particularly numerous where tillage is reduced and stubbles are retained—just the situation where earthworm numbers are likely to be encouraged.

INTRODUCTIONS OF NEW EARTHWORM TAXA

The introduction of earthworms to lacking soils has resulted in significant increases in plant production in several countries. Perhaps the best known cases in the scientific literature include the introduction of *A. caliginosa* to pastures in New Zealand, where pasture production was increased initially by 72% and then by 25% in the longer term (Stockdill 1982); the introduction of a mixture of *A. caliginosa, A. longa, L. rubellus,* and *L. terrestris* in polder grasslands in the Netherlands (10% increase) (Hoogerkamp et al. 1983); and the introduction of *L. terrestris* and *A. caliginosa* to grassland on reclaimed peat bog in Ireland (25–49% increase after two to three years) (Curry and Boyle 1987). Springett (1985) introduced *A. longa* to a pasture in New Zealand which already contained *A. caliginosa* and *L. rubellus* and recorded an increase in plant production of up to 27% in subsequent seasons. Edwards and Lofty (1980) inoculated *L. terrestris* and *A. longa* into sterilized soil in England and recorded increased root growth and grain yield in direct-drilled cereals. In contrast, James (1991) reported that the introduction of *A. caliginosa* and *Octolasion cyaneum* to tallgrass prairie in the U.S.A. had a negative influence on soil properties through a reduction in the numbers of more useful native species (*Diplocardia* spp).

A simple method for inoculating earthworms into unpopulated soils was developed by Stockdill (1982) which involved cutting shallow sods of soil from heavily populated fields and placing them in unpopulated sites. This method is suitable for epigeic and endogeic species (e.g., *L. rubellus* and *A. caliginosa*), which are likely to be harvested in the sods. Butt (1992) and Butt et al. (1992) have developed a simple method for mass-producing and distributing deep-burrowing, anecic species (e.g., *L. terrestris*).

The rates of dispersal of earthworms following introduction to new habitats have been measured by several authors in New Zealand and Europe (Stockdill 1982; Hoogerkamp et al. 1983; Curry and Boyle 1987; Marinissen 1991; Marinissen and van den Bosch 1992; Stein et al. 1992) and vary between 2–15 m yr^{-1}, according to the fecundities and burrowing behaviors of the different species. Recent studies in modeling (Marinissen and van den Bosch 1992) and the use of geostatistics to measure environmental features resulting from earthworm activities (e.g., A horizon depth and number of pores) (Stein et al. 1992) represent exciting new developments in research on earthworm dispersal.

The earthworm fauna in agricultural soils in southern Australia is dominated by accidentally-introduced species that are now distributed patchily. While edaphic and climatic factors explain much of this patchiness in distribution, it is reasonable to assume that many areas that lack particular species do so because of lack of opportunity to colonize. Increasing the distributions of the most beneficial species through deliberate introductions, to sites where they are thought likely to establish, may prove very profitable. However, few such field introductions of earthworms have been made to date. *A. caliginosa* and *A. longa* have been introduced into pastures in Tasmania with resultant increases in production (Temple-Smith et al. 1993; Garnsey 1994). Introductions of *A. caliginosa* to irrigated pastures in New South Wales led to a breakdown of a thick litter mat and a decline in bulk density (Noble et al. 1970), and introductions of *Aporrectodea* spp. and *Eukeria saltensis* (Ocnerodrilidae) into irrigated wheat in New South Wales increased air permeability of the soil (Blackwell and Blackwell 1989).

The distribution of the deep-burrowing *A. longa* is currently restricted within Australia to Tasmania and a few experimental release sites in South Australia and Victoria (Baker et al. 1997a). The climate-matching software package "CLIMEX" (Sutherst and Maywald 1985) has been used to predict where *A. longa* might colonize within mainland Australia (Figure 11). Field trials are currently evaluating the environmental factors affecting the establishment of *A. longa*, optimal inoculation rates, dispersal, and the influences of this species on soil properties and plant production at a range of sites within its potential mainland distribution (e.g., Figures 6–8 and G. Baker, unpubl. data). These studies are also determining the thresholds of abundance that are required for *A. longa* to influence soil fertility and plant production.

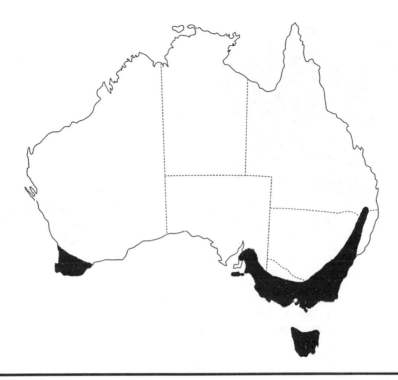

Figure 11. Potential distribution of *Aporrectodea longa* in Australia, based on climatic data for sites near where it currently occurs in large numbers in northern Tasmania.

The possibility also exists to introduce additional earthworm species into southern Australia from climatically-matched regions overseas. No deliberate attempts to do this have yet been recorded, although such a strategy was suggested by Barley (1959c) and Lee (1985). Broad-scale surveys and intensive, seasonal monitoring of field populations (Baker et al. 1992, 1993c,d) suggest that the current fauna in agricultural fields is poorly represented with deep-burrowing species. Virtually all earthworm activity is confined to the top 10 cm or less during winter and spring (four to seven months). The further spread of *A. longa* within Australia will possibly help to redress this limitation of the earthworm fauna, but it is unlikely that *A. longa* will successfully colonize the strictly mediterranean climatic regions. The natural distribution of *A. longa* does not extend into mediterranean regions of countries such as France (Figure 12). Instead, other anecic species such as *Scherotheca* spp. are found there. These latter species might be considered for importation to Australia.

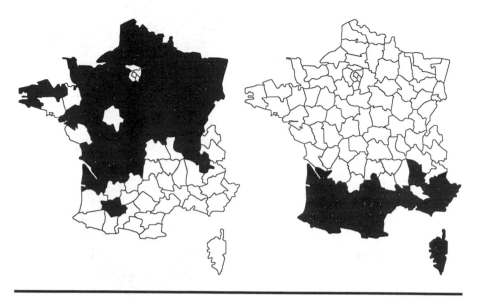

Figure 12. Distributions of (left) *Aporrectodea longa* **and (right)** *Scherotheca* **spp. in France. Source: The maps are based on departmental records listed in Bouché (1972).**

The native European distributions of several of the lumbricid species now found in Australia are broad, ranging from the Mediterranean to Scandinavia (e.g., *A. caliginosa* and *A. chlorotica*). The majority of early European migrants to Australia, who presumably brought these lumbricids with them accidentally (e.g., in potted plants), were mainly from countries with cool, temperate climates, such as the United Kingdom, Ireland, and Germany. It is sensible to question the likely suitability of strains of earthworms from such countries, when faced with the warmer and drier habitats in much of southern Australia, and if mediterranean strains of the same species might be more appropriate. Current research is using modern molecular biological techniques (e.g., Polymerase Chain Reaction, Randomly Amplified Polymorphic DNA) to identify strains within lumbricid earthworms in Australia and trace their origins (G. Baker, C. Fowler, A. Dyer, unpubl. data). Some related research has isolated and sequenced diagnostic clones for the two closely related species *A. trapezoides* and *A. caliginosa*. This work verified the identification of juveniles of these two species on the rather subjective basis of body pigmentation. Similar molecular biological methods to those now being used on earthworms have been used to identify genetic variability within insect biological control agents (Edwards and

Hoy 1993). These DNA-based methods have been argued to be more sensitive than protein-based methods. Nevertheless, Terhivuo and Saura (1993) have demonstrated much genetic variation within species such as *A. rosea* using enzyme electrophoresis, as well as morphological variation.

EARTHWORMS AS INDICATORS OF THE SUSTAINABILITY OF AGRICULTURE

Earthworms are popularly believed to reflect soil health. They often make up a large proportion of the biomass of the soil fauna and respond numerically to many agricultural management practices (see above). Earthworm abundance and biomass are also correlated with a range of edaphic variables. It is therefore not surprising that earthworms have been suggested as potential indicators of the sustainability of agricultural practices that farmers might use (Oades and Walters 1994).

A useful indicator of sustainability must be attractive to farmers so that they will understand and adopt it, easy to measure reliably, and responsive to environmental change in a timely fashion. Farmers know that earthworms are beneficial. However, few are aware of the species they have on their land and, like scientists, they are unclear just how many earthworms they need in their soil (i.e., what are the abundance thresholds they need to aim at?). It is important that farmers recognize the species of earthworms they have on their farms, realize the varying abilities of species to influence soil properties and plant production, and note the strengths and weaknesses of their resource. Simple keys have been devised for the common earthworm species in Australia that farmers might use (e.g., Baker and Barrett 1994).

Sampling for earthworms, whichever method is used, is notoriously labor intensive and fraught with inaccuracies (Baker and Lee 1992). Earthworms are patchily distributed within fields (Baker et al. 1992, 1993b). Soil moisture can vary within short periods of time and greatly affect the numbers of earthworms collected (Baker et al. 1993c). Farmers are busy people, but they must take care to collect sufficient samples to make their data meaningful and enable detection of differences in abundance through time or space. Some earthworms have large reproductive potential (e.g., epigeic species) but the earthworms that predominate in Australian agricultural fields probably do not (Lee 1985). While drastic physical or chemical disturbance might quickly reduce earthworm numbers, numerical recovery may well take several years.

The fact that the earthworm fauna of Australian agricultural habitats is dominated mainly by introduced species raises an immediate question: How far have these species spread to occupy sites suitable for them? The answer is not known, but it seems likely that there are many sites yet to be occupied. More than 40% of pastures in one region of western Victoria lack *A. trapezoides*, but no good reason other than lack of opportunity to colonize can be given for its absence from these pastures. While the presence of large numbers of a diverse community of earthworms can only be a healthy sign, there is a strong risk that low numbers or indeed absence of earthworms might be misinterpreted as a "problem" at a particular site when the real problem is not with the soil *per se* but the chance of earthworm dispersal to it. Some seemingly "healthy" soils in Australia lack earthworms (e.g., some kraznozems). That is not to say that these soils would not be *more* productive with the arrival of appropriate species of earthworms!

CONCLUSIONS

The world literature on earthworms in agricultural soils is huge. Much of the available information has been comprehensively reviewed by Edwards and Lofty (1977), Lee (1985), and Curry (1994). Therefore, rather than rework this extensive literature, this paper has considered recent research on the earthworm fauna of agricultural soils in one region of the world, southern Australia.

The average abundance and species richness of earthworm communities in agricultural soils in southern Australia are generally low, especially in fields used for cereal production. However, the range in abundance is large (0–1262 m^{-2}). The greatest abundances found in southern Australia compare favorably with the densest populations recorded elsewhere in the world (Lee 1985; Curry 1994). Research has identified the environmental factors most closely correlated with earthworm abundance in Australian soils (e.g., rainfall, soil N and C) and agricultural management practices (e.g., minimum tillage, stubble retention) which can greatly encourage dense populations. Lack of opportunity to colonize very probably also explains much of the observed patchiness in the distributions of some of the common introduced species.

The most common species in Australian agricultural soils are the introduced lumbricids, *A. caliginosa*, *A. trapezoides,* and *A. rosea,* which are also common in other regions of the world with similar climates. Native Australian megascolecid species (e.g., *Spenceriella* spp.) are generally rare but can occasionally be dominant. Whether or not the introduced lumbricids compete for resources with the native species is not known.

Field and laboratory experiments have demonstrated the different abilities of some of the most common species to influence soil properties and plant production. For example, *A. trapezoides* appears to be a much more beneficial species than *A. rosea* in terms of promoting wheat grain yield and quality. Unfortunately, *A. trapezoides* is currently much rarer than *A. rosea* in fields used for cereal production. It is important to realize that the numbers of earthworms used in experiments to demonstrate potential benefits (often about 400 m^{-2}) may exceed observed field densities. These experiments should therefore be interpreted cautiously. Measures are needed of the threshold densities required to obtain benefits in the field.

There is much potential to introduce beneficial species to sites lacking them, either by further spread of species already present but patchily distributed within Australia, or the introduction of novel species or strains from climatically matched regions overseas. The introduced lumbricid, *A. longa*, is currently restricted to Tasmania, but its potential distribution within Australia is predicted to be much larger. Preliminary results from introductions of *A. longa* into pastures in South Australia and Victoria suggest that substantial increases in pasture production may accrue from redistributing this species further and augmenting the earthworm fauna where deep-burrowing species are lacking.

Earthworms have been proposed as useful indicators of agricultural sustainability. With a great deal of care in sampling, earthworms might be combined with other physical and chemical indicators to monitor performance in local areas. However, because of the patchy distributions of the most common species, it seems unlikely that very meaningful comparisons can be made across broad geographic regions.

ACKNOWLEDGMENTS

I wish to thank the many colleagues who have contributed to the research reported here, especially Vicki Barrett, John Buckerfield, Penny Carter, Paul Dalby, Robyn Grey-Gardner, Peter Williams, and Jason Woods. I also wish to thank the Wool, Grains, Dairy, and Land and Water Research and Development Corporations for their financial assistance.

REFERENCES CITED

Abbott, I., and C.A. Parker. 1980. The occurrence of earthworms in the wheat-belt of western Australia in relation to land use and rainfall. Australian Journal of Soil Research 18, 343–352.

Abbott, I., and C.A. Parker. 1981. Interactions between earthworms and their soil environment. Soil Biology and Biochemistry 13, 191–197.

Baker, G.H. 1983. Distribution, abundance, and species associations of earthworms (Lumbricidae) in a reclaimed peat soil in Ireland. Holarctic Ecology 6, 74–80.

Baker, G.H. 1989. Damage, population dynamics, movement and control of pest helicid snails in southern Australia. In Slugs and Snails in World Agriculture. British Crop Protection Council Monograph No. 41. I. Henderson (ed.), pp. 175–185. BCPC, Thornton Heath, U.K.

Baker, G.H. 1992. Optimising earthworm activity in soils. Proceedings of the 33rd Annual Conference of the Grassland Society of Victoria, pp. 59–66.

Baker, G.H., and V.J. Barrett. 1994. Earthworm Identifier. CSIRO, Melbourne.

Baker, G.H., and K.E. Lee. 1992. Earthworms. In Soil Sampling and Methods of Analysis. M.R. Carter (ed.), pp. 359–371. Canadian Society of Soil Science. Lewis Publishers, Boca Raton, FL.

Baker, G.H., V.J. Barrett, R. Grey-Gardner, and J.C. Buckerfield. 1992. The life history and abundance of the introduced earthworms *Aporrectodea trapezoides* and *A. caliginosa* (Annelida: Lumbricidae) in pasture soils in the Mount Lofty Ranges, South Australia. Australian Journal of Ecology 17, 177–188.

Baker, G.H., V.J. Barrett, P.J. Carter, J.W.D. Cayley, and G.R. Saul. 1993a. The influence of fertiliser on the abundance and diversity of earthworms in pastures in western Victoria. Proceedings of the 7th Australian Agronomy Conference, pp. 312–315.

Baker, G.H., V.J. Barrett, P.J. Carter, J.W.D. Cayley, and G.R. Saul. 1993b. The influence of phosphate application and stocking rate on the abundance of earthworms in a Victorian pasture. Proceedings of the 6th Australasian Conference on Grassland Invertebrate Ecology, pp. 85–91.

Baker, G.H., V.J. Barrett, P.J. Carter, P.M.L. Williams, and J.C. Buckerfield. 1993c. Seasonal changes in the abundance of earthworms (Annelida: Lumbricidae and Acanthodrilidae) in soils used for cereal and lucerne production in South Australia. Australian Journal of Agricultural Research 44, 1291–1301.

Baker, G.H., V.J Barrett, R. Grey-Gardner, and J.C. Buckerfield. 1993d. Abundance and life history of native and introduced earthworms (Annelida: Megascolecidae and Lumbricidae) in pasture soils in the Mount Lofty Ranges, South Australia. Transactions of the Royal Society of South Australia 117, 47–53.

Baker, G.H., P.M.L. Williams, V.J. Barrett, and P.J. Carter. 1993e. Burial of surface-applied lime by earthworms in South Australian pastures. Proceedings of the 17th International Grassland Congress 1, 939–941.

Baker, G.H., P.J. Carter, V.J. Barrett, G.P Kilpin, J.C. Buckerfield, and P.R. Dalby. 1994. The introduction and management of earthworms to improve soil structure and fertility in south-eastern Australia. In Soil Biota. Management in Sustainable Farming Systems. C.E. Pankhurst, B.M. Doube, V.V.S.R. Gupta, and P.R. Grace (eds.), pp. 42–49. CSIRO, Melbourne.

Baker, G.H., V.J. Barrett, P.J. Carter, J.C. Buckerfield, P.M.L. Williams, and G.P. Kilpin. 1995. Abundance of earthworms in soils used for cereal production in south-eastern Australia and their role in reducing soil acidity. In Plant Soil Interactions at Low pH. R.A. Date, N.J. Grundon, G.E. Rayment, and M.E. Probert (eds.), pp. 213–218. Kluwer Academic Publishers, Dordrecht.

Baker, G.H., T.A. Thumlert, L.S. Meisel, P.J. Carter, and G.P. Kilpin. 1997a. "Earthworms Downunder." A survey of the earthworm fauna of urban and agricultural soils in Australia. Soil Biology and Biochemistry. In press.

Baker, G.H., P.M.L. Williams, P.J. Carter, and N.R. Long. 1997b. Influence of lumbricid earthworms on yield and quality of wheat and clover. Soil Biology and Biochemistry. In press.

Barley, K.P. 1959a. The influence of earthworms on soil fertility. I. Earthworm populations found in agricultural land near Adelaide. Australian Journal of Agricultural Research 10, 171–178.

Barley, K.P. 1959b. The influence of earthworms on soil fertility. II. Consumption of soil and organic matter by the earthworm *Allolobophora caliginosa*. Australian Journal of Agricultural Research 10, 179–185.

Barley, K.P. 1959c. Earthworms and soil fertility. IV. The influence of earthworms on the physical properties of a red-brown earth. Australian Journal of Agricultural Research 10, 371–376.

Barley, K.P., and A.C. Jennings. 1959. Earthworms and soil fertility. III. The influence of earthworms on the availability of nitrogen. Australian Journal of Agricultural Research 10, 364–370.

Barnes, B.T., and F.B. Ellis. 1979. Effects of different methods of cultivation and direct drilling, and disposal of straw residues, on populations of earthworms. Journal of Soil Science 30, 669–679.

Blackwell, P.S., and J. Blackwell. 1989. The introduction of earthworms to an ameliorated, irrigated duplex soil in south-eastern Australia and the influence on macropores. Australian Journal of Soil Research 27, 807–814.

Bouché, M.B. 1972. Lombriciens de France. Ecologie et Systematique. Annales de Zoologie-Ecologie Animale Numero hors-serie, 1–671.

Buckerfield, J.C. 1993a. Pastures in crop rotations enhance earthworm populations in southern Australia. Proceedings of the 17th International Grassland Congress 1, 942–944.

Buckerfield, J.C. 1993b. Long-term responses of native and introduced earthworms to pasture soil applications of fungicides. Proceedings of the 6th Australasian Conference on Grassland Invertebrate Ecology, pp. 92–99.

Buckerfield, J.C. 1994. Appropriate earthworms for agriculture and vermiculture. Technical Report 2/1994. CSIRO Australia, Division of Soils, Adelaide.

Buckerfield, J.C., and Auhl, L.H. 1994. Earthworms as indicators of sustainable production in intensive cereal cropping. In Soil Biota. Management in Sustainable Farming Systems. Poster Papers. C.E. Pankhurst (ed.), pp. 169–172. CSIRO, Melbourne.

Butt, K.R. 1992. Development of an earthworm cultivation and soil-inoculation technique for land restoration. Proceedings of the 3rd British Grassland Society Conference, pp. 6–7.

Butt, K.R., J. Frederickson, and R.M. Morris. 1992. The intensive production of *Lumbricus terrestris* L. for soil amelioration. Soil Biology and Biochemistry 24, 1321–1325.

Chartres, C.J., K.R. Helyar, R.W. Fitzpatrick, and J. Williams. 1992. Land degradation as a result of European settlement of Australia and its influence on soil properties. In Australia's Renewable Resources: Sustainability and Global Change. Bureau of Rural Resources Proceedings No. 14. R.M. Gifford and M.M. Barson (eds.), pp. 3–33. Government Printing Service, Canberra.

Chin, J. 1990. Underground drainage increases the production of lucerne but not pasture. In Research Review 1989–90, J. Cayley, N. Draffen, and J. Graham (eds.), p. 49. Department of Agriculture and Rural Affairs, Pastoral Research Institute, Hamilton, Victoria, Australia.

Coventry, D.R. 1985. Changes in agricultural systems on acid soils in southern Australia. Proceedings 3rd Australian Agronomy Conference, pp. 126–145.

Curry, J.P. 1994. Grassland Invertebrates. Ecology, Influence on Soil Fertility and Effects on Plant Growth. Chapman & Hall, London.

Curry, J.P., and K.E. Boyle. 1987. Growth rates, establishment, and effects on herbage yield of introduced earthworms in grassland on reclaimed cutover peat. Biology and Fertility of Soils 3, 95–98.

Dalby, P.R. 1996. Competition between earthworms in high rainfall pastures in the Mt. Lofty Ranges, South Australia. Ph.D. Thesis, University of Adelaide.

Doube, B.M., P.M. Stephens, C.W. Davoren, and M.H. Ryder. 1994. Earthworms and the introduction and management of beneficial microorganisms. In Soil Biota. Management in Sustainable Farming Systems. C.E. Pankhurst, B.M. Doube, V.V.S.R. Gupta, and P.R. Grace (eds.), pp. 32–41. CSIRO, Melbourne.

Edwards, C.A., and P.J. Bohlen. 1992. The effects of toxic chemicals on earthworms. Reviews of Environmental Contamination and Toxicology 125, 23–99.

Edwards, C.A., and J.R. Lofty. 1977. Biology of Earthworms. 2nd Edition. Chapman and Hall, London.

Edwards, C.A., and J.R. Lofty. 1980. Effects of earthworm inoculation upon the root growth of direct drilled cereals. Journal of Applied Ecology 17, 533–543.

Edwards, C.A., and J.R. Lofty. 1982a. The effect of direct drilling and minimal cultivation on earthworm populations. Journal of Applied Ecology 19, 723–734.

Edwards, C.A., and J.R. Lofty. 1982b. Nitrogenous fertilizers and earthworm populations in agricultural soils. Soil Biology and Biochemistry 14, 515–521.

Edwards, O.R., and M.A. Hoy. 1993. Polymorphism in two parasitoids detected using random amplified polymorphic DNA polymerase chain reaction. Biological Control 3, 243–257.

Fender, W.M. 1985. Earthworms of the western United States. Part I. Lumbricidae. Megadrilogica 4, 93–129.

Ferrar, P. 1975. Disintegration of dung pads in north Queensland before the introduction of exotic dung beetles. Australian Journal of Experimental Agriculture and Animal Husbandry 15, 325–329.

Fraser, P.M. 1994. The impact of soil and crop management practices on soil macrofauna. In Soil Biota. Management in Sustainable Farming Systems. C.E. Pankhurst, B.M. Doube, V.V.S.R. Gupta, and P.R. Grace (eds.), pp. 125–132. CSIRO, Melbourne.

Fraser, P.M., R.J. Haynes, and P.H. Williams. 1994. Effect of pasture improvement and intensive cultivation on size of microbial biomass, enzyme activities and composition and size of earthworm populations. Biology and Fertility of Soils 17, 185–190.

Garnsey, R.B. 1994. Increasing earthworm populations and pasture production in the Midlands of Tasmania through management and the introduction of the earthworm *Aporrectodea longa*. In Soil Biota. Management in Sustainable Farming Systems. Poster Papers. C.E. Pankhurst (ed.), pp. 27–30. CSIRO, Melbourne.

Gerard, B.M., and R.K.M. Hay. 1979. The effect on earthworms of plowing, tined cultivation, direct drilling and nitrogen in a barley monoculture system. Journal of Agricultural Science, Cambridge 93, 147–155.

Haines, P.J., and N.C. Uren. 1990. Effects of conservation tillage farming on soil microbial biomass, organic matter and earthworm populations, in north-eastern Victoria. Australian Journal of Experimental Agriculture 30, 365–371.

Helyar, K.R. 1991. The management of acid soils. In Plant-Soil Interactions at Low pH. R.J. Wright, V.C. Baligar, and R.P. Murrmann (eds.), pp. 365–382. Kluwer Academic Publishers, Dordrecht

Hindell, R.P., B.M. McKenzie, and J.M. Tisdall. 1994. Destabilisation of soil aggregates by geophagous earthworms—a comparison between earthworm and artificial casts. In Soil Biota. Management in Sustainable Farming Systems. Poster Papers. C.E. Pankhurst (ed.), pp. 131–132. CSIRO, Melbourne.

Hirth, J.R., B.M. McKenzie, and J.M. Tisdall. 1994. Some physical characteristics of earthworm casts in burrows. In Soil Biota. Management in Sustainable Farming Systems. Poster Papers. C.E. Pankhurst (ed.), pp. 129–130. CSIRO, Melbourne.

Holter, P. 1979. Effect of dung-beetles (*Aphodius* spp.) and earthworms on the disappearance of cattle dung. Oikos 32, 393–402.

Hoogerkamp, M., H. Rogaar, and H.J.P. Eijsackers. 1983. Effect of earthworms on grassland on recently reclaimed polder soils in the Netherlands. In Earthworm Ecology, J.E. Satchell (ed.), pp. 85–105. Chapman and Hall, London.

Hutchinson, K.J., and K.L. King. 1980. The effects of sheep stocking level on invertebrate abundance, biomass and energy utilisation in a temperate, sown grassland. Journal of Applied Ecology 17, 369–387.

James, S.W. 1991. Soil, nitrogen, phosphorus, and organic matter processing by earthworms in tallgrass prairie. Ecology 72, 2101–2109.

Jensen, M.B. 1985. Interactions between soil invertebrates and straw in arable soil. Pedobiologia 28, 59–69.

Kingston, T.J. 1989. *Aporrectodea caliginosa* and *Lumbricus rubellus* populations under irrigated and dryland pastures in northern Tasmania. Proceedings of the 5th Australasian Conference on Grassland Invertebrate Ecology, pp. 199–205.

Kingston, T.J., and M.G. Temple-Smith. 1989. Earthworm populations under Tasmanian pastureland. Proceedings of the 5th Australasian Conference on Grassland Invertebrate Ecology, pp. 192–198.

Lavelle, P. 1988. Earthworm activities and the soil system. Biology and Fertility of Soils 6, 237–251.

Lavelle, P., I. Barois, A. Martin, Z. Zaidi, and R. Schaefer. 1989. Management of earthworm populations in agro-ecosystems: a possible way to maintain soil quality? In Ecology of Arable Land. M. Clarholm and L. Bergstrom (eds.), pp. 109–122. Kluwer Academic Publishers, Dordrecht.

Lee, K.E. 1985. Earthworms. Their Ecology and Relationships with Soils and Land Use. Academic Press, Sydney.

Lobry de Bruyn, L.A. 1993. Changes in earthworm numbers and soil structure with the advent of summer irrigation in dairy pastures. Proceedings of the 6th Australasian Conference on Grassland Invertebrate Ecology, pp. 114–121.

Marinissen, J.C.Y. 1991. Colonization of arable fields by earthworms in a newly reclaimed polder in the Netherlands—preliminary results. Proceedings of the 11th International Soil Zoology Colloquium, pp. 341–348.

Marinissen, J.C.Y., and F. van den Bosch. 1992. Colonisation of new habitats by earthworms. Oecologia 91, 371–376.

Martin, N.A., and J.C. Charles. 1979. Lumbricid earthworms and cattle dung in New Zealand pastures. Proceedings of the 2nd Australasian Conference on Grassland Invertebrate Ecology, pp. 52–54

McColl, H.P., P.B.S. Hart, and F.J. Cook. 1982. Influence of earthworms on some soil chemical and physical properties, and the growth of ryegrass on a soil after topsoil stripping—a pot experiment. New Zealand Journal of Agricultural Research 25, 239–243.

Mele, P.M. 1991. What species, and how many, on local farms. Australian Institute of Agricultural Science Occasional Publication No. 62, 20–26.

Noble, J.C., and P.A. Mills. 1974. Soil moisture status and its effect on earthworm populations under irrigated pastures in southern Australia. Proceedings of the 12th International Grassland Congress 1, 470–476.

Noble, J.C., W.T. Gordon, and C.R. Kleinig. 1970. The influence of earthworms on the development of mats of organic matter under irrigated pastures in southern Australia. Proceedings of the 11th International Grassland Congress, pp. 465–468.

Oades, J.M., and L.J. Walters. 1994. Indicators for sustainable agriculture: policies to paddock. In Soil Biota. Management in Sustainable Farming Systems. C.E. Pankhurst, B.M. Doube, V.V.S.R. Gupta, and P.R. Grace (eds.), pp. 219–223. CSIRO, Melbourne.

Pizl, V. 1992. Effect of soil compaction on earthworms (Lumbricidae) in apple orchard soil. Soil Biology and Biochemistry 24, 1573–1575.

Reed, K.F.M., and P.S. Cocks. 1982. Some limitations of pasture species in southern Australia. Proceedings 2nd Australian Agronomy Conference, pp. 142–160.

Reinecke, A.J., and F.A. Visser. 1980. The influence of agricultural land use practices on the population densities of *Allolobophora trapezoides* and *Eisenia rosea* (Oligochaeta) in southern Africa. In Soil Biology as Related to Land Use Practices. D.L. Dindal (ed.), pp. 310–324. EPA, Washington.

Rovira, A.D. 1992. Dryland mediterranean farming systems in Australia. Australian Journal of Experimental Agriculture 32, 801–809.

Rovira, A.D., K.R.J. Smettem, and K.E. Lee. 1987. Effect of rotation and conservation tillage on earthworms in a red–brown earth under wheat. Australian Journal of Agricultural Research 38, 829–834.

Sharpley, A.N., J.K. Syers, and J.A. Springett. 1979. Effect of surface-casting earthworms on the transport of phosphorus and nitrogen in surface runoff from pasture. Soil Biology and Biochemistry 11, 459–462.

Sochtig, W., and O. Larink. 1992. Effect of soil compaction on activity and biomass of endogeic lumbricids in arable soils. Soil Biology and Biochemistry 24, 1595–1599.

Springett, J.A. 1983. Effect of five species of earthworm on some soil properties. Journal of Applied Ecology 20, 865–872.

Springett, J.A. 1985. Effect of introducing *Allolobophora longa* Ude on root distribution and some soil properties in New Zealand pastures. In Ecological Interactions in Soil. A.H. Fitter (ed.), pp. 330–405. Blackwell, Oxford.

Springett, J.A. 1992. Distribution of lumbricid earthworms in New Zealand. Soil Biology and Biochemistry 24, 1377–1381.

Springett, J.A., and J.K. Syers. 1984. Effect of pH and calcium content of soil on earthworm cast production in the laboratory. Soil Biology and Biochemistry 16, 185–189.

Springett, J.A., R.A. Gray, and J.B. Reid. 1992. Effect of introducing earthworms into horticultural land previously denuded of earthworms. Soil Biology and Biochemistry 24, 1615–1622.

Stein, A., R.M. Bekker, J.H.C. Blom, and H. Rogaar. 1992. Spatial variability of earthworm populations in a permanent polder grassland. Biology and Fertility of Soils 14, 260–266.

Stephens, P.M., C.W. Davoren, B.M. Doube, M.H. Ryder, A.M. Benger, and S.M. Neate. 1993a. Reduced severity of *Rhizoctonia solani* disease on wheat seedlings associated with the presence of the earthworm *Aporrectodea trapezoides* (Lumbricidae). Soil Biology and Biochemistry 25, 1477–1484.

Stephens, P.M., C.W. Davoren, M.H. Ryder, and B.M. Doube. 1993b. Influence of the lumbricid earthworm *Aporrectodea trapezoides* on the colonisation of wheat roots by *Pseudomonas corrugata* strain 2140R in soil. Soil Biology and Biochemistry 25, 1719–1724.

Stephens, P.M., C.W. Davoren, B.M. Doube, and M.H. Ryder. 1994. Ability of the earthworms *Aporrectodea rosea* and *Aporrectodea trapezoides* to increase plant growth and the foliar concentration of elements in wheat (*Triticum aestivum* cv. Spear) in a sandy loam soil. Biology and Fertility of Soils 18, 150–154.

Stephens, P.M., C.W. Davoren, M.H. Ryder, B.M. Doube, and R.J. Correll. 1995. Field evidence for reduced severity of *Rhizoctonia* bare patch disease of wheat, due to the presence of the earthworms *Aporrectodea rosea* and *Aporrectodea trapezoides*. Soil Biology and Biochemistry 26, 1495–1500.

Stockdill, S.M.J. 1982. Effects of introduced earthworms on the productivity of New Zealand pastures. Pedobiologia 24, 29–35.

Stockdill, S.M.J., and G.G. Cossens. 1966. The role of earthworms in pasture production and moisture conservation. Proceedings of the New Zealand Grassland Association, pp. 168–183.

Sutherst, R.W., and G.F. Maywald. 1985. A computerised system for matching climates in ecology. Agriculture Ecosystems and Environment 13, 281–299.

Temple-Smith, M.G., and T. Pinkard. 1996. The Role of Earthworms in Agriculture and Land Management. Department of Primary Industry and Fisheries, Tasmania.

Temple-Smith, M.G., T.J. Kingston, T.L. Furlonge, and R.B. Garnsey. 1993. The effect of introduction of the earthworms *Aporrectodea caliginosa* and *Aporrectodea longa* on pasture production in Tasmania. Proceedings of the 7th Australian Agronomy Conference, p. 373.

Terhivuo, J., and A. Saura. 1993. Genic and morphological variation of the parthenogenetic earthworm *Aporrectodea rosea* in southern Finland (Oligochaeta, Lumbricidae). Annals Zoologica Fennici 30, 215–224.

Tyndale-Biscoe, M. 1990. Common Dung Beetles in Pastures in South-eastern Australia. CSIRO, Melbourne.

Waterhouse, D.F. 1974. The biological control of dung. Scientific American 230, 101–108.

Earthworms in Agroecosystems: A Summary of Current Research

12

Paul F. Hendrix
Institute of Ecology and Department of Crop and Soil Sciences
at the University of Georgia

T he impacts of earthworms on soil processes and their potential utility in agriculture are currently of wide interest. As suggested by Baker (this volume) it would be futile to attempt to review the vast literature on this subject, which ranges from scientific treatises to popular articles in magazines and newspapers; several recent works have covered the subject in detail (Lee 1985; Curry 1994; Edwards and Bohlen 1996; Edwards et al. 1995, Lee 1995). Instead of an extensive literature review, this paper presents a broad overview of current research on earthworms in agroecosystems, identifying recent trends and future directions for research. As a gauge of recent progress, comparisons are made between contributions at the last two International Symposia on Earthworm Ecology held, respectively, in Avignon, France, in 1990 (ISEE IV, Kretschmar 1992) and in Columbus, Ohio, USA, in 1994 (ISEE V). Priorities for future research, promising directions, and critical problems needing attention are summarized from ISEE V and from papers contributed at the Workshop on Earthworm Ecology in Forest, Rangeland and Crop Ecosystems in North America, held in Helen, Georgia, USA, in 1993 (Hendrix 1995).

RECENT TRENDS

Implications for agriculture can be found in nearly all the range of topics covered at both ISEE IV and ISEE V. This is partly due to the fact that many

1-884015-74-3/98/$0.00/$.50
©1998 by CRC Press LLC

researchers are interested specifically in agriculture and the potential influences of earthworms on agricultural production, soil conservation, environmental quality, and so on. But from a broader perspective, agricultural systems often are more easily studied than more complex natural ecosystems, and earthworm effects on soil processes and plant growth are more conspicuous in agroecosystems than in natural ecosystems. Thus, agricultural systems provide a crucible in which to test ideas about earthworms, beyond their role in agriculture.

Topics relevant to agriculture from ISEE IV and ISEE V include earthworm systematics, biogeography, ecology, and behavior; effects on soil processes (nutrient and organic matter dynamics, soil structure, and hydrology); uses in waste management and land management; and ecotoxicology. A listing of such topics was compiled from the programs of both meetings (A. Kretzschmar and C. Edwards, pers. comm.) and is presented in Table 1. This compilation also includes numbers of presentations (talks and posters) within each topic category. Although it is not intended that firm conclusions be drawn from such a small sampling of the literature, a few interesting trends can be seen.

First, there was an increase in the total numbers of agriculturally-related contributions at ISEE V (111) compared to ISEE IV (91). These contributions represent about 69% and 63%, respectively, of the total numbers of papers

Table 1. Numbers of contributions within various topics relevant to agroecosystems summarized from International Symposium on Earthworm Ecology (ISEE) IV and V

	Number of contributions		
	ISEE IV	*ISEE V*	*% Change*
1) Biogeography in managed landscapes	11	12	+9
2) Management effects on abundance/distribution (tillage, cropping systems)	20	15	−25
3) Managed introductions and land use	7	5	−29
4) Nutrient cycling processes (decomposition, mineralization, microbiology)	13	19	+46
5) Soil physical properties (aggregation, porosity, infiltration, leaching)	12	16	+33
6) Effects on plant growth (rhizosphere effects, disease suppression)	3	9	+200
7) Waste processing and vermicomposting	14	21	+50
8) Ecotoxicology (effects of pesticides and heavy metals)	11	14	+27
TOTAL	91	111	

presented at the two meetings (160 at ISEE V and 145 at ISEE IV). Agricultural contributions increased in number because, first, proportionately more of the papers at ISEE IV dealt with basic biological questions about oligochaetes generally, and thus were not counted as directly relevant to agroecology, and second, there was a larger total number of participants at ISEE V (206) than at ISEE IV (161). Whether these numbers reflect a worldwide increase in research interest in earthworms in agroecosystems is not known. The meeting in Avignon in southern France (ISEE IV) appeared to attract more participants from Europe, where there is a very strong tradition of basic research in soil biology, whereas the Columbus, Ohio, meeting was probably more accessible to researchers in the western hemisphere with applied interests (representatives from 26 countries attended ISEE V).

A second trend appears to be an increase in numbers of contributions in all categories except "management effects on earthworm abundance and distribution" and "managed introductions and land use." Although the decline in actual numbers of contributions in these categories is small, these topics have received considerable attention over the past several decades (Satchell 1983; Lee 1985); the fact that their numbers did not increase may be a hint that interest or perhaps funding opportunities are shifting to other areas of research. The categories of "biogeography in managed landscapes" and "ecotoxicology" showed little to modest increases, although ecotoxicology papers were numerous at both meetings. The largest increases (>30%) in contributions were in the topics of "nutrient cycling," "soil physical properties," "effects on plant growth," and "waste processing and vermicomposting." The first three may reflect growing interest in mechanisms of earthworm influences on soil processes in agroecosystems (this point is addressed again later); the latter is consistent with increasing scientific and societal interest in waste recycling and management.

Highlights from several of the presentations from ISEE V reflect some of these trends. The microbial connection with earthworm activity is emerging as a central theme in soil nutrient process studies. For example, it is clear that earthworm activity accelerates crop residue decomposition and nutrient mineralization, and there is growing evidence that microbes serve as a primary source of nutrition for earthworms. In an ecological sense, the relationship might be considered a "keystone" association (Parmelee et al., this volume). With respect to residue quality, earthworms may selectively ingest high-quality residues (Bohlen et al. 1995), but their relative effects on decomposition may be greater on low-quality residues which earthworms fragment, inoculate with microbes, and incorporate into soil. High-quality substrates tend to decompose rapidly even in the absence of earthworms. This idea has also been suggested for other soil fauna (e.g., microarthropods) involved in forest litter decomposition (Seastedt et al. 1983).

Lavelle et al. (this volume) made the interesting point that the cost of earthworm activity in terms of organic carbon in agroecosystems must be considered, because earthworms tend to stimulate microbial activity and accelerate turnover and possibly loss of soil carbon, if adequate organic inputs are not maintained. The management implication of this is that some "base" amount of organic substrates must be added to soil periodically to feed microbes and earthworms, with additional amounts needed to build organic matter into soil.

As mentioned previously, substrate quality has a strong influence on the interaction between earthworms and microbes. These observations also have implications for mixed residue management in agroecosystems. While the mineralization of rapidly decomposing residues may contribute to short-term nutrient availability, more slowly decomposing materials (i.e., with higher C/N) may immobilize nutrients and add to pools with longer turnover times and more sustained nutrient availability (Tian et al. 1995). Further, very recalcitrant materials, especially those left on the soil surface, contribute to a "mulch effect," which protects soil surfaces from erosive forces (e.g., rainfall impact, wind) and ameliorates soil microclimate (Lal 1991; Hendrix et al. 1992).

With respect to earthworm effects on plant growth, a number of interesting observations have been reported. Several papers indicated that earthworm effects on plants vary with earthworm species, plant species, and soil type (Lavelle et al., this volume). For example, Gilot-Villenave (1995), Pashanasi (1995), Baker et al. (1995), Blakemore (1995), and Brown et al. (1995) all reported greater plant production or nutrient uptake in soils where earthworms were present, compared to controls without earthworms. However, Devliegher and Verstraete (1995) found reduced plant growth in the presence of *Lumbricus terrestris* and Baker et al. (1995) found no effect of *Aporrectodea rosea* on clover growth. Lavelle et al. (this volume) further reported that legumes generally did not seem to respond to earthworm additions, whereas maize and rice did. Several possible mechanisms were proposed to account for increased plant growth in the presence of earthworms, including reduced incidence of plant disease (i.e., earthworms may consume disease fungi or make soil inhibitory to them), increased availability of nutrients (e.g., through stimulation of mineralization), and enhanced soil structure (e.g., reduced bulk density), creating a more favorable environment for root growth, or combinations of these factors.

Despite all of the beneficial effects (documented and hypothesized) of earthworms on plant growth, nutrient dynamics, and soil structure, Parmelee et al. (this volume) reviewed aspects of earthworm activities that may be considered undesirable in agricultural systems. These include removal or burial of surface residues that would otherwise protect soil surfaces from erosion; increasing erosion and surface sealing via freshly produced, unstable casts that are susceptible to raindrop impact; riddling of irrigation ditches, making them less able to carry water; increasing nitrogen losses through leaching and denitrification; and increasing carbon loss through enhanced microbial respiration. Parmelee et al. (this volume) suggest that it is the net result of positive and negative effects of earthworms that is important in determining whether or not they have detrimental impacts in agroecosystems.

As pointed out by Curry (this volume), any management applied to soil is likely to have some effect on earthworm populations. The well-used diagram of Edwards and Lofty (1969) and Wallwork (1976) is modified in Figure 1 to illustrate this point. Thus, management effects may have positive or negative effects on earthworm abundance and diversity. Apart from direct toxicity of some agricultural chemicals or substances in soil amendments (e.g., heavy metals in sewage sludge), these effects are primarily the result of changes in soil temperature, soil water, and organic matter quantity or quality, the principal driving variables of soil biological activity.

A final interesting trend comes from Australia, where scientists studying earthworm ecology are developing a tradition of interacting closely with farmers

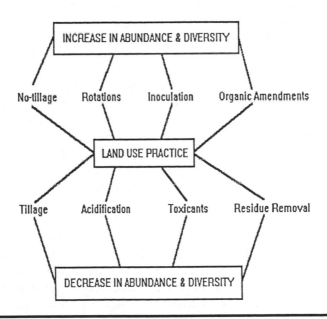

Figure 1. Illustration of the effects of soil management on the abundance and diversity of earthworms in agricultural soils (simplified from Edwards and Lofty 1969 and Wallwork 1976).

and with the public. The "Earthworms Downunder" program (Baker et al. 1995), which involved young people in the collection and census of earthworms nation-wide, not only accumulated useful information for agricultural purposes but also stimulated public interest in earthworm research and may serve to recruit new scientists into agricultural research.

RESEARCH NEEDS

Priorities for earthworm research, relevant to agriculture, include both earthworm influences on soil processes and plant growth, and the impacts of agricultural management on earthworm populations. A number of potentially important areas for future research are summarized below from contributions at ISEE V and from papers in Hendrix (1995).

With respect to earthworm effects on biogeochemical cycles, Blair et al. (1995) identified several topic areas. Understanding of earthworm effects on soil nutrient and organic matter dynamics must come from studies over a range of spatial scales, from short-term physiological processes within the earthworm gut to long-term patterns of nutrient storage and loss in ecosystems. Equally important is the need for a clear linkage between results derived from short-term laboratory experiments and long-term field studies. In particular, means of translating microsite phenomena (e.g., trace gas flux, nutrient mineralization) to ecosystem and landscape scales under field conditions deserve attention.

A useful way to examine earthworm effects on nutrient cycling processes is through studies of isotopic tracers, such as ^{13}C, ^{14}C, ^{32}P, and ^{15}N. Recent studies using both natural abundance and enriched materials have quantified nutrient flux and turnover due to earthworm activity (Cortez et al. 1989; Spain et al. 1992; Binet and Trehen 1992; Martin et al. 1992; Zhang and Hendrix 1995). Further research utilizing these techniques can be expected to increase our understanding of earthworm influences on biogeochemical mechanisms and pathways in agricultural and native ecosystems.

Interesting deviations from the widely-held view of earthworm functional groupings (i.e., Bouché 1977) suggest a possible need for revision of the current scheme. In particular, species-specific activities of earthworms may preclude their inclusion into broad ecological categories. Reexamination of functional groupings may be appropriate for at least certain tropical and subtropical (i.e., non-European lumbricid) taxa. Further, because much of our understanding of earthworm biology and ecology is based on European lumbricid species, the relative importance of native versus exotic species to ecosystem processes in a given area should be examined. There may be cases where native species are better adapted and are more effective in enhancing nutrient cycling (e.g., James 1991), and are possibly of greater agricultural utility than the familiar Lumbricidae or other exotic species.

Interactions of earthworms with plant roots and other soil biota have important implications in agroecosystems. Enhanced plant production due to earthworm activity has been discussed previously, but the mechanisms involved are not always clear. Earthworm-microbial interactions deserve particular attention. However, entire soil food webs, their roles in nutrient cycling, and the influence of earthworms on them also need further study.

The impacts of earthworm activity on soil structure in agroecosystems are receiving increasing attention. Tomlin et al. (1995) identified several potentially fruitful lines for further research. Although increased soil porosity and water infiltration are well-known consequences of earthworm activity, relatively little is known of the mechanisms by which solutes (e.g., agricultural chemicals) are transported through earthworm burrows. Because burrow linings may act both as sources and sinks for solutes, better understanding is needed of their physical, chemical, and microbial characteristics (e.g., organic chemical nature and exchange properties).

Aggregation may be one of the most important soil properties affected by earthworms in agricultural and natural ecosystems. Under laboratory conditions, earthworms may enhance aggregate stability, depending on water content, organic matter quality, time since cast production, etc. (Shipitalo and Protz 1989). But it is not known if these results can be extrapolated into earthworms improving soil structure under field conditions. The key to understanding this phenomenon may lie in the nature and dynamics of organic compounds and their interaction with soil minerals, as influenced by earthworms. Field and laboratory studies are needed to address this problem adequately. This should be a profitable area for future research. The stability of casts also has implications for the storage and turnover of nutrients in soil.

Edwards et al. (1995) and Lee (1995) made a number of recommendations for research specifically on earthworms in agroecosystems Many ecological questions about earthworms remain unanswered, including basic habitat requirements and distribution and abundance patterns in many geographical areas. Projects such as the "Earthworms Downunder" study (Baker et al. 1995) are needed in agricultural regions worldwide to assess the resource base available for further earthworm research. Such efforts will also provide information for earthworm inoculation studies, which often are conducted in the laboratory but which need to be conducted on a field scale to assess the potential for earthworms to enhance crop growth and improve soil properties in agroecosystems.

We need a better understanding of the impacts of various earthworm species and community assemblages on soil organic matter dynamics in agroecosystems, especially those under no-tillage or receiving organic inputs. Earthworms may be a primary mechanism for incorporation and decomposition of organic residues in these systems. Also, it might prove fruitful to include earthworms in simulation models of soil organic matter, which typically do not explicitly include soil biota other than microbes and roots.

Finally, there is continuing need for studies of the effects of crop rotations and management systems (including use of cultivation, chemicals, irrigation, etc.) on earthworm abundance, diversity, and distribution. This is particularly true where new management systems are tested and where management goals include buildup and maintenance of earthworm populations. More information along these lines is needed to improve our ability to manage earthworms in the field.

CONCLUSION

The growing numbers of participants at each successive ISEE attest to the increasing interest in many aspects of earthworm biology and ecology. This paper has covered only selected highlights of some of the presentations at the most recent symposium (ISEE V); the reader is referred to other papers in this volume and to the proceedings of that meeting for a wealth of details from current research.

Despite the large literature on earthworms, much remains to be known before we are able to exploit the beneficial activities of these creatures in agriculture fully. Results from papers presented at ISEE IV and ISEE V show that progress is being made in a number of areas, as outlined above. The ultimate test of our efforts will be demonstrated by how successfully we are able to make predictions about earthworm effects on ecosystem processes and about management effects on earthworm populations and communities. Our models at this stage are mostly empirical and perhaps adequate for some management purposes (e.g., site-, species-, or management-specific conditions). However, as our knowledge base grows and questions become more focused and refined, we should expect to see better understanding of processes and the development of mechanistic models that predict behaviors over wide ranges of conditions. Steps in this direction have been made by Martin and Lavelle (1992) and Monestiez and Kretzschmar (1992) at ISEE IV, and by Klok et al. (1995) and Baveco et al. (1995) at ISEE V. Future ISEE gatherings undoubtedly will reveal further progress.

ACKNOWLEDGMENTS

Travel and other support for this work was provided by the Department of Crop and Soil Sciences, University of Georgia, and by grant BSR-8818302 from the National Science Foundation. The author is grateful to G.G. Brown, M.A. Callaham, Jr., and D.A. Crossley, Jr. for helpful discussions during preparation of this paper.

REFERENCES CITED

Baker, G.H., T. Thumlert, L. Meisel, P.J. Carter, and G.P. Kilpin. 1995. "Earthworms Downunder": A survey of the earthworm fauna in urban and agricultural soils in Australia. Proceedings of Fifth International Symposium on Earthworm Ecology. Soil Biology and Biochemistry (in press).

Baker, G.H., P.M.L. Williams, P.J. Carter, and N.R. Long. 1995. Influence of lumbricid earthworms on wheat and clover yield and quality. Proceedings of Fifth International Symposium on Earthworm Ecology. Soil Biology and Biochemistry (in press).

Baveco, H.M., A.M. de Roos, C. Klok, J.C.Y. Marinissen, and W. Ma. 1995. Modelling the population dynamics of the earthworm *Lumbricus rubellus*. II. Effects of toxicants on predator-regulated populations. Proceedings of Fifth International Symposium on Earthworm Ecology. Soil Biology and Biochemistry (in press).

Binet, F., and P. Trehen. 1992. Experimental microcosm study of the role of *Lumbricus terrestris* (Oligochaeta:Lumbricidae) on nitrogen dynamics in cultivated soils. Soil Biology and Biochemistry 24:1501–1506.

Blair, J.M., R.W. Parmelee, and P. Lavelle. 1995. Influences of earthworms on biogeochemistry. In Ecology and biogeography of earthworms in North America, P.F. Hendrix (ed.). Lewis Publishers, Boca Raton, FL, pp. 125–156.

Blakemore, R.J. 1995. Earthworms and pasture production in south-east Queensland. Proceedings of Fifth International Symposium on Earthworm Ecology. Soil Biology and Biochemistry (in press).

Bohlen, P.J., R.W. Parmelee, and C.A. Edwards. 1995. Decomposition of crop residues in maize (*Zea mays*) agroecosystems with modified earthworm populations. Proceedings of Fifth International Symposium on Earthworm Ecology. Soil Biology and Biochemistry (in press).

Bouche, M.B. 1977. Strategies lombriciennes. In Soil organisms as components of ecosystems: Proceedings of the 6th Int. colloquium on soil zoology, U. Lohm and T. Persson (eds.). Swedish Natural Science Research Council Ecological Bulletin No. 25, Stockholm, pp. 122–133.

Brown, G.G., P. F. Hendrix, and M.H. Beare. 1995. Earthworms (*Lumbricus rubellus*) and the transfer of ^{15}N from surface-applied sorghum residues into different soil pools and uptake by plants. Proceedings of Fifth International Symposium on Earthworm Ecology. Soil Biology and Biochemistry (in press).

Cortez, J., R. Hameed, and M.B. Bouche. 1989. C and N transfer in soil with or without earthworms fed with ^{14}C- and ^{15}N-labelled wheat straw. Soil Biology and Biochemistry 21:491–497.

Curry, J.P. 1994. Grassland invertebrates: Ecology, influence on soil fertility and effects on plant growth. Chapman & Hall, London.

Curry, J.P. 1995. Factors affecting earthworm abundance in soils. Proceedings of Fifth International Symposium on Earthworm Ecology. Soil Biology and Biochemistry (in press).

Devliegher, W., and W. Verstraete. 1995. The effect of *Lumbricus terrestris* on soil in relation to plant growth. Proceedings of Fifth International Symposium on Earthworm Ecology. Soil Biology and Biochemistry (in press).

Edwards, C.A., and P.J. Bohlen. 1996. Biology and ecology of earthworms, 3rd ed. Chapman and Hall, New York.

Edwards, C.A., and J.R. Lofty. 1969. The influence of agricultural practice on soil microarthropod populations. In The soil ecosystem, J.G. Sheals (ed.). Systematics Association, London.

Edwards, C.A., P.J. Bohlen, D.R. Linden, and S. Subler. 1995. Earthworms in agroecosystems. In Ecology and biogeography of earthworms in North America, P.F. Hendrix (ed.). Lewis Publishers, Boca Raton, FL, pp. 185–214.

Gilot-Villenave, C. 1995. Effects of inoculation with the tropical endogeic earthworm *M. anomala* on soil characteristics and yam production in Cote d'Ivoire. Proceedings of Fifth International Symposium on Earthworm Ecology. Soil Biology and Biochemistry (in press).

Hendrix, P.F. (ed.). 1995. Ecology and biogeography of earthworms in North America. Lewis Publishers, Boca Raton, FL.

Hendrix, P.F., D.C. Coleman, and D.A. Crossley, Jr. 1992. Using knowledge of soil nutrient cycling processes to design sustainable agriculture. Journal of Sustainable Agriculture 2:63–82.

James, S.W. 1991. Soil, nitrogen, phosphorus, and organic matter processing by earthworms in tallgrass prairie. Ecology 72(6):2101–2109.

James, S.W., and M.R. Cunningham. 1989. Feeding ecology of some earthworms in Kansas tallgrass prairie. American Midland Naturalist 121:78–83.

Klok, C., A.M. de Roos, H.M. Baveco, J.C.Y. Marinissen, and W. Ma. 1995. Modelling population dynamics of the earthworm *Lumbricus rubellus*. I. Identification of most sensitive life history parameters. Proceedings of Fifth International Symposium on Earthworm Ecology. Soil Biology and Biochemistry (in press).

Lal, R. 1991. Soil conservation and biodiversity. In The biodiversity of microorganisms and invertebrates: Its role in sustainable agriculture, D.L. Hawksworth (ed.). CAB International, pp. 89–104.

Lavelle, P. 1995. Large-scale effects of earthworms on soil organic matter and nutrient dynamics: Hypotheses and preliminary results. Proceedings of Fifth International Symposium on Earthworm Ecology. Soil Biology and Biochemistry (in press).

Lee, K.E. 1985. Earthworms: Their ecology and relationships with soils and land use. Academic Press, Sydney.

Lee, K.E. 1991. The diversity of soil organisms. In The biodiversity of microorganisms and invertebrates: Its role in sustainable agriculture, D.L. Hawksworth (ed.). CAB International, pp. 73–87.

Lee, K.E. 1995. Earthworms and sustainable land use. In Ecology and biogeography of earthworms in North America, P.F. Hendrix (ed.). Lewis Publishers, Boca Raton, FL, pp. 215–234.

Martin, S., and P. Lavelle. 1992. A simulation model of vertical movements of an earthworm population (*Millsonia anomala* Omodeo, Megascolecidae) in an African savanna (Lamto, Ivory Coast). Soil Biology and Biochemistry 24:1419–1424.

Martin, A., A. Mariotti, J. Balesdent, and P. Lavelle. 1992. Soil organic matter assimilation by a geophagous tropical earthworm based on deltaC 13 measurements. Ecology 73: 118–128.

Monestiez, P., and A. Kretzchmar. 1992. Estimation of the relationship between structural parameters of simulated burrow systems and their partitioning effect. Soil Biology and Biochemistry 24:1549–1554.

Parmelee, R.W., P.J. Bohlen, and J.M. Blair. 1995. Earthworms and nutrient cycling processes: Summary and research imperatives. Proceedings of Fifth International Symposium on Earthworm Ecology. Soil Biology and Biochemistry (in press).

Pashanasi, B., J. Alegre, R. Schaeffer, and P. Lavelle. 1995. Effects of inoculation with the earthworm *Pontoscolex corethururs* in low input cropping systems of Peruvian Amazonia on soil parameters and plant growth during six successive cropping cycles. Soil Biology and Biochemistry (in press).

Satchels J.E. (ed.). 1983. Earthworm ecology, from Darwin to vermiculture. Chapman and Hall, London.

Seastedt, T.R., D.A. Crossley, Jr., V. Meentemeyer, and J.B. Waide. 1983. A two year study of leaf litter decomposition as related to macroclimatic factors and microarthropod abundance in the southern Appalachians. Holarctic Ecology 6:11–16.

Shipitalo, M.J., and R. Protz. 1988. Factors influencing the dispersibility of clay in worm casts. Soil Science Society of America Journal 52:764–769.

Shipitalo, M.J., and R. Protz. 1989. Chemistry and micromorphology of aggregation in earthworm casts. Geoderma 45:357–374.

Spain, A.V., P. Lavelle, and A. Mariotti. 1992. Stimulation of plant growth by tropical earthworms. Soil Biology and Biochemistry 24:1629–1634.

Tian, G., B.T. Kang, and L. Brussaard. 1995. Earthworm activity and substrate chemical composition interaction during decomposition of plant residue. Proceedings of Fifth International Symposium on Earthworm Ecology. Soil Biology and Biochemistry (in press).

Tomlin, A.D., M.J. Shipitalo, W.M. Edwards, and R. Protz. 1995. Earthworms and their influence on soil structure and infiltration. In Ecology and biogeography of earthworms in North America, P.F. Hendrix (ed.). Lewis Publishers, Boca Raton, FL, pp. 157–181.

Wallwork, J.A. 1976. The distribution and diversity of soil fauna. Academic Press, London.

Zhang, Q.L., and P.F. Hendrix. 1995. Earthworm (*Lumbricus rubellus* and *Aporrectodea caliginosa*) effects on carbon flux in soil. Soil Science Society of America Journal 59:816–823.

Earthworms and the Environment

The Use of Earthworms in Ecotoxicological Evaluation and Risk Assessment: New Approaches

13

A.J. Reinecke and S.A. Reinecke
Department of Zoology, University of Stellenbosch,
Stellenbosch, South Africa

oncerns about soil fertility, risks of chemicals leaching into drinking water, contamination of soil, and detrimental effects of contaminants on the living environment have resulted in a strong and growing interest in soil organisms among environmental scientists and legislators.

Legislation in many countries has recently focused the attention of scientists on the need for sensitive organisms from the soil environment for use in research and environmental monitoring, as indicators of contamination and for regulatory testing, similar to the developments in the aquatic field.

Many toxic materials accumulate along food webs and the detritivore-decomposer levels are frequently the first to be affected since the organic matter and the soil are the ultimate sink for most contaminants.

Earthworms play an important role in a variety of soils where they contribute to the complex processes of decomposition while affecting aeration, water transport, and soil structure. Van Hook (1974) concluded that earthworms could serve as useful biological indicators of contamination because of the fairly consistent relationships between the concentrations of certain contaminants in earthworms.

Because earthworms are common in many soils they are vulnerable to the impacts on soil. First, they are selected for assessment of environmental risk for various reasons. They are beneficial for promoting soil fertility and serve as food for a variety of animals. Not only are they general representatives of soil fauna but they are also practical to use in both laboratory and field tests. They are convenient to handle because of their relatively large size and can reach a relatively high biomass in some soils. Many species are suitable for captive breeding, which makes them readily available. Their behavior brings them in close contact with the soil and they have relatively short life cycles, allowing for long-term studies of successive generations.

New trends in toxicity testing have not yet rendered earthworm testing obsolete. The use of aquatic toxicity tests for predicting the toxicity of soil samples (Gälli et al. 1994) is a useful new development that cannot, however, replace the need for tests with soil-dwelling organisms. This method extracts an aqueous leachate from the soil which is then bioassayed aquatically. Compounds that are not sufficiently water soluble or adsorbed very strongly on soil particles therefore could not be evaluated by aquatic bioassays.

The use of earthworms for ecotoxicological evaluation has undergone considerable development in the last few years. Acute toxicity testing has been well established and standardized. As pointed out by Tomlin (1992), Bouché (1992), and Van Gestel (1992), these tests *per se* do not provide sufficient information to predict the effect of a chemical applied in field situations. Various new approaches have been adopted to refine and simplify procedures that could lead to more ecologically relevant information since ecotoxicological test methods for soils are relatively underdeveloped (Van Straalen and Van Gestel 1993). Various problems remain however, and although some have been addressed by adopting compromises, there is an urgent need to develop new approaches (Forbes and Forbes 1994). In this review, an attempt has been made to discuss the latest approaches to the various problems and to explain new routes of investigation with some emphasis on the recommendations of the International Workshop on Earthworm Ecotoxicology, held in Sheffield, England, in 1991.

THE TEST ORGANISMS

There have been doubts about using *Eisenia fetida* as "typical" earthworm in toxicity testing. In acute toxicity testing the position of this species, however, seems to be well established. The basic requirement of finding a species easy to rear and genetically homogenous (Bouché 1992) could be fulfilled by using representatives of this species. Bouché (1992) argues for the use of *Eisenia andrei* or a genetically controlled single strain of the *Eisenia fetida* complex. No firm evidence of considerable variation in response has yet been brought forward if either of these approaches is adopted. Heimbach (1985) is of the opinion that the sensitivity of *E. fetida andrei* is sufficiently comparable to that of *Lumbricus terrestris* in spite of the ecological differences between these species. Heimbach (1992) obtained good correlations between LC_{50} values from the Artificial Soil Test (using this species) and a standardized field test. Callahan et al. (1994) have suggested that *Eisenia fetida* may be representative of four other species based on the concentration-response relationships for 62 chemicals and after applying the Weibull function. All these species, however, are to a large extent representative of the same ecological group. Extrapolation to other earthworm species may be less successful.

As reviewed by Edwards and Coulson (1992) in 42 pesticide comparisons by various researchers, involving 2 to 5 species, there was no consistent relationship between species. It must be kept in mind, however, that the toxicity tests were seldom conducted under identical experimental conditions. A factor of 10 was suggested to bring *E. fetida* in line with the most sensitive species (Heimbach 1992). This approach allows for the continued use of *E. fetida* in many toxicity tests. In the sense that *E. fetida* combines sensitivity, economic importance, and ecological relevance, it can be seen as the selected earthworm species for routine toxicity testing.

In chronic toxicity tests as well as bio-accumulation studies the ideal is to include a representative of each ecological type. The three main ecological types (Bouché 1972) are the endogeics, epigeics, and anecics.

Sublethal effects on growth and reproduction have been measured in the laboratory (Lofs-Holmin 1980; Martin 1986; Van Gestel et al. 1989), but lack of sufficient comparative data for sublethal effects has made comparisons in species susceptibility impossible. Reproduction toxicity tests on *Eisenia fetida* (Van Gestel et al. 1988, 1989) will most probably lead the way in determining whether this species could also be considered as standard laboratory species for studying sublethal effects. Edwards and Coulson (1992) emphasize the need for a new approach. They advocate a program of cooperative research to compare the susceptibility of different species under identical conditions at different laboratories.

There is clearly a need to distinguish between the purposes of the various tests. While *Eisenia fetida* may be suitable for some tests and there are also sufficient grounds to extrapolate to certain other species and soils, it can never serve solely as representative species of the soil environment for the purpose of assessing ecological risk. A much broader based approach, although less practical for regulatory purposes, is required of an in-depth understanding of the effects of chemicals on ecosystems. In this context the earthworm has only a limited contributory role to play. Earthworm researchers in the field of ecotoxicology should therefore not limit themselves to the requirements proposed for regulatory purposes but should follow a more holistic approach in recognizing that earthworms are but one component of a very complex soil environment of which there is only a very limited understanding. The fact that *Eisenia fetida* is useful as an organism for toxicity testing does not necessarily make it a useful biological indicator species in the ecological sense or a more useful biomonitor species.

ACUTE TOXICITY TESTING

Acute toxicity studies are conducted to ascertain the total adverse biological effects caused during a finite period of time, following the administration of single, normally large doses of a chemical. The effects are often severe without always causing mortality. Acute toxicity studies are designed to express potency of the toxicant in terms of median lethal dose (LD_{50}) causing death of 50% of the universal population of the species exposed under the defined conditions of the test. Where indirect administering is done, the potency is expressed as the median lethal concentration (LC_{50}), which is more often the case in earthworm studies.

These tests on earthworms are now conducted with well-established protocols. They (Reinecke 1992; Van Straalen and Van Gestel 1993) have preliminary screening value and provide information on relative toxicity of chemicals. Edwards and Coulson (1992) recommended that initial screening by using OECD guideline 207 remain the standard laboratory practice and Van Gestel (1992) supports this view based on the results of Van Gestel and Ma (1990) and Van Gestel et al. (1991) after studying the influence of soil characteristics on the toxicity of chemicals.

To a large extent, the evaluation of environmental risk of chemicals has until now relied on acute toxicity tests, in spite of the fact that no clear foundation for the validity of such an approach existed. These laboratory tests have been conducted over a wide range of chemicals and earthworms (Goats and Edwards 1982; Neuhauser et al. 1983, 1986; Roberts and Dorough 1983), but the application of these test results for environmental risk analysis is lacking. Callahan et al. (1994) followed a new approach towards comparing species toxicity by integrating an extensive database on acute toxicity of chemicals to earthworms based on the Weibull function (Weibull 1951) used by Shirazi and Lowrie (1988, 1991) for fish. This technique generalized the relationship between the chemical and the organism in terms of two parameters—toxicity (scale factor k) and tolerance (form factor a). Their analysis provided an assessment of the relative tolerance of four species to each of the 62 chemicals and in relationship to each other using two test protocols, the contact test and the soil test. Their results suggested that *Eisenia fetida* may be representative of the species *Allolobophora tuberculata, Eudrilus eugeniae,* and *Perionyx excavatus.*

The question whether responses to "acute" exposure can predict the effect of "chronic" exposure in the field has been answered in different ways in recent times. Although laboratory tests cannot fully simulate the structure of soil or behavior of earthworms in the field, certain endpoints other than mortality can be obtained from these tests. The use of the same test protocol to study body weight changes and reproduction does provide useful data when integrated with results of field tests but does not preclude the latter. Acute toxicity tests in artificial soil can probably be extrapolated to natural soils, but data is still lacking.

The artificial soil test, which is now widely accepted as the standard procedure, needs further refinement. Differences in peat and kaolin clay could result in differences in adsorption, moisture retention, and bio-availability of chemicals. Particle size of peat and clay should be defined more precisely. Furthermore, pH changes (Van Gestel 1992) can occur during the testing procedure, affecting chemical behavior and uptake considerably.

Acute toxicity tests are designed for the purpose of identifying highly dangerous chemicals that have immediate effects and not to determine acceptable environmental concentrations. They can serve however as a qualitative screen for detection of other toxicological effects and also give a first estimate of the NOEC level for continuous exposure. These tests do not necessarily clear any chemical from further testing but do assist in practice in setting priorities for further testing of sublethal effects.

CHRONIC TOXICITY TESTS, SUBLETHAL EFFECTS, AND BIOMARKERS

Living earthworms in the soil are more frequently exposed over much longer periods of time to agents at levels lower than those that are fatal. In order to simulate such exposure, short-term (subchronic) and long-term (chronic) studies are required. The former is usually conducted over 14 days and longer, while the latter is conducted over one or two years. Sublethal tests are designed to detect subtle effects such as disturbances in behavior, retarded development, lowered fertility, teratogenic effects, etc., that may cause population changes without necessarily leading to mortality. Data referring to the impairment of vital functions of organisms has a greater ecological relevance than those obtained from measurement of acute toxicity (Ma 1984).

Standardization of a chronic toxicity test for earthworms has not been achieved yet. Procedures vary and standardization is limited. The ecological significance of findings is still uncertain and reproducibility is limited. A variety of tests have been suggested. The pesticide test for sublethal effects (Kokta 1992) that was subjected to a ring test in Germany and the artificial soil test proposed by Van Gestel et al. (1989) provide an adequate starting point for the development of a standardized test.

Useful endpoints that have emerged from various studies are the following:

- Growth of juveniles
- Changes in body weight of adults
- Reproduction
  - rate of cocoon production
  - hatchling numbers
  - hatching success
  - incubation time
  - sperm parameters
- Behavior
- Morphological effects
- Physiological effects
- Decomposition in the soil

Undertaking chronic toxicity tests is labor-intensive and time-consuming but seems to be the next logical step after the acute toxicity level of a chemical has been established in screening tests, was found to be within certain toxic limits (Kokta and Rothert 1992), and the estimated exposure concentration was high. It must be kept in mind that environmental behavior and other factors associated with a chemical may warrant that chronic toxicity testing be performed in spite of the fact that the chemical has "passed" the acute toxicity test and was rated as "probably a low risk."

The relevance of life-history parameters in earthworm ecotoxicology was clearly demonstrated by Cluzeau et al. (1992). These authors have shown that disturbance in non-target population dynamics could affect the quality of cultivated soils. It is especially relevant in the context of recovery after a disturbance (Edwards and Brown 1982).

The use of sensitive biomarkers represents a fairly new approach. A biomarker is defined as a xenobiotically-induced variation in cellular or biochemical components or processes, structures, or functions that is measurable in a biological system or sample. Major biomarkers that are available are discussed by Peakall (1992). Very little research has so far been undertaken on biomarkers in earthworms. Biomarkers have been evaluated in *Lumbricus terrestris* and *Eisenia fetida* (Goven et al. 1988; Venables et al. 1988; Rodriquez et al. 1989; Fitzpatrick et al. 1992). A broad spectrum of xenobiotics can alter immune function. The immunobiology of earthworms has been studied intensively, which may provide for the development of assays for immunotoxicological studies (Fitzpatrick et al. 1990; Venables et al. 1992; Goven et al. 1994). Although a number of coelomocyte-based endpoints have been shown to be sensitive indicators of sublethal toxicity of chemicals (Venables et al. 1992) and hold promise to provide cost-effective assessment of potential risk, evidence of ecological relevance is still lacking. This, however, represents a new approach that may yield promising results.

Another new approach, as far as earthworm research is concerned, is the potential use of sperm parameters as a biomarker (Reinecke et al. 1994). These authors posed the question whether effects on sperm ultrastructure could be related to sublethal concentrations of an environmental pollutant and thus provide a novel way of determining effects on biological systems. They found ultrastructural damage in sperm after exposing earthworms to various sublethal concentrations of the organochloride dieldrin. They argued that quantification of sperm damage as well as other parameters such as sperm density and sperm motility may be correlated with chemical concentration. Subsequent research on the effects of heavy metals (Reinecke et al. in press) showed that certain metals slowed down growth of worms at very low concentrations and extensive ultrastructural damage of the spermatozoa was observed. If it can also be shown that sperm damage will manifest in reproduction changes at the population level, this approach may provide a novel toxicity tool with ecological relevance.

Earthworm sperm counts show potential as a rapid-measurement endpoint biomarker for measuring sublethal effects of chemical pollutants on reproduction (Cikatovic et al. 1993).

One aspect that is frequently overlooked in chronic toxicity studies is the question of survival and reversibility. When designing chronic studies, adequate numbers of earthworms should be included so that, at the termination of the treatment period, sufficient worms would remain to study the reversibility of effects and recovery from the toxicity. This approach will bring earthworm toxicity studies closer in line with well-established practices for higher animals and could facilitate risk assessment.

ESTIMATING EXPOSURE

In order to obtain some idea of the exposure to a chemical, the application rate per unit area is taken into account in an effort to determine the actual exposure experienced by the earthworms in the soil. The behavior of both the worms and the particular chemical will give an indication whether the worms are in fact exposed to the chemical. By assuming that the soil is evenly packed and the chemical is evenly distributed, the critical depth limit can be estimated and will vary according to soil type and soil cover. All the factors affecting exposure should be considered but are difficult to measure. Various authors have made different assumptions in determining the estimated environmental concentration (EEC). The following assumptions advanced by Kokta and Rothert (1992) and others seem to be useful for purposes of estimating exposure following liquid applications:

- Even distribution of the chemical in the upper 2.5 cm of soil.
- Bulk density of soil is 1.5 g/cm^3.
- The full amount if applied on bare soil.
- Fifty percent of total if plant cover exists.
- For pesticides with less than three applications per season the total amount is added up making allowance for persistence.

Field Tests Using Earthworms

Field tests can be undertaken in field plots or by continuously monitoring in the field. These tests have obvious advantages such as being realistic since they are undertaken under natural climatic conditions. Different species are exposed, and a broad data base is obtained. The logical sequence of events would be to undertake these long-term, labor-intensive tests only after the toxic effects of a chemical have been reliably established after both acute and chronic toxicity testings (see Figure 1).

As pointed out by Lofs (1992), the aim is to determine whether an ecologically significant population change will occur as a result of exposure to the chemical, taking full cognizance of the fact that earthworm populations can fluctuate enormously due to seasonal changes. The importance of a sensitive and carefully designed test is obvious. Test designs were proposed by Edwards (1992), Lofs (1992), and Kula (1992) since the literature showed that field experiments are extremely diverse and do not allow for meaningful comparisons due to poor design and inadequate replications. Distribution of chemicals in soils is also highly variable (Beyer 1992).

Field tests can also provide valuable data on the indirect effects of chemicals such as effects on food supply and soil cover. Limitations of field tests for assessing toxicity of chemicals to earthworms are discussed fully by Edwards (1992). The latter author proposed a standardized field test design along the following lines:

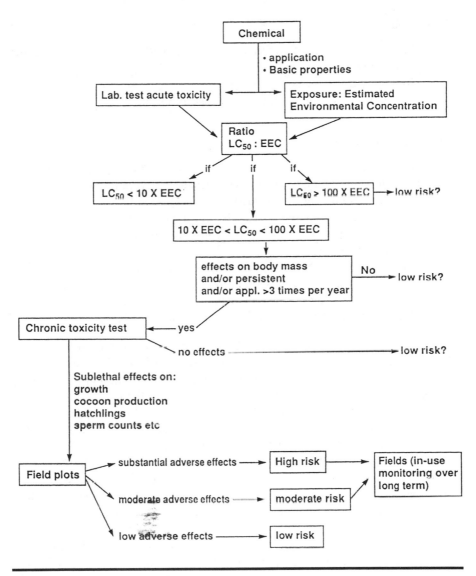

Figure 1. Risk assessment scheme for earthworms (after Kokta and Rothert 1992 and others).

Site Variables

- At least six species of common earthworms with at least 100 worms per square meter
- Preferably a loam-based soil type
- No history of chemical use for at least five years

Treatment Variables

- Clearly define chemical with known physico-chemical properties such as solubility, water/lipid partition coefficient, and volatility
- Dose, the highest recommended
- A minimum of four replicates, also for the control
- Plot size at least between 5 and 10 meters square
- Defined cropping
- Timing of the experiment when earthworms are most active with a duration of at least six months but preferably longer for persistent chemicals
- Use of toxic standards such as benomyl or carbaryl
- Determination of residues in worms and soil to assess bioconcentration

The assessment of earthworm populations is extremely difficult (Edwards 1991) and a "worst case approach" is suggested (Lofs 1992) to determine a biologically significant effect. A combination of hand-sorting and formalin extraction could be used (Edwards 1992). Earthworms in the top 5–10 cm of soil are hand-sorted, after which the quadrate is treated with formalin. This method recovers both the species that live close to the soil surface (endogeic) as well as those that penetrate deep into the soil (anecic).

Until more data can be obtained from well-designed and standardized field experiments, comparison with data from standardized laboratory experiments is not feasible. In order to obtain a balanced judgment on the potential toxicity and environmental hazard of a chemical a suitable data bank of results of both laboratory and field experiments is needed. Heimbach (1992) has obtained promising results in such a comparative study. He obtained a good correlation ($r = 0.86$) between LC_{50} values from the "Artificial Soil Test" and a "Standardized Field Test" based on a test design by Edwards and Brown (1982). There is a growing body of evidence that LC_{50} tests in the laboratory could be used to predict field results by using a compensation factor. Further evidence is, however, needed before the validity of this approach could be generally accepted.

Earthworms in Bioassays and Microcosms

The use of earthworms as tools in the detection of chemical contamination involves bioassays at contaminated sites in the field or in the laboratory using soil taken from the contaminated site.

Contaminated sites are frequently characterized by complex chemical mixtures rather than single chemicals. Adverse biological effects associated with a site can seldom be ascribed to a single chemical. Determining causal relationships between specific chemicals and observed effects is not possible because of the complexity and variability of biological responses. To determine the environmental impact associated with complex mixtures in a site, a toxicity-based approach rather than a chemically-based approach should be adopted (Callahan and Linder 1992), thus incorporating biological information into the assessment process.

For the assessment of environmental hazard potential a measurement of contaminant bio-availability is required as well as other biological effects. This is provided for by a bioassay (Callahan et al. 1985, 1991).

Model ecosystems (also called microcosms) that approximate real ecosystems have been used by various authors. Design features are discussed by Van Straalen and Van Gestel (1993). The effects of toxicants are assessed by two or more interacting organisms being exposed simultaneously. The development of microcosms as ecotoxicological tools has not proceeded beyond the laboratory experimentation phase and there seems to be much scope for future development in this field.

Residues in Earthworms and Their Role as Biomonitors and Bio-indicators

The concentration of a chemical in earthworms is sometimes a useful indicator of whether the chemical is near toxic levels in the environment. This makes earthworms useful monitoring organisms for the soil environment. A classic example of the importance of earthworms as biological monitors was presented by Ma (1987), in which he showed that heavy metal concentration in moles was closely related to the concentration in earthworms but not to the concentrations in soils.

The presence of toxic amounts of a chemical in earthworms poses a risk of secondary poisoning of predators. It is, therefore, important not only to know what the body burdens of any particular toxic chemicals are, but to understand the various pathways of metabolism and detoxification.

The use of organisms as indicators implies that the organisms can indicate the presence or absence of a particular factor or condition. The presence or absence of a particular species tells us about the environment. The use of earthworms in this sense as indicators of contamination is a topic of considerable interest but of limited practicality. Their use as indicators is limited by the fact that a variety of environmental influences could be responsible for the observed condition, making the establishment of causal relationships between population density and the degree of pollution very difficult. The term indicator has also been used loosely to refer to biological monitors. Biological monitors (over and above their possible role as indicators) are usually available in abundance throughout the area of study (Martin and Coughtrey 1982). They respond to change in the degree of pollution and retain the pollutant progressively during the exposure period. Earthworms have been used extensively in environmental monitoring, especially as biological monitors of heavy metal and organochlorine pollution. A clear relationship has been shown between the concentration of some metals in earthworms and in the surrounding soils. Concentrations of lead and cadmium in earthworms are related closely to those in soil, making earthworms good monitors for at least these two metals, while data on others are mostly lacking or not showing such a clear relationship. The interpretation of results should, however, take interspecific variation into account as well as soil characteristics and other physical factors. Perämäki et al. (1992) have clearly demonstrated the importance of pH and soil calcium. Their results showed an increasing accumulation of cadmium in the earthworm *Aporrectodea caliginosa* at lower pH values and confirm the findings of Ma et al. (1982, 1983) on the importance of pH.

The use of earthworms as biological monitors to determine the accumulated concentrations of pollutants in their tissue as integrative estimate of the degrees of pollution is an attractive idea but is fraught with practical difficulties (Morgan et al. 1992). Closely related species differ in the way they accumulate pollutants and factors such as age, size, season, and diet influence accumulation. Furthermore, the possibility of genetic adaptation to selection pressures complicates matters even more. The use of slope-intercept plots (Morgan et al. 1992) under certain circumstances provides insight into bio-availabilities.

To use earthworms effectively as biomonitoring tools, it is important to know the body burdens of any particular toxic chemical and also to know the various pathways of metabolism and detoxification. Chemical analysis over a wide range is an expensive undertaking, but in cases where the vertebrate toxicity of a chemical is relatively high, residue analyses should be undertaken, especially if the long-term persistence and the potential for bio-accumulation is high.

Measuring levels of pollutants in organisms indicates how much is present at a particular time but does not indicate fluxes or rates of metabolic breakdown. Considerable research has been undertaken on the uptake of trace contaminants but no standard protocols exist for measuring bio-accumulation in terrestrial ecosystems (Phillips 1993), but more research along the lines of modeling done by Connell and Markwel (1990) for bio-accumulation of lipophilic compounds in earthworms is needed.

A very recent development in toxicity assessment that has the potential to change toxicant monitoring considerably in the near future is biosensors. The aim is to incorporate relevant biological systems into sensor systems by bringing biological material and transducers into intimate association. Apart from the work by Drewes and Lingamneni (1992), very little effort by earthworm researchers has gone in this direction.

RISK ESTIMATION

The objective of ecological risk assessment is to use available toxicological and ecological information to estimate the probability that some undesired ecological event will occur (Wilson and Crouch 1987). These events or ecological endpoints (as opposed to toxicity endpoints) are not confined to specific taxa and are clouded with uncertainties and require an ecosystem approach. The final estimated effect on the ecosystem level is expressed as a probability. The identification of critical ecological endpoints is of prime importance (Bartell et al. 1992).

Risk assessment is normally aimed at the protection of human health or at the protection of the ecosystem (and biodiversity) as such. The interrelationship of these two aims is obvious.

The use of earthworms in risk assessment schemes is therefore twofold. Apart from protecting earthworms as beneficial organisms, earthworms are used to obtain information on environmental quality and to ensure environmental safety in general. The aim is to derive "acceptable" concentrations of toxicants in soil. The earthworm is therefore used as sensitive "indicator" or "responder." The general consensus seems to be that, although there is no single species of earthworm that is most sensitive to all chemicals, the species *Eisenia fetida* can still play this role to some extent. But extrapolating directly to other species is seldom useful. Species vary greatly in their response to toxicants. Van Straalen and Van Gestel (1993) approach this problem by applying a safety factor to data on indicator species to ensure protection of "all" species in an ecosystem.

This safety factor is based on the variability of the toxicity data. Van Straalen and Denneman (1989) followed Kooijman (1987) in developing a new approach for estimating a benchmark concentration (HCp). These statistical methods apply only to toxicity data for single species and provide a useful way of deriving quality criteria. Application of this model on earthworm toxicity data has been attempted by Van Straalen (1990). A comparison between NOEC values of five substances in soil for *Eisenia fetida* and other soil invertebrates suggested a safety factor greater than 20, preferably 100, to protect sensitive species. The use of these types of extrapolation methods is discussed by Forbes and Forbes (1994).

Risk of ecological damage is also dependent on what happens to the toxicant after it reaches the soil. Toxicity as such may be very misleading, especially if the chemical will degrade quickly or become detoxified. The extent of the initial damage may be such that speedy recovery can minimize damage within a short time. The size and duration of effects are therefore important characteristics for categorizing chemicals (Kokta and Rothert 1992).

Regulatory schemes are operated in many countries to ensure environmental safety of chemicals. These schemes rely on experimental data obtained under laboratory and field conditions. In some schemes the chemicals must also be examined for potential effects on earthworms (Greig-Smith 1992).

The International Workshop on Ecotoxicology of Earthworms held in Sheffield in 1991 recommended that risk assessment should be carried out for each type of land in which a product is used and should be flexible. Consistent criteria should be agreed upon for placing chemicals into categories of "high," "intermediate," "low," and "negligible" risk to earthworms. Products should be labeled to indicate the level of risk for earthworms.

The risk assessment scheme (Figure 1) adopted from Kokta and Rothert (1992) provides a useful procedure for earthworms.

Ecological risk assessment in a broader sense is not only concerned with effects on earthworms but endeavors to extrapolate to complex ecosystems. Ecological risk assessment requires an interdisciplinary approach and earthworm researchers should remain vigilant regarding useful developments and approaches in other fields. Advances in expert systems and artificial intelligence capabilities will in the future contribute to the coordination of models and data.

The use of mathematical models for forecasting ecological effects (Bartell et al. 1992) is well-established in the aquatic field but less so for the soil environment. Bartell et al. (1992) have shown that although the original contention was that direct extrapolation of laboratory toxicity data was ill advised because of the complexity of ecological systems, results from bioassays will continue to generate information since effects measured in laboratory microcosms can be compared with mathematical model results.

Researchers in earthworm ecology can therefore still contribute extensively toward an understanding of the basic functions of the soil ecosystems and the effects of chemicals and toward the development of a useful risk estimation methodology.

Decisions on Managing Estimated Risk

Once a regulatory scheme has been applied and it is certain that earthworms are adversely affected by the chemical, the next step obviously is to protect the earthworms. Most agricultural pesticides are used in soils where earthworms may be affected. Since this is unavoidable, the second best option would be to decide whether the effects will be "acceptably low." Another possibility is to decide if the effect will be reversible within a reasonably short period of time, thus not affecting the earthworm population too severely in the long term. Knowledge of earthworm life cycles and reproduction rates becomes relevant if population recovery is to be considered. Kokta and Rothert (1992) advocate that at least the pre-treatment population level should be restored before the next application of the same chemical is undertaken.

Whatever the approach may be, making decisions will remain difficult in spite of the fact that a more scientific basis for decision making is being provided by researchers, simply because there are conflicting interests requiring wise compromises. Good decisions will only be taken if a thorough appreciation of the role of earthworms in soil exists.

SUMMARY

- Earthworms are playing a useful role in ecotoxicological evaluation.
- In spite of doubts about using *Eisenia fetida* as "typical" earthworm in toxicological studies, this species' position in acute toxicity tests seems to be secured. By using a correction factor as proposed by some researchers, this species may also continue to be used in chronic toxicity studies. Since studies on the effects of toxicants on reproduction have gained in importance, this prolific species will also continue to be used in these studies.
- Researchers should not allow the requirements for the development of useful regulatory tests to narrow their research approach toward understanding the complex soil environment. Basic research on other species and communities should continue.
- Acute toxicity testing with earthworms is now done with well-established protocols but minor refinements in the procedure are still needed. Particle size of peat and clay, for instance, should be more precisely defined.

- Chronic toxicity tests for earthworms have not been standardized yet. Useful endpoints have been identified and the importance of various sublethal effects, especially on reproduction, have been pointed out. The relevance of life-history parameters has been demonstrated and various new approaches to the development of earthworm biomarkers have been adopted.
- The use of earthworm sperm parameters as a biomarker could provide a novel toxicity tool with ecological relevance.
- Assumptions for determining exposure to chemicals in the soil vary, but basic guidelines have been advanced which could lead to more consistent approaches.
- Since estimating exposure has inherent uncertainties, residue analysis should still be undertaken in cases where vertebrate toxicity of a chemical is high and where the application rate is also high and long-term persistence is a possibility.
- Field tests to determine whether an ecologically significant population change has occurred remain important. Field tests can provide valuable data but require standardization or at least guidelines.
- Earthworms can play a useful role in bioassays and in microcosm research and more research is required in this field.
- There is a need to develop a standardized protocol for bio-accumulation tests.
- Ecological risk estimation is a broadly based, multi-disciplinary field.

The use of earthworms to derive "acceptable" concentrations of toxicants in soils seems well-founded, but extrapolating directly to other species is seldom useful since species vary greatly in their response. Safety factors have been suggested to enhance the validity of quality criteria, but much more research is required, especially on the duration of toxic effects and recovery of damage.

Contaminants exert their effects at all levels of biological organization but research in environmental toxicology has concentrated on understanding effects at individual and lower levels. Ecotoxicology is primarily about the effects of contaminants on the levels of populations, communities, and ecosystems.

The usefulness of sublethal endpoints and other responses is recognized but there is a need to determine their ecological significance. Very little integration of earthworm ecology and earthworm toxicology has taken place, probably due to the fact that results from community and ecosystem studies are complex, highly variable, and difficult to interpret because contaminants exert their effects both directly and indirectly.

The challenge therefore remains to interpret responses observed at lower levels of observation (cell, individual, etc.) in terms of ecosystems as a whole or, as Forbes and Forbes (1994) suggest, to improve the state of ecosystem theory so that it can be more effectively applied to practical problems.

REFERENCES CITED

Bartell, S.M., R.H. Gardener, and R.V. O'Neil. 1992. Biological risk estimation. Lewis Publishers, Boca Raton, FL.

Beyer, W.N. 1992. Relating results from earthworm toxicity tests to agricultural soil. In Ecotoxicology of Earthworms, P.W. Greig-Smith et al. (eds.), pp. 109–115. Intercept Ltd., Hants, U.K.

Bouché, M.B. 1972. Lombriciens de France. Écologie et Systématique. Publ. Institut National de la Recherche Agronomique, Paris.

Bouché, M.B. 1992. Earthworm species and ecotoxicological studies. In Ecotoxicology of Earthworms, P.W. Greig-Smith et al. (eds.), pp. 20–35. Intercept Ltd., Hants, U.K.

Callahan, C.A., and G. Linder. 1992. Assessment of contaminated soils using earthworm test procedures. In Ecotoxicology of Earthworms, P.W. Greig-Smith et al. (eds.), pp. 187–196. Intercept Ltd., Hants, U.K.

Callahan, C.A., L.K. Russell, and S.A. Peterson. 1985. A comparison of three earthworm bioassay procedures for the assessment of environmental samples containing hazardous wastes. Biology and Fertility of Soils 1, 195–200.

Callahan, C.A., G.A. Menzie, D.D. Willbornd, and T. Ernst. 1991. On site methods for assessing chemical impact on the soil environment using earthworms; a case study at the Baird & McGuire Superfund Site, Holbrook, M.A. Environmental Toxicology and Chemistry 10, 817–826.

Callahan, C.A., M.A. Shirazi, and E.F. Neuhauser. 1994. Comparative toxicity of chemicals to earthworms. Environmental Toxicology and Chemistry 13, 291–298.

Cikutovic, M.A., L.D. Fitzpatrick, B.J. Venables, and A.J. Goven. 1993. Sperm count in earthworms for environmental toxicology: effects of cadmium and chlordane. Environmental Pollution 81, 123–125.

Cluzeau, D., R. Lagarde, G. Texier, and L. Fayolle. 1992. Relevance of life-history parameters in earthworm ecotoxicology. In Ecotoxicology of Earthworms, P.W. Greig-Smith et al. (eds.), pp. 225–229. Intercept Ltd., Hants, U.K.

Connell, D.W., and R.D. Markwell. 1990. Bio-accumulation in the soil to earthworm system. Chemosphere 20, 91–100.

Drewes, C.D., and A. Lingamneni. 1992. Use of earthworms in eco-neurotoxicity: effects of carbo furan in Lumbricus terrestris. In Ecotoxicology of Earthworms, P.W. Greig-Smith et al. (eds.), pp. 63–72. Intercept Ltd., Hants, U.K.

Edwards, C.A. 1991. Methods for assessing populations of soil-inhabiting invertebrates. Agriculture, Ecosystems and Environment 34, 145–176.

Edwards, C.A. 1992. Testing the effects of chemicals on earthworms: the advantages and limitations of field tests. In Ecotoxicology of Earthworms, P.W. Greig-Smith et al. (eds.), pp. 75–84. Intercept Ltd., Hants, U.K.

Edwards, P.J., and S.M. Brown. 1982. Use of grassland plots to study the effects of pesticides on earthworms. Pedobiologia 24, 145–150.

Edwards, P.J., and J.M. Coulson. 1992. Choice of earthworm species for laboratory tests. In Ecotoxicology of Earthworms, P.W. Greig-Smith et al. (eds.), pp. 36–43. Intercept Ltd., Hants, U.K.

Fitzpatrick, L.C., A.J. Goven, B.J. Venables, and E.L. Cooper. 1990. Earthworm immunoassays for evaluating biological effects of exposure to hazardous materials. In In Situ Evaluation of Biological Hazards of Environmental Pollutants, S.S. Sandhu (ed.), pp. 119–129. Plenum Press, New York.

Fitzpatrick, L.C., R. Sassani, B.J. Venables, and A.J. Goven. 1992. Comparative toxicity of polychlorinated biphenyls to earthworms *Eisenia foetida* and *Lumbricus terrestris*. Environmental Pollution. In press.

Forbes, V.E., and T.L. Forbes. 1994. Ecotoxicology in theory and practice. Chapman & Hall, London.

Gälli, R., C.D. Munz, and R. Scholtz. 1994. Evaluation and application of aquatic toxicity tests: use of the Microtox test for the prediction of toxicity based upon concentrations of contaminants in soil. Hydrobiologia 273, 179–189.

Goats, G.C., and C.A. Edwards. 1982. The prediction of field toxicity of chemicals to earthworms by laboratory methods. In Earthworms in Waste and Environmental Management, C.A. Edwards and E.F. Nauhauser (eds.), pp. 283–294. SPB Academic Publishing, The Hague, The Netherlands.

Goven, A.J., B.J. Venables, L.C. Fitzpatrick, and E.L. Cooper. 1988. An invertebrate model for analyzing effects of environmental xenobiotics on immunity. Clinical Ecology 4, 150–154.

Goven, A.J., S.C. Chen, L.C. Fitzpatrick, and B.J. Venables. 1994. Lysozyme activity in earthworm (*Lumbricus terrestris*) coelomic fluid and coelomocytes: enzyme assay for immunotoxicity of xenobiotics. Environmental Toxicology and Chemistry, 13, 607–613.

Greig-Smith, P.W. 1992. Risk assessment approaches in the U.K. for the side effects of pesticides on earthworms. In Ecotoxicology of Earthworms, P.W. Greig-Smith et al. (eds.), pp. 159–168. Intercept Ltd., Hants, U.K.

Heimbach, F. 1985. Comparison of laboratory methods, using *Eisenia foetida* and *Lumbricus terrestris*, for the assessment of the hazard of chemicals to earthworms. Zeitschrift für Pflanzenkrankheiten und Pflanzenschutz 92(2), 186–193.

Heimbach, F. 1992. Effects of pesticides on earthworms populations: comparison of results from laboratory and field tests. In Ecotoxicology of Earthworms, P.W. Greig-Smith et al. (eds.). Intercept Ltd., Hants, U.K.

Kokta, C. 1992. Measuring effects of chemicals in the laboratory: effect criteria and endpoints. In Ecotoxicology of Earthworms, P.W. Greig-Smith, H. Becker, P.J. Edwards, and F. Heimbach (eds.), pp. 55–62. Intercept Ltd., Hants, U.K.

Kokta, C., and H. Rothert. 1992. Hazard and risk assessment for effects of pesticides on earthworms—the approach in the Federal Republic of Germany. In Ecotoxicology of Earthworms, P.W. Greig-Smith et al. (eds.), pp. 169–176. Intercept Ltd., Hants, U.K.

Kooijman, S.A.L.M. 1987. A safety factor for LC_{50} values allowing for differences in sensitivity among species. Water Research 17, 527–538.

Kula, H. 1992. Measuring effects of pesticides on earthworms in the field: test design and sampling methods. In Ecotoxicology of Earthworms, P.W. Greig-Smith et al. (eds.), pp. 90–99. Intercept Ltd., Hants, U.K.

Lofs, A. 1992. Measuring effects of pesticides on earthworms in the field: effect criteria and endpoints. In Ecotoxicology of Earthworms, P.W. Greig-Smith et al. (eds.), pp. 85–89. Intercept Ltd., Hants, U.K.

Lofs-Holmin, A. 1980. Measuring growth of earthworms as a method of testing sublethal toxicity of pesticides. Swedish Journal of Agricultural Research, 10, 25–33.

Ma, W.C. 1982. The influence of soil properties and worm related factors on the concentration of heavy metals in earthworms. Pedobiologia, 24, 109–119.

Ma, W.C. 1984. Sublethal toxic effects of copper on growth, reproduction and litter breakdown activity in the earthworm *Lumbricus rubellus*, with observations on the influence of temperature and soil pH. Environmental Pollution (Series A) 33, 207–219.

Ma, W.C. 1987. Heavy metal accumulation in the mole, *Talpa europa*, and earthworms as an indicator of metal bioavailability in terrestrial environments. Bulletin of Environmental Contamination and Toxicology 39, 933–938.

Ma, W.C., T. Edelman, I. Van Deersum, and T. Jans. 1983. Uptake of cadmium, zinc, lead and copper by earthworms near a zinc-smelting complex: influence of soil pH and organic matter. Bulletin of Environmental Contamination and Toxicology 30, 424–427.

Martin, N.A. 1986. Toxicity of pesticides to *Allolobophora caliginosa*. New Zealand Journal of Agricultural Research 29, 699–706.

Martin, M.H., and P.J. Coughtrey. 1982. Biological monitoring of heavy metal pollution. Land and air. Applied Science Publishers, London.

Morgan, J.E., A.J. Morgan, and N. Corp. 1992. Assessing soil metal pollution with earthworms: indices derived from regression analyses. In Ecotoxicology of Earthworms, P.W. Greig-Smith et al. (eds.), pp. 233–237. Intercept Ltd., Hants, U.K.

Neuhauser, E.F., M.R. Malecki, and R.C. Loehr. 1983. Methods using earthworms for the evaluation of potentially toxic materials in soils. In Hazardous and Industrial Solid Waste Trading, Vol. 2, STP 805, R.A. Conway and W.P. Gulledge (eds.), pp. 313–320. American Society for Testing and Materials, Philadelphia, PA.

Neuhauser, E.F., M.R. Malecki, and R.C. Loehr. 1984. Growth and reproduction of the earthworm *Eisenia fetida,* after exposure to sublethal concentrations of metals. Pedobiologia 27, 89–97.

Neuhauser, E.F., M.R. Malecki, and M. Adnatra. 1986. Comparative toxicity of ten organic chemicals to four earthworm species. Comparative Biochemistry and Physiology 83C, 197–200.

Peakall, D. 1992. Animal biomarkers as pollution indicators. Ecotoxicology series 1. Chapman & Hall, London.

Perämäki, P., J. Itämies, V. Karttunen, L.H.J. Lajunen, and E. Pulliainen. 1992. Influence of pH on the accumulation of cadmium and lead in earthworms (*Aporrectodea caliginosa*) under controlled conditions. Ann. Zool. Fennici 29, 105–111.

Phillips, D.J.H. 1993. Bioaccumulation. In Handbook of Ecotoxicology, Vol. 1, P. Calow (ed.), pp. 378–396. Blackwell Scientific, London.

Reinecke, A.J. 1992. A review of ecotoxicological test methods using earthworms. In Ecotoxicology of Earthworms, P.W. Greig-Smith et al. (eds.), pp. 7–19. Intercept Ltd., Hants, U.K.

Reinecke, S.A., and A.J. Reinecke. 1997. The influence of toxic heavy metals on growth and reproduction of *Eisenia fetida* (Oligochaeta)—a laboratory study. Soil Biology and Biochemistry. In press.

Reinecke, A.J., S.A. Reinecke, and M. Froneman. 1994. The sublethal effects of the organochlorines dieldrin and lindane on growth and reproduction of *Eudrilus eugeniae* and *Eisenia fetida* (Oligochaeta). S.A. Tydskrif vir Natuurwetenskap en Tegnologie 13(1), 21–24.

Roberts, B.L., and W.H. Dorough. 1983. Relative toxicity of chemicals to the earthworm *Eisenia foetida*. Environmental Toxicology and Chemistry 3, 66–78.

Rodriquez, J., B.J. Venables, L.C. Fitzpatrick, A.J. Goven, and E.L. Cooper. 1989. Suppression of secretory rosette formation by PCBs in *Lumbricus terrestris*: an earthworm immunoassay for humoral immunotoxicity of xenobiotics. Environmental Toxicology and Chemistry 8, 1201–1207.

Shirazi, M.A., and L.N. Lowrie. 1988. Comparative toxicity based on similar asymptotic endpoints. Archives of Environmental Contamination and Toxicology 17, 273–280.

Tomlin, A.D. 1992. Behaviour as a source of earthworm susceptibility to ecotoxicants. In Ecotoxicology of Earthworms, P.W. Greig-Smith et al. (eds.), pp. 116–125. Intercept Ltd., Hants, U.K.

Van Gestel, C.A.M. 1992. The influence of soil characteristics on the toxicity of chemicals for earthworms: a review. In Ecotoxicology of Earthworms, P.W. Greig-Smith et al. (eds.), pp. 44–54. Intercept Ltd., Hants, U.K.

Van Gestel, C.A.M., and W.C. Ma. 1988. Toxicity and bioaccumulation of chlorophenols in earthworms, in relation to bioavailability in soil. Ecotoxicology and Environmental Safety 15, 289–297.

Van Gestel, C.A.M., and W.C. Ma. 1990. An approach to quantitative structure-activity relationships (QSARs) in earthworm toxicity studies. Chemosphere 21, 1023–1033.

Van Gestel, C.A.M., and W.A. Van Dis. 1989. The influence of soil characteristics on the toxicity of four chemicals to the earthworm *Eisenia fetida andrei* (Oligochaeta). Biology and Fertility of Soils 6, 262–265.

Van Gestel, C.A.M., W.A. Van Dis, E.M. Van Breemen, and P.M. Sparenburg. 1989. Development of a standardized reproduction toxicity test with the earthworm species *Eisenia fetida andrei* using copper, pentachlorophenol, and 2,4-dichloroaniline. Ecotoxicology and Environmental Safety 18, 305–312.

Van Gestel, C.A.M., W.C. Ma., and C.E. Smit. 1991. Development of QSARs in terrestrial ecotoxicology: earthworm toxicity and soil sorption of chlorophenols, chlorobenzenes and dichloroaniline. Science of the Total Environment 109/110, 589–604.

Van Gestel, C.A.M., E.M. Dirven-van Breeman, and R. Baerselman. 1992. Influence of environmental conditions of the growth and reproduction of the earthworm *Eisenia andrei* in an artificial soil substrate. Pedobiologia 36, 109–120.

Van Hook, R.I. 1974. Cadmium, lead and zinc distributions between earthworms and soils: potentials for biological accumulation. Bulletin of Environmental Contamination and Toxicology 2, 509–512.

Van Straalen, N.M. 1990. New methodologies for estimating the ecological risk of chemicals in the environment. In Proceedings 6th International Congress, Int. Assoc. Engineering Geology, D.G. Price (ed.), pp. 165–173. A.A. Balkema, Rotterdam.

Van Straalen, N.M., and C.A.J. Denneman. 1989. Ecotoxicological evaluation of soil quality criteria. Ecotoxicology and Environmental Safety 18, 241–251.

Van Straalen, N.M., and C.A.M. Van Gestel. 1993. Soil invertebrates and micro-organisms. In Handbook of Ecotoxicology, Vol. 1, P. Calow (ed.), pp. 251–277. Blackwell Scientific, London.

Venables, B.J., K.E. Daugherty, A.J. Goven, and O.O. Ohlsson. 1988. Characterization of toxicity of fly ash from the combustion of refuse-derived fuel. Proceedings 81st Annual Meeting of Air Pollution Association, Dallas, TX, 88–26 pp. 3–16.

Venables, B.J., L.C. Fitzpatrick, and A.J. Goven. 1992. Earthworms as indicators of toxicity. In Ecotoxicology of Earthworms, P.W. Greig-Smith et al. (eds.), pp. 197–206. Intercept Ltd., Hants, U.K.

Weibull, W. 1951. A statistical distribution function of wide application. Journal of Applied Mechanics 18, 293–297.

Wilson, R., and E.A.C. Crouch. 1987. Risk assessment and comparisons: an introduction. Science 236, 267–270.

Earthworms in Environmental Research: Still a Promising Tool

14

H. Eijsackers
Netherlands Integrated Soil Research Programme, Wageningen, The Netherlands*

After the very successful 4th International Symposium on Earthworm Ecology (Avignon, September 1990) and the most productive international workshop on Earthworm Ecotoxicology (Sheffield, April 1991), earthworm assays seemed to have been accepted fully in environmental management and research. Earthworms were acknowledged as general tools in various fields of environmental research and management. At the workshop, a number of methodologies with respect to pre-application testing, post-application bioassays, monitoring, waste management, and risk assessment were presented (Greig-Smith et al. 1992).

However, five years later, how much progress has really been made? Much effort has been put into further standardization of the tests proposed, and a number of interesting studies have been published on different aspects of testing and on new, better tests. But have earthworms really been accepted in the general field of ecotoxicological research and environmental management?

The main purpose of this chapter is to review progress in earthworm ecotoxicology during this last five-year period. It will be based on the presentations in the session "Earthworms and Environmental Research" of the 5th International Symposium on Earthworm Ecology, the results within the Nether-

* Present address: National Institute of Human Health and the Environment, Department of Ecotoxicology, POB1, NL 3720 BA Bilthoven, The Netherlands.

lands Integrated Soil Research Programme, and a number of other Western European programs in this field, supplemented with appropriate examples from other research.

After a brief introduction to the attention to earthworm ecotoxicological research in this last period, this overview starts with uptake and elimination processes (bioaccumulation and toxicokinetics). This is followed by different aspects of laboratory testing, field studies, and sampling programs. Next, food chain transfer is described as a process of species interaction. Finally, some integrated studies at higher biological integration levels (community, ecosystem) are described that include earthworm responses to population dynamics and soil structure.

CURRENT INTEREST IN EARTHWORM ECOTOXICOLOGY

What makes earthworms a favorite "model animal" in ecotoxicological research? Given the general attitude towards earthworms—those slimy, squirming creatures—it seems rather remarkable at first glance that earthworms are so popular. However, this same attitude indicates that earthworms are easily recognized. Their usefulness in nature is easily acknowledged as food for birds and bait for fish. Moreover, they execute a well-defined and positive role in the formation of soil, which can be easily observed. Next to that, from a technical-experimental point of view, they are easy to breed, culture, and handle.

In the past few years, some new soil ecotoxicity-oriented research programs have been carried out or initiated: the Netherlands Integrated Soil Research Programme (NISRP), the Swedish MATS program (Soil Biological Variables in Environmental Hazard Assessment) last year succeeded by ISA (Integrated Soil Analysis), the European network SERAS (Soil Ecotoxicity Risk Assessment Systems), and the EU SECOFASE (development, improvement, and standardization of test systems for assessing sublethal effects of chemicals on fauna in the soil ecosystem). In each of these programs earthworm testing is included. In NISRP and MATS more fundamental aspects also are covered.

Analyzing the current interest in ecotoxicological research with earthworms by screening the programs of a number of major ecotoxicological conferences of the Society for Environmental Toxicity and Chemistry (SETAC) and the Society of Ecotoxicology and Environmental Safety (SECOTOX) reveals a somewhat different picture. In the SETAC conference in Sheffield (1991), seven papers on earthworms were presented of a total of 142 presentations (5%), compiled with other soil ecotoxicological aspects in Donkers et al. (1994). For the SECOTOX conference in Amsterdam (1992), these figures were four out of 171 papers (<4%); for the SETAC conference in Lisbon (1993), eight earthworm papers (including three on vermicomposting) out of 594 (2%) platform and poster contributions; and for the SETAC conference in Houston (1994), even fewer: five out of more than 1,500 contributions. Hence, the conclusion that interest in earthworm testing is still growing is not always valid.

Much effort has been put into earthworm test development; the Organization for Economic Coordination and Development (OECD) and the International Standards Organization (ISO) have carried out a number of ring tests and standardization studies. Notwithstanding all these efforts, in a recent study for OECD on the selection of a set of laboratory ecotoxity tests (Léon and Van Gestel, pers. comm.), the earthworm tests scored relatively low with a 6th position (of 44 tests in total) for the OECD test, 13th for the test of the Environmental Protection Agency (EPA), and 18th for the ISO test. Standardization was the main factor, which was underrated, and therefore newly-developed tests by the International Organization for Biological Control (IOBC) and the National Institute for Human Health and the Environment (RIVM-NL), with a higher ecological relevance than the artificial soil/*Eisenia fetida* test, scored very low (#38, 39, 40).

In conclusion, if more ecologically relevant earthworm test should be accepted, quite a lot of work has to be done yet. This was also recognized in the Sheffield workshop, resulting in a number of recommendations for further research (Table 1).

Table 1. Future research on earthworm ecotoxicology as recommended in the International Workshop on Earthworm Ecotoxicology, Sheffield, April 1991

1. Encourage improvement of standard artificial soil test.
2. Develop reliable extrapolation models from standard test conditions to natural soils to improve likely field exposure and predict population effect levels.
3. Develop new laboratory methods and extrapolate to present field methods.
4. Initiate a common data base.
5. Develop a standard field protocol.
6. Determine most suitable plot size for standard field tests.
7. Improve knowledge on ecological significance of population-level effects.
8. Develop methods for behavioral responses and incorporate in standard tests.
9. Develop research approach to understand differences in sensitivity between species on biochemical/physiological mechanisms.
10. Improve knowledge on safety factors based on exposure-toxicity ratios.
11. Develop consistent criteria to categorize chemicals for high, intermediate, low, and negligible risk for earthworms.
12. Improve knowledge on potential indirect effects on earthworms.

TOXICOKINETIC BEHAVIOR BY EARTHWORMS (UPTAKE, ELIMINATION, BIOACCUMULATION)

Ecotoxicological work is typically split into a number of phases. The first question is how the organism is exposed to a contaminant. How is the contaminant chemically available in the soil, by what routes and mechanisms are earthworms taking up the contaminant, and how is it internally processed; is it broken down, excreted, or stored? This is summarized under the headings of environmental chemistry and toxicokinetics. These aspects will be further discussed in this section.

The next questions—what are the effects of a chemical on the individual earthworm, what are the implications for the earthworm population, and what impacts does this have on soil ecosystems and food chains—are treated in following sections.

Much work has already been done on the factors influencing the uptake, internal distribution, and elimination of heavy metals in earthworms (Beeby 1993). Next to the characteristics of the metal, soil and earthworm factors play significant roles.

Nieboer and Richardson (1980) distinguished two groups of metals, one that tends to bind metals to oxygen sites in biological ligands and acts as macronutrients, and one that forms strong bonds with N or S and exerts toxicity by affecting protein structure and enzyme function (Figure 1). As a consequence, some heavy metals will be regulated after uptake by earthworms (e.g., Zn) while others will be accumulated continuously (e.g., Cd) and become tightly

Period	Class A		Borderline					Class B			
2	Li	Be									
3	Na	Mg									
4	K	Ca	Cr	Mn	Fe Co Ni	Cu	Zn		Cu		
5	Rb	Sr					Cd	Sn	Ag		
6	Cs							Pb	Au	Hg	Pb

Figure 1. Biological classification of metals, arranged according to periodic table and working mechanism: class A macronutrients forming O-bonds and class B toxicants forming N- and S-bonds.

bound. These last ones remain in earthworms also after a transfer to clean soil as observed for Cd by van Gestel et al. (1993a). A second characteristic of Cd that reinforces accumulation is its low toxicity for earthworms. The metals in the group of macronutrients may become toxic as well, given dose, conditions, and endpoints. Fischer and Molnar (1997) observed that Na, K, and Ba all negatively affected cocoon production, presumably by influencing osmotic relations.

Toxic metals interact with trace metals and these metal macronutrients. Substitution is an important process in this context as shown for Ca-Cd and Ca-Pb interactions by Ma (1993). In general, invertebrates with a high Ca requirement actively accumulate heavy metals. In addition Janssen et al. (1992, 1993) showed that potassium affects uptake of ^{134}Cesium but not of sodium.

In most contaminated sites, a mixture of various contaminants will be present, so we also have to assess their combined toxicity. Posthuma (1997) tested a number of combinations of Cd, Zn, and Cu and observed both synergism and antagonism. Antagonistic responses mean that just adding up toxicities of separately tested metals can largely overestimate the impact of the combined heavy metals in field conditions.

Of the different soil factors (soil acidity, pH, cation exchange capacity, percentage organic matter), pH plays the most important role. It affects both the physico-chemical binding and the biological uptake processes, as shown by Marinussen and Van der Zee (1997). Moreover, Marinussen and Van der Zee illustrated the importance of soil moisture; with increased soil moisture the Cu content in the pore water decreased. This illustrates that bioaccumulation has both a physico-chemical and a biological aspect. Moreover, as well as the biological uptake processes, soil moisture also affects earthworm behavior and metabolism in general. Negative observations on the effects of soil moisture on pesticide uptake by earthworms are reported with respect to the impact of parathion with *E. fetida* by Bauer and Römbke (pers. comm.). The soil acidity (pH) influences the physico-chemical behavior of heavy metals in soil and also has a general impact on feeding rate and metabolic turnover of earthworms as suggested for Pb uptake by Bengtsson and Rundgren (1992). This impact of pH also happened to be important for the ecotoxicological assessment of different soil clean-up techniques. One of the clean-up methods is washing the contaminated soil with acids, thereby extracting the heavy metals present in those soils. To test the ecological value of the cleaned soil, Van Gestel et al. (1993b) carried out some earthworm bioassays. They showed that these extractive treatments may even increase uptake by earthworms of metal residues from remediated soils.

Biological factors can also have an impact on the seasonal fluctuations of uptake processes in earthworms. Bengtsson and Rundgren (1992) observed, in an outdoor experiment with *Lumbricus terrestris*, that uptake of Pb was lower during wintertime. The steady state of the lead burden of the earthworm during the cold winter period indicates that uptake is an active process, presumably related to feeding, in which soil temperature, pH, and moisture play important roles. Morgan and Morgan (1993) observed that the epigeic *Lumbricus rubellus* showed higher Zn concentration during winter and early spring, which in general show distinct earthworm activity (the authors did not mention any cold spell). The endogeic earthworm species *Aporrectodea caliginosa* had lower Cd and Zn concentrations during diapause, which was explained by active elimination and a significantly higher Pb content. The higher Pb content was explained by retainment of Pb, in combination with a decreased biomass. In monitoring activities these aspects have to be taken into account.

For organic compounds van Gestel (1992) and van Gestel and Ma (1993) developed a soil-pore-water partitioning approach and derived QSAR relationships for a number of chlorinated hydrocarbons (Figure 2). This concept has

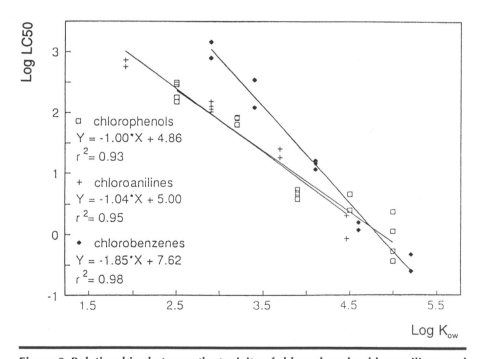

Figure 2. Relationships between the toxicity of chlorophenols, chloroanilines, and chlorabenzenes to *Eisenia andrei* and log K_{ow}. Note: For *Lumbricus rubellus* the relation with chlorophenols is log LC_{50} (µmol.l^{-1}) = −0.72*log K_{ow} + 4.46 (r^2 = 0.87).

been extended further in studies by Belfroid (1994) and Loonen (1994) on the toxicokinetics of uptake and elimination mechanisms in earthworms, for hydrophobic chemicals and dioxins/furans respectively. In a series of studies on uptake of these chemicals by earthworms from water, moist soil, and soil plus food, they showed that the uptake proceeds in a monophasic way. The elimination in soil is biphasic (Figure 3) with a slow second phase. This is in agreement with the elimination rate from water (Belfroid 1994). The first fast elimination must therefore be ascribed to emptying soil from the gut. Loonen (1997) observed that in the presence of sediment the aquatic earthworm species *L. variegatus* showed additional accumulation of chemicals, which was not accounted for by the soil-pore-water partitioning model, suggesting also an active uptake from sediment particles. Intestinal uptake from food also occurs and has been measured separately in laboratory experiments by Belfroid. In relation to the uptake in the gut from soil and through the skin from water, this uptake route appeared to be quantitatively less important, but depends on the organic matter content of the soil. In organic rich soils this can be of importance. Relating these data to field conditions is still not possible (Belfroid et al., in press). As a consequence, there is a good argument to use the potential or critical body burden (or better critical body concentration) as a measure for actual exposure instead of applied doses (Fitzgerald et al. 1997; Lanno and McCarty 1997).

Loonen (1994) also observed, when repeating an accumulation study in earthworms after a contact period of more than two years, a clearly decreased bioavailability (Figure 4). This indicates that contaminants may become bound to or in organic matter, mineral particles, and micropores and become less available for uptake or other biological processes. For pesticides this process is known as bound residues.

TESTING WITH EARTHWORMS

When we know how a contaminant is taken up by the earthworm and how it becomes distributed over the earthworm body, our next question is what kind of effects will result. Concentration of contaminants in the reproductive organs will exert a different effect than accumulation in the cerebral ganglion or in special storage organs. Moreover, these various effects—or so-called testing endpoints—will have a different impact on the ultimate survival of the earthworm or, when looking at the population level, on the intrinsic rate of increase or maintenance of the earthworm population.

Much effort has been put into standardization of earthworm tests during these last years. The OECD test with artificial soil and *Eisenia fetida* has proven

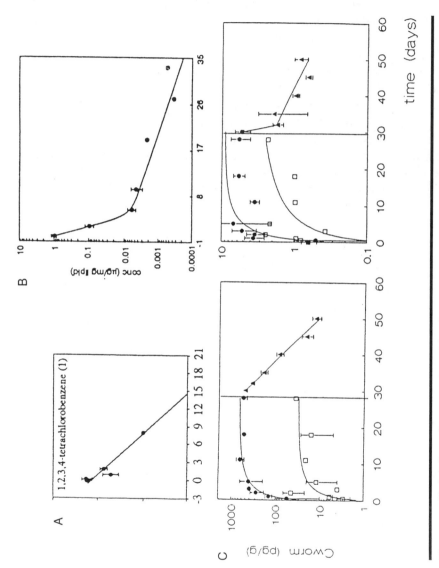

Figure 3. Elimination of 1,2,3,4-tetrachlorobenzene from (A) *E. fetida* in water and (B) in soil. (C) Accumulation and elimination of TCDD by *L. variegatus* in the presence and absence of sediment.

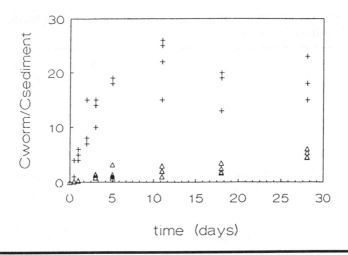

Figure 4. Organism/sediment ratios of *L. variegatus* 3 weeks (+) and 21 months (Δ) after mixing sediment with TCDD.

to be highly reproducible. By adding a small pellet of cow manure as food, the survival of the earthworms improves greatly. The nutritive value of the peat, clay, and sand mixture of the artificial soil has proved to be rather low. Moreover, an improved protocol has been introduced (Van Gestel et al. 1989) in which a more sensitive chronic endpoint (reproduction instead of survival) is used, and a recovery period is introduced that also gives the opportunity to study the hatchability of the cocoons produced. Together with cocoon production this gives a potential estimate of the population maintenance rate. As a next step, Kula (1994) adapted the method for assessment of pesticides by applying the pesticide to the soil surface. Comparing the effect of surface application of a compound with the effect of mixing it through the total test soil mass revealed reasonably similar results with benomyl (Table 2).

Slimak (1997) tested the impact of earthworm avoidance behavior for diazinon, mecoprop, carbaryl, and potassium-fatty acid salts. Earthworms actively avoided these compounds, as was observed also for heavy metals (Eijsackers 1981), fly ash (Ma and Eijsackers 1989), harbor sludge (Ma 1997), and pesticides (Bauer and Römbke 1997), so avoidance should be incorporated as assessment in test procedures.

Biomarkers are a new concept in earthworm testing. These have been developed based on a number of enzyme functions (Goven et al. 1993, 1994; Wang 1997) for macrophage phagocytosis, a cytometric assay by Fugère et al. (1997),

Table 2. Effects of benomyl after surface application or total mixture with the OECD artificial soil test

	Control	0.5 kg.ha^{-1}	2.5 kg.ha^{-1}
Number of juveniles			
surface application	11.8 ± 3.6	8.7 ± 1.7	1.8 ± 0.4
total contamination	11.8 ± 3.6	6.9 ± 2.5	0
Body weight			
surface application	124.4 ± 0.3	130.1 ± 5.3	65.0 ± 1.3
total contamination	124.4 ± 0.3	136.7 ± 3.6	49.9 ± 2.0

hemoglobin content (Rozen and Mazur 1997), and for sperm production and fertility (Reinecke and Reinecke 1997; Cikutovic et al. 1993).

The major limitation in all these test approaches is, however, the question why tests using earthworms should be better than those using other organisms. A similar question is whether earthworm biomarkers would be generally applicable for other soil organisms. Combining the general validity of these biomarkers with a proper assessment of their ecological relevance is therefore a necessity before they can become widely used.

For the further improvement of testing the effects of chemicals on earthworms, the following topics still need further attention: statistical interpretation of dose-effect curves, inter-compound testing, inter-species testing, testing realistic (low and repeated) field doses, and testing artificial versus natural soil.

In interpreting the results of earthworm ecotoxicology tests we have to realize that when using the LC$_{50}$, the form of the dose-effect curves is not critical. However, in using more sensitive endpoints like reproduction and NOECs, this form certainly matters. For a number of heavy metals and combinations of heavy metals, Spurgeon et al. (1994) found a dose-response step function for Cd and a gradual decrease for Zn, whereas Posthuma et al. (1993) could describe the combined effects of Cd/Cu and Cd/Zn on reproduction using a linear logarithmic model and the effect of Cu/Zn with a hormesic model (Figure 5). Especially when deriving NOEC values, the model used and the statistical variation affect the outcome very much as these values are the highest concentrations in a series that do not show a significant difference with the control. Therefore, the set-up of the experiment and the variability of the resulting data set influence the NOEC derivation greatly. Moreover, it is only an approximation and as a consequence, e.g., for step functions, it is not possible to derive NOECs. Hence, to fully understand and interpret the different response patterns much more work is necessary.

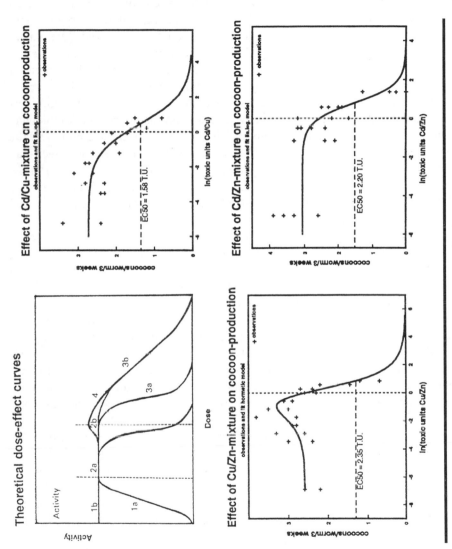

Figure 5. Dose-effect curves of different heavy metal mixtures.

Studies on inter-compound testing (e.g., Neuhauser et al. [1986], van Gestel and Ma [1993], Kula [1994], and Larink [1994] on the effects of organic compounds and Posthuma et al. [1993] and Diaz-Lopez and Mancha [1994] on the effects of heavy metals) show that for a number of compound groups generalized relationships can be observed. For generally acting (narcotic) organic compounds (van Gestel and Ma 1993) it is possible to derive so-called Quantitative Structure Activity Relationships (QSARs). For heavy metals, Posthuma et al. (1993, 1997) developed an approach in which they "summed" the effects of heavy metals on the basis of their LC_{50}s, expressed in toxicity units. Diaz-Lopez and Mancha (1994) investigated the effects of different anions and the additions of different fertilizers on the toxicity of Cu. Various copper salts (sulphate, nitrate, and chlorides) have different toxicities to earthworms, and moreover the combination of NH_4NO_3 and $CuSO_4$ exerts a much stronger toxic effect than when tested separately. Fischer and Molnar (1997) reported that a number of the macro-nutrient metals—$NaCl$, KCl, $CaCl_2$, $MgCl_2$, $BaCl_2$, and $MnCl_2$—reduced reproduction, as well as $SnCl_2$, $SrCl_2$, $AlCl_3$, and $FeCl_3$, while $CoCl_2$, $CuCl_2$, and $NiCl_2$ proved to be acutely toxic.

Studies on inter-species testing produced distinctly different results. Neuhauser et al. (1986) claimed that the four species they tested showed good correlation, while Haque and Ebing (1983) found a significant relationship between *E. fetida* and *L. terrestris* for the effects of a series of pesticides. Heimbach (1985) found in general a factor of 2–3 when comparing *E. fetida* and *L. terrestris*. On the contrary, Kula (1994) found differences between *E. fetida* and three other earthworm species (*A. caliginosa, A. chlorotica,* and *A. longa*) from a factor of 4 up to a factor of 80. Callahan et al. (1994) observed with four species (*E. fetida, Allolobophora tuberculata, Euctrilus eugeniae,* and *Periomyx excavatus*), 62 chemicals, and the filter paper and artificial soil test a similar range of toxicity for all four species, but a difference of up to four orders of magnitude between the two test systems.

Presumably this difference between test systems is the consequence of using nominal concentrations and not taking the actual concentrations into account. In the filter paper test, these may be similar, but in soil the real availability can differ considerably depending on the type of chemical and soil. According to Kratz and Pöhhacker (1994) two closely related species like *Eisenia fetida fetida* and *E. fetida andrei* show distinctly different responses to carbendazim and phenmedipham.

Ma and Bodt (1993), testing the toxicity of chemicals to six earthworm species, suggested a genus-related variation in toxicity to chlorpyrifos, with increasing sensitivity in the order *Eisenia* spec. < *Aporrectodea* spec. < *Lumbricus* spec. These differences were not related to body weight, according to the authors; it seemed more likely that some physiological factor is involved. This is supported by the observation of Stenersen et al. (1992) that the different sensitivity of the closely related *Eisenia* species (*E. fetida* and *E. andrei*) and *Eiseniella veneta* to carbaryl was related to the possession of a carbaryl-resistant enzyme by the first two species. This also supports the results from Kratz and Pöhhacker (1994), who also found a different sensitivity for the two *Eisenia* species. These last studies call for further investigation of a taxonomically related sensitivity pattern at different levels (species, genus, or family), in order to achieve a quantified differentiation of a safety factor that can be included in risk assessment procedures to cover differences in sensitivity.

In the test proposed by Kula (1994) and also in the recommendation of the Sheffield ecotoxicology workshop (Greig-Smith et al. 1992), field relevant doses are suggested as being the dose used in practice and five times this dose.

However, as shown by Springett and Gray (1992), far lower doses (20, 10, and 5% of recommended field rate) could exert toxic effects when applied regularly for a longer period (100 days at two-week intervals), which is more relevant for the actual growing period and agronomic practice.

The use of artificial soil as a replacement for natural soils has been scrutinized, and there are reports pointing toward good as well as limited correlation. Both with respect to heavy metals (Posthuma et al. 1993) and organic pesticides, the artificial soil test seems to over- as well as underestimate the toxicity in real soil conditions. Fayolle and Chabert (1997) found a good correlation between laboratory and field testing of the effects of lindane, carbofuran, imidachloride, and chlormephos using *E. fetida, L. terrestris,* and *A. chlorotica.* Lanno et al. (1997) observed a marked influence of soil type comparing three soil types with respect to the impact of benomyl, 2-chloroacetamide, diazinon, and pentachlorophenol. Different toxicant availability is a main governing factor, because both organic matter and clay adsorb chemicals differently. Van Gestel and van Straalen (1994) state that the organic matter content in combination with sorption data provided a good basis for a translation formula from artificial soil to real soil conditions. This has been worked out further by Belfroid (1994), but further study is still needed.

FIELD STUDIES

The ultimate relevance of all this testing lies in a proper maintenance of the earthworm population as being the natural motor of soil ecosystems, turning the soil upside down continuously, thereby creating an optimal soil condition, and degrading organic matter and working it into the soil. Especially in agronomy systems, a proper combination of management of these "underground forces" and chemical pest treatment should be achieved by proper preventive test assessment procedures.

In addition to the state-of-the-art field tests presented at the Sheffield ecotoxicology workshop by Edwards (1992), Kula (1992), and Heimbach (1992), further progress has been made.

Kula (pers. comm.) proposed a standardized approach for field experimentation, in which he gives working rules for representative sites (both grass and arable land), plot sizes (10 × 10 m) with a 2-m protection zone with four replicates, sampling procedures, and intervals, and suggests *L. terrestris* and *A. caliginosa* as relevant species, which usually occur in sufficient densities in these kinds of environments. Heimbach (1997) has experimented with barriers between plots and also included the indirect impact of a changed food supply (grass cut or mulched). His conclusions are that lateral earthworm dispersal is limited and can be neglected in field sampling, whereas the impact of plowing and reseeding can be rather drastic. The observations of Mather and Christensen (1997) on the quite extensive lateral dispersal of earthworms suggest the need for caution in the design of field experiments.

With respect to the correlating of laboratory test results with field sampling, in two field studies Spurgeon et al. (1994) and Posthuma et al. (1997) report on samplings in the vicinity of large smelter works. Spatial distribution in a "dose-effect" relation was expressed by Spurgeon et al. (1994), based on the OECD 14-day LC_{50}s of the heavy metals present, in terms of km^2 from the source in the vicinity of the smelter works which should be devoid of earthworms. For Zn this was 75 km^2, Cu 42 km^2, and Pb 4.7 km^2. Posthuma et al. (1997) plotted the numbers of earthworms found in a sigmoid distance-response curve, which enabled calculation of an EC_{50} that could then be compared with the outcomes of standard OECD tests. Both Posthuma et al. and Spurgeon et al. observed an overestimation of the potential toxic effect of the heavy metals using the OECD test. Posthuma et al. explained this by a difference in uptake rate that they actually observed for Cd accumulation (Figure 6) and, hence, a difference in bioavailability. This is confirmed by the observation of Spurgeon et al. (1994) that despite their extrapolation that no earthworms should be present in the close vicinity of the smelter, they are still present. In addition, Posthuma et al. pointed at a possible antagonistic effect of binary mixtures of heavy metals compared to the single-metal OECD test (see above, "Toxicokinetic Behavior by Earthworms").

What is still missing, nevertheless, is a proper validation of laboratory versus field tests. Heimbach (1992, 1994) has made a good approach but had to make many assumptions to bring laboratory and field studies properly in line. A recent desk study on validation (Hamers, pers. comm.) concludes that the

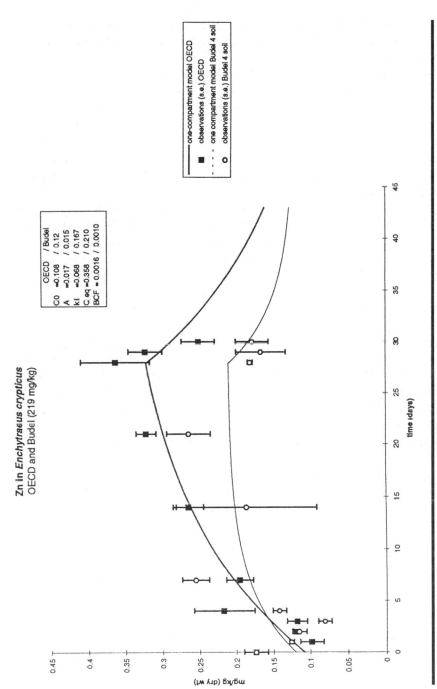

Figure 6. Uptake of zinc by *Enchytraeus crypticus* from OECD artificial soil and Budel sandy soil, showing reduced bioavailability in the last one (L. Posthuma, pers. comm.).

proper and statistically sound data base needed for such validation is very small. More studies combining statistically-based laboratory and field experiments are needed.

Callahan and Linder (1992) sampled contaminated soil from a field site and tested this in the laboratory or under outdoor conditions for toxicity to earthworms. This last approach was also used by Bengtsson et al. (1992) when they studied the possible adaptation of earthworms to long-term exposure in the soil surrounding a copper brass mill dating from the 17th century. They pointed at the occurrence of seasonality in the uptake of heavy metals by earthworms, as was suggested by Morgan and Morgan (1993), an important aspect in designing proper monitoring schemes.

Moreover, Bengtsson et al. (1993) discussed the possibilities for recovery, or better maintenance, of the observed scattered and low-density *D. octaedra* population in the near vicinity of the old mill (as also observed for other species in the surroundings of the Avonmouth smelter by Spurgeon et al.).

This potential for recovery or maintenance is a further aspect to consider in field studies. It has been studied especially in relation to repeated application of pesticides, but not in relation to remediation of more persistently contaminated areas. In their studies at the brass mill, Bengtsson et al. (1993) ascribed the maintenance of *D. octaedra* populations to either immigration of juveniles from less polluted areas or spatial heterogeneity in metal distribution in the soil. This last explanation is not supported by their own field data, since the heavy metal contents in the various plots sampled by them show approximately the same coefficient of variation; hence heterogeneity at the old mill is not greater than elsewhere. Immigration is perhaps a more relevant explanation than has been supposed previously. This perspective of (re)immigration therefore needs further attention. It should be investigated also in the framework of restoration of acidified and limed coniferous soils as studied by Rundgren (in press) or further soil-ecological recovery of remediated sites as described by Bradshaw (1994) and Tamis et al. (1994). The last study showed, for some thermically and biologically cleaned sites, distinct recovery of earthworm populations.

FOOD CHAIN RESEARCH INVOLVING EARTHWORMS

The best recognized "performance" of earthworms for the general public is as fish bait. However, many other animals prefer earthworms as food. Next to songbirds, raptors (buzzard and tawny owl), various mammals (hedgehogs, badgers, and boars), and amphibians and reptiles like earthworms. Because of the considerable ability of earthworms to accumulate contaminants from the soil matrix into their body parts, earthworms are an important transfer route from the soil to the terrestrial ecosystems. Therefore earthworms play an important role in food chain transfer.

With respect to food chain research, considerable progress has been made, and a number of models on food chain transfer have been developed in The Netherlands and elsewhere. This started with rather simple models by Romijn et al. (1991) and Luttik et al. (1993), in which the maximal permissible concentration (MPC) is calculated by dividing the no observed effect concentration for these bird or mammal predators ($NOEC_{bird/mammal}$) by the bioconcentration factor of the contaminant from the soil into the earthworm ($BCF_{earthworm}$). MPCs were calculated for standard soil situations and compared to MPCs for other terrestrial organisms. This revealed that secondary poisoning could be a critical pathway with earthworms for cadmium and methylmercury.

As a next, more complicated step, biological characteristics of the predator were introduced. Noppert et al. (1994) combined BCFs for earthworms with a formula for the uptake rate of chemicals by predators. This was based on their uptake efficiency, feeding rate, elimination rate, and life expectancy. Gorree and Tamis (1993) extended this approach further in their BioMagnification model (BIOMAG-2) and introduced the bioavailable proportion of a compound by using a soil-pore-water partitioning approach (see the section above on toxicokinetic behavior). As a further improvement, Everts et al. (1993) introduced the basal, existence, and field metabolic rates for predators both in laboratory feeding experiments and (based on general assumptions) in the field, and developed the following formula:

$$NOEC_{prey} = NOEC_{lab.food} \cdot \frac{E_{prey}}{E_{lab.food}} \cdot \frac{EMR_{total\ bird}}{EMR_{species\ concern}} \cdot \frac{FMR_{norm.condition}}{FMR_{peak\ activity}}$$

where E = energy content, FMR = field metabolic rate, EMR = existence metabolic rate, and BMR = basal metabolic rate.

These last three models all assume a stochastic exposure of earthworms to chemicals and so introduce a certain probability in the risk estimates derived.

The third step in these model developments introduces population dynamic elements: by which factors earthworm populations vary yearly in the field. In the model of Ma and Van der Voet (1993) an explicit analysis of original field data is carried out. Next to the earlier used $BCF_{earthworm}$ plus the bioavailable fraction of the chemical in the soil, a complicated (non-linear) age-dependent relation is calculated (by regression) of the data of the predators in combination with a theoretical model on actual uptake rates in the various organs of the predators. In this way it was possible to predict target organ loads as functions of ingestion of the contaminant, its assimilation rate, and internal partitioning.

A fourth step is combining these uptake mechanisms with the other processes steering the cycling of biomass through an ecosystem. The amount of biomass cycling is combined with the accumulation rate of a contaminant. The resulting load of the biomass with the contaminants defines how much of a contaminant ends up in various parts of the ecosystem. This approach is used in the CATS model. This model analyzes the cadmium cycle in a particular ecosystem (a meadow) based on the C- and N-cycles and the resulting biomass transfers between the different elemental pools in the system; cadmium is carried by this biomass from one pool to another (Figure 7 from Traas and Aldenberg 1992). Because this model also used a soil availability model it was possible to calculate what happens when agricultural areas that have been contaminated with cadmium (by emission from a nearby smelter plus the application of fertilizer that contains cadmium) are set aside (Knoop and Traas 1993). Due to the cessation of liming, cadmium can become more available and accumulated in the food chain, resulting in toxic kidney levels in moles (Figure 8).

The results and estimates used in the other models are expressed in different ways. It can be as the relation between the potential environmental concentration and the no effect concentration: the PEC/NEC ratio (Romijn et al. 1991; Luttik et al. 1993; Noppert et al. 1994). It can also be expressed as a risk for passerine birds due to uptake of diazinon by earthworms in combination with the toxicity of these birds for this pesticide (Stephenson et al. 1997) or in a potential risk area around a point pollution source (Gorree and Tamis 1992) or in an exposure risk for target organs (Ma and van der Voet 1993).

In all food chain uptake studies the role of earthworms or soil invertebrates in general as the intermediate between soil and terrestrial predators proved to be crucial. BCFs for soil-earthworms, in all cases, had the highest levels, as exemplified by data of Ma (1994) (Table 3). Because of their high bioaccumulation potential and relatively low sensitivity to certain toxic compounds, earthworms are major intoxication sources for terrestrial predators.

Only the last study by Ma (1994) used original field data, however. This illustrates clearly the main limitation of food chain modeling at present: the lack of suitable field data. In a combined field and laboratory study, Denneman et al. (1992) investigated the food chain transfer of Cd and Zn via earthworms into moles (Table 4) and further confirmed the direct cause-response relationship by feeding moles experimentally with cadmium-loaded earthworms. In 25- and 50-day feeding experiments, earthworms with an approximate load of 60.7 mg/kg caused distinct kidney damage, typical of cadmium in the Malpighian tubuli and bulboses, and hypertrophy in the mesangial cells of the glomerulus.

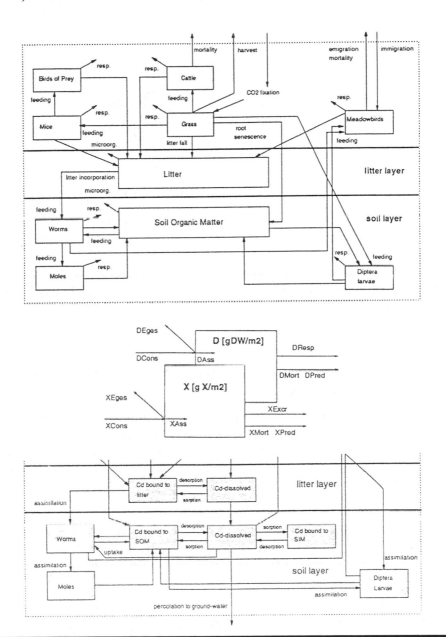

Figure 7. Upper graph: Flow sheet of the CATS model giving the boxes and fluxes of the biomass cycling (inset: the toxicant transport due to biomass fluxes). Lower graph: Resulting boxes and fluxes of the cadmium cycling in the system.

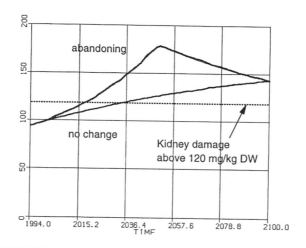

Figure 8. Mobilized cadmium (µg dissolved/liter soil) due to cessation of liming after abandoning cadmium-loaded arable land in relation to the toxic level for moles (kidneys).

Indirect Effects and Effects of Chemicals at Ecosystem Level Related to Earthworms

The important function of earthworms as food for other organisms is not only important in the context of food chain transfer. When earthworms are getting scarce because they are negatively affected by a specific contaminant, this will cause food shortage for their predators. When this causes negative effects these are mentioned as "indirect effects."

Table 3. Concentration factors (CF) for cadmium and lead in herbivore and decomposer-based terrestrial food chains

Species group	$CF_{cadmium}$	CF_{lead}
Coleoptera	1.3–6.5	0.2–0.5
Carabidae	1.5–9.5	0.0–0.3
Aranea	18–86	0.3–0.5
Opiliones	5.5–23	0.1–0.8
Lumbricidae	32–136	1.3–3.0
grass	0.5–2.5	0.0–0.3
soil (mg/kg)	0.2–2.9	20–130

Table 4. Cadmium and zinc contents of mole kidneys, earthworms (L. rubellus), and soil in heavy metal contaminated sandy soils (Kempen area) and clean sandy (2 areas) and clayey reference soils

	Cadmium			Zinc		
	cont.sand	ref.sand	ref.clay	cont.sand	ref.sand	ref.clay
mole kidney	197	18/47	43	202	131/118	132
earthworms	77	3/8	26	1599	286/426	725
soil (0–10 cm)	1.8	0.2/0.2	1.5	103	35/46	272

As stated already with respect to food chain research, the main limitation in ecosystem-level research into earthworm ecotoxicology is the shortage of suitable field data. At the recent conferences of the Society for Environmental Toxicology and Chemistry in Lisbon and Houston special sessions were organized on indirect effects of contaminants in ecosystems, without any presentations on earthworms. Heimbach (1997) gave data on the implications of different management of field plots—grass cover cut and removed, mulched, or plowed—on the toxicity of applied chemicals to earthworms. He incorporated a change in food availability, mechanical damage, and a change in soil structure as indirect effects in the test. He concluded that these last effects seemed to be more important than the impacts of the applied chemicals.

There are several studies, but a proper population dynamic analysis or modeling is still lacking. Klok et al. (1997) and Baveco et al. (1997), however, present some results of a model that combines population development with energy budgets and distinguishes between the various approaches in population biology. Do we have to make a distinction between the development stage of the earthworm or merely its size? Can we use defined (discrete) time steps or a continuous time frame? Should we include density-dependent processes or not?

Another approach is to model the structure of the soil ecosystem, as described (Knoop and Traas 1993) in the previous paragraph. The soil ecology groups at the Institute for Soil Fertility (present name: Institute for Agrobiological Research, Haren, NL) and the Natural Resource Ecology Laboratory (Fort Collins, Colorado, US) have built a model that generates the structure of an arable or grassland soil ecosystem. With this model they have simulated the changes in C- and N-cycles under the influence of different management practices (de Ruiter et al. 1993). As a further extension, work has been started in which the removal of a specific microbivore or predatory group—due to a relatively large sensitivity to a specific toxic compound—is simulated with respect to its consequences for C- and N-cycles and general biomass turnover (de Ruiter and Moore 1994). In a study by Marinissen and de Ruiter (1994) the impact of earthworms on these systems has been analyzed; therefore, it should be possible to assess removal of earthworms from the system in a similar way. However, this has still to be done.

A major weakness, with respect to the validation of these ecosystem structure studies, is the general lack of studies on interactions between earthworms and other soil faunal groups (see Chapter 9). Recently, Hyvönen et al. (1994) published a study on the interactions between earthworms and nematodes. Bengtsson et al. (1986) already observed that nematode infection of earthworm cocoons causes a lower hatchability. Acidity and heavy metal contamination may interfere with the impact of this infection. Further studies in this field might provide tools to study influences on species interactions as elements of ecosystem structure.

Another type of indirect relationship that deserves further study is between earthworm and soil structure. Tomlin et al. (1993) observed the impact of three types of treated sewage sludge and reported that earthworm burrows are lined with fecal material that had higher heavy metal concentrations than the surrounding soil. Moreover, soluble forms of heavy metals could be leached more easily through these burrows.

An element we have to encounter in all these studies is the temporal scale of our studies. In a number of studies on adaptation of earthworms to heavy metals, the presence of metal-binding metallothioneines has been reported. Parallel to that there have been studies on the better survival of adapted earthworm populations, or a decreased uptake by adapted earthworm population (Terhivuo et al. 1994; Marino and Morgan 1997).

However, up till now it has not been possible to prove that very long-term exposure to heavy metals induced the presence of particular proteins, even after several centuries of exposure, as studied by Bengtsson et al. (1992). These last authors put their study in the framework of evolutionary responses. A major element in these discussions is a trade-off between different strategies to optimize earthworm survival. Indications for this might be derived from short-term studies concentrating on trade-off between different responses of earthworms to chemicals. Although there are some indications of such interactions, studies focusing on these basic questions are still lacking.

RISK ASSESSMENT BASED ON EARTHWORM STUDIES

The ultimate goal of all research described previously is to assess the overall environmental impact of specific chemical compounds (pesticides, chemical compounds, heavy metals), specific contaminated substrates (sewage sludge, building materials), or generally or specifically contaminated situations (abandoned waste dumps, contaminated and dredged harbor sludges). For all these purposes earthworm tests, bioassays, field studies, and monitoring programs can be useful.

We have to realize that there are some prerequisites for a proper ecological risk assessment. As Menzie et al. (1993) stated, "the 'problem formulation' phase of ecological risk assessment is probably the most important aspect. Sensitivity and validation studies have been frequently insufficient to ensure the relevance of ecological exposure and effect models to real world situations."

Jepson (1993) claimed that the current emphasis on toxicological criteria, at the expense of ecological factors, results in a detailed description of local toxic effects, meanwhile neglecting the consequences at the population level. In this context he recommends long-term risk analysis at the scale of total populations, hence not just the field or the farm but the whole agricultural landscape. In this way the total pattern and frequency of exposure to toxic chemicals is combined for pollutants with short or long persistence, small or large application areas, high and low application frequencies. Moreover, this includes impacts of pollutants in temporary habitats or pollutants affecting dispersive invertebrates. The SCARAB project that was recently started in the UK (Tarrant 1997) compares total agricultural management systems with normal versus low input of pesticides over a long period. These kinds of studies may provide the data for the above suggested long-term assessment at the landscape scale.

Burger and Gochfeld (1992) call for incorporating appropriate temporal time scales and critical life stages into ecological risk assessment.

During the conference of the Society of Ecology and Environmental Safety in Amsterdam in 1992, a special round table discussion was devoted to uncertainties in hazard assessment procedures (Løkke and Hoekstra 1993). The main points mentioned were as follows:

- Environmental conditions in ecosystems differ strongly from laboratory conditions.
- Numerous species are and will stay untested.
- Species do interact with each other, which is not covered at all in single species testing.
- Many chemical compounds are present simultaneously.

If we keep in mind that soil ecosystems are under stress from other impacts, such as desiccation, acidification, and a too high nutrient level by excessive manuring (in aquatic ecosystems called eutrification), much work still has to be done to develop ecologically sound risk assessment systems.

SUMMARY AND GENERAL CONCLUSIONS

If we want to achieve an ecologically relevant laboratory test system using earthworms, the currently available test systems must be intercalibrated with tests using ecologically more relevant test species and conditions. Next, these tests have to be standardized further to become fully accepted at the international standardization (ISO) and environmental policy level (OECD, EU). Field validation must also be secured as part of this standardization.

For field studies we need a much more integrated approach. This includes an integration from the population to the community (species interactions) or ecosystem (structure and function) level. But it also includes soil physico-chemical and soil structural aspects.

Only in this way can an ecologically sound risk assessment of environmental contaminants and potential contaminating activities and situations be achieved.

REFERENCES CITED

Bauer, C., and J. Römbke. 1997. Factors influencing the toxicity of two pesticides on three lumbricid species in laboratory tests. 5th International Symposium for Earthworm Ecology, Ohio, 1994.

Baveco, H.M., A.M. de Roos, C. Klok, J.C.Y. Marinissen, and W. Ma. 1997. Modeling population dynamics of the earthworm *Lumbricus rubellus*. II. Effects of toxicants on predator-regulated populations. 5th International Symposium for Earthworm Ecology, Ohio, 1994. Soil Biology and Biochemistry (in press).

Beeby, A. 1993. Toxic metal uptake and essential metal regulation in terrestrial invertebrates. In R. Dallinger and P.S. Rainbow (eds.). Ecotoxicology of metals in invertebrates. Lewis Publishers, Boca Raton, FL.

Belfroid, A.C. 1994. Toxicokinetics of hydrophobic chemicals in earthworms. Ph.D. thesis, University of Utrecht.

Belfroid, A.C., J. Meiling, D. Sijm, J. Hermens, W. Seinen, and C.A.M. van Gestel. 1994. Uptake of hydrophobic halogenated aromatic hydrocarbons from food by earthworms (*Eisenia andrei*). Archives of Environmental Contamination and Toxicology 27: 260–265.

Bengtsson, G., and S. Rundgren. 1992. Seasonal variation of lead uptake in the earthworm *Lumbricus terrestris* and the influence of liming and acidification. Archives of Environmental Contamination and Toxicology 23: 198–205.

Bengtsson, G.A., T. Gunnarsson, and S. Rundgren. 1986. Effects of metal pollution on the earthworm *Dendrobaena rubida* (Sav.) in acidified soils. Water, Air and Soil Pollution 28: 361–383.

Bengtsson, G., H. Ek, and S. Rundgren. 1992. Evolutionary response of earthworms to long-term metal exposure. Oikos 63: 289–297.

Bradshaw, A.D. 1994. Natural rehabilitation strategies. In H.J.P. Eijsackers and T. Hamers (eds.). Integrated soil and sediment research: a basis for proper protection. Kluwer, Dordrecht, pp. 577–587.

Burger, J., and M. Gochfeld. 1992. Temporal scales in ecological risk assessment. Archives of Environmental Contamination and Toxicology 23: 484–488.

Callahan, C.A., and G. Linder. 1992. Assessment of contaminated soils using earthworm test procedures. In P.W. Greig-Smith, H. Becker, P.J. Edwards, and F. Heimbach (eds.). Ecotoxicology of earthworms. Intercept Publishers, Andover, U.K., pp. 187–196.

Callahan, C.A., M.A. Shirazi, and E.F. Neuhauser. 1994. Comparative toxicity of chemicals to earthworms. Environmental Toxicology and Chemistry 13: 291–298.

Cikutovic, M.A., L.C. Fitzpatrick, B.J. Venables, and A.J. Goven. 1993. Sperm counts in earthworm (*L. terrestris*) as a biomarker for environmental toxicology—effects of cadmium and chlordane. Environmental Pollution 81: 123–125.

Denneman, W.D., M. Hoven-Steggink, and G.K. Korthals. 1992. Doorgifte van Cd en Zn in de voedselketen bodem-regenworm-mol. Eindrapport Speerpuntprogramma Bodemonderzoek. Final report Netherlands Integrated Soil Research Programme, Wageningen, Netherlands.

Diaz Lopez, G., and R. Mancha. 1994. Usefulness of testing with *Eisenia foetida* for the evaluation of agrochemicals in soil. In M. Donkers, H. Eijsackers, and F. Heimbach (eds.). Ecotoxicology of soil organisms. Lewis Publishers, Boca Raton, FL, pp. 251–256.

Edwards, C.A. 1992. Testing the effects of chemicals on earthworms: the advantages and limitation of field tests. In P.W. Greig-Smith, H. Becker, P.J. Edwards, and F. Heimbach (eds.). Ecotoxicology of earthworms. Intercept Publishers, Andover, U.K., pp. 75–84.

Eijsackers, H. 1981. Effecten van koperhoudende varkensmest op regenwormen en op de kwaliteit van grasland. Landbouwkundig Tijdschrift 93: 307–314.

Eijsackers, H. 1994. Soil ecotoxicology: finding the way in a pitch dark labyrinth. In M. Donkers, H. Eijsackers, and F. Heimbach (eds.). Ecotoxicology of soil organisms. Lewis Publishers, Boca Raton, FL, pp. 1–23.

Everts, J.W., Y. Eys, M. Ruys, J. Pijnenburg, H. Visser, and R. Luttik. 1993. Assessing the risk of biomagnification: a physiological approach. The Science of the Total Environment, Supplement 1993: 1501–1506.

Fayolle, L., and A. Chabert. 1997. Effect on earthworm populations of soil insecticides in corn crop: laboratory and field results. 5th International Symposium on Earthworm Ecology. Soil Biology and Biochemistry (in press).

Fischer, E., and L. Molnar. 1997. The effect of metal chlorides on growth and reproduction of *Eisenia fetida* (Oligochaeta Lumbricidae). 5th International Symposium on Earthworm Ecology. Soil Biology and Biochemistry (in press).

Fitzgerald, D., R.P. Lanno, A. Farwell, and D.G. Dixon. 1997. Critical body residues (CBRs) in the assessment of pentachlorophenol toxicity to three earthworm species in artificial soil. 5th International Symposium on Earthworm Ecology. Soil Biology and Biochemistry (in press).

Fugère, N., D. Flipo, K. Krzystuniak, D. Nadeau, G. Poirier, and M. Fournier. 1997. Evaluation of earthworm exposure to contaminated soil by cytometric assay of macrophage phagocytosis in *Lumbricus terrestris*. 5th International Symposium on Earthworm Ecology.

van Gestel, C.A.M. 1992. Earthworms in ecotoxicology. Ph.D. thesis, University of Utrecht.

van Gestel, C.A.M., and W.-C. Ma. 1993. Development of QSAR's in soil ecotoxicology:

earthworm toxicity and soil sorption of chlorophenols, chlorobenzenes, and chloroanilines. Water, Air and Soil Pollution 69: 265–276.

van Gestel, C.A.M., and N.M. van Straalen. 1994. Ecotoxicological test systems for terrestrial invertebrates. In M. Donkers, H. Eijsackers, and F. Heimbach (eds.). Ecotoxicology of soil organisms. Lewis Publishers, Boca Raton, FL, pp. 205–228.

van Gestel, C.A.M., W.A. van Dis, E.M. van Breemen, and P.M. Sparenburg. 1989. Development of a standardized toxicity test with the earthworm species *Eisenia fetida andrei* using copper, pentachlorophenol, and 2,4-dichloroaniline. Ecotoxicology and Environmental Safety 18: 305–312.

van Gestel, C.A.M., E.M. Dirven-van Breemen, and R. Baerselman. 1993a. Accumulation and elimination of cadmium, chromium, and zinc and effects on growth and reproduction in *Eisenia andrei* (Oligochaeta, Lumbricidae). Science of the Total Environment, Suppl. 585–597.

van Gestel, C.A.M., E.M. Dirven-van Breemen, and J.W. Kamerman. 1993b. The influence of soil clean up on the availability of heavy metals for earthworms and plants. In H.J.P. Eijsackers and T. Hamers (eds.). Integrated soil and sediment research: a basis for proper protection. Kluwer, Dordrecht, pp. 345–348.

Gorree, M.A., and W.L.M. Tamis. 1992. BIOMAG-2: risk assessment of soil pollution for terrestrial vertebrates; adaptation and evaluation. Centre Environmental Studies, Leiden report 97 (in Dutch).

Goven, A.J., G.S. Eyambe, L.C. Fitzpatrick, B.J. Venables, and E.L. Cooper. 1993. Cellular biomarkers for measuring toxicity of xenobiotics: effects of polychlorinated biphenyls on earthworm *L. terrestris.* Environmental Toxicology and Chemistry 12: 863–870.

Goven, A.J., S.C. Chen, L.C. Fitzpatrick, and B.J. Venables. 1994. Lysozyme activity in earthworms (*L. terrestris*) coelomic fluid and coelomocytes—enzyme array for immunotoxicity of xenobiotics. Environmental Toxicology and Chemistry 13: 607–613.

Greig-Smith, P.W., H. Becker, P.J. Edwards, and F. Heimbach. 1992. Ecotoxicology of earthworms. Intercept Publishers, Andover, U.K., 269 pp.

Haque, A., and W. Ebing. 1983. Toxicity determination of pesticides to earthworms in the soil substrate. Zeitschrift für Pflanzenkrankheiten und Pflanzenschutz 90: 395–408.

Heimbach, F. 1985. Comparison of laboratory methods using *E. fetida* and *L. terrestris* for the assessment of the hazard of chemicals to earthworms. Zeitschrift für Pflanzenkrankheiten und Pflanzenschutz 92: 186–193.

Heimbach, F. 1992. Effects of pesticides on earthworm populations: comparison of results from laboratory and field tests. In P.W. Greig-Smith, H. Becker, P.J. Edwards, and F. Heimbach (eds.). Ecotoxicology of earthworms. Intercept Publishers, Andover, U.K., pp. 100–108.

Heimbach, F. 1992. Correlation between data from laboratory and field tests for investigating the toxicity of pesticides to earthworms. Soil Biology and Biochemistry 24: 1749–1753.

Heimbach, F. 1994. Use of laboratory toxicity tests for the hazard assessment of chemicals to earthworms representing the soil fauna. In H.J.P. Eijsackers and T. Hamers (eds.). Integrated soil and sediment research: a basis for proper protection. Kluwer, Dordrecht, pp. 299–302.

Heimbach, H. 1997. Field tests on side effects of pesticides on earthworms: influence of plot size and cultivation practices. 5th International Symposium on Earthworm Ecology. Soil Biology and Biochemistry (in press).

Hyvonen, R., S. Andersson, M. Clarholm, and T. Persson. 1994. Effects of lumbricids and enchytraeids on nematodes in limed and unlimed coniferous mor humus. Biology and Fertility of Soils 17: 201–205.

Jepson, P.C. 1993. Ecological insights into risk analysis: the side effects of pesticides as a case study. Science of the Total Environment, Suppl. 1993: 1547–1566.

Klok, C., A.M. de Roos, H.M. Baveco, J.C.Y. Marinissen, and W. Ma. 1997. Modeling population dynamics of the earthworm *Lumbricus rubellus*. I. Identification of most sensitive life history parameters. 5th International Symposium on Earthworm Ecology. Soil Biology and Biochemistry (in press).

Knoop, J., and Th. Traas. 1993. Acidification, changing land use, and cadmium mobilization: a modeling approach. In G.R.B. Meulen, W.M. Stigliani, W. Salomons, E.M. Bridges, and A.C. Imeson (eds.). Chemical time bombs. Proc. Eur. state-of-the-art conf. on delayed effects of chemicals in soils and sediments, Veldhoven, Foundation for Ecodevelopment, Hoofddorp, Netherlands, pp. 107–118.

Kratz, W., and R. Pöhhacker. 1994. The development of soil ecotoxicity test systems with lumbricids to assess sublethal and lethal effects. In M. Donkers, H. Eijsackers, and F. Heimbach (eds.). Ecotoxicology of soil organisms. Lewis Publishers, Boca Raton, FL, pp. 263–272.

Kula, H. 1992. Measuring effects of pesticides on earthworms in the field: test design and sampling methods. In Greig-Smith, P.W., H. Becker, P.J. Edwards, and F. Heimbach (eds.). Ecotoxicology of earthworms. Intercept Publishers, Andover, U.K., pp. 90–99.

Kula, C. 1994. A prolonged laboratory test on sublethal effects of pesticides on *Eisenia fetida*. In M. Donkers, H. Eijsackers, and F. Heimbach (eds.). Ecotoxicology of soil organisms. Lewis Publishers, Boca Raton, FL, pp. 257–262.

Lanno, R.P., C.D. Wren, and G.L. Stephenson. 1997. The use of acute lethality thresholds in assessing the toxicity of four chemicals to the earthworm *Lumbricus terrestris* in three natural soils. 5th International Symposium on Earthworm Ecology. Soil Biology and Biochemistry (in press).

Larink, O., and H. Kula. 1994. Development and standardization of acute and sublethal laboratory test methods with different earthworm species. SECOFASE 2nd Technical Report, pp. 19–24.

Loonen, H. 1994. Bioavailability of chlorinated dioxins and furans in the aquatic environment. Ph.D. thesis, University of Amsterdam.

Løkke, H., and J. Hoekstra. 1993. Uncertainties in hazard assessment procedures. The Science of the Total Environment, Suppl. 1993: 1799–1800.

Luttik, R., C.A.F.M. Romijn, and J.H. Canton. 1993. Presentation of a general algorithm to include secondary poisoning in effect assessment. The Science of the Total Environment, Suppl. 1993: 1491–1500.

Ma, W.-C. 1993. Speciation of heavy metals in relation to their availability to soil macrobiota (earthworms). Final report project C4-12, Netherlands Integrated Soil Research Programme, Wageningen.

Ma, W.-C., and J. Bodt. 1993. Difference in toxicity of the insecticide chlorpyriphos to six species of earthworms (Oligochaeta, Lumbricidae) in standardized soil tests. Bulletin of Environmental Contamination and Toxicology 50: 864–870.

Ma, W.-C., and H. Eijsackers. 1989. The influence of substrate toxicity on soil fauna return in reclaimed land. In J.D. Majer (ed.). Animals in primary succession: the role of fauna in reclaimed land. Cambridge University Press, pp. 1–23.

Ma, W.-C., and H. van der Voet. 1993. A risk-assessment model for toxic exposure of small mammalian carnivores to cadmium in contaminated natural environments. The Science of the Total Environment, Suppl. 1993: 1701–1714.

Marinissen, J.C.Y., and P.C. de Ruiter. 1993. Contribution of earthworms to carbon and nitrogen cycling in agro-ecosystems. Agriculture, Ecosystems and Environment 47: 59–74.

Marino, F., and A.J. Morgan. 1997. Evidence for inter-population differentiation in earthworm metal relationships revealed by prolonged maintenance on metalliferous soils in the laboratory. 5th International Symposium on Earthworm Ecology. Soil Biology and Biochemistry (in press).

Marinussen, M.P.J.C., and S.E.A.T.M. van der Zee. 1997. Cu uptake by *L. rubellus* as affected by total amount of Cu in soil, soil pH and moisture, and soil heterogeneity. 5th International Symposium on Earthworm Ecology.

Mather, G., and O. Christensen. 1988. Surface movements of earthworms in agricultural land. Pedobiologia 32: 399–405.

Menzie, C.A., W. van der Schalie, and R. Landy. 1993. Lessons learned from ecological risk assessment studies in the United States. Abstract book SETAC, Lisbon, 1993, p. 41.

Morgan, J.E., and A.J. Morgan. 1993. Seasonal changes in the tissue-metal (Cd, Zn, and Pb) concentration in 2 ecophysiologically dissimilar earthworm species—pollution-monitoring implications. Environmental Pollution 82: 1–7.

Neuhauser, E.F., P.R. Durkin, M.R. Malecki, and M. Anatra. 1986. Comparative toxicity of ten organic chemicals to four earthworm species. Comparative Biochemistry and Physiology 83C: 197–216.

Nieboer, E., and D.H.S. Richardson. 1980. The replacement of the nondescript term "heavy metals" by a biologically and chemically significant classification of metal ions. Environmental Pollution 1B: 3–26.

Noppert, F., J.W. Dogger, F. Balk, and A.J.M. Smits. 1994. Secondary poisoning in terrestrial food chain; a probabilistic approach. In H.J.P. Eijsackers and T. Hamers (eds.). Integrated soil and sediment research: a basis for proper protection. Kluwer, Dordrecht, pp. 303–307.

Posthuma, L., L. Weltje, F. Mogo, and R. Baerselman. 1993. Combinatietoxiciteit van zware metalen bij de regenworm *Eisenia andrei*. Poster National Symposium Netherlands Integrated Soil Research Programme 1993, Wageningen.

Posthuma, L., R. Baerselman, H. Boonman, and L. Weltje. 1997. On the validity of laboratory toxicity tests with *Eisenia andrei* for earthworms in the field. 5th International Symposium on Earthworm Ecology.

Reinecke, S.A., and A.J. Reinecke. 1997. The influence of cadmium, lead, and manganese on spermatozoa and reproduction of *Eisenia fetida* (Oligochaeta). 5th International Symposium on Earthworm Ecology. Soil Biology and Biochemistry (in press).

Romijn, C.A.F.M., R. Luttik, W. Slooff, and J.H. Canton. 1991. Presentation and analysis of a general algorithm for effect-assessment on secondary poisoning. Terrestrial food chains. RIVM Report 679102007, Bilthoven, Netherlands.

Rozen, A., and L. Mazur. 1997. Influence of different levels of traffic pollution on haemoglobin content in earthworm *Lumbricus terrestris*. 5th International Symposium on Earthworm Ecology. Soil Biology and Biochemistry (in press).

de Ruiter, P.C., and J.C. Moore. 1994. Simulation of the effects of contamination on the functioning of below ground food webs. In H.J.P. Eijsackers and T. Hamers (eds.). Integrated soil and sediment research: a basis for proper protection. Kluwer, Dordrecht, pp. 309–312.

de Ruiter, P.C., J.C. Moore, K.B. Zwart, L.A. Bouwman, J. Hassink, J. Bloem, J.A. de Vos, J.C.Y. Marinissen, W.A.M. Didden, G. Lebbink, and L. Brussaard. 1993. Simulation of nitrogen mineralization in the below-ground food webs of two winter wheat fields. Journal of Applied Ecology 30: 95–106.

Rundgren, S. 1995. Earthworms and soil remediation. Liming of acidic coniferous forest soils in Southern Sweden. Pedobiologia 38: 519–529.

Springett, J., and R.A.J. Gray. 1992. Effect of repeated low doses of biocides on the earthworm *Aporrectodea caliginosa* in laboratory cultures. Soil Biology and Biochemistry 24: 1739–1744.

Spurgeon, D.J., S.P. Hopkin, and D.T. Jones. 1994. Effects of cadmium, copper, lead, and zinc on growth, reproduction, and survival of the earthworm *Eisenia fetida* (Savigny): assessing the environmental impact of point-source metal contamination in terrestrial ecosystems. Environmental Pollution 84: 123–130.

Stenersen, J., E. Brekke, and F. Engelstadt. 1992. Earthworms for toxicity testing; species differences in response towards cholinesterase inhibiting insecticides. Soil Biology and Biochemistry 24: 1761–1764.

Stephenson, G.L., I.C.J. Middelraad, C.D. Wren, and J. Warner. 1997. The exposure of earthworms (*Lumbricus terrestris*) to diazinon and risk assessment to passerine birds. 5th International Symposium on Earthworm Ecology. Soil Biology and Biochemistry (in press).

Tamis, W.L.M., H.A. Udo de Haes, and A.J. Schouten. 1994. Ecological recovery of some thermally and biologically cleaned field soils. In H.J.P. Eijsackers and T. Hamers (eds.). Integrated soil and sediment research: a basis for proper protection. Kluwer, Dordrecht, pp. 341–344.

Tarrant, K.A. 1997. Effects on earthworm populations of reducing pesticide use: part of the UK SCARAB Project. 5th International Symposium on Earthworm Ecology. Soil Biology and Biochemistry (in press).

Terhivuo, J., E. Pankakoski, H. Hyvarinen, and I. Koivisto. 1994. Pb uptake by ecologically dissimilar earthworms (Lumbricidae) species near a lead smelter in South Finland. Environmental Pollution 85: 87–96.

Tomlin, A.D., R. Protz, R.R. Martin, D.C. MacCabe, and R.J. Lagace. 1993. Relationships amongst organic matter content, heavy metal concentrations, earthworm activity, and soil microfabric on a sewage sludge disposal site. Geoderma 57: 89–103.

Traas, Th., and T. Aldenberg. 1992. CATS-1: a model for predicting contaminant accumulation in a meadow ecosystem. The case of cadmium. RIVM Report 719103001. RIVM Bilthoven, Netherlands.

Wang, Z. 1997. The study of soil heavy metal pollution monitored with earthworms. 5th International Symposium on Earthworm Ecology. Soil Biology and Biochemistry (in press).

Earthworms in
Waste Management

The Use of Earthworms in the Breakdown and Management of Organic Wastes

15

Clive A. Edwards
Professor of Entomology at The Ohio State University, Columbus, Ohio

It has long been known that earthworms are important in the breakdown of organic matter and the release of the nutrients that it contains (Darwin 1881). In recent years, it has been demonstrated clearly that some species of earthworms are specialized to live in decaying organic matter and can degrade it into fine particulate materials, high in available nutrients, with considerable potential as soil additives. For instance, earthworms are able to process sewage sludges and solids from waste water (Neuhauser et al. 1988), brewery wastes (Butt 1993), processed potato waste (Edwards 1983), waste from the paper industries (Butt 1993), wastes from supermarkets and restaurants (Edwards 1995), animal wastes from poultry, pigs, cattle, sheep, goats, horses, and rabbits (Edwards et al. 1985; Edwards 1988), as well as horticultural residues from dead plants, yard wastes (Edwards 1995), and wastes from the mushroom industry (Edwards 1988).

Traditionally, certain species of earthworms have been bred for fish bait in a wide range of different organic wastes. Since 1978, there has been increasing interest in possible methods of processing organic wastes using earthworms to produce valuable soil additives and protein for animal feed. This interest has resulted in a series of conferences aimed at reviewing and promoting such processes. The first of these, titled "Utilization of Soil Organisms in Sludge Management" (Hartenstein 1978), held in Syracuse, New York, U.S.A., focused on the processing of sewage sludge by earthworms, as did the second, a "Workshop

1-884015-74-3/98/$0.00/$.50
©1998 by CRC Press LLC

on the Role of Earthworms in the Stabilization of Organic Residues" (Appelhof 1981), held in Kalamazoo, Michigan, U.S.A. These were followed by an "International Symposium on Agricultural Prospects in Earthworm Farming" (Tomati and Grappelli 1983), held in Rome, Italy, and the largest, a "Symposium on the Use of Earthworms in Waste Management and Environmental Management" (Edwards and Neuhauser 1988), held in Cambridge, U.K. Additionally, sessions on earthworms and waste management have been held at International Earthworm Symposia in Bologna, Italy, in 1985 (Pagliai and Omodeo 1987); Avignon, France, in 1990 (Kretschmar 1992); and Columbus, Ohio, U.S.A in 1994 (Edwards 1997).

Research has been initiated and commercial projects have been developed in many countries, including England, France, The Netherlands, Germany, Italy, Spain, the United States, Japan, the Philippines, India and other parts of Southeast Asia, Australia, Cuba, the Bahamas, and many countries in South America. In particular, research in the U.S.A. on earthworms in waste breakdown has concentrated mainly on the utilization of sewage sludges and solids (Neuhauser et al. 1988) and research in the U.K. has focused on processing animal, vegetable, and industrial wastes (Edwards 1988) until recent years.

BREAKDOWN OF SEWAGE WASTES BY EARTHWORMS

Research into the potential use of earthworms to break down and manage sewage sludge began at the State University of New York (SUNY), Syracuse, in the late 1970s (Hartenstein 1978). It was demonstrated quite early on a laboratory scale that aerobic sewage sludge can be ingested by the earthworm *E. fetida* and egested as casts, and in the process the sludge is decomposed and stabilized (i.e., rendered innocuous) about three times as fast as non-ingested sludge, apparently because of the increases in rates of microbial decomposition in the casts. During this process, relative to non-earthworm ingested sludge, objectionable odors disappear quickly and there is a marked reduction in populations of the pathogenic microorganisms *Salmonella enteriditis*, *Escherichia coli*, and other Enterobacteriaceae. Although most of the sludge produced in sewage plants is anaerobic, and when fresh can be toxic to *E. fetida,* after becoming aerobic it becomes readily acceptable to this species.

It was found that mixing sewage sludge with other materials, e.g., garden wastes, paper pulp sludge, or other lignin-rich wastes, and composting the mixture using earthworms, can accelerate their decomposition, due to maceration and mixing of such materials during passage through the earthworm gut and passage into earthworm casts. There are many possibilities for the utilization of garden, paper, and timber mill wastes and other materials as bulking agents, for simultaneous disposal of these materials together with municipal sewage sludge. The use of earthworms in sludge management has been termed *vermicomposting*, or *vermistabilization* (Neuhauser et al. 1988; Loehr et al. 1984). Because these processes have not been studied well, there are still many fundamental aspects that need to be researched, evaluated, and resolved to assure the success of such a process.

Factors about which we need more information include the following: (i) how earthworms are affected by sludge characteristics, (ii) the comparative ability of different species of earthworms to grow and reproduce in sludge, (iii) the need for pre-processing sludge to make it acceptable to earthworms, and (iv) the effect of mixed earthworm species on sewage sludge breakdown in a vermistabilization system. For earthworms to be useful in stabilizing sludge, they must increase the stabilization rate, which can be demonstrated best if the presence of earthworms in sludge causes an increase in the rate of volatile solids reduction. Maximum reduction of volatile solids is a main goal of any sludge stabilization system.

Research at SUNY, in New York State, was along two complementary lines: (i) basic studies to identify fundamental factors that affect the performance of the vermistabilization process, and (ii) applied studies to determine the design and management relationships (Neuhauser et al. 1988). The earthworm *E. fetida* has been shown to increase the rates of destruction of sludge volatile solids in aerobic sludge greatly. This increase in the rate of volatile solids destruction reduces the probability of putrefaction occurring in the sludge due to anaerobic conditions. The main cause of the increased rate of degradation of the sludge is probably the increased aeration and turnover due to the earthworms. A series of experiments were conducted to determine the most desirable moisture content for sludges used in vermistabilization units, since both excessive and insufficient moisture can impact the growth of earthworms adversely.

A range of sludges with different moisture contents were tested, using *E. fetida,* at a temperature of 25°C (Neuhauser et al. 1988). Earthworm growth at the lower and higher total solids levels (6.3 to 7.9% and 17.9 to 25.1% solids) differed statistically, at the 1% level, from the earthworm growth at the middle range of solids (9.3 to 15.9% solids). This indicated that optimum earthworm growth occurred over a range of total solids, in the media to which the worms were exposed on a wet basis, from about 9% to 16% (i.e., 84% to 91% moisture content).

However, more liquid wastes can be used in the vermistabilization process, so long as they are added slowly and the liquid can drain readily from the sludge, the organics are retained, and aerobic conditions are maintained. The desirability of maintaining the total solids content of the media in the range quoted above does not mean that wetter sludge slurries cannot be processed with vermistabilization. In practice it might be necessary to add moisture to materials in a vermistabilization process, if the media should become too dry. It is also important to relate rates of earthworm growth to the age of the sludge, i.e., the time after the sludge was removed from the aerobic reactor and dewatered (Neuhauser et al. 1988). As sludge ages, its nutritive value to earthworms decreases rapidly, whereas the ash content of the sludge increases with time, a further indication of sludge stabilization.

The practical feasibility of using earthworms to stabilize wastewater treatment sludges has been investigated (Loehr et al. 1984). These workers concluded that a liquid sludge vermistabilization process was feasible and provided data on the rates of stabilization and the physical and chemical characteristics of the residual stabilized solids, resulting from vermistabilization, a conclusion that was supported by Pincince et al. (1980).

There have been various practical attempts to utilize earthworms in sewage sludge breakdown in the U.S.A. (Loehr et al. 1984; Pincince et al. 1980; Green and Penton 1981), in the U.K. (Edwards and Neuhauser 1988), and in Italy (Tomati and Grappelli 1984), but full-scale successful vermiprocessing of sewage sludge has not yet been achieved. The potential of such commercial operations was reviewed by Hartenstein (1978), Appelhof (1981), and Edwards and Neuhauser (1988), who concluded that a major obstacle to be overcome is to avoid exposure of the earthworms used in vermistabilization to toxic chemicals that might enter the wastewater stream.

BREAKDOWN OF ANIMAL, VEGETABLE, AND URBAN INDUSTRIAL ORGANIC WASTES BY EARTHWORMS

There has been extensive research into using earthworms to break down various animal manures, such as pig and cattle solids and slurries; wastes from laying chickens, broilers, turkeys, and ducks; horse manure; and rabbit droppings in the U.K. (Edwards 1983). This research was extended later to studies using earthworms to break down vegetable wastes, including those from the mushroom industry, processed potato industry, brewery industry, paper pulp and supermarket industries, and yard wastes, including grass clippings and leaves. This work began as a fundamental interdisciplinary research program on a laboratory scale, involving both biologists and engineers, and was extended to large-scale developmental research on a field scale, engineering technology, and eventual commercialization.

The U.K. research had two main aims: first, to convert animal and vegetable wastes into useful materials that could be added to agricultural land to improve soil structure and fertility or be marketed for horticultural use as a plant growth medium or a component of commercial potting composts, and second, to assess the potential of harvesting worms from the worked waste and processing them into a protein supplement for fish, poultry, and pigs. To accomplish these aims, a complex network of interdisciplinary collaborative research was initiated involving six research stations, six university or college departments, and eight commercial organizations. The following main areas of research and development were involved:

1. A laboratory screening program into the suitability of five different earthworm species in processing ten different organic waste materials. The aim was to assess their biological and economic potentials, and study the biology and ecology of these worms in different organic wastes (Edwards 1988).
2. Studies to assess the source of nutrition of those species of earthworms that live on organic wastes; the relative importance of bacteria, protozoa, fungi, and nematodes in their diet; and which microorganisms are essential to their survival (Morgan 1988; Edwards and Fletcher 1988).
3. Evaluation of rates of conversion of different organic wastes into earthworm biomass in relation to type of waste, earthworm stocking rate, and environmental factors (Edwards et al. 1985) (Figure 3).
4. Methods of harvesting and processing of earthworms into animal feed protein, animal feeding trials, and toxicological tests (Edwards 1985; (Edwards and Niederer 1988).
5. Development of a range of technologies and systems of production of earthworm protein and earthworm processed waste (Edwards 1985, 1995).
6. Production of plant growth media processed by earthworms from organic wastes, plant growth trials. Amendment of these media to produce maximum plant growth (Edwards 1983; Edwards et al. 1985; Edwards and Burrows 1988).

Five earthworm species were identified as potentially useful species to break down organic wastes. These were *Eisenia fetida*, *Dendrobaena veneta*, and *Lumbricus rubellus*, from temperate areas, and *Eudrilus eugeniae* and *Perionyx excavatus* from the tropics. The survival, growth, mortality, and reproduction of these species were studied in detail in the laboratory, using a range of organic wastes, including pig, cattle, duck, turkey, poultry, potato, brewery, paper wastes, and activated sewage sludge. All the species could grow and survive in a wide range of organic wastes but some were very prolific, others grew rapidly, and yet others attained a large biomass quickly, all characters contributing to the practical usefulness of the earthworms. However, there were many species-specific differences in the biology and ecology of these earthworms.

Most organic wastes can be broken down by earthworms, but some have to be pretreated in various ways to make them acceptable and not all organic wastes grow earthworms equally well. The characteristics of the different wastes tested are as follows:

1. *Cattle solids* are the easiest animal waste in which to grow earthworms. They usually contain no materials that are unfavorable to growing earthworms except when they are very fresh. Solids have to be separated from slurries before they can be used to grow earthworms satisfactorily, but the liquids can be added back to the solids at a later stage.

2. *Horse manure* is an excellent material for growing earthworms and needs very little modification other than maintenance of good environmental factors in the waste.

3. *Pig solids* are probably the most productive waste for growing earthworms. If the waste is in the form of a slurry, the solids must be separated mechanically or by sedimentation. Pig waste tends to contain some ammonia and inorganic salts and, unless these are washed out, may have to be composted for about two weeks or longer prior to inoculation with earthworms. Pig wastes may have a content of heavy metals, particularly copper (Edwards et al. 1988; Wong and Griffiths 1991). The processed wastes are high in nutrients.

4. *Poultry wastes,* including chicken, duck, and turkey manures, contain significant amounts of inorganic salts and ammonia that may kill worms in freshly-deposited waste. After removal of these materials through composting, washing, or aging, earthworms grow well in them and the compost produced is high in nutrients.

5. *Potato waste,* in the form of peel from the processed potato and frozen potato industry, is an ideal growth medium for earthworms and needs little modification in terms of moisture content or other preprocessing (Edwards et al. 1985).

6. *Paper pulp solids* are produced by mechanical separation or sedimentation of solids from the press washings. These solids are an excellent material for growth of earthworms with no need for preprocessing or additives.

7. *Brewery waste* needs no modification, in terms of moisture content, to grow earthworms. Worms can process it very quickly and grow and multiply rapidly in it.

8. *Spent mushroom compost* is a good medium for growing earthworms, which are able to break down the straw it contains into small fragments and produce a finely-structured material. However, it may be low in plant nutrients.

9. *Urban wastes,* including grass clippings and tree leaves, as well as food wastes from supermarkets and restaurants, are all good growth media for earthworms, particularly when they are first macerated and thoroughly mixed before use (Huhta and Haimi 1988; Edwards 1995).

Systems of growing earthworms range from very simple methods involving low technology such as windrows, waste heaps, or boxes, through moderately complex to completely automated continuous-flow reactors (Jensen 1993; Edwards 1995). The basic principle of all of the successful processing systems is to add the wastes frequently in small, thin layers and allow the earthworms to process successive aerobic layers of wastes. The earthworms will always be concentrated in the upper 15 cm of waste and move upwards as each successive waste layer is added. Many of the operations can be mechanized, a suitable balance being needed between the costs of mechanization and the savings in labor resulting. The key to combining maximum productivity of vermicompost and earthworm growth is to maintain aerobicity and optimal moisture and temperature conditions, and to avoid excessive amounts of ammonia and salts. The adding of wastes in thin layers avoids overheating through thermophilic composting, but is usually enough to maintain suitable temperatures for worm growth during cold periods. Hence, for year-round production in temperate climates, the processing should be done under cover, although heating is not usually necessary if the waste additions are managed well.

SPECIES OF EARTHWORMS SUITABLE FOR PROCESSING ORGANIC WASTES

Biology and Ecology of Suitable Species

Many species of earthworms have potential for use in organic waste processing, but relatively few have been used on a widespread scale and researched adequately. The species used most commonly include *Eisenia fetida* and *Eisenia andrei* (brandling or tiger worms), *Eudrilus eugeniae* (African night crawler), *Lumbricus rubellus* (red worm), *Dendrobaena veneta, Perionyx excavatus,* and *Perionyx hawayana.*

The growth of *E. fetida, E. eugeniae, P. excavatus,* and *P. hawayana* in sewage sludge has been studied (Neuhauser et al. 1988). These researchers concluded that all these species have a range of optimum temperatures for growth in sludge of between 15° and 25°C and all four species produced most cocoons at 25°C. Over a period of 20 weeks, *P. excavatus* had the lowest rate of increase in weight and *E. fetida* grew slightly slower than before. Both *P. hawayana* and *E. eugeniae* reached peak biomass in about 10 to 12 weeks, and *E. eugeniae,* which grew faster, began to lose weight after 14 weeks. *D. veneta* increased most in weight and took 16 weeks to achieve maximum weight. *P. excavatus* produced the largest number of cocoons, and *D. veneta,* which produced the lowest number of cocoons, did not start producing cocoons for 10 weeks. The other three species, *E. fetida, E. eugeniae,* and *P. hawayana*, all produced similar numbers of cocoons, with peak cocoon production after 10 weeks.

It is important to evaluate the number of live young earthworms that would be obtained from the cocoons of each species. Cocoons from five species of earthworms, *D. veneta, E. fetida, E. eugeniae, P. excavatus,* and *P. hawayana*, were collected and allowed to hatch (Edwards 1988). Individual cocoons were kept under non-stressed conditions, at 25°C, and were checked twice per week to determine the number of cocoons that hatched and the number of worms that were produced per hatched cocoon.

They concluded from these data that *E. fetida* produced 6 cocoons per worm per week (19 young worms), *D. veneta* 5 cocoons (19 young worms), *E. eugeniae* 11 cocoons (20 young worms), *P. excavatus* 24 cocoons (13 young worms), and *P. hawayana* 10 cocoons (9.5 young worms) per parent worm. These researchers also studied the growth of different combinations of these species in polyculture. Although the total earthworm biomass tended to be greater in polyculture, the results were not clear-cut.

Edwards (1988) studied the life cycles and optimal conditions for growth and survival of *E. fetida, D. veneta, E. eugeniae,* and *P. excavatus* in animal and vegetable wastes (Tables 1 and 2). Each of the four species differed considerably in terms of their response to and tolerance of different temperatures. The optimum temperature for *E. fetida* was 25°C, with a temperature tolerance from 0°

Table 1. Maximum reproduction rate of earthworms in animal and vegetable wastes—cocoon production

Species	No. of cocoons	% hatch	No. of hatchlings	Net reproductive rates per week
Eisenia fetida	3.8	83.2	3.3	10.4
Eudrilus eugeniae	3.6	81.0	2.3	6.7
Perionyx excavatus	19.5	90.7	1.1	19.4
Dendrobaena veneta	1.6	81.2	1.1	1.4

Table 2. Productivity of earthworms in animal and vegetable waste—length of life cycle

Species	Time for cocoons to hatch (days)	Time to sexual maturity (days)	Time egg to maturity (days)
Eisenia fetida	32–73	53–76	85–149
Eudrilus eugeniae	13–27	32–95	43–122
Perionyx excavatus	16–21	28–56	44–71
Dendrobaena veneta	40–126	57–86	97–214

to 35°C. *D. veneta* had a rather lower temperature optimum and less tolerance of extreme temperatures. The optimum temperatures for *E. eugeniae* and *P. excavatus* were also about 25°C, but they died at temperatures below 9°C and above 30°C. The optimum temperatures for cocoon production were much lower than for growth for all species (Figure 1).

These four species also differed in their optimum moisture requirements from those of *E. fetida* but not greatly (Figure 2). The range over which the worm grew optimally was quite narrow, with optimal growth at 80–55% M.C., with considerable decreases in growth at moisture content of 70% and 90%. However, *D. veneta* was able to withstand a much wider range of moisture than others, such as *P. excavatus*.

All four species of earthworms were very sensitive to ammonia, and did not survive in organic wastes containing much ammonia, e.g., fresh poultry litter. They also died in wastes with large quantities of inorganic salts. Both ammonia and inorganic salts have very sharp cutoff points between being toxic and non-toxic, i.e., <0.5 mg per g of ammonia and <0.5% salts. However, wastes that have too much ammonia became acceptable after it was removed by a period of composting or when both excessive ammonia and salts were washed out of the waste. Earthworms are relatively tolerant with regard to pH, but when given a choice in a pH gradient, they moved towards the more acid material with a pH preference of 5.0. The optimal conditions for breeding *E. fetida* are summarized in Table 3. These do not differ much from those suitable for the other species.

Characteristics of Different Earthworm Species that Process Organic Wastes

Different earthworm species have quite different requirements for optimal development, growth, and productivity in organic wastes. I shall review the characteristics of the more commonly-used species.

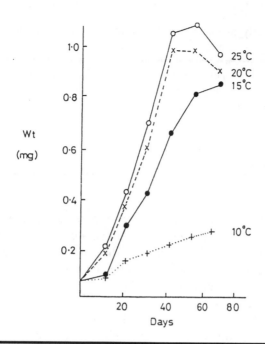

Figure 1. Growth of *Eisenia fetida* at different temperatures.

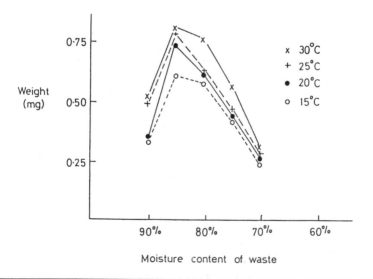

Figure 2. Growth of *Eisenia fetida* at different moisture contents.

Table 3. Optimal conditions for breeding *E. fetida* in animal and vegetable wastes

Condition	Requirements
Temperature	15–20°C (limits 4–30°C)
Moisture content	80–90% (limits 60–90%)
Oxygen requirement	Aerobicity
Ammonia content of waste	Low: <0.5 mg/g
Salt content of waste	Low: <0.5%
pH	>5 and <9

Eisenia fetida

The species most commonly used for breaking down organic wastes is *E. fetida* or the closely related species *E. andrei*. There are a number of reasons why these species are preferred all over the world. They are ubiquitous and many organic wastes became colonized naturally by these species. They have a wide temperature tolerance and can live in organic wastes with a range of moisture content. They are tough worms, readily-handled, and in mixed species cultures one of these species usually becomes dominant, so that even when field systems begin with other species, they often end by being dominated by *E. fetida*. Although they are so similar, *E. fetida* and *E. andrei* (the "tiger worm" and the closely related "red tiger worm") have been distinguished as separate species, but their morphological characteristics and overall reproductive performances and environmental requirements do not differ significantly (Reinecke and Viljeon 1991). These species are widely distributed throughout the temperate regions of the world and are the species most commonly used in commercial vermiculture and waste reduction. Graff (1974), Watanabe and Tsukamoto (1976), Tsukamoto and Watanabe (1977), Hartenstein et al. (1978), Kaplan et al. (1980), Edwards (1988), and Neuhauser et al. (1988) all investigated the productivity, growth, and population biology of *E. fetida,* when fed on animal manures, or sewage sludge, so we have a great deal of critical information on this species.

In surveys of commercial earthworm farms in the U.S. and Europe by Edwards (1988) and in Australia, the earthworms sold under the name *L. rubellus* were all *E. fetida* or *E. andrei*. Data on the biology and ecology and environmental requirement of *E. fetida* is summarized in the previous section.

Eudrilus eugeniae

This is a large earthworm, native to Africa, commonly known as the African night-crawler, that grows extremely rapidly and is quite prolific. It is cultured

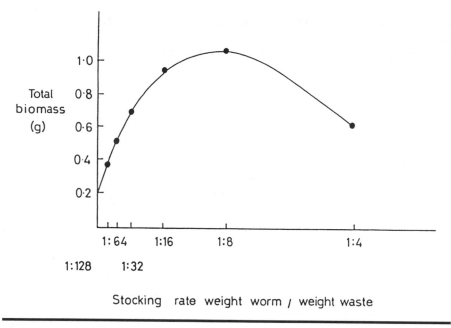

Figure 3. Optimum stocking rates with *E. foetida* for maximum biomass production.

extensively in the U.S., and under optimum conditions it would seem to be ideal for earthworm protein production. Its main disadvantages are its poor temperature tolerance and poor handling capabilities, so that it is easily damaged and can be difficult to harvest. *E. eugeniae* has high rates of reproduction (Bano and Kale 1991; Edwards 1988), and is capable of decomposing large quantities of organic wastes rapidly (Neuhauser et al. 1988; Kale and Bano 1991; Edwards 1988). However, *E. eugeniae* has a preference for higher temperatures and cannot tolerate extended periods below 16°C (Viljoen and Reinecke 1992) and it does not survive below 10°C. Its use in outdoor vermiculture may therefore be limited to tropical and sub-tropical regions, unless lower winter temperatures in the wastes are controlled.

Perionyx excavatus

This tropical earthworm is extremely prolific, and it is almost as easy to handle as *E. fetida* and very easy to harvest. Its main drawback for use under temperate conditions is it inability to withstand temperature conditions below 5°C, but for tropical conditions, it is an ideal species. It has an extremely high reproductive rate (Neuhauser et al. 1988; Edwards et al. 1988) (Figures 1 and 2). It is a very common species in Asia and is used extensively in vermiculture in the Philippines and Australia and India.

Dendrobaena veneta

This species is a large worm with some potential for use in vermiculture, and can also survive in soil, but is not very prolific and does not grow very rapidly (Edwards 1988). It is probably the least suitable species for organic matter breakdown out of the species that have been studied in detail, but it can be bred readily in organic wastes for transfer and use in agricultural soils.

Polypheretima elongata

This species has been tested for use in reduction of organic solids, including municipal and slaughterhouse wastes; human, poultry, and dairy manures; and mushroom compost in India. A project in India, using this species, claimed to have a commercially-viable facility for the "vermistabilization" of 8 tons of solid wastes per day. They have developed a "vermifilter," packed with vermicompost and live earthworms, that produces reusable water from sewage sludges, manure slurries, and organic wastewaters from food processing. *P. elongata* appears to be restricted to tropical regions, and may not survive temperate winters.

Lumbricus rubellus

This is a common species of earthworm that is usually found in moister soils, particularly those to which animal manure or sewage solids have been applied (Cotton and Curry 1980). It can be used for organic waste breakdown but increased research into its potential is needed before major adoption for this purpose.

VERMICOMPOSTS AS PLANT GROWTH MEDIA AND SOIL ADDITIVES

Earthworm composts (vermicomposts) can be produced from almost all kinds of organic wastes with suitable preprocessing and controlled processing conditions. They grow plants extremely well, and they can also be used as structural additives for poorer soils to provide nutrients and minimize erosion.

Characteristics of Vermicomposts Produced by Earthworms from Organic Wastes

The final physical structure of the plant growth media or vermicomposts produced from organic wastes depends very much on the parent waste from which they were produced. Some wastes, such as cattle, pig, and poultry manures from indoor breeding systems as well as spent mushroom compost, all contain straw, which takes considerably longer for the earthworms to fragment than the more particulate materials, such as animal solids and slurries, brewery wastes, paper pulp, and similar materials. However, the final product from most organic wastes is usually a finely-divided peat-like material with excellent structure, porosity, aeration, drainage, and moisture-holding capacity (Edwards 1982, 1983). Structurally, it has the appearance and many of the characteristics of peat and additionally contains plant nutrients.

The nutrient content of vermicomposts differs greatly depending on the parent material. However, when their nutrient content is compared with that of a commercial plant growth medium to which inorganic nutrients have been added, they usually contain more of most of the necessary mineral elements for plants, although there is often a deficiency of magnesium (Table 4). An important feature of vermicomposts is that, during the processing of the various organic wastes by earthworms, many of the nutrients that they contain are changed to forms that are more readily taken up by plants, such as nitrate or ammonium nitrogen, exchangeable phosphorus, and soluble potassium, calcium, and magnesium (Table 5). Moreover, many earthworm-processed animal wastes tend to be on the alkaline side of neutral (>7.0), whereas most plants prefer a growth medium on the acid side of neutral, e.g., with a pH of 6.0. The processing of wastes by earthworms does not change the pH of the material appreciably, so

Table 4. Major plant nutrient elements in earthworm-processed animal wastes

	Element content (% dry wt.)					
Waste material	*N*	*P*	*K*	*Ca*	*Mg*	*Mn*
Separated cattle solids	2.20	0.40	0.90	1.20	0.25	0.02
Separated pig solids	2.60	1.70	1.40	3.40	0.55	0.03
Cattle solids on straw	2.50	0.50	2.50	1.55	0.30	0.05
Pig solids on straw	3.00	1.60	2.40	4.00	0.60	0.05
Duck solids on straw	2.60	2.90	1.70	9.50	1.00	0.10
Chicken solids on shavings	1.80	2.70	2.10	4.80	0.70	0.08
Commercial plant growth medium	1.80	0.21	0.48	0.94	2.20	0.92

Table 5. Effect of earthworm activity on nutrients in organic wastes

Organic waste	Nitrate nitrogen (ppm)	Readily soluble P (% d.m.)	Exchangeable (% d.m.)		
			K	Ca	Mg
Cattle waste					
Unworked	8.8	0.11	0.19	0.35	0.05
Worm-worked	259.4	0.18	0.41	0.59	0.08
Pig waste					
Unworked	31.6	1.05	1.49	1.56	0.45
Worm-worked	110.3	1.64	1.76	2.27	0.72
Potato waste					
Unworked	74.6	0.19	1.94	0.91	0.24
Worm-worked	1428.0	0.22	3.09	1.37	0.34

worm-worked wastes benefit from some acidification or from mixing with an acid medium such as peat.

Growth of Plants in Vermicomposts

There is very good evidence that vermicomposts can promote the growth of plants. For instance, Fosgate and Babb (1972) grew earthworms in cattle wastes and reported that the vermicompost produced was equal to greenhouse potting mixes for production of flowering plants. Reddy (1988) reported increased growth of *Vinca rosea* and *Oryza sativa,* after addition of cast material from *Pheretima alexandri.* Buchanan et al. (1988) suggested that most vermicomposts had higher levels of available nutrients than the wastes from which they were formed. Edwards (1988) reported that samples of vermicomposts had relatively high levels of available nitrogen. Handreck (1986) reviewed the utilization of vermicomposts as horticultural potting media, and concluded that although they could supply most of the trace element needs of plants, many vermicomposts may not have sufficient nitrogen to supply all the needs of the plants. However, it seems difficult to justify this conclusion, since most organic wastes have excess amounts of nutrients and usually only a small proportion is lost during efficient and rapid vermicomposting (Edwards et al. 1985). It seems probable that the vermicomposts that he tested had been produced very slowly and had lost most of their nutrients through volatilization or leaching.

In extensive trials, testing the growth of a wide range of plants in a variety of worm-worked wastes (Edwards and Burrows 1988), most plants germinated earlier and grew better than in commercial plant growth media. A wide range of plants were grown successfully in both undiluted worm-worked wastes as well as in a range of dilutions and mixes, including 3:1 or 1:1 ratios of worm-worked wastes to peat, pine bark, or Kettering loam.

Plants tested for their growth in vermicomposts by Edwards and Burrows (1988) include vegetables such as aubergine (eggplant), cabbage, peppers, cucumber, lettuce, radish, and tomato; bedding plants such as *Alyssum, Antirrhinum, Aster, Campanula, Calceolaria, Cineraria, Coleus,* French marigold, plumose asparagus, sweet pea, *Polyanthus,* and *Salvia* (Edwards and Burrows 1988); and ornamental shrubs such as *Eleagnus pungens, Cotoneaster conspicua, Pyracantha, Viburnum bodnantense, Chaemaecyparis lawsonia,* and *Juniperus communis* (Scott 1988).

The vermicomposts after processing usually have about 75% moisture content and may need some drying. Additionally, some form of partial sterilization, such as heating to between 60° and 80°C for 24 hours, or passing through a flame-sterilizer, can be used to kill residual earthworms, their cocoons, insects and their eggs, and avoid some pathogens problems. If the waste is likely to contain human pathogens, a brief precomposting for 3 to 4 days may be advisable as a precaution. Usually, a magnesium sulfate supplement is necessary to rectify magnesium deficiencies that occur in most animal wastes, and the pH is adjusted in some way, such as by adding acid peat, to bring the medium to a pH of about 6.0. Such vermicomposts seemed to accelerate the emergence and subsequent growth of seedlings of most species of plants tested.

A wide range of tests of seedling emergence of pea, lettuce, wheat, cabbage, tomato, and radish were made in small pots and trays, using the standard European Economic Community recommended seedling-emergence test. The emergence of tomatoes, cabbage, and radish seedlings tended to be as good, and usually better, in vermicomposts than in commercial plant growth media, and much better than in composted animal wastes with no earthworms. Similarly, the early growth of seedlings of ornamentals up to the stage when they were transplanted into larger pots or outdoors was as good or better in the earthworm-worked animal wastes mixed with peat than in a commercial plant growth medium.

The growth of eggplants, dahlias, coleus, ornamental peppers, and polyanthus was also good in both worm-worked animal wastes and in mixtures of these processed wastes with peat, and was often better than in commercial plant growth media. Some of the ornamentals, particularly chrysanthemums, salvias, and petunias, flowered much earlier in worm-worked waste mixtures, and this could possibly be due to a hormonal effect resulting from microbial action, since it is well known that microorganisms can produce phytohormones (Tomati and Galli 1995). A number of other species of plants followed significantly different growth patterns in vermicomposts, another indication of a possible phytohormonal effect.

Tomatoes and cabbages germinated well and grew better in mixtures of worm-worked wastes with peat and sand than in a commercial plant growth medium, or than in 100% peat, or in a peat/sand mixture. Worm-worked paper waste was one of the best vermicomposts tested and there were no problems in processing it, or producing a standardized material from it without a need for many nutrient additives.

The effects of dilution with a commercial plant growth medium of worm-worked animal wastes on the growth of three bush ornamentals at a range of levels were quite dramatic (Scott 1988). When a 50/50 mixture of worm-worked pig and cattle animal wastes was diluted at a range of levels, ranging from 5% to 10%, with a commercial plant growth medium, all of the mixtures, even at the lowest dilutions, caused improved growth in *Chaemaecyparis lawsoniana, Pyracantha* sp., and *Viburnum bodnantense,* even better than in the recommended commercial medium itself. All of the dilutions and different mixtures also tended to grow better plants than the 100% worm-worked animal wastes, which had a tendency to dry out more rapidly than the different mixtures. These results, where even small amounts of worm-worked wastes have significant effects on growth, indicate that the response must not be based only on the nutrient content of vermicomposts.

Worm-worked animal wastes were also used as "blocking" materials to grow seedlings for transplanting into the field. Cabbages were grown in machine-compressed blocks made from either a commercial seedling medium or from worm-worked cattle or pig wastes. The seedlings were transplanted into the field in the same blocks and their subsequent growth followed and measured. Those seedlings grown in blocks of worm-worked pig waste produced cabbages almost twice as large at harvest than those grown in the commercial blocking material (Edwards and Burrows 1988).

Thus, although much more research is needed, there is evidence that good vermicomposts, when mixed with peat and other materials, make excellent plant growth media. They need some standardization to ensure an adequate plant nutrient status, possible addition of any deficient nutrients, adjustment of pH, and sterilization to kill insects and pathogens, and so on, but have a considerable commercial horticultural potential if produced rapidly and efficiently. We need more information on the potential markets for such materials.

THE USE OF EARTHWORMS AS A SOURCE OF PROTEIN FOR ANIMAL FEEDS

It was first suggested that earthworms contained sufficient protein to be considered as animal food by Lawrence and Millar (1948), and this potential as animal feed has been confirmed in the last decade, when full analyses of the body tissues of earthworms have been available, to show the kinds of amino acids they contain and the nature of the other chemical body constituents. The first successful animal feeding trials were by Sabine (1978), but subsequently there have been a number of other such trials by various workers (Edwards and Niederer 1988).

Nutrient Value of Earthworms as Animal Feed

The first analyses of the constituents of the tissues of different species of earthworms were by Lawrence and Millan (1945) and by McInroy (1971), and there have been various other analyses since this (Schulz and Graff 1977; Sabine 1978; Yoshida and Hoshii 1978; Mekada et al. 1979; Taboga 1980; Graff 1982; Edwards 1985; Edwards and Niederer 1988), and some of these show clearly that the essential amino acid spectrum for earthworm tissues, as reported by these different authors, compares well with those from other currently-used sources of animal feed protein, and that the mean amounts of essential amino acids recorded are very adequate for a good animal feed. In addition, earthworm tissues contain a preponderance of long-chain fatty acids, many of which cannot be synthesized by non-ruminant animals, and an adequate mineral content. They have an excellent range of vitamins and are rich in niacin, which is a valuable component of animal feeds, and are an unusual source of vitamin B_{12}. The overall nutrient spectrum of worm tissues shows an excellent potential as a protein supplement to feed for fish, poultry, pigs, or domestic animals.

Production of Earthworms for Animal Feed in Animal, Vegetable, and Industrial Wastes

The growth patterns of individual earthworms or whole populations in organic wastes follow classical sigmoid growth curves, with a rapid initial growth phase followed by a steadier phase and a subsequent leveling off. The maximum protein production per unit time can be achieved by inoculating relatively large volumes of animal wastes with small numbers of young worms to take advantage of the initial phase of population growth. Dry-matter conversion ratios of waste to earthworm biomass, which range from 10% for cattle and pig waste to 2% for duck waste, have been achieved readily in the laboratory, although rather lower conversion rates have been attained in the field.

Practical Production of Earthworm Feed Protein for Animals

The efficient production of earthworm protein depends mainly upon detailed knowledge and management of the population dynamics of the appropriate species, maintenance of optimal environmental conditions, and upon the engineering of suitable production methods, and particularly upon development and use of systems of harvesting earthworms from wastes, that involve small labor inputs.

Earthworms that process organic wastes grow best at relatively high moisture levels (80–90% M.C.), and this raises subsequent harvesting problems, since it is not easy to separate worms mechanically from the finely-divided organic matter at such high moisture contents, and some drying of the vermicompost before harvesting is usually necessary. There are various methods of separating earthworms from fully worked organic materials, but they tend to be labor-intensive, and an improved method was developed at Rothamsted and the National Institute for Agricultural Engineering, Silsoe, U.K. (Price and Phillips 1990). The efficiency of this machinery, in terms of percentage recovery of earthworms, is very high. The machine described will separate the worms from about one tonne of waste per hour, and can be automated and scaled up to increase its output and efficiency.

After worms are collected from the separating machine, they may have small particles of waste attached to their bodies and are likely to contain waste in their guts. The worms must be washed thoroughly and left standing in water for several hours, in order to evacuate the residual waste particles from their guts completely. A range of different methods of processing the worms into materials suitable for animal feed have been developed (Edwards and Niederer 1988). Two of these methods produced a moist paste product and the other four produced dry meals; all of the products were acceptable formulations for particular types of animal feeds, and the ultimate choice of a method of processing depends upon (a) the animal to be fed, (b) the type of animal feed required, (c) minimal loss of dry matter, (d) minimal loss of nutrient value, and (e) the cost of production. The following were the methods developed:

1. Incorporation with molasses
2. Ensiling with formic acid
3. Air-drying at room temperature
4. Freeze-drying
5. Oven-drying at 95°C
6. Acetone immersion followed by oven-drying at 95°C

The different processing methods used affected the amounts of total and essential amino acids very little; however, the lysine content was decreased slightly by ensiling with molasses using formic acid and by freeze-drying, compared to the other methods. The dry weight matter yield differed slightly between methods. Clearly, a stable protein feed can be produced by any of the methods listed and the choice of method must depend mainly on the use to which the protein is to be put, the animal that is to be fed, and the cost of the processing method in relation to the value of the protein.

The Value of Worm Protein as Feed for Fish, Poultry, and Pigs

The main outlets suggested for utilization of earthworm protein have been in fish farming and poultry and pig feeds. All of these have been tested experimentally (Sabine 1978; Edwards 1985; Edwards and Niederer 1988).

Fish Feeding Trials

The first use of earthworms as a protein source in fish feed was reported by Tacon et al. (1983). The growth of trout fed on *E. fetida*, *A. longa*, and *L. terrestris* as a total feed was compared with that of fish fed on a commercial formula. The fish fed frozen *A. longa* and *L. terrestris* grew as well as or better than fish fed on commercial trout pellets. However, trout did not grow so well on a whole diet of freeze-dried *E. fetida*, although they grew almost as well on *E. fetida* that had been blanched in boiling water before freezing. Protein makes up only 15–30% of commercial fish diets, and dried earthworm meal derived from *E. fetida*, which had not been blanched satisfactorily, replaced the fishmeal component of formulated trout pellets at the normal levels of inclusion between 5% and 30%. Clearly, earthworms have good potential both as complete feed or protein supplement for trout or other fish. Guerrero (1983) reported that *Tilapia* fish grew better on diets containing earthworm protein supplements from *P. excavatus* than those provided with other fish meal supplements. Velasquez et al. (1991) reported that earthworm meal produced from *E. fetida* produced satisfactory growth of rainbow trout with a significant increase in lipid content.

Chicken Feeding Trials

The first reports of the growth of chickens on a diet with earthworm protein were by Harwood and Sabine (1978). They found no significant difference in growth of chickens between those fed earthworm and those fed meat meal protein supplement. Similar results were reported by Taboga (1980) and Mekada et al. (1979), and Jin-you et al. (1982) reported that chickens fed on earthworms put on weight faster that those given other diets (including fish meal), had more breast muscle, and they consumed less food.

Freeze-dried earthworm protein was used by Fisher (1988) and chickens fed this protein supplement grew well, had a good weight gain per unit of food, and an excellent nitrogen retention when fed on diets with levels of worm meal from 72 to 215 g/kg.

Pig Feeding Trials

In feeding trials with both starter and grower pigs (Sabine 1978), young pigs fed on an earthworm protein supplement grew equally well and had similar feed conversion ratios to those grown on regular commercial feeds. Jin-you et al. (1982) also reported that piglets grew better on diets with earthworm protein supplements than on other protein supplements, weaning was accelerated, estrus in sows was earlier, and there was increased disease resistance and a decreased incidence of white diarrhea. Good growth of young pigs on earthworm protein was also reported by Edwards and Niederer (1988).

Economic Potential of the Production of Earthworm Protein for Animal Feed

A detailed study of the economics of production of earthworm protein concluded that the earthworm meal must be produced at an economic price, although the value of the compost can also be taken into account as complementary income. Earthworms can be produced economically with relatively low labor inputs. The labor-intensive part of earthworm protein production is the harvesting process, and this remains the main barrier to successful commercial production of earthworm protein. More efficient methods of harvesting have been tested and hold considerable promise for the future.

In a computer analysis of the economic value of earthworm protein based on its amino acid, fatty acid, mineral, and vitamin contents, it can be seen that it is extremely valuable as feed for certain animals, particularly eels and young turkeys, and it has the same value for fish, pig, and poultry feed as fish meal or meat.

METHODS OF ORGANIC WASTE MANAGEMENT BY EARTHWORMS

Methods of managing organic wastes by earthworms range from simple outdoor windrows to complex continuous reactors (Price 1987). We cannot deal with the technology of worm production in detail, but it is clear that simple windrow systems on the soil surface are relatively inefficient unless managed extremely well. It has been found that growing earthworms in beds filled with animal waste to a depth of about 50 cm, in successive shallow layers at regular intervals by manually or automatically operated gantries, are easy systems and relatively non-labor-intensive. In colder climates, some form of insulated housing over the earthworm processing system is necessary. Different forms of batch production in crates or boxes are useful and systems of continuous processing of wastes with automatic addition and removal of wastes have been developed. The technology to maximize earthworm and/or compost production is still evolving, but holds considerable promise for development into well-engineered, highly productive non-labor-intensive systems. A rapid rate of growth and multiplication of earthworms is essential for the efficient conversion of organic wastes into earthworm tissue protein and maintenance of large earthworm populations for vermicomposting. If these can be achieved, systems could be developed using a minimum of labor or sophisticated technology.

Organic wastes range from almost liquid slurries to relatively dry and finely dispersed solids. All of these wastes must be brought to a suitable moisture content and temperature and their ammonia and salt contents reduced to acceptable levels by leaching, composting, or some other method, before the earthworms can be grown successfully and productivity maximized.

Processing of each kind of organic waste involves different problems (Edwards and Neuhauser 1988). Animal wastes such as pig and cattle wastes can be processed by earthworms, when they are either straw-based animal wastes or solids separated from slurries, using a commercially-available mechanical slurry separator. Cattle solids become acceptable to earthworms a few days after collection and/or separation, but pig solids may take up to two weeks before the worms will enter them and feed satisfactorily. Duck, turkey, or chicken wastes with straw or wood shavings pose an even greater problem, since they contain considerable amounts of ammonia and, until this falls to below 0.5 mg per g, the earthworms will not enter or utilize it. The key to successful processing of poultry waste is to monitor adverse factors closely and use different techniques to accelerate its acceptability for vermistabilization. Once processed, poultry wastes, which are rich in nutrients, can be diluted with other materials to make excellent plant growth media. Industrial wastes such as paper wastes, brewery wastes, processed potato wastes, restaurant wastes, and garden wastes are much easier to preprocess and make acceptable to earthworms.

The technologies available for processing organic wastes with earthworms are of three main types. These differ in cost and complexity, the simplest costing the least, initially, and the high-technology systems costing much more to set up, but being much less labor-intensive and efficient in operation repayment. Wastes are processed very much faster in the higher technology automated systems. The relative economic performances of the three systems depend upon land availability, labor availability, and types of waste to be processed.

Low-Cost Floor Beds or Windrows

Outdoor windrows or beds with low simple walls are the simplest type of process generally used. The size of such beds is flexible, but the width of the beds should not exceed 8 feet (2.4 m), which allows the entire bed to be inspected easily. Without the need to walk on the bed, it is also compatible with the sizes of many suitable surface coverings and construction materials. The length is less important and depends on the area available. They can be laid on soil which drains freely and is not subject to waterlogging. Concrete areas are ideal for earthworm-processing systems since they provide a firm surface for tractor operations. However, it is essential for precautions to be taken to prevent too much water from entering the beds and to allow excess water to drain away from the bed. Often, such floor beds are covered and the covers removed only for watering and addition of new waste materials. Windrows and floor beds process organic wastes relatively slowly, often taking 6–12 months. During this period there may be losses of plant nutrients through volatilization or leaching.

Gantry-Fed Beds

An important principle in improving the efficiency of organic wastes by earthworms is to be able to add the wastes to beds as deep as one meter, in thin layers 1 to 2 cm thick at frequent intervals. This can be done most readily by adding the wastes by means of an overhead gantry, running on wheels on the walls of the beds (Figure 4). This gradual addition of waste maximizes waste processing, minimizes the generation of heat through composting, and ensures that earthworms are continually processing the fresh wastes near the surface.

Containers or Box Systems

Edwards (1988) discussed methods of batch vermicomposting, in large or small stacked boxes or containers, and suggested that most of the methods tested were too labor-intensive, since batches had to be moved in order to add more wastes or water. There have been various attempts to develop efficient batch systems and modular container systems. More research into such methods is needed.

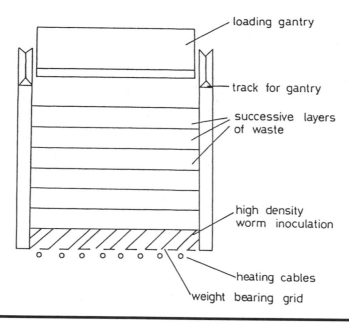

Figure 4. Design of automatic loading earthworm bed.

Raised Gantry-Fed Beds

Earthworm activity is usually confined to the top 10 to 15 cm of a bed of organic wastes, and as successive layers of waste are added the bed becomes full and needs to be emptied. The efficiency and rate of processing of the wastes can be increased considerably by raising the bed on legs above the ground and collecting the waste through the bottom. If the bed has a mesh base, the worm-processed organic matter can be passed through the mesh by some mechanical means and collected on a moving belt below the bed or from the floor with a slurry scraper. If waste is added to the top of the waste, in thin layers from a mobile gantry daily and collected through the base, continual processing of the waste can be achieved, without disturbing the earthworms in the bed. Such a system can become much more sophisticated and automated through complete mechanization of the addition of wastes and the collection systems. Such automated continuous-processing reactors have been operated successfully for as long as two years, with no problems and excellent efficiency (Price and Phillips 1990; Edwards 1995).

COMPLETE RECYCLING SYSTEMS

A complete, vermiculture-based, urban waste recycling system (SOVADEC) has been developed in France. This involves putting waste through a selector that breaks up plastic and removes it, followed by manual sorting, sorting of rolling objects such as bottles, and separation of ferrous metal objects with magnets. The waste is then transported to a compost for 30 days followed by vermicomposting for about 60 days before storing and packaging. This system can turn as much as 27% of the total urban waste stream into vermicompost.

REFERENCES CITED

Appelhof, M. 1981. Workshop on the Role of Earthworms in the Stabilization of Organic Residues, Vol. 1, Proceedings. Beech Leaf Press, Kalamazoo, Michigan, 315 pp.

Buchanan, M.A., E. Russell, and S.D. Block. 1988. Chemical characterization and nitrogen mineralization potentials of vermicomposts derived from differing organic wastes. In Earthworms in Environmental and Waste Management. C.A. Edwards and E.F. Neuhauser (eds.). SPB Academic Publishing, The Netherlands, 231–240.

Butt, K.R. 1993. Utilization of solid paper mill sludge and spent brewery yeast as a feed for soil-dwelling earthworms. Bioresource Technology 44: 105–107.

Darwin, C. 1881. The formation of vegetable mound through the action of worms, with observations of their habits. Murray, London, 326 pp.

Edwards, C.A. 1982. Production of earthworm protein for animal feed from potato waste. In Upgrading Waste for Feed and Food. D.A. Ledward, A.J. Taylor, and R. Laurio (eds.). Butterworths, London, 321 pp.

Edwards, C.A. 1983. Earthworms, organic wastes and food. Span. Shell Chemical Co. 26(3): 106–108.

Edwards, C.A. 1985. Production of feed protein from animal wastes by earthworms. Philosophical Transactions of the Royal Society of London 310: 299–307.

Edwards, C.A. 1988. Breakdown of animal, vegetable, and industrial organic wastes by earthworms. Agriculture, Ecosystems and Environment 24: 21–31.

Edwards, C.A. 1995. Commercial and environmental potential of vermicomposting: A historical overview. BioCycle June: 62–63.

Edwards, C.A., and I. Burrows. 1988. The potential of earthworm composts as plant growth media. In Earthworms in Environmental and Waste Management. C.A. Edwards and E.F. Neuhauser (eds.). SPB Academic Publishing, The Netherlands, 211–220.

Edwards, C.A., and K.E. Fletcher. 1988. Interactions between earthworms and microorganisms in organic-matter breakdown. Agriculture Ecosystems and Environment 24: 235–247.

Edwards, C.A., and E.F. Neuhauser. 1988. Earthworms in waste and environmental management. SPB Academic Publishing, The Hague, The Netherlands, 388 pp.

Edwards, C.A., and A. Niederer. 1988. The production and processing of earthworm protein.

In Earthworms in Waste and Environmental Management. C.A. Edwards and E.F. Neuhauser (eds.). SPB Academic Publishing, The Netherlands, 169–180.

Edwards, C.A., and A.R. Thompson. 1973. Pesticides and the soil fauna. Residue Reviews 45: 1–79.

Edwards, C.A., I. Burrows, K.E. Fletcher, and B.A. Jones. 1985. The use of earthworms for composting farm wastes. In Composting of Agricultural and Other Wastes. J.K.R. Gasser (ed.). Elsevier, Amsterdam, 229–242.

Fisher, C. 1988. The nutritional value of earthworm meal for poultry. In Earthworms in Waste and Environmental Management. C.A. Edwards and E.F. Neuhauser (eds.). SPB Academic Publishing, The Netherlands, 181–192.

Fosgate, O.T., and M.R. Babb. 1972. Biodegradation of animal waste by *Lumbricus terrestris*. Journal of Dairy Science 55: 870–872.

Graff, O. 1974. Gewinnung von Biomasse aus Abfallstoffen durch Kultur des Kompostregenwurms *Eisenia foetida* (Savigny 1826). Landbauforsch Volkenrode 2: 137–142.

Graff, O. 1982. Vergleich der Regenwurmarten *Eisenia foetida* und *Eudrilus eugeniae* hinsichtlich ihrer Eignung zur Proteingewinnung aus Abfallstoffen. Pedobiologia 23: 277–282.

Green, E., and S. Penton. 1981. Full scale vermicomposting at the Lufkin water pollution control plant. In Proc. Workshop on the Role of Earthworms in the Stabilization of Organic Residues, Vol. 1. M. Appelhof (ed.). Beach Leaf Press, Kalamazoo, Michigan, 229–231.

Guerrero, R.D. 1983. The culture and use of *Perionyx excavatus* as a protein resource in the Philippines. In Earthworm Ecology from Darwin to Vermiculture. J.E. Satchell (ed.). Chapman & Hall, London, 309–313.

Handreck, K.A. 1986. Vermicomposting as components of potting media. Biocycle October: 58–62.

Hartenstein, R. 1978. The most important problem in sludge management as seen by a biologist. In Utilization of Soil Organisms in Sludge Management. R. Hartenstein (ed.). National Technical Information Service, PB286932, Springfield, Virginia, 2–8.

Harwood, M., and J.R. Sabine. 1978. The nutritive value of worm meal. In Proceedings of 1st Australasian Poultry Stockfeed Convention, Sydney, 164–171.

Huhta, V., and J. Haimi. 1988. Reproduction and biomass of *Eisenia foetida* in domestic waste. In Earthworms in Waste and Environmental Management. C.A. Edwards and E.F. Neuhauser (eds.). SPB Academic Publishing, The Netherlands, 65–70.

Jensen, J. 1993. Applications of vermiculture technology for managing organic waste resources. Proceedings of the Ninth International Conference on Solid Waste Management, November 14–17, 1993, 1–8.

Jin-you, X., Z. Xian-Kuan, P. Zhi-ren, et al. 1982. Experimental research on the substitution of earthworm for fish meal in feeding broilers. Journal of South China Normal College 1: 88–94.

Kale, R.D., and K. Bano. 1991. Time and space relative population growth of *Eudrilus eugeniae*. In Advances in Management and Conservation of Soil Fauna. G.K. Veeresh, D. Rajagopal, and C.A. Virakamath (eds.). Oxford & IBH, New Dehli, 657–664.

Kale, R.D., K. Bano, and R.V. Krishnamoorthy. 1982. Potential of *Perionyx excavatus* for utilizing organic wastes. Pedobiologia 23: 419–425.

Kaplan, D.L., R. Hartenstein, E.F. Neuhauser, and M.R. Malecki. 1980. Physicochemical requirements in the environment of the earthworm *Eisenia foetida*. Soil Biology and Biochemistry 12: 347–352.

Kretzschmar, A. (ed.). 1992. ISEE 4, Fourth International Symposium on Earthworm Ecology. Soil Biology and Biochemistry 24(12): 1193–1774.

Lawrence, R.D., and H.R. Millar. 1945. Protein content of earthworms. Nature, London 155(39): 517.

Loehr, R.C., J.H. Martin, E.F. Neuhauser, and M.R. Malecki. 1984. Waste Management Using Earthworms—Engineering and Scientific Relationships Final Report, Project ISP-8016764. National Science Foundation, 76 pp.

Mcinroy, D. 1971. Evaluation of the earthworm *Eisenia foetida* as food for man and domestic animals. Feedstuffs 43: 37–47.

Mekada, H., N. Hayashi, H Yokota, and J. Olcomura. 1979. Performance of growing and laying chickens fed diets containing earthworms. Journal of Poultry Science 16: 293–297.

Morgan, M.H. 1988. The role of microorganisms in the nutrition of *Eisenia foetida*. In Earthworms and Waste Management. C.A. Edwards and E.F. Neuhauser (eds.). SPB Academic Publishing, The Netherlands, 71–82.

Neuhauser, E.F., R.C. Loehr, and M.R. Malecki. 1988. The potential of earthworms for managing sewage sludge. In Earthworms and Waste Management. C.A. Edwards and E.F. Neuhauser (eds.). SPB Academic Publishing, The Netherlands, 9–20.

Pincince, A.B., J.F. Donovan, and J.E. Bates. 1980. Vermicomposting municipal sludge: an economical stabilization alternative. Sludge 23: 30.

Price, J.S. 1987. Development of a vermicomposting system. Proceedings of the 4th International CIEC Symposium on Agricultural Waste and Management Environmental Protection 1: 294–300.

Price, J.S., and V.R. Phillips. 1990. An improved mechanical separator for removing live worms from worm-worked organic wastes. Biological Wastes 33: 25–37.

Reddy, M.V. 1988. The effect of casts of *Pheretima alexandri* on the growth of *Vinca rosea* and *Oryza sativa*. In Earthworms in Environmental and Waste Management. C.A. Edwards and E.F. Neuhauser (eds.). SPB Academic Publishing, The Netherlands, 241–248.

Reinecke, A.J., and S.A. Viljoen. 1991. Vertical deposition of cocoons by the compost worm *Eisenia fetida*. Pedobiologia 35.

Sabine, J.R. 1978. The nutritive value of earthworm meal. In Utilization of Soil Organisms in Sludge Management. R. Hartenstein (ed.). National Technical Information Services, PB286932, Springfield, Virginia, pp. 285–296.

Schultz, E., and O. Graff. 1977. Zur Bewertung von Regenwurmmehl aus *Eisenia foetida* als Eiweissfuttermittel. Landbouw Forschung Volkenrode 27: 216–218.

Scott, M.A. 1988. The use of worm-digested animal waste as a supplement to peat in loamless composts for hardy nursery stock. In Earthworms in Environmental and Waste Management. C.A. Edwards and E.F. Neuhauser (eds.). SPB Academic Publishing, The Netherlands, 231–229.

Taboga, L. 1980. The nutritional value of earthworms for chickens. British Poultry Science 21: 405–410.

Tacon, A.G.J., E.A. Stafford, and C.A. Edwards. 1983. A preliminary investigation of the nutritive value of three terrestrial earthworms for rainbow trout. Aquaculture 35: 187–199.

Tomati, U., and A. Grappelli (eds.). 1984. Proceedings: International Symposium on Agricultural and Environmental Prospects in Earthworm Farming. Publ. Minist. Ric. Sci. Tech., Rome, Tipolitografia Euromodena, 183.

Tsukamoto, J., and H. Watanabe. 1977. Influence of temperature on hatching and growth of *Eisenia foetida* (Oligochaeta, Lumbricidae). Pedobiologia 17: 338–342.

Velasquez, L., I. Ibanez, C. Herrera, and M. Oyarzun. 1991. A note on the nutritional evaluation of worm meal (*Eisinia foetida*) in diets for rainbow trout. Animal Products 53(1): 119–122.

Viljoen, S.A., and A.J. Reinecke. 1992. The temperature requirements of the epigeic earthworm species *Eudrilus eugeniae* (Oligochaeta)—a laboratory study. Soil Biology and Biochemistry 24: 1345–1350.

Watanabe, H., and J. Tsukamoto. 1976. Seasonal change in size, class, and stage structure of lumbricid *Eisenia foetida* population in a field compost, and its practical application as the decomposer of organic waste matter. Revue d'Ecologie Biologie du Sol 13: 141–146.

Wong, S. H., and D.A. Griffiths. 1991. Vermicomposting in the management of pig waste in Hong Kong. World Journal of Microbiological Biotechnology 7(6): 593–595.

Yoshida, M., and H. Hoshii. 1978. Nutritional value of earthworms for poultry feed. Japanese Journal of Poultry Science 15(6): 308–311.

Earthworms: Nature's Gift for Utilization of Organic Wastes

16

Radha D. Kale
Department of Zoology, University of Agricultural Sciences (GKVK),
Bangalore, India

E arthworms are one of the major soil macroinvertebrates and are known for their contributions to soil formation and turnover with their widespread global distribution. The role of earthworms in the breakdown of organic debris on the soil surface and in the soil turnover process was first highlighted by Darwin (1881). Since then, it has taken almost a century to appreciate their important contribution in curbing organic pollution and providing topsoil in impoverished lands. This realization, although late, has awakened the global population to serious thought on utilizing them for ecological benefit. By the turn of the century, earthworms' potential as a biological tool should be much better understood to make organic farming and sustainable development a reality with the use of selected species of earthworms. The number of papers presented at the session at ISEE 5 on earthworms in waste management authenticates how this field of study is gaining a priority status and I should like to comment on some of these presentations.

Different laboratories have tried the possibility of utilizing earthworms to break down organic wastes which have been the causative agents of much organic pollution. By regulating the moisture levels and mixing the ingredients in proper ratios that can be accepted by the earthworms, coffee pulp (Arellano et al. 1995), sugar factory waste (Kale et al. 1994), and pig solids (Dominquez and Edwards 1994) could all be converted into good quality soil additives, along with the biomass production of earthworms.

1-884015-74-3/98/$0.00/$.50
©1998 by CRC Press LLC

The reports of Vinceslas-Apka and Loquet (1994) and Fredrickson et al. (1994) have shown that the involvement of earthworms in the composting process decreases the time of stabilization of the waste and produces an efficient organic pool with energy reserves as vermicompost. Garcia et al. (1994) showed in their studies that the sludges from both agribased industries and domestic sewage plants not accepted as soil additives directly on fields can be a food source for composting earthworms, with suitable organic amendments such as plant litter or animal waste to produce the worm biomass and obtain better quality soil additives.

In the case of earthworms that are used for composting of organic waste, the relationship between biomass production and population increase is of utmost importance. Meyer and Bouwman (1994) provided an explanation for the possibility of not getting expected population increases in these earthworms. They suggested that anisopary, a physiological behavioral pattern of worms where some percentage of the population remains only as sperm donors and fails to produce cocoons, as well as various extrinsic factors like the available food sources and climatic factors, can also contribute to their reproductive potential. Similarly, the levels of hazardous heavy metals in the organic wastes fed to worms can affect spermatogenesis and spermateleosis. This was made clear in the ultrastructural studies carried out by Reinecke and Reinecke (1994) that were based on exposing the worms to different concentrations of cadmium, lead, and manganese mixed with cattle dung. The tissue burden of any of these hazardous materials in earthworms may at some point enter the higher level food chain, as was demonstrated in studies on the earthworm population at a hazardous waste site (Stair et al. 1994).

In developing countries, where the trend is to switch over to more ecofriendly organic farming, Jambekar (1994) demonstrated improvements in the fertility status of the soil in vineyards due to earthworms and their effects on yield of grapes, which is very encouraging. Similarly, Mba (1994) highlighted the effect of vermicompost on the ground cover crop *Telfaria occidentalis* and its influence on increasing earthworm activity in the soil. Encouraging the endogeic populations of earthworms by amending soil with organic manures and ground cover crops can contribute significantly to the soil fertility in tropical countries.

It is true that clear-cut demarcations of the role of epigeic and endogeic species of earthworms and their limitations have to be made, as was summarized by Buckerfield (1994). If there is any confusion, it has to be clarified by highlighting the importance of endogeic species of earthworm and the inability of epigeic species of earthworm to overcome adverse physical conditions in nature. Once this is clarified, it should be possible to specify the species of earthworm that can work best on organic waste. Mitchell (1994) discussed composting using epigeic earthworms to overcome organic pollution.

In most of the presentations at ISEE 5, *Eisenia fetida* and *Eisenia andrei* were chosen for vermicomposting. Although there is information about other worms like *Perionyx excavatus* or *Eudrilus eugeniae*, it is very scanty. Fayolle et al. (1994) reported the possibility of rearing *Dendrobaena veneta* on organic waste, such as horse manure and paper sludges. Studies of the life cycle of this earthworm on other kinds of organic waste can increase the number of earthworms available to work on organic wastes. In tropical and subtropical conditions, *E. eugeniae* and *P. excavatus* are the best vermicomposting earthworms. Work is in progress to test the possibility of using other species from forest lands in vermicomposting.

The application of epigeic species of earthworms in combating organic pollution and producing high-quality organic soil additives and earthworm biomass is moving at a very slow pace in most scientific laboratories compared with the enthusiastic group of workers in the United States who have been successful in promoting the technology of vermicomposting. Appelhof (1995) and Bisesi and Appelhof (1994) have initiated this as programs in schools and have prepared worksheets and manuals to create interest and awareness among youngsters. White (1994) has come out with the publication of a quarterly newsletter, *Worm Digest*, in which he points out that earthworms may be the answer to solving waste disposal and rejuvenating neglected land.

From my personal experience and from the presentations in the session on "Earthworms and Waste Management" at ISEE 5, this is a challenging field for scientists to bridge the gap between the laboratory and field. The whole human race will be the beneficiary if vermicomposting technology is accepted and adopted. The activity in the small state of Karnataka, India, described here shows its general acceptance by agriculturists, urban residents, and industrialists.

The papers presented touched upon various aspects of biology that hitherto have not received much attention. The changing scenario with regard to use of earthworms in organic waste management, especially the voluminous waste from agri-based industries, was a welcome feature. It is incredible to see the efforts made to tap the talent of resourceful schoolchildren and initiate them to use earthworms to handle problems of urban solid waste. Finally, it could be discerned from the presentations that, though *E. fetida* predominates as the composting earthworm, there are various attempts to test the efficiencies of other earthworms, in order to encourage the use of locally-available species or the species that can adapt best to the different zoogeographic regions.

An aspect not covered in the presentations was the implementation of the benefits of vermicomposting technology in developmental programs. The efforts of researchers to involve the public through various media have to be strengthened further by publication of scientific data to confirm earthworms as one of the best means of abating organic pollution and minimizing indiscriminate use of inorganic fertilizers. The proper monitoring of the production of earthworm biomass can also add to animal protein substitutes in animal feed production units.

The countryside and agricultural lands are vanishing sights in many countries moving toward industrialization and away from an agrarian emphasis. Increased poverty, brought about by a decline in available fertile land to grow food grains, is accompanied by greed to use the land for cash crops. Under such circumstances, the present problem depends upon improving the fertility of available land to overcome the problem of hunger and starvation.

With these points in view, a program of research and extension activities initiated by using *E. eugeniae* as a composting worm in this sub-tropical part of India is presented with the aim of furthering research on waste management through earthworms.

A SPECTRUM OF RURAL AND URBAN SOLID WASTE GENERATION

The Indian sub-continent, with its varied physiographic and agroclimatic zones and cultural practices, produces a great deal of agricultural waste. Depending on the major crop of the zone, agroindustries are established in different townships. The kinds of waste generated in these units are extremely diverse. They are of plant or animal origin and can undergo degradation to release plant nutrients from the bound complex form. As the complex structural composition of these substances resists easy breakdown, the decomposition is a slow process. This has resulted in accumulations of these materials without proper utilization. Stubbles, weeds, and litter are the main biomass that form major farm wastes. The wastes released from dairy farms can be added. Table 1 lists the major farm wastes and agroindustrial wastes that are posing disposal problems.

The growth of cities has resulted in an ever-increasing accumulation of organic wastes. Most farm produce enters cities to cater to the food needs of the urban population. Thus, most agricultural produce is moved away from the place of origin. The unutilized and unwanted part of organic crop residues is often put into landfills. Organic material in farmland that could have returned to the bio-geo-chemical cycle to enrich the nutrient status of soil has been turned into a pollutant in the city. In India, domestic waste is mostly of organic nature and contributes 70% to 80% of urban solid waste. Each household of four family members generates 0.5–0.75 kg kitchen waste per day (Kale and Sunita 1993).

Table 1. List of wastes tested for vermicomposting

Sl. no.	Source of waste generation	Utilizable waste for vermicomposting
I	Agricultural waste	
	1. Agricultural fields	Stubble, weeds, husk, straw, and farmyard manure
	2. Plantations	Stems, leaf matter, fruit rind, pulp, and stubble
	3. Animal waste	Dung, urine, and biogas slurry
II	Urban solid waste	Kitchen waste from households and restaurants, waste from market yards and places of worship, and sludge from sewage treatment plants
III	Agro-industries waste	
	1. Food processing units	Peel, rind, and unused pulp of fruits and vegetables
	2. Vegetable oil refineries	Pressmud and seed husk
	3. Sugar factories	Pressmud, fine bagasse, and boiler ash
	4. Breweries and distilleries	Spent wash, barley waste, and yeast sludge
	5. Seed production units	Core of fruits, paper, and date expired seeds
	6. Aromatic oil extraction units	Stems, leaves, and flowers after extraction of oil
	7. Coir industries	Coir pith

STATE OF AGRICULTURE IN KARNATAKA STATE, INDIA

Food production is the primary concern of any country. When productive lands are scarce and population growth is increasing at an alarming rate, maximum productivity must be achieved from available land. A little more than 71% of the population of Karnataka state lives in rural areas. Among this rural population, 94% depend on agriculture. Reports from the Directorate of Agriculture, Economics, and Statistics and Economic Survey show that land utilization for agriculture over the state averages 1.2 ha/individual. In this area nearly 56.2% is used for sowing crops once a year and 8.8% is cultivated more than once. Only 12% of agricultural land is irrigated. For every ton of food grains produced, an average consumption of chemical fertilizers as an energy subsidy is 50 kg N, 30 kg P, and 90 kg K. Inorganic fertilizer utilization has more than doubled in a decade and so has the use of pesticides for pest control. These increases in chemical application have not boosted agricultural yields significantly, except those of sugarcane. For the rest of the crops, production has either remained the same or has declined in the last five years. It is costlier to maintain plants in hot climates than in temperate areas because of the high temperatures and water stresses (Best 1962). A mere 3% of the agricultural community in Karnataka owns more than 10 ha of land and the rest of the landholders are marginal to medium farmers with less than 10 ha. The current strategy of a ten-fold increase in use of fertilizers, pesticides, and machinery to get a mere two-fold increase in agricultural production is economically unviable under the existing situations in the state (Bennett and Robinson 1967).

In recent times, reduction of the levels of pollution caused by different sources has been emphasized. Factory production units of fertilizers are releasing various hazardous by-products that can pollute air, water, and soil, if proper preventive measures are not taken. Similarly, sludges from sewage treatment plants and other organic degradable refuse are causing harm to the ecosystem. The same organic refuses can be utilized for the agricultural system if regulated properly. To utilize the nutrients in these materials, detritus consumption on agricultural land has to be activated. To meet the needs of short duration crops, which have evolved in the present-day agricultural systems, more and more chemical fertilizers are currently used. The repeated use of chemicals in tropical lands is showing an increasingly adverse effect on soil properties, productivity, and fertility. However, this alarming situation has produced a reverse in this strategy of agricultural practice by a small percentage of agriculturists in the state. Their practices involve selecting varieties of plants that are most resistant to pest attack and have low demand for inorganic nutrient inputs, and practicing multiple cropping systems. This also includes the production of biological insecticides and biomass for organic soil additives. By tapping the organic detritus as a resource, it is realized that it is possible to rejuvenate the topsoil and increase harvests. In this organic detritus group, earthworms can be managed to feed on varieties of organic wastes, thereby serving as tools to hasten the process of degradation and release of nutrients and improving the nutrient status of the tropical soils. The propagation of earthworms for humus production under seminatural conditions is developing rapidly in the state and is revolutionizing agriculture.

EARTHWORMS AS BIODEGRADERS OF WASTE BIOMASS

The loss of topsoil due to practices associated with the indiscriminate use of chemicals is a major cause of the decline in productivity status of these tropical soils. The realization of this fact has begun to increase the use of organic wastes on the fields. There is a decline in the availability of cattle dung and the current need is to get the required organic soil additives from unutilized available plant biomass residues in minimum time. Various methods have come into practice, in addition to the old practice of pit composting. Engineering skills are employed to provide good aeration of composting materials, to minimize the time of composting. Selected groups of fungi are used in different places for composting of lignocellulose-based materials.

Much of the importance given to earthworm activity in temperate soils is lacking in tropical regions, although earthworm species diversity and richness is not much less than in temperate regions (Bano and Kale 1991). Food niches and strategies that have developed among different species of earthworms have helped to broaden their use in waste breakdown. Epigeic earthworm species showing a greater affinity for nitrogen and rich organic matter live in a more unstable environment. They resemble the spiral stages of ecological development, with a smaller body size, higher metabolic rate, higher fecundity, and shorter life cycle. In natural conditions, their survival depends on the environment and degree of biotic pressure from predators. These earthworms form the components of the tropical forest floor community. With the loss of natural forests, they have entered the agricultural plantations.

Higher yields from the use of chemical fertilizers have led the farming community to neglect the importance of organic manures and additives. Farmers have been unaware that organic manures are essential to restore the cycle of events in the soil in order to keep it productive. In recent years, chemicals applied to the soil short-circuited this cycle of events and deprived the soil organisms of their energy source to restore the health of the soil through their activity.

When earthworms are isolated to work on waste organic matter, their major contribution is in fragmenting the organic matter. The microenvironment they provide for the establishment of microorganisms is of utmost importance in the composting process. Their excretions of ammonia and urea add to the nitrogen content. Other organic acids and mucus secretions provide nourishment for microbial populations. With the organic amendments to the fields and use of minimum tillage practices, the soil organisms become more important.

SOLID WASTE UTILIZATION FOR COMPOST PRODUCTION USING EARTHWORMS

We tried composting animal waste under laboratory conditions using *P. excavatus* (Kale et al. 1982), a species distributed all over India. These earthworms can be found congregated near cattle sheds and in biogas slurry pits. Plantations with a good litter cover also form a habitat for these worms. Similarly *P. sansibaricus* in Kerala and *P. pallus* in Maharashtra have been tested for their use in organic waste degradation. Apart from these species, polyhumic worms such as *Lampito mauritii* have also been tried for vermicomposting. As in temperate countries, *E. eugeniae* and *E. fetida* are also gaining importance as the ideal species for humus production.

E. eugeniae, being a tropical species, is establishing well in southern peninsular India whereas *E. fetida* establishes best in the more temperate part of the country. *E. eugeniae* is preferred for the degradation of agricultural waste and *E. fetida* for urban waste degradation at the community level and in households. The systems for utilizing these earthworms were developed at different stages in the laboratory. Methods were aimed at minimizing the time of composting, improving the quality of the compost, minimizing the cost of labor, and making it an economic venture for the spread of the technology to the rural areas.

It started with using organic matter that breaks down slowly to form the first tier in a composting container followed by a layer of finely sieved sand and garden soil respectively. Populations of *E. eugeniae*, *E. fetida,* or *P. excavatus* were introduced into these prepared containers. Soft organic wastes like animal waste or vegetable waste were spread on the surface. In the initial stages, worms fed on the surface layer and produced casts. The feed mix was added as needed after collecting the cast. Every three months, the contents of the culture containers were emptied and by this time the entire organic matter including stubbles from agriculture fields, sugarcane trash, or coir waste had decomposed. This was shown by the reduction in levels of residual cellulose and lignin in the worm-worked materials (Kale et al. 1991). Since this procedure was not viable for the farming community, an alternative and a much simpler method evolved.

In older agricultural practices, when the available land area for food production per individual was more, farmers were in the habit of reserving a part of their land for growing certain shrubs and grazing cattle. These shrubs were pruned periodically to mix the green matter into the soil to serve as green manure. Most of these plants had a high level of nitrogen.

Based on this practice, green leaves from different plants, weeds, hedge cuttings, and dry leaves were mixed with cow dung slurry and left in the culture containers for two weeks. During this period, two turns were given to the mix to aerate the material. After two weeks of conditioning, the worms were released on the waste surface where they fed on the surface materials and moved down as most of the material was converted into worm casts. Occasionally, water was sprinkled on the surface. Worms, fed on the soft material to begin with and the hard and unfed material, were mixed again with fresh material. The collection and preparation of organic mixes being simple and time-saving,

Table 2. Range of nutrients in vermicompost

1. Organic carbon (%)	9.15–17.98
2. Total nitrogen (%)	0.50–1.50
3. Available phosphorus (%)	0.10–0.30
4. Available potassium (%)	0.15–0.56
5. Available sodium (%)	0.06–0.30
6. Calcium and magnesium (meq/100 g)	22.67–47.60
7. Copper (ppm)	2.00–9.50
8. Iron (ppm)	2.00–9.30
9. Zinc (ppm)	5.70–11.50
10. Available sulphur (ppm)	128.00–548.00

farmers further simplified the method and have developed their own techniques for vermicomposting the wastes listed in Table 1.

To minimize the nutrient loss from the materials during composting and to provide a vent for the released carbon dioxide or other gases during the decomposition process, a 2.5-cm-thick mud pack was placed on the surface of the decomposing material and PVC tubes 3 cm in diameter with a series of holes or even the hollow shoots of the plants were inserted into the packed material 30 cm apart. After two weeks, worms were released into the vermicompost pits through temporary holes made on the mud pack. By this method moisture loss from the waste was minimized. Thus, the light and oxygen keep the worms active beneath the surface of the mud pack in the organic wastes. This increases the biomass of the worms and also the nutrient status of the compost produced in a short interval of time (Table 2). The species *E. eugeniae, E. fetida,* and *P. excavatus* all work well under these conditions, whereas *Dichogaster curgensis,* which needs a soil base, failed to survive. The large size and low carrying capacity of *E. eugeniae* have led us to depend more on *E. fetida*, which tolerates high population density pressure in its use for urban solid organic wastes. Neuhauser et al. (1979, 1980), in their studies, have shown the sensitivity of *E. eugeniae* to density pressure. A similar carrying capacity of *E. eugeniae* on organic wastes under laboratory conditions was studied and was measured to be 0.015 g/cc (Kale and Bano 1991).

URBAN SOLID WASTE MANAGEMENT

The practice of waste segregation is growing both at the community level and in individual households. The waste is segregated in the home before handing

Table 3. Composting of household waste using three species of earthworms: *Eudrilus eugeniae, Eisenia fetida,* **and** *Perionyx excavatus* **(Kale and Sunita 1993)**

Earthworm species	Organic waste (kg)	Time taken for composting (days)	Compost recovery (kg)	Initial biomass (g)	Final biomass of worms (g)	Population increase (no. of young ones)
I set						
Eudrilus eugeniae	200	60	160	300	1,500	32,000
Eisenia fetida	200	90	160	150	350	30,000
Perionyx excavatus	200	90	160	100	205	6,000
II set						
Eudrilus eugeniae	400	60	250	1,500	1,800	100,000
Eisenia fetida	400	100	250	350	500	80,000
Perionyx excavatus	400	100	250	205	280	20,000

Note: Initially 1,000 non-clitellate worms of each species were introduced into different pits. The population of *Eudrilus eugeniae* has reached carrying capacity by the end of 5 months.

over the same to garbage collectors. Only the compostable waste is dumped in pits constructed in public parks of residential areas for vermicomposting. The pits are covered with metallic mesh to keep away predators. A low level and sloped roofs protect the pits from inundation during heavy rains and from direct sunshine. Care is taken to maintain the aesthetic look of the parks while constructing the pits. Similar composting activity is done in houses in small tubs or even in knitted sacks.

The daily garbage production in Bangalore (Karnataka) averages 2,000 tons per day. In the residential localities 70% to 80% of the solid waste is biodegradable organic waste. Table 3 provides information on the composting of such urban wastes in a residential area. The organic matter can result in air pollution and groundwater pollution both by the obnoxious odors at the dump sites and by the released leachates. As an alternative, by collecting the waste into impermeable pits, under aerobic conditions with selected species of earthworms, the entire material is converted in a short time into good vermicompost. The wastes that cause pollution and are a source of epidemiological problems now become a source of income for those who have begun vermicomposting and this compost provides a high nutrient source that is very beneficial and evokes biological activity in impoverished soils.

Interest in processing kitchen waste is increasing, so several designs of vermicomposting vessels have evolved to suit different places. One of the containers is a cylindrical drum erected horizontally on a stand. Mesh covers on either side of the drum provide ventilation. The capacity of the drum is about 5 kg. Rotation at an interval ranging from 48 h to 72 h (maximum five rotations) provides good aeration in the medium. Such a closed and compact system can be maintained easily in any household without occupying much space. Two drums of this capacity are ideal for a typical Indian house with four to five family members. Different cities in the country are planning to devise methods to utilize such a vermicomposting technology.

VERMICOMPOSTING OPERATIONS BY AGRO-INDUSTRIES

An average pressmud (a by-product of the sugar processing industry containing the elements added to clarify juice and sediments, solids like bagacillo, the smaller fibers of cane sugar, and particulates and mud) production per ton of sugarcane is 35 kg. A sugar factory that has taken up vermicomposting has a unit capacity for crushing 2,000 tons of sugarcane per day. The resulting pressmud released into lagoons averages 2,000 tons per month. The other organic wastes in lesser quantities are the fine bagasse and ash from boilers. These are currently using large areas of land around the factory units as dump sites. The pressmud as such can be a good soil additive for its nutrient status, but the farmers are not willing to apply this to their lands for fear of developing complications in the fields.

The pressmud has no use other than to become a water and air pollutant if no alternative way is available for its safe disposal, and vermicomposting is one of the only alternatives. Khoday's group of companies are converting this waste into vermicompost together with the waste from their dairy farm and crop residues from their plantations. They started with 5,000 E. eugeniae in June 1993, multiplied them in cement cisterns, and within one year they had a production level of 20 tons of compost per month. This prompted them to develop a unit to convert all the waste from the sugar factory and the sludge from the distillery into vermicompost by investing Rs 25,000,000 ($710,000 US) in this single production unit.

Similarly, an aromatic oil extraction unit, near Bangalore city, had a problem in disposal of flower and plant wastes after extracting the oils using organic solvents. The quantity of the waste generated was very high, relative to the quantity of the oil extracted. The materials disposed of in the dump sites caused bad odors and were not properly decomposed, even after one year. Now the unit has tested the efficiency of earthworms at converting this material into vermicompost. Encouraging results both in terms of composting time and the nutrient value of the recovered compost have prompted this unit to enter into much larger scale production.

Similarly, distillery sludge, an effluent with spent grain, and yeast sludges are used for composting. A public sector machine tool factory has taken up vermicomposting of the sludges from a domestic sewage plant. The agriculturists from the surrounding areas are not prepared to use the sludge directly on the fields and it is not used for the gardens in the factory. Instead it is heaped up near the treatment plant and wasted. Now the factory is mixing other plant residues from pruning with the sludge and converting the sludge successfully into vermicompost.

The competition and awareness of the potential of using the organic wastes will maintain the cost of the wastes at reasonable levels to meet the needs of the users. For big units, since this is only a means to dispose of the unwanted wastes, it is only additional income to the units and provides a job opportunity for the unemployed. The organic waste has turned into profits with the use of earthworms in these units. A vegetable seed production and tissue culture division in Bangalore produces organic waste in the form of ripened rind of fruit, after the seeds are separated. Since they are producing a large number of plants by adopting tissue culture techniques, from agar to cotton buds and paper, lots of organic waste is generated. The unsold seeds after the expiration date have to be destroyed. This unit is now using these materials for vermicomposting. As the nature of the waste generated is of different kinds, vermicompost is produced by using different suitable combinations of these wastes.

DEVELOPMENT OF VERMICOMPOSTING TECHNOLOGY IN RURAL AREAS

The green revolution in India encouraged the indiscriminate use of fertilizers to obtain two to three crop yields per year using irrigation. As a result, tropical soils, which are prone to loss of nutrients and depletion of carbon levels, are turning unproductive. Now there is concern about sustaining productivity rather than enjoying the high but short-lived yields and financial returns.

High temperatures during most of the year and the unequal and unpredictable rainfall provide much less scope for the activity of soil organisms. Only termites and ants can be active in such situations. Moisture-sensitive organisms such as earthworms are active only for very short periods. Low moisture contents in the rain-fed soil, regular plowing, little available organic matter in the land, and heavy pesticide applications have further decreased their population. All these factors contribute to an unawareness among farmers about biological processes in soil and the importance of earthworms in these in particular. The overall populations of soil organisms that contribute to the formation of topsoil by fragmenting the organic material and mixing into the soil strata are declining. The productivity status of the soil is showing the same downward trend. At this juncture, a lack of availability of manure at the right time in required quantities, many farmers are looking for different resources to build up the topsoil. It is essential to restore the carbon level in tropical soils where the depletion of carbon takes place at a rapid rate.

A technology using suitable species of earthworms for degradation of any organic wastes of plant and animal origin for a minimum of six weeks was released for the benefit of farmers in 1984 from the University of Agricultural Sciences, Bangalore. Nevertheless, few farmers came forward to make use of the technology because of the heavy subsidy at that time on chemical fertilizers. The ill effects of using only inorganic chemicals were not realized at that time. Applying fertilizers, pesticides, and herbicides was time-saving and less labor-intensive. By 1990, farmers realized that the subsidy on inorganic chemicals was not an ever-lasting feature. To get the same yield from their fields, they had to continually increase the quantity of the fertilizers. Pest populations developed resistance to pesticides and pesticides, instead of bringing down the incidence of pest attack, started to destroy the crops. Thereby, farming has become uneconomical. The nightmare of losing soil fertility combined with uncontrollable pest attacks has made Indian farmers look for alternative methods of production available through a more sustainable agriculture.

From 1990, vermicompost production, using available waste biomass and epigeic worms like *E. eugeniae,* has advanced rapidly. Table 4 provides information on the spread of this technology in the area from February 1983 to April 1994. Direct dialogue between the farmers and representatives of various organizations had led them to try out different degradable materials and improvise methods to suit the local conditions. Farmers are accepting this as a highly viable technology and are convinced that with minimum expense they can produce better quality organic soil additive. The feedback from farmers has revealed that our farmers are more optimistic due to this technology and innovation. In some of the districts of this state, almost all the farmers know about this new technology and as the well-known slogan goes, a process of "each one teach one" has started. The message of protecting the soil for future generations to enjoy is spreading and boosting the morale of farmers. The art of mass rearing and maintenance of earthworm cultures and the tapping of organic wastes for

Table 4. Dissemination of vermicomposting technology from UAS Bangalore from 1983 to 1994

Year	Within Karnataka	Outside Karnataka
1983	2	MAH/1
1984	1	TN/1 AP/1 MAH/1
1985	1	TN/1 KER/1 MAH/1
1986	0	0
1987	1	AP/1
1988	0	MAH/1
1989	0	TN/1 KER/1 PUN/1
1990	4	TN/3 MAH/1
1991	51	KER/4 AP/4 MAH/3 TN/6
1992	290	KER/10 MAH/5 GUJ/2 AP/2 PUN/1 MAN/1 DEL/1 HP/1 MP/1 RAJ/1 OR/3 BEN/1 UP/1 HAR/1
1993	361	TN/22 KER/17 AP/19 OR/4 GUJ/2 PUN/1 MAH/10 DEL/2 BEN/1 SIK/1 POND/1
1994 (Mar)	116	AP/3 MAH/1 TN/3 KER/1

AP = Andrha Pradesh, BEN = Bengal, DEL = Delhi, GUJ = Gujurat, HAR = Haryana, HP = Himachal Pradesh, KER = Kerala, MAH = Maharashtra, MAN = Manipur, MP = Madhya Pradesh, POND = Pondichery, PUN = Punjab, RAJ = Rajasthan, SIK = Sikkim, TN = Tamil Nadu, UP = Uttar Pradesh.

their maintenance have provided good scope for developing vermicomposting as a cottage industry in this country, where there is no dearth of organic wastes and labor. The tapping of a resourceful technology is of utmost importance for the present day since "soil is the placenta of life."

HUMUS PRODUCED BY EARTHWORM ACTIVITY— "WASTE TO SOIL"

Joshi and Kelkar (1952) have reported higher electrical conductivity in casts, which denotes an increase in the levels of soluble salts over the surrounding soil. They have shown that casts have greater nitrifying power than the soil. Earthworm casts being aggregates, make the site more aerobic. The stability of the casts depends on the concentration and type of organic matter present and the bacterial and fungal polysaccharides (Dutt 1948; Bhandari et al. 1967). Earthworm casts are a better source of organic manure than other anaerobically degraded compost because of the following factors:

They are loosely packed granular aggregates of semi-digested organic matter that provide energy for the establishment of various microorganisms. Some of the microorganisms associated with the casts remove the bad odor from decomposing materials (Watanabe et al. 1982). The casts also form a suitable base for free-living beneficial microbes whose activity is essential for the release of nutrients to plants (Atlavinyte and Daciulyte 1969; Atlavinyte and Vanagas 1982; Ross and Cairns 1982). An establishment of a microenvironment takes place in the presence of worms in the given medium (Kale et al. 1987). Especially in tropical countries, earthworms cannot remain active throughout the year (Roy 1957; Reddy and Alfred 1978; Chauhan 1980). Nutrients from the soil leach out at a rapid rate under ambient soil and environmental conditions in tropical countries. Under such circumstances, application of earthworm casts to fields can improve the physico-chemical and biological properties of the soil (Kale et al. 1992).

The bio-chemical activity of established microorganisms and earthworm exudates has a stimulatory effect on plant growth (Ross and Cairns 1982). The presence of earthworms in culture pots improved the germination, growth, and yield of barley crop (Atlavinyte and Zinkuviene 1985). A higher level of vitamin B_{12} in the medium due to worm activity was reported by Atlavinyte and Daciulyte (1969). Nielson (1965) isolated IAA-like substances from homogenates of different species of earthworms. Springett and Syers (1979) have reported an increase in net crop production on application of worm casts. Similar information is available on improvement in the growth and yield of crops influenced by the worm exudates (Graff and Makeschin 1980). Tomati et al. (1990) have reported about the presence of growth regulator substances in worm-worked soils. Increase in the protein synthesis of *Agaricus bisporus* and radish *Raphanus sativam* was recorded in plants grown in the presence of worm cast (Galli et al. 1990; Tomati et al. 1990). Increase in the rates of uptake of nutrients with the increase in a symbiotic microbial association in cereal and ornamental plants on using vermicompost as a source of organic manure was observed (Kale et al. 1987, 1992). Similarly, in a perennial crop like mulberry, there was no difference in the uptake of nutrients in plants grown on vermicompost or chemical fertilizers. Although the NPK concentrations applied to land in the form of chemicals was higher than the level of the same components in vermicompost, the level that entered the plant tissues remained the same irrespective of the concentrations that entered the soil (unpublished data). Table 5 provides the information on the yield data of different crops for which vermicompost was used as source of organic matter. These findings authenticate that when earthworms work on organic matter they improve the quality of the humus produced by their activity.

Table 5. Effect of vermicompost on growth and yield of tested crops

Sl. No.	Station	Crop Variety	Parameters	Inferences	Reference
1	Wet land at Bangalore north	Summer variety paddy (4.5 months crop)	1. Nutrient uptake in plants 2. Nutrient levels in soil after harvest 3. Microbial load in soil before and after harvest 4. Mycorrhizal association with roots	Improved uptake of nutrients, increased level of N, P, and microbial load. Higher level of symbiotic association.	Kale et al. (1992)
2	Vegetable garden with irrigation facility in Bangalore north	*Solanum melongena, Lycopersicon esculentum, Raphanus sativus,* and *Daucus carota*	Yield	Yield unaffected on reducing the chemical dosage by 50% of recommended dose when applied with vermicompost.	Bano et al. (1994)
3	Botanical garden GKVK Bangalore	Different ornamental plants	Vegetative growth and flower yield	Some flowering plants needed minimum fertilizers along with vermicompost and no need for additional fertilizers when vermicompost was used in some cases.	Bano et al. (1994)
4	Botanical Garden GKVK Bangalore	Two varieties of *Helianthus annus* EC 68415 and Morden	Vegetative growth and seed yield	No change in vegetative characters with different combinations of fertilizers. Vermicompost with half the recommended dose of chemicals increased the yield.	Kale et al. (1991)
5	Farm land at Bangalore south	*Arachis hypogea* and *Glycine max*	Same as above	Same as above.	Kale et al. (1993)

Note: To study treatment effects on various crops, the recommended dosages of fertilizers given in package of practices of UAS, Bangalore, were taken as control to compare the treatments using vermicompost.

The production of degradable organic waste and the problem of its disposal is a global problem. To protect the topsoil, to restore the sustainability of productive soils, and to rejuvenate the degraded soils are a major concern at the international level. Provision of a suitable environment in the soil by amending good quality organic soil additives enhances the development of resistance in plants to pests and diseases. Minimizing the use of fertilizers and pesticides or herbicides brings down the level of air, water, and soil pollution. When farmers are asked to use more manure or soil additives to revive the productivity status of their soils the question that arises is from where to get the required quantity of materials needed to feed the soil. No doubt, the crop varieties used require heavy energy subsidies to give the expected yields. By minimizing the time of humification of organic material, by optimizing the production, and by evolving the methods to minimize the loss of nutrients during the course of decomposition, the fantasy becomes fact. Earthworms can serve as tools to facilitate these functions. Just as the truth lies in their serving as "nature's plowman," they form nature's gift to produce good humus, which is the most precious material to fulfill the need of crops. Table 6 provides information on the feedback received from randomly-selected persons who are using earthworms to produce the vermicompost. The quality of compost produced by them, its utility, and their opinion on the use of manure for different crops is furnished to summarize the success story of vermicomposting in the state of Karnataka.

Table 6(a). Response to media use by UAS, Bangalore, for dissemination of technology and the range of vermicompost production by different groups on random data collection

(a) Media response		(b) Different categories		(c) Average vermicompost production (kg/month)	
Different media	Response (%)	Activity groups	%	Range	%
1. Newspapers, magazines and books	48	1. Individuals from rural areas	55	1. <100	35
	,			2. 100–200	23
2. Radio and television	7	2. Individuals from urban areas	15	3. 200–500	12
				4. 500–1000	12
3. Workshops and exhibitions	10	3. Non-government organizations	10	5. 1000–2000	10
				6. 2000–3000	3
4. From the Centre (UAS)	14	4. Entrepreneurs	10	7. 3000–5000	2
				8. 5000–10,000	2
5. Other than UAS	20	5. Industrial units	5	9. >10,000	1

Table 6(b). Opinion of the farmers on using vermicompost for different crops

I. Cereal		II. Pulses		III. Oilseeds	
Crop variety	Opinion	Crop variety	Opinion	Crop variety	Opinion
1. Jowar	+++	1. *Pisum sativum* (garden pea)	+++	1. *Helianthus annuum* (sunflower)	++++
2. *Oriza sativa* (rice)	++++	2. *Phaseolus mungo* (blackgum)	+++		
3. *Zea mays* (maize)	+++	3. *Cajanus cajan* (Tuvar Dal/ pegiongram)	+++	2. *Arachis hypogea* (groundnut)	+++
4. *Eleusine coracana* (ragi)	+++	4. *Dolichos lablab* (country bean)	+++	3. *Glycine max* (soyabean)	++++
				4. *Brassica compestris* (mustard)	+++

IV. Spices		V. Vegetables		VI. Fruits	
Crop variety	Opinion	Crop variety	Opinion	Crop variety	Opinion
1. Cardamom	++++	1. *Brassica oleracea* var. *capitala* (cabbage)	++++	1. *Mangifura indica* (mango)	+++
2. *Piper nigrum* (pepper)	++++	2. *Raphanus sativus* (radish)	++++	2. *Musa paradisiaca* (banana)	++++
3. *Murrya paniculata* (curry leaf plant)	++++	3. *Daucus carrota* (carrot)	++++	3. Chickku	+++
		4. *Solanum tuberosum* (potato)	++++	4. *Citrullus lanatus* (watermelon)	++++
4. *Curcuma longa* (turmeric)	+++	5. *Lycopersium esculentum* (tomato)	++++	5. *Citrus* spp. (lemon)	+++
		6. *Capsicum annuum* (chillies)	++++	6. *Vitis vinifera* (grapes)	++++
5. *Cinnamomum zeylanicum* (cinnamon)	+++	7. *Cucurbita pepo* (pumpkin)	++++	7. *Artocarpus heterophyllus* (jacktree)	+++
		8. *Luffa acutangula* (ribbed gourd)	++++	8. Ber	++++
6. Clove	+++	9. Cluster beans	+++	9. *Punica granatum* (pomogranate)	++++
		10. *Cucumis sativus* (cucumber)	+++	10. *Annona squamosa* (custard apple)	++++
		11. *Ipomoea batatas* (sweet potato)	+++		

Crop variety	Opinion
11. *Tamarindus indica* (tamarind)	+++
12. *Phaseolus vulgaris* (French beans)	++++
13. *Abelmoschus esculentus* (lady's finger)	+++
14. *Solanum melongena* (brinjal)	++++
15. Snakegourd	+++

VII. Ornamental plants

Crop variety	Opinion
1. Roses	++++
2. *Pyrethrum* sp. (chrysanthemum)	++++
3. *Vanda roxburghi* (orchids, vanilla)	++++
4. *Impatiens balsamina* (balsam)	+++
5. *Tagetes patula* (marigold)	++++
6. *Pimpinella anisa* (lady's lace)	++++
7. *Polianthes tuberosa* (tuberose)	++++
8. Celotia	+++
9. Zinnia	+++
10. Anthurium	++++

VIII. Cash crops

Crop variety	Opinion
1. *Theobroma cocao* (cocoa)	++
2. *Coffea arabica* (coffee)	+++
3. *Thea sinensis* (tea)	++
4. *Morus alba* (mulberry)	++++
5. *Saccharum officinaum* (sugarcane)	++++
6. Beetle leaf	++++
7. *Gossypium hirsutum* (cotton)	+++

IX. Plantation crops

Crop variety	Opinion
1. *Cocos nucifera* (coconut)	++++
2. *Areca catechu* (arecanut)	++++
3. *Teetona grandis* (teak)	+++

++++ = excellent, +++ = very good, ++ = good, + = no difference.

REFERENCES CITED

Appelhof, M. 1995. Vermicomposting school lunchroom waste utilizing *Eisenia fetida*. Soil Biology and Biochemistry (in press).

Arellano, R.P., I. Barois, and E. Arand. 1995. Earthworm carrying capacity for coffee pulp using *Eisenia andrei* and *Perionyx excavatus*. Soil Biology and Biochemistry (in press).

Atlavinyte, O., and J. Daciulyte. 1969. The effects of earthworms on the accumulation of vitamin B12 in soil. Pedobiologia 9: 165–170.

Atlavinyte, O., and J. Vanagas. 1982. The effect of earthworms on the quality of barley and rye grain. Pedobiologia 23: 256–262.

Atlavinyte, O., and Zimkuviene. 1985. The effect of earthworms on the barley in the soil of various density. Pedobiologia 28: 305–310.

Bano, K., and Kale, R.D. 1991. Earthworm fauna of southern Karnataka, India. In Advances in management and conservation of soil fauna. G.K Veeresh, D. Rajagopal, and C.A. Viraktamath (eds.), pp. 627–634. Oxford & IBH, New Delhi.

Bennett, I.L., and H.L. Robinson. 1967. The World Food Problem. A report of the President's Science Advisory Committee, Panel on the World Food Supply. Superintendent of Documents, Washington D.C. 3 vols.

Best, R. 1962. Production factors in the tropics. In Fundamentals of dry matter production and distribution. Netherland Journal of Agricultural Science 10 (No. 5, Special Issue): 347–353.

Bhandari, G.S., N.S. Randhawa, and M.S. Maskina. 1967. Polysaccharide content of earthworm casts. Current Science 36: 519–520.

Bisesi, M., and M. Appelhof. 1994. Qualitative evaluation of a Worm-A-Way Composter. Paper presented at ISEE5.

Blussee, P.A. 1994. Start and development of Zeeland Wormicultures Frusan, Netherlands. Paper presented at ISEE5.

Buckerfield, J. 1994. Appropriate earthworms for agriculture and vermiculture in Australia. Paper presented at ISEE5.

Chauhan, T.P.S. 1980. Seasonal changes in activities of some tropical earthworms. Comparative Physiology and Ecology 5: 288–298.

Darwin, C. 1881. The formation of vegetable mould through the action of worms with observations of their habits. Murray, London, pp. 326.

Dominguez, J., and C.A. Edwards. 1994. Effects of stocking rate and moisture content on the growth and maturation of *Eisenia fetida* (Oligochaeta) in pig manure. Paper presented at ISEE5.

Dutt, A.K. 1948. Earthworm and soil aggregation. Journal of the American Society of Agronomy 40: 407–410.

Elvira, C., L. Sampedro, and S. Mato. 1994. Vermicomposting of waste water sludge from paper industry with some other material rich in nitrogen. Paper presented at ISEE5.

Fayolle, L., H. Michaud, D. Cluzeau, and J. Stawiecki. 1994. Influence of temperature and feeding patterns on the life cycle of the earthworm *Dendrobaena veneta* (Oligochaeta). Paper presented at ISEE5.

Frederickson, J., K.R. Butt, R.M. Morris, and C. Daniel. 1994. Combining vermiculture with traditional green waste composting systems. Paper presented at ISEE5.

Galli, E., V. Tomati, A. Grappelli, and G. de Lena. 1990. Effect of earthworm cast on protein synthesis in *Agaricus bisporus*. Biology and Fertility of Soil 9: 1–2.

Garcia, M., D. Otero, and S. Mato. 1994. Reproductive behaviour of *E. andrei* (Oligochaeta; Lumbricidae) in individual cultures with sewage sludge. Paper presented at ISEE5.

Graff, O., and F. Makeschin. 1980. Beeinflussung des Ertrags von Weidelgras (*Lolium multiforum*) durch Ausscheidungen von Regenwurmen drei verschiendenen Arten. Pedobiologia 20: 176–180.

Jambhekar, H. 1994. Vermicompost experience in grape cultivation. Paper presented at ISEE5.

Joshi, N.V., and B.V. Kelkar. 1952. The role of earthworms in soil fertility. Indian Journal of Agricultural Science 22: 189–196.

Kale, R.D., and K. Bano. 1991. Time and space relative population growth of *Eudrilus eugeniae*. In Advances in management and conservation of soil fauna. G.K. Veeresh, D. Rajagopal, and C.A. Viraktamath (eds.), pp. 657–664. Oxford & IBH, New Delhi.

Kale, R.D., and N.S. Sunita. 1993. Utilization of earthworms in recycling of household refuse—a case study. In Biogas slurry utilization, pp. 75–79. CORT, New Delhi.

Kale, R.D., K. Bano, and R.V. Krishnamoorthy. 1982. Potential of *Perionyx excavatus* for utilization of organic wastes. Pedobiologia 23: 419–425.

Kale, R.D., K. Bano, M.N. Sreenivasa, and D.J. Bagyaraj. 1987. Influence of worm cast (vee Comp E UAS 83) on the growth and mycorrhizal colonization of two ornamental plants. South Indian Horticulture 35: 433–437.

Kale, R.D., B.C. Mallesh, K. Bano, and D.J. Bagyaraj. 1992. Influence of vermicompost application on the available macronutrients and selected microbial populations in a paddy field. Soil Biology and Biochemistry 24: 1317–1320.

Kale, R.D., K. Bano, M.N. Sreenivasa, K. Vinayak, and D.J. Bagyaraj. 1991. Incidence of cellulolytic and lignolytic organisms in the earthworm worked soils. In Advances in management and conservation of soil fauna. G.K. Veeresh, D. Rajagopal, and C.A. Viraktamath (eds.), pp. 599–604. Oxford & IBH, New Delhi.

Kale, R.D., S.N. Seenappa, and C.B.J. Rao. 1994. Sugar factory refuse for production of vermicompost and worm biomass. Paper presented at ISEE5.

Mba, C.C. 1994. Interaction of *Tolfaria occidentalis* with two vermicomposts. Paper presented at ISEE5.

Meyer, W.J., and W.J. Bouwman. 1994. Anisopary in compost earthworm reproductive strategies (Oligochaeta). Paper presented at ISEE5.

Mitchell, A. 1994. Exploitation and stabilization of waste materials by earthworm-driven polarization and separation of their potential resources. Paper presented at ISEE5.

Neuhauser, F., D.L. Kaplan, and R. Hartenstein. 1979. Life history of earthworm *Eudrilus eugeniae*. Revue des Ecologie du Biologie du Sol 16: 525–534.

Neuhauser, F., R. Hartenstein, and D.L. Kaplan. 1980. Growth of earthworm *Eisenia fetida* in relation to population density and food rationing. Oikos 35: 93–98.

Nielson, R.L. 1965. Presence of plant growth substances in earthworms demonstrated by paper chromatography and Went Pea test. Nature (London) 208: 1113–1114.

Reddy, M.V., and J.R.B. Alfred. 1978. Some observations on the earthworm population and biomass in subtropical pine forest soil. In Soil biology and ecology in India. C.A Edwards and G.K. Veeresh (eds.), pp. 78–82. UAS Technical Series No. 22.

Reinecke, S.A., and A.J. Reinecke. 1994. The influence of cadmium, lead, and manganese on spermatozoa and reproduction of *Eisenia fetida* (Oligochaeta). Paper presented at ISEE5.

Salazar, T., E. Aranda, and L. Barois. 1994. Comparative vermicompost production by *Eisenia andrei, E. fetida* and *Perionyx excavatus* using coffee pulp; and carrying capacity for coffee pulp using *Eisenia andrei* and *Perionyx excavatus*. Paper presented at ISEE5.

Stair, D.M., T.W. Hensen, M.M. Suggs, T.L. Ashwood, G.W. Suter, and B.E. Sample. 1994. Sampling of resident earthworms to evaluate ecological risk at a hazardous waste site. Paper presented at ISEE5.

Tomati, U., E. Galli, A. Grappelli, and G. Di lena. 1990. Effect of earthworm casts on protein synthesis in radish (*Raphanus sativam*) and lettuce (*Lactuga sativa*) seedlings. Biology and Fertility of Soils 9: 1–2.

Vinceslas-Akpa, and M. Loquet. 1994. Organic matter transformation in ligno-cellulosic waste products composted and vermicomposted (*Eisenia fetida andrei*) chemical analysis and 13C CPMAS NMR spectroscopy. Paper presented at ISEE5.

Watanabe, H., I. Hattori, Y.R. Takai, and H. Hasegava. 1982. Effect of excrement of earthworms on deodorization of ammonia. Journal of Tokyo University of Fisheries 69: 11–18.

White, S. 1994. The art of small scale vermicomposting. Paper presented at ISEE5.

Index

377

.